TALKING ABOUT WORLDVIEWS

A CONVERSATIONAL INTRODUCTION TO THINKING PHILOSOPHICALLY

MICHAEL S. JONES • MARK J. FARNHAM
AND DAVID L. SAXON

Talking About Worldviews: A Conversational Introduction to Thinking Philosophically

Published by Kregel Academic, an imprint of Kregel Publications, 2450 Oak Industrial Dr. NE, Grand Rapids, MI 49505-6020.

Cataloging-in-Publication Data is available from the Library of Congress.

ISBN 978-0-8254-4843-0, print
ISBN 978-0-8254-7145-2, epub
ISBN 978-0-8254-7144-5, Kindle

Printed in the United States of America
26 27 28 29 30 31 32 33 34 35 / 5 4 3 2 1

"Approach is imperative in communication. Pursuing a certain line of argument, appreciating different tactics, or creating intrigue in messaging is an art form in the exchange of ideas. Presenting a topic of conversation, then, makes the opportunity for transformation possible. In full transparency, it is uncommon to be introduced to a philosophy text that addresses the meta questions of life while putting readers at ease—inviting them to a fireside chat. When someone picks up *Talking About Worldviews*, a warm reception awaits. Worldview ideas can summon thoughts of erudite philosophers at some unreachable height. Yet Michael Jones, Mark Farnham, and David Saxon have used the conversational approach to make every reader feel at home. Where can you go to find a book of in-depth analysis, structured learning, clarity of definition, compare-and-contrast method of worldview investigation, and a dialogical engagement of ideas? Look no further than this text. As the authors suggest in their conclusion, they hope you 'plunder the treasures' of *Talking About Worldviews*."

—Mark Eckel, Executive Director, The Center for Biblical Integration, Liberty University

"Many textbooks claim to be different or unique in various ways. This volume by Jones, Farnham, and Saxon may be entitled to the strongest claim of this nature for any introductory philosophy text. Mixing fiction with nonfiction in every chapter, the authors tell about four friends who meet regularly to deliberate upon various philosophical issues and who are unintentionally caught up in a crime scene. Their discussions—plus the events in each episode—serve to introduce the topic of that respective chapter, working through the volume in a way that makes for far more interesting reading for students who are generally required to take philosophy but too often find it to be tough sledding. This text could make such a philosophy course both a better learning experience and an enjoyable process."

—Gary R. Habermas, Distinguished Research Professor, Liberty University

"Philosophy can often feel abstract or inaccessible, but *Talking About Worldviews* makes it both inviting and essential. Through the creative blend of story and analysis, the authors show readers why philosophical questions matter for everyday life and how our unspoken assumptions shape the way we see the world. At the same time, in a cultural moment where fruitful dialogue is rare, this book offers a compelling model of how to disagree with conviction while still showing respect. What emerges is a resource that is philosophically substantive, genuinely enjoyable to read, and deeply relevant to our times. I highly recommend it."

—Kevin Richard, Director, Center for Apologetics and Cultural Engagement, Liberty University

"*Talking About Worldviews* is a really good and engaging book. I love the conversational style and illustrative stories in the ongoing dialogue with fictitious characters. They make a big difference in the material being interesting, understandable, and practical. Moreover, the range of content and the careful progression of that content make this book a great introduction to philosophy for individual readers and classrooms. I highly recommend it."

—JP Moreland, Distinguished Professor of Philosophy, Talbot School of Theology, Biola University, and author of *Love Your God with All Your Mind*

"There seems to me to be at least two undoubted qualities of *Talking About Worldviews*: its eminently, thoroughly proved pedagogical character and the excellent idea of combining inspired fictional (conversational) content with relevant nonfictional sections within the chapters. These two qualities—but not only these—make this volume one to be recommended as extremely useful and enjoyable to read, but also one that can be seen as even necessary for a philosophical education in the true sense of the word, a plenary one, not restricted to a dry, technical perspective, as is most often the case."

—Viorel Vizureanu, Dean, Faculty of Philosophy, University of Bucharest

"One of my primary goals as a philosophy teacher is to connect my students with the answer to their question, 'Why should I learn philosophy?' *Talking About Worldviews* provides the foundation that I am looking for in my students to be able to consider their own worldview and to relate to people who differ from them. The authors' novel approach of the use of narrative to introduce the key lessons of philosophy as they relate to worldview formation is interesting and engaging. The characters' journeys in seeking to apply the lessons of philosophy reflect what my students experience in discovering philosophy for themselves. The narrative written by the authors does not shy away from showing the inward uncertainty of seeking to understand one's philosophical reasoning using difficult and exciting situations. The topical sections apply philosophy to worldview formation for the student and provide great discussion questions that the teacher can utilize to apply the chapter's lessons in class. *Talking About Worldviews* is a great text for teaching philosophy and for applying those lessons to important topics of today."

—Timothy Johns, Associate Professor, Maranatha Baptist University

"*Talking About Worldviews* takes readers on an engaging journey that makes philosophy both clear and captivating. With remarkable accessibility, this book shines in three key ways: It presents a wide range of worldviews with balance and fairness, explains complex ideas with striking clarity, and weaves it all into a narrative that keeps you turning the pages. Inspiring, insightful, and refreshingly readable, this is a book I wholeheartedly recommend and a true credit to its authors' creativity and scholarship."

—Bryan Brock, Assistant Dean, Maranatha Baptist Seminary, and Professor, Maranatha Baptist University

"The authors set out in *Talking About Worldviews* to provide a textbook for an Introduction to Philosophy or Worldviews course that today's students will actually 'get into' reading. The attempt is masterfully pulled off, presenting a two-layer textbook, where 'dialogue' and 'theory' are interwoven to great success. The narrative portion with four friends who start a philosophical study group constantly has the comparative and contrastive worldview elements interwoven with considerable philosophical legerdemain. Then, the accompanying 'theory' sections offer remarkable insight by laying out a well-meshed, clear, and readable introduction to philosophical ideas in the history of philosophy supporting and explaining what 'all the racket is about' in the appealing and intellectually stimulating dialogue among the friends—touching on both Eastern and Western branches of worldview analysis. The reader is thus creatively and systematically exposed to how Christian and other leading Western worldviews—in the diverse areas of logic, metaphysics, epistemology, ethics, and even philosophy of law and cognate areas—do (or should) interact with interest and civility along with these Eastern views, which is a bonus. Bravo and high fives (and perhaps namaste with clapping of hands)! Highly recommended for adoption for undergraduate Introduction to Philosophy, Intercultural Studies, Apologetics, or Worldview courses!"

—Edward N. Martin, Professor of Philosophy, Liberty University

"*Talking About Worldviews* is an ingenious and engaging introduction to thinking philosophically. It's organized around a series of fictional meetings between four people with very different ways of seeing the world, and it uses this frame to explore some of the most important and fundamental big-picture questions in our discipline: the nature of reality, knowledge, value, and, of course, God. This is an engrossing and clear presentation of our discipline, written with an eye toward demonstrating why philosophy matters. A great text to draw students into philosophical thinking; as much of a page-turner as an intro text can be. While it is friendly to Christianity, it is not at all doctrinaire—the text is fair and open-minded and takes pains to make skeptical students see their views are taken seriously."

—David Merli, Professor of Philosophy, Franklin and Marshall College

CONTENTS

RELIGION

ETHICS

JURISPRUDENCE

PHILOSOPHICAL ANTHROPOLOGY

PREFACE

Nearly everyone has beliefs about the nature of reality. We have beliefs about what's real, where reality came from, what its purpose is, how long it will last, and more. This is your view of the world—your *worldview*. How you view the world influences how you interpret your experiences and live your life. Therefore, your worldview must be accurate.

Most people haven't self-consciously examined the beliefs that make up their worldview. Some of these beliefs may be false, even though people think they are true. We believe it's both important and useful to give some careful thought to your worldview so that you can be assured that it's true. That's one of the chief reasons that we've written this book.

Another reason is that people need a model of how to disagree respectfully. Thanks to modern technology, we have more opportunities to interact with others than we've ever had before. Unfortunately, this hasn't resulted in people improving their skill of respectful disagreement. We believe it's possible to disagree with people while still respecting them. In fact, we think that respecting other people can help you have more fruitful disagreements—that it's beneficial to disagree respectfully.

A third reason for this book is the need for a readable textbook about worldviews that communicates effectively on an introductory level but is still philosophically informed and enjoyable to read.

A UNIQUE SOLUTION

Talking About Worldviews takes a unique approach to addressing these needs. Each chapter contains both fiction and nonfiction. The fictional portions of this book follow the developing friendship between four young professionals who join a reading group to discuss a philosophy book. Each person comes from a very different background: One is an atheist, another an existentialist, the third finds inspiration in Hinduism and Buddhism, and the fourth is a Christian. Over the course of *Talking About Worldviews,* we get to know these people and watch their friendship grow as they wrestle with big philosophical questions from the perspective of each of their worldviews.

The fictional component is designed to accomplish several things. First, it makes reading *Talking About Worldviews* more engaging and relatable. It also provides real-life examples of the philosophical issues that will be discussed in the nonfiction portions of each chapter. Finally, it gives an example of civil disagreement, for although each of the four friends has their own convictions, they also respect (and like) each other. Their disagreements lead to genuine learning and personal growth.

The second half of each chapter is more like a traditional textbook. It clarifies and elaborates the philosophical issues that our four friends encountered and discussed in the first half of the chapter. It defines terms and explains the arguments for and against each perspective.

The result of this unique approach is a textbook that is fun to read, approachable, and philosophically satisfying. We want *Talking About Worldviews* to cause you to fall in love with studying worldviews philosophically. We want it to become a habit, or even a passion, to ask philosophical questions and pursue philosophical understanding. And we want to inspire you to engage in respectful dialogue with your friends.

FEATURES OF *TALKING ABOUT WORLDVIEWS*

Below are some of the unique features of this book.

- Fiction and nonfiction are combined for an engaging format.
- Philosophical concepts are used to clarify worldview differences.
- All issues needed for an introductory philosophy course are covered.
- Each chapter begins with a synopsis and ends with questions to ponder, vocabulary terms, and suggestions for further reading.
- Lessons on critical thinking are integrated into the fictional portions.
- An extensive index is included in the back.
- This book is available in paperback or as an ebook.

NOTE TO THE READER

The story told in the fiction sections builds gradually from chapter 1 through to the end of the book, so it's important to read the chapters in order. If you're just interested in the story and don't care much about the philosophical content, you could read the first half of each chapter and skip the second half. However, that would pretty much miss the point of the book, which is to help you think critically about the major worldview issues and the arguments that support the various perspectives on them.

Conversely, if you are interested only in the philosophical concepts and not the story itself, then you could read the second half of each chapter, skipping all the fictional portions. That would allow you to cover all the philosophical content more rapidly. (It would be less fun, of course.) If you take this approach, you do not need to read all the chapters in order, but you should definitely read the chapters on worldview, philosophy, logic, and abstract objects before reading the other chapters, as they introduce terms and teach critical thinking skills upon which the other chapters build.

Finally, please do not read this book expecting it to tell you what to believe or what the correct view is on the issues. That's not the purpose of the book. This volume is intended to help you understand issues more deeply, expose you to a range of arguments supporting opposing perspectives on important issues, and most of all, spark your thinking about worldviews.

NOTE TO THE INSTRUCTOR

Talking About Worldviews is intended as a theoretically informed introduction to the study of philosophy through the prism of worldviews. It can be read for pleasure or personal enrichment, and we believe it would be an excellent book for a reading circle. However, its primary purpose is as an undergraduate college textbook. In that context, it could be paired with an anthology of primary texts.

As was pointed out to the reader, each chapter of *Talking About Worldviews* begins with a fiction section and ends with a nonfiction section. The story in the fiction sections builds gradually from chapter 1 through to the end of the book, so it's important to read the chapters in order. If you are not going to have the students read all the chapters, it would be good to inform the students that they may wish to read the fictional portions of the unassigned chapters so that they don't miss an aspect of the plot as it develops.

Also mentioned in our note to the reader is that this book makes no attempt to present what we view as the correct position on the issues addressed. The purpose of this volume is to spur the reader's thinking on these issues rather than settling the issues for the reader. We leave it up to the instructor to provide further guidance, and we have confidence that a book that leaves this task in your competent hands is exactly what is needed to produce fruitful classroom discussions that will lead to transformative learning experiences.

ACKNOWLEDGMENTS

While all three of the authors had a hand in the production of each chapter, Michael S. Jones was the lead author of all the nonfiction sections, as well as the preface and introduction. Mark J. Farnham was the lead author of chapters 1, 2, 6, 8–10, 14–16, 19, 21, 24, and the conclusion. David L. Saxon was the lead author of chapters 3–5, 7, 11–13, 17–18, 20, 22–23, and he compiled the bibliography. Each of us is grateful for the cordial and fruitful collaboration we have enjoyed.

We extend our thanks to the good people at Kregel Academic. Their expertise in editing and publishing was invaluable to the production of this volume. We also acknowledge the very important role played by our wives, Adrienne Farnham, Jamie Saxon, and Laura Jones, who have supported us, advised us, proofread some of the chapters, and helped in other ways as the book developed. Without our better halves, this book would not exist. Finally, our greatest gratitude is to God, whom we view as the foundation of our worldview. "For us there is one God, the Father, from whom are all things and for whom we live, and one Lord, Jesus Christ, through whom are all things and through whom we live" (1 Cor 8:6).

INTRODUCTION: WHY LEARN ABOUT WORLDVIEWS?

The twenty-first century is a contentious time in which to live. People disagree on everything, from what the smallest particle that makes up the universe is to what the largest object in existence is, from how old the universe is to what the youngest possible age of a human being is, from whether there is a multitude of gods to whether there are any gods at all. Not only do we disagree about a great number of things; we also argue about them. At work and at school, via social media, texts, and telephone calls, people in the twenty-first century air their opinions and attempt to influence other people's beliefs. Unfortunately, this is often done in a fractious way.

This book aims to give you an example of a better way. Many disagreements arise because people approach issues from different presuppositions about the fundamental nature of reality. In other words, they have different *worldviews*. However, different starting points can be opportunities for growth and learning if the differences are discussed respectfully and constructively. Philosophy can provide us with tools to critically evaluate such worldview differences. This book is about three things: worldviews; friendly, respectful dialogue as a tool for achieving an objective understanding of new perspectives; and philosophical analysis as a tool for evaluating such perspectives.

WORLDVIEW

It has often been said that everyone has a worldview, an opinion on the fundamental nature of reality. This may be a bit of an overstatement,[1] but it does seem likely that the vast majority of people have a worldview. However, most people have never even heard the term and are not aware that they have one. Nonetheless, it would be good if people were aware that they have a worldview, and if they had a solid understanding of their worldview, that they were aware of their reasons for believing it and what alternatives are possible. That's because a worldview isn't merely an abstract set of ideals: *Your worldview shapes how you interpret your daily experiences and live your life.*

This truth is easily illustrated. Imagine two people who experience something highly unusual and difficult to explain. One of them believes in supernatural powers and the like; the other believes only in the natural world and the laws of nature. The first person might say, "Hey, I think we just experienced a miracle!" To this the other would probably respond, "I don't believe in miracles. Whatever that was, I'm sure there's a reasonable, scientific explanation." The second person's worldview doesn't have room for miracles, while the first person's does.

DIALOGUE

One great way to learn about worldviews is to read books about them. The book that you're holding is a great place to begin studying worldviews, and several other books are recommended at the end of the first chapter. Another good way to learn about worldviews is to make friends who have different perspectives and discuss your differences with them. Some people shy away from controversial discussions, but such conversations can be fun!

---

1. Much depends on how one defines personhood. If we define a worldview as a set of beliefs about the fundamental nature of reality, and if the category of "human person" includes people who are unable to have such beliefs because they are too young (or in some way mentally incapacitated so that they are incapable of having such beliefs), then there are some people who do not have a worldview. However, it seems likely that everyone who is capable of having such beliefs does have a worldview.

In fact, one goal of this book is to illustrate how such discussions can be both informative and enjoyable.

That brings us to the most unique feature of this book: Every chapter contains a fiction section followed by a nonfiction section. The fiction portions narrate the development of a friendship between four people who join a reading circle that's working its way through a philosophy book. They come from disparate backgrounds, but they have at least one thing in common: They want to understand life more deeply. From the outset they are open-minded and friendly toward one another. Each has his or her own personal convictions, but rather than viewing the opinions of their newfound friends as a threat or as uninformed and unjustified, they begin with the assumption that their friends may have good reasons for their strange views, and they have a healthy curiosity and a strong commitment to treating others as they would want to be treated: with respect.

"Treat others in the same way that you would want them to treat you."
–Jesus

PHILOSOPHY

The nonfiction part of each chapter explains the philosophical concepts that the four friends discussed in the fiction portion. This includes critical thinking concepts like formal and informal fallacies, how to reason inductively and deductively, evidential belief justification, and the like. It also includes important metaphysical issues that underlie many disagreements and their applications in areas like ethics, politics, and anthropology.

The exact topics covered can be seen in the table of contents. They range from logic through epistemology, metaphysics, philosophy of religion, ethics, and philosophy of law, to philosophical anthropology. Twenty-four topics are covered, which gives the book twenty-four chapters. There are other issues in philosophy, but this is a broad range of topics for an introductory text.

PROGRESSION

The chapters of this book have a logical progression. Readers should begin with chapter 1 and work their way through the chapters, always reading the fiction portion of each chapter before the nonfiction portion. In the later chapters, the nonfiction parts of the book sometimes assume familiarity with concepts that are introduced in earlier chapters. It's also helpful to read the fiction part of each chapter before the nonfiction section because the fiction portion introduces and illustrates concepts that are then explained and expanded in the nonfiction part of the chapter. Additionally, the fiction portions of the book tell a story that builds from chapter 1 through the climax and resolution found in chapters 23–24. If you skip around, the story won't make sense.

It is possible to read the fiction sections without reading the nonfiction ones, but that might leave you wondering about certain concepts that are utilized but not explained in detail in the fiction sections. It's also possible to read the nonfiction portions without reading the fiction sections, but that would be much less fun! And it's possible to omit some of the chapters entirely if the topics are not of interest or if time does not permit reading them, but in that situation, we recommend that you still read the fiction portion so that there aren't gaps in the storyline.

PURPOSE

This book presents multiple perspectives on every issue discussed. While some of the three authors did not grow up in Christian homes, all of us are practicing Christians, have read widely, and have interacted extensively with people with other worldviews. We do not want to convince you to "take our side" on the issues. We want you to practice the critical thinking skills introduced in the first few chapters and apply them to the issues discussed in the subsequent chapters so that you can reason your way to whatever conclusion is most likely to be true.

> **"The first to state his case seems right, until his opponent begins to cross-examine him."**
> **–King Solomon**

As you read *Talking About Worldviews*, we hope you will find it entertaining and even inspiring. More than that, we hope it will help you to rethink your beliefs, not necessarily with the goal of changing them, although that might be a good thing, but rather with the goal of better understanding what you believe and why you believe it. After all, your worldview determines, in a sense, how you interpret everything around you, and it greatly influences the choices you make. We pray that you will take the challenge of Socrates, one of the greatest philosophers ever, who famously stated, "The unexamined life is not worth living."[2]

2. Plato, *Five Dialogues: Euthyphro, Apology, Crito, Meno, Phaedo*, 2nd ed., trans. G. M. A. Grube and John M. Cooper (Hackett, 2002), 41.

INTRODUCTORY ISSUES

1

WORLDVIEWS

SYNOPSIS

This chapter introduces the concept of worldviews and the idea that, although almost everyone has a worldview, many people are not aware of it. Then the chapter illustrates how people from different perspectives can begin to dialogue about their beliefs and learn from one another.

DIALOGUE

Hannah walked tentatively into the coffee shop, wondering what this gathering would be like. She scanned the room and realized she didn't know who or what she was looking for. The group had agreed to meet at 7:00 p.m. at Brews Brothers Café on Prince Street, but it seemed that everyone assumed they'd somehow recognize each other.

Hannah ordered and found a high table away from the more crowded low tables. It was about six feet long, in a well-lit area, and looked like a good spot for a discussion. She hoped no one else would sit there so the group could spread out a little. She pulled the philosophy book they had agreed to read out of her bag and placed it on the table. Maybe the other group members would see the book and make their way over to her.

Hannah sipped at her vanilla latte with just a hint of anxiety. Would she be able to contribute to the discussion? Would it be friendly, or would tempers flare? She didn't know what the others believed or their backgrounds.

She simply knew from the Get Together website that three men would be joining her—Angelo, Zach, and Suresh.

Customers filtered into the shop in ones and twos, some chatting and others obviously in a hurry. No one looked around or made eye contact with her. Finally, a sharply dressed man in his midthirties entered, looked around the shop, made eye contact with Hannah, and held up a copy of the same book. He flashed a huge smile, waved, and pointed to the line of customers to motion that he was going to order first.

Hannah heaved a sigh of relief. He seemed friendly enough. Two minutes later, he made his way over, carrying a black coffee in a house mug.

"Hannah? Hi, I'm Zach," he said, extending his hand.

"Yes, so nice to meet you." Hannah smiled as she shook his hand. "Is this a good spot?"

"It seems a little quieter than over by the espresso machine," Zach said, just as the machine hissed and hummed loudly.

"Are you the one who organized this group?" Hannah asked.

Zach nodded, taking a seat at the table. "I recently moved back to the area and have been wanting to have serious discussions with thoughtful people. I grew up in Greenfield, so I have a few high school and college friends nearby, but not many are interested in these kinds of conversations. I guess our interests changed when I moved out of state for my doctorate."

"You have a doctorate in philosophy?" Hannah's eyes widened. "I wasn't expecting an advanced discussion. This is all pretty new for me."

Zach waved his hand. "Oh no, my degree is in chemistry. I'm starting at the beginning with this stuff."

"Oh good," Hannah said. "I don't want to slow down the discussion. Have you started on the book yet?" She wanted to make sure she wasn't already behind.

"I thought we could get to know each other first and then start reading together next time?"

"Sounds good to me."

"So tell me about yourself," Zach said, taking a sip of his coffee. "Where are you from? What do you do?"

Just then, Hannah noticed a dark-haired young man looking around over by the register. She waited until his eyes met hers, and then she held up the book. He nodded, smiled, and made his way over to the long table. She turned back to Zach. "Why don't we wait until everyone is here to make introductions?"

"Is this the philosophy reading group?" the young man asked as he approached the table. He seemed a little nervous.

"Yes!" Hannah and Zach said in unison.

"Welcome," Zach said, extending his hand. "Glad you could make it! What's your name?"

"I'm Angelo. Nice to meet you!"

Hannah and Zach introduced themselves and offered Angelo a seat.

"Let me grab something to drink first," he said, turning to walk back to the counter.

Angelo reached the barista just as a man about the same age as him walked through the door. They made eye contact, and Angelo, noticing the book in his hand, said, "Are you here for the philosophy reading group?"

The man nodded and grinned. "My name is Suresh. Are we the first ones here?"

Angelo shook his head and pointed across the room to Hannah and Zach. "We're the last ones, actually. I was going to get a drink before we get started. Do you want something too?"

"Definitely! I need something to get the intellectual juices flowing if I'm going to discuss philosophy."

Both men ordered espressos and, when they had their drinks, walked to the table and sat down. The four exchanged greetings and made small talk for a few moments.

Finally, Zach spoke up.

"I'm so glad everyone could come. I think this will be a helpful time together. I organized this because I've been having interesting discussions with people at work about issues I've never really thought about. My education is in the hard sciences, and I just earned a doctorate in chemistry, but I've never really thought much about philosophical issues until recently. I work in the pharmaceutical industry and just moved back to the area. I'm thirty-six, single, and I live with my border collie, Brady. I've always been focused on science, but in the last year or so, I've started to realize that there's more to life than work and formulas and statistics. A few of my colleagues have challenged me about some of my beliefs, so I've turned to philosophy to look for answers. I was hoping a reading group would be a low-key way to learn with others."

Angelo spoke next. "My name is Angelo. I'm thirty-two. I was excited to see this group advertised on the Get Together website. I've been looking for a place to talk about important issues and beliefs for a while now. I went to college for computer programming but couldn't find the type of job I hoped for here in Greenfield. I come from a tight-knit Italian family and didn't want to leave town, so I got a job as a security guard at the courthouse, and that got me interested in the law. I'm hoping to apply for law school next year and learned that some training in philosophy would help get me ready for the LSAT. Rather than taking a class, I thought I'd try to learn philosophy outside my work schedule."

Hannah introduced herself. "I'm thirty-two as well, and I was thrilled to see the ad in Get Together about this philosophy discussion. I've been having somewhat of an existential crisis about what I believe recently. I've been wanting to talk to someone, but most of my friends and coworkers don't seem interested in these kinds of conversations. I grew up Pentecostal and was deeply immersed in that world until I began working as a case manager in social work. The sad cases I've handled have really made me question my faith and wander away from the religion of my family and childhood. I've explored several philosophies over the last few years and have found them somewhat helpful but not completely satisfying. I'm hoping this group will be a place where I can bounce ideas off you and look for some clarity."

Suresh leaned forward in his seat with excitement. "That's what I want too!" he said. "Discussing ideas and challenging each other is exactly what I'm looking for. I'm Indian and grew up in an immigrant family that came to the States when I was ten. My beliefs are a mix of Eastern and Western thought, but I don't really know where I belong. My family has shaped me tremendously, but American education has always been at odds with my Eastern upbringing. I'm thirty now. I've wanted to be a chef from the time I was a teenager, but a restaurant kitchen can be hostile and brutal, with little space for introspection. I've been struggling to maintain my humanity. Recently, I reunited with an old friend, Disha, and she has reintroduced me to my Eastern roots. I'm trying to sort out the conflicting cultures in my life to find some peace of mind."

Hannah looked at Zach. "So where do we begin?"

Zach tapped the cover of the book they'd all brought. "Well, I read ahead a bit. The book begins by introducing the concept of *worldview*, so that seems like a good place to start. My understanding is that a worldview is a set of beliefs about the fundamental nature of reality that grounds and influences our thoughts, perceptions, and actions.

Hannah pulled out a notebook as Zach was talking.

"In other words," he said, "we each look at the world in a way that helps make sense of our experiences and that we think accurately describes reality. A worldview answers questions about what we think the world is, who we are, the meaning of life, the purpose for everything, where it's all going, what's wrong with the world, and what would make everything right."

"Wow," Suresh said. "That's a lot to think about . . . I'm not sure I've worked through all those questions yet."

"I don't think we have to have everything figured out right now," Hannah said. "I guess I understand Zach to be saying that we live and act each day from at least a vague idea of how we'd answer these questions. Like I said, I grew up in a Pentecostal home. God was central to everything in our lives and the way we thought about everything. In recent years, as I have cared for people with severe disabilities and seen people experience very difficult life situations, the idea of a loving God has seemed less and less believable."

Hannah looked down at her hands. "For a while, I was what you might call a nihilist. The world seemed absurd and pointless. But I couldn't shake this longing for meaning and purpose, and I was motivated to relieve suffering. So I moved back a bit into what I think would be called an existentialist approach. I believe there is no given purpose in life, so we're left to make our own purpose and to decide for ourselves who we are. I go back and forth between believing in God and doubting God's existence. Either way, I don't think it really matters. But I'm still trying to figure out my beliefs. I'm not sure what to think about where it's all going. I do believe there are such things as right and wrong, but I'm not sure how to objectively determine the difference. I sort of intuit morality, if that makes sense, but I don't expect that others will find that convincing."

Everyone nodded thoughtfully.

"That was helpful," Zach said. "I think you got us moving in the right direction."

There was a short pause as everyone looked around the table to see who would go next.

"Okay, I'll go," Zach said. "I feel pretty settled in my view of the world. As a scientist, I don't believe in God and tend to look at everything through the lens of the material. I think the universe is simply matter and energy, including us humans. I think science is the best way to explain the questions of life, although I have to admit that some questions are more easily answered than others. The universe began with the Big Bang, it's guided by natural selection, and life in the universe will end with a whimper when the sun burns out."

"Wow. You oughta write for Hallmark," Angelo said.

Everyone laughed, including Zach.

"I believe that *morality* simply describes those behaviors that help society flourish," Zach said, "so *good* is what promotes flourishing, and *evil* is whatever doesn't. Social scientists help us know what those things are. Now, I admit that the differences between societies are difficult to explain only using science, but I still think science is the best way to figure that out. Religion tends to make a mess out of things and cultivates blind belief, so I don't put much stock in religious opinions. But I do respect those who find religion helpful, as long as they don't try to override science."

Suresh spoke up. "I appreciate this little exercise so much. It's making me think! I'm with Hannah in that I'm still figuring out what I believe. I grew up believing in many deities and the supernatural. We prayed to the gods who are the source of life, and our purpose was to seek enlightenment through various practices. Since we had accumulated karma in previous lives, one of the purposes of life was to do good to pay off that karma. My education in an elite private school and my immersion in the restaurant world made me more secular in my thinking. Quite frankly, it has left me feeling empty. Recently my friend Disha has been 'reenchanting' the world for me with her renewed commitment to the ways of our culture. I am seeing life in a new way, with a sense of wonder at the sacred aspects of nature and the rhythms of daily life. For me, morality is rooted in care for the earth, other creatures, and people. Life has purpose because the divine permeates every aspect of the universe, including other people. I like Eastern religion because you can avoid dogmatism, since the specific beliefs are not as critical as they seem to be in other religions."

"That is such an interesting approach, Suresh," Hannah said. "So far, it seems like we're all very different from each other in the way we view the world." She looked over at Angelo. "How about you, Angelo? Are you going to diversify our group even more?"

Angelo laughed. "I am, in fact! I was born and raised Catholic, like many Italians, but now I would call myself an evangelical Christian. When it comes to the worldview questions, however, evangelicals and Catholics are mostly in agreement. The world is the creation of an eternal God who made everything. So the beauty and design of the universe are intentional and reflect God's infinite character and love for his creation, especially humanity. The world was made to be a blessing for humans, but the first humans disobeyed God and brought a curse on the world. That would explain the brokenness and ugliness in the world."

Angelo paused. "Is this a familiar story to everyone?"

The other three nodded.

"Go on," said Zach.

"Okay. I believe that we find our identity in the declaration that God made us in his image, which speaks of our rationality, sense of morality, and natural knowledge of God. We were made to glorify God and cultivate the earth, with all its potential. Not only was nature cursed after the first human disobeyed God, but people were also corrupted by their disobedience, and so we are all morally depraved and guilty before God. Morality is essentially the character of God revealed in his commands to people, both what is apparent in nature and what he specifically revealed in the Bible. God remedied our situation by sending his Son, Jesus Christ, to atone for our sins through his death and resurrection and to reconcile us to himself. Our moral debt before God can be paid by repenting of our sin and trusting in the work of Christ on the cross. We will all stand before God at the end of time to give account for our actions. Those who have repented of their sin and placed their trust in Jesus alone for salvation will enter eternal bliss in the new heaven and new earth, and those who don't will suffer torment in hell."

"This is very interesting!" Suresh said. "Two of us—Hannah and me—feel like our worldview is still developing, and two of us—Zach and Angelo—seem quite settled in their beliefs. Yet we could divide the group another way. Angelo and I are convinced that there are deities in the world, while Hannah and Zach are skeptical or reject the idea. In addition, Hannah and Angelo have a background in Christianity, while Zach and I do not. This is going to be fun!"

Everyone else looked around and smiled at Suresh's enthusiasm. It did seem like the group was going to be more than simply educational. On the broader social level, they all might enjoy this weekly meeting more than they had expected. Their differences and similarities would make for endless varieties of discussion.

Zach looked around the table. "Should we break here for the night?"

Angelo nodded. "I feel energized by this start! I'm so eager to come back to discuss more. You all have put my mind at ease about talking about topics many people might feel are impolite. I appreciate everyone being so open and encouraging."

"Same," Hannah said. "I'll be thinking about this conversation all week."

"Same time and place next week?" Zach said, sliding out of his chair and collecting his things.

Everyone got up and said their goodbyes.

It's going to be a fascinating ride, that's for sure, Zach thought.

THEORY

Have you ever noticed that your beliefs tend to fit together like the pieces of a puzzle? Ideally, your beliefs don't contradict each other, but instead they complement each other, forming a coherent belief system. Continuing with the puzzle analogy, once you complete a puzzle, you probably step back from it and admire how the pieces now form a coherent picture. Likewise, if you could step back from a person's network of beliefs and look at it, hopefully you'd see a coherent picture of how he or she views reality.

This is what we call a "worldview." A **worldview** is a set of beliefs about the fundamental nature of reality that grounds and influences all of one's perceiving, thinking, and doing. The term originated with the German philosopher Immanuel Kant and represents a useful concept for understanding how your presuppositions impact how you interpret your experiences.[1]

You may have noticed that the definition of a worldview implies that the beliefs that comprise a worldview are only those that concern the fundamental nature of reality. Your worldview is not "everything you believe." There's another term for that: **belief system**. Your worldview is what you believe about the really big issues. The rest of your beliefs fill in the details.

It's difficult to decide which belief is the most central to a worldview: It could be the belief that we can know truth, or it could be belief in or denial of the supernatural, or perhaps it is the fundamental belief in existence itself. Radical skeptics have sometimes denied that any beliefs are true, which is a belief that, if true, would impact all of one's worldview to some degree.[2] Radical solipsists believe that only they exist, each solipsist believing that he or she is the only reality.[3]

Certainly, belief or disbelief in the supernatural has been a major distinction between rival worldviews throughout history. This has been true both in the East and the West.[4] If a person believes in the supernatural, then it is easy to accept the possibility of miraculous cures and the power of prayer. Similarly, inasmuch as such belief usually goes hand-in-hand with a belief in things that are spiritual rather than physical, it is easy for such a belief to extend to the existence of other types of immaterial existents, such as universal human rights, as were invoked by the theistic framers of the Declaration of Independence.[5]

---

1. David K. Naugle, *Worldview: The History of a Concept* (Eerdmans, 2002), 58.
2. Although this sort of skepticism sounds self-contradictory, it may be possible to formulate it more carefully so that it avoids this problem.
3. Stephen P. Thornton, "Solipsism and the Problem of Other Minds," in *Internet Encyclopedia of Philosophy*, https://iep.utm.edu/solipsis/.
4. In the West, the contrast between polytheism and Epicureanism in ancient Greece provides an excellent example of this, as does the contrast between theism and naturalism in the modern period. While supernaturalistic perspectives like Hinduism, Buddhism, Sikhism, and Jainism are dominant in India, Carvaka provided a historical and intellectual counterpoint that was very important. In China, the supernaturalism in Neo-Confucianism and Taoism had an early counterpoint in the philosopher Yang-tse and a much later one in Maoist Marxism.
5. The opening lines of the Declaration of Independence are one of the most famous statements exemplifying the complementarity of theism and universal human

In contrast, if a person believes that nothing exists beyond the physical world, then he is probably going to deny the existence of gods, ghosts, angels, and devils; he may also have difficulty rationalizing belief in the existence of universal human rights, timeless moral truths, immutable laws of logic, and other, similar immaterial entities. After all, such things are not physical. Such skepticism may serve the naturalist well: It may serve to immunize him from belief in things that are little more than superstitions handed down from previous ages. On the other hand, it may also be an impediment to accepting beliefs that are rationally justified.

In fact, the question of the supernatural can be used to chart the possible worldviews:

TYPES OF WORLDVIEWS

Naturalism	Supernaturalism	Blended
Nihilism	Monotheism	Deism
Secular Humanism	Polytheism	Panentheism
Pantheism	Paganism	Eastern Monism

As this chart illustrates, worldviews can be grouped into three broad categories. **Naturalism** is the view that nothing exists except the natural world. It entails the denial of the supernatural. Naturalism often amounts to **physicalism**, the view that everything that exists is physical.[6] Physicalism involves the belief that everything that exists is material and denies the existence of immaterial things such as spirits, incorporeal souls, and non-physical objects like human rights, moral absolutes, abstract numbers, the

rights: "We hold these Truths to be self-evident, that all Men are created equal, that they are endowed by their Creator with certain unalienable Rights, that among these are Life, Liberty, and the Pursuit of Happiness." Harvard University, "The Democratic Knowledge Project," https://declaration.fas.harvard.edu/resources/text.

6. Materialism used to be the common label for what many philosophers now call physicalism. However, since the term "materialism" can also be used to refer to the perspective that what's most important in life is the accumulation of material possessions, in an effort to disambiguate our vocabulary, many philosophers now prefer the term "physicalism" when referring to the view that everything is material.

laws of logic, etc. Physicalists who want to affirm that any of these things exist must find a way to explain them in physical terms.

One form of naturalism is **nihilism**, which is the view that there are no gods, there is no life after death, it is not possible to know truth, there are no objective moral values, and life has no purpose. It's a pretty depressing philosophy. There are various forms of nihilism, some of which are less extreme than this, but the general tendency is toward skepticism about truth, value, and meaning in life. Nihilism fits well with physicalism.

Another form of naturalism is **secular humanism**, which is similar to nihilism in some ways but different in others. Like nihilism, secular humanism holds that there are no gods, there is no life after death, there are no objective moral values, and life has no intrinsic purpose. However, secular humanism argues that humans can create moral values and can give life extrinsic purpose.[7] Humans, being intelligent and creative creatures, can do things that no other known creature can—hence the name "humanism."

A rather surprising form of naturalism is **pantheism**, which is the view that all that exists is the natural world, and the natural world is, after a fashion, God. In pantheism, the concept of God is not the idea of God found in classical monotheistic religions like Judaism, Christianity, and Islam, which see God as an omnipotent, omniscient, omnipresent, personal being who exists alongside creation.[8] Instead, pantheism sees the natural world as containing all the power that exists, and therefore it is inherently omnipotent. Similarly, it contains all the information that exists, so in a sense, it is omniscient. Since all the places that exist are places in the natural world, the natural world is inherently omnipresent. Hence, the natural world is omnipotent, omniscient, and omnipresent, and thus has the attributes of God. It's not a personal God: The natural world doesn't have thoughts and feelings like people do. But it does contain all the thoughts and feelings of the people who exist within it, so in that specific sense it has thoughts and

---

7. The difference between intrinsic and extrinsic purpose will be explained in the chapter on the meaning of life (ch. 23).
8. "Omnipotent" means all powerful, "omniscient" means all knowing, and "omnipresent" means that God is everywhere at once.

feelings. When viewed this way, pantheism manages to believe in God while still affirming naturalism.

Supernaturalism is the name we give to another group of worldviews. These are the worldviews that affirm the existence of things outside or in addition to the natural world. They are called "super-natural" because they exist, in a way, "above" the natural world. Such things can include gods, ghosts, angels, human souls, and other non-physical things like human rights, moral absolutes, abstract numbers, the laws of logic, etc. It's not the case that all forms of supernaturalism affirm the existence of all imaginable immaterial existents. What is the case is that all forms of supernaturalism affirm the existence of at least some immaterial existents.

The most familiar form of supernaturalism in the Western world is **monotheism**, the belief in the existence of one God who is simultaneously present within and outside the natural world.[9] Judaism, Christianity, and Islam are religions that embrace a monotheistic worldview. In addition to teaching about God, these religions also teach the existence of human souls, angels, and some immaterial objects like abstract numbers, moral truths, etc.

Polytheism is another supernaturalist worldview. It's similar to monotheism, except it teaches that multiple gods exist. Examples of polytheism include the pantheons of ancient Greece and Rome, and in our day, Hinduism and Mormonism.[10] Polytheistic religions typically embrace the existence of various immaterial entities in addition to gods, but on the other hand, they sometimes construe the gods themselves as being material or quasi-material.

Paganism is also a supernaturalist worldview, though the term "paganism" is somewhat difficult to define. It originated in the ancient world and has, over the centuries, been used to designate a wide range of religious

---

9. The term **theism** is often used as a synonym for monotheism. Technically they are not identical: Theism is belief in the existence of *at least* one god, while monotheism is belief in the existence of *only* one god. Hence one could theoretically claim to be a theist even if one is a polytheist. However, in this book we'll follow the common practice of using "theism" as shorthand for "monotheism."
10. Although many Mormons deny that Mormonism is polytheistic, it does seem to fit the criteria of polytheism.

and quasi-religious belief systems. Today the term is often used to designate the view that the world contains more than just the material universe and the laws of nature: It is full of spirits of many kinds, including the spirits of humans, animals, plants, streams and rivers, and those that inhabit many other natural phenomena. In addition to the laws of nature, there is magic that supersedes these laws. Belief in a God or multiple gods, as well as belief in other types of incorporeal entities (numbers, timeless moral truths, laws of logic, etc.), is compatible with paganism. This worldview is highly supernaturalistic. Wicca is an example of paganism that is fairly common in the West; in India, Jainism could be considered a form of paganism.[11]

In addition to worldviews that are explicitly naturalist or explicitly supernaturalist, there are some that blend aspects of naturalism and supernaturalism. Inasmuch as naturalism denies the existence of the supernatural, it seems like this should be impossible, but it's not. A few examples will make this clear.

Deism is a blended worldview. Deism is like monotheism in that it believes in one god. This seems to make it a version of supernaturalism. However, deists believe that God, being all-wise, created a world that is so perfect that it does not need his presence or his interference in order to continue to function. In effect, God created a perpetual motion machine. Therefore, God is not present and active in the world. In fact, he is absent from it. Because deism says there is no god present in this world, deism seems like a form of naturalism. That said, nothing in deism rules out belief in ghosts, souls, incorporeal minds, and the like, nor immaterial entities like abstract numbers, moral principles, human rights, etc. A deist who holds to an absentee God but grants that various sorts of immaterial entities exist is closer to supernaturalism than naturalism.

Panentheism is also a blended worldview. It is similar to pantheism in that it holds that the natural world is God. However, while pantheism downplays any immaterial element in the universe/God, panentheism boldly

---

11. The term "pagan" is sometimes used as a pejorative, but in this book the term is being used in its academic sense. Hence, when Wicca and Jainism are classified as pagan, this is not intended as a slight in any way. It is merely an academic classification.

affirms the existence of the immaterial. Panentheism sees the physical universe as the body of God, and it holds that there is a mind or spirit that permeates this body. This explains the appearance in the universe of things that seem intelligently designed: They are a reflection of the intelligence that pervades the physical world.

Like deists, panentheists have room in their worldview for incorporeal entities other than God. A panentheist who believes that the physical universe has an immaterial mind or spirit and also believes that humans have immaterial minds and/or spirits—while believing in ghosts, angels, abstract numbers, timeless moral truths, and the like—is clearly closer to supernaturalism than naturalism. However, inasmuch as panentheism views all these as aspects of the natural world, even if they are not all physical, we can see that panentheism blurs the lines between naturalism and supernaturalism.

A final example of a blended worldview is what is sometimes called **Eastern monism**. Various Eastern religions, including Advaita Vedanta Hinduism, Mahayana Buddhism, and Taoism, affirm, in essence, that all reality is one organism. That's called monism, which basically means "one-ism." In some ways this is similar to pantheism, and it's even closer to panentheism, both of which are monistic. Different religions work out the details in various ways, but the central idea is that our failure to recognize that we are one with the universe is the central aspect of the human dilemma. They view the bifurcations between physical and spiritual, between natural and supernatural, between human and non-human, as the main cause of our problems, large and small. They don't necessarily deny these bifurcations, but they affirm that there is a much higher truth: that everything is one.

The attentive reader may wonder where **postmodernism** fits into this chart of possible worldviews. Actually, postmodernism doesn't fit very well into the chart. That's because postmodernism involves rejecting the possibility of developing a fully coherent worldview. Postmodernism replaces the overreach of modernism with a sort of skepticism about the possibility, and even the value, of developing a "theory of everything." This skepticism itself may constitute a sort of worldview—but that's not how a postmodernist would view it.

So now that we understand what the term "worldview" means and we've seen examples of different kinds of worldviews, several questions arise naturally. Must a person have a worldview? How does a person acquire a worldview, and can one change one's worldview? What's the value of a worldview? Zach, Hannah, Angelo, and Suresh will be wrestling with these issues throughout the book. These and related questions will be dealt with in our next chapter on philosophy.

QUESTIONS TO PONDER

- What kind of people have a worldview?
- Do you have a worldview?
- What is your worldview?
- Why does it matter what your worldview is?

TERMS TO KNOW

- worldview
- belief system
- naturalism
- supernaturalism
- physicalism
- nihilism
- secular humanism
- pantheism
- monotheism
- theism
- polytheism
- paganism
- deism
- panentheism
- Eastern monism
- postmodernism

FOR FURTHER READING

Naugle, David K. *Worldview: The History of a Concept*. Eerdmans, 2002. This is a thoroughly researched study of the development and meaning of the term "worldview" that also manages to be quite readable (for an academic work).

Sire, James. *Naming the Elephant: Worldview as a Concept*. 2nd ed. IVP Academic, 2015. A sort of sequel to *The Universe Next Door*, this is Sire's more academic study of worldviews.

Sire, James. *The Universe Next Door*. 5th ed. IVP Academic, 2009. This has become the standard survey of worldviews: It's both readable and comprehensive.

Sunshine, Glenn S. *Why You Think the Way You Do: The Story of Western Worldviews from Rome to Home*. Zondervan Academic, 2009. This volume traces the development of the worldviews that dominate the Western world, thus helping us understand how we arrived at the worldviews that we find in our midst today.

PHILOSOPHY

SYNOPSIS

As a discipline, philosophy is intimidating to many people, even though we informally philosophize about many things in our lives. By starting with the basics, almost anyone can gain philosophical knowledge and skill with enough practice and encouragement.

DIALOGUE

It had been a busy week for everyone. At various points, each member of the new group had felt some doubts about whether joining this group and committing to weekly meetings had been a good idea.

The first meeting had been great, but as the next meeting drew closer, they all began to question themselves. *Is this really worth it?* What about all the other things they could be doing with their time instead of spending hours reading a philosophy book and then meeting with this group of strangers? Each person also struggled with impostor syndrome, feeling that the others were more suited for the discussion than they were. Would they have anything to contribute? Would the others view them as dead weight? What were they thinking, committing to this weekly meeting?

But once they started trickling into the coffee shop, any negative feelings quickly dissolved. Everyone greeted each other warmly, and that sense of ease they'd felt at their first meeting quickly emerged. Before they knew it, they were talking about their weeks and reacquainting themselves with each other's life stories. Everyone relaxed into cheerful conversation.

After some time catching up, Zach pulled out his book. "Should we get started?"

"Yes, let's," Hannah said.

"Our reading for this week was still somewhat introductory—an overview of the various topics addressed by philosophy. Maybe we could go through the topics and talk about how each of us understands them?"

"Sounds good to me," Suresh said. "I wonder if we could also try to apply this chapter to some of the issues going on in the world today."

"Like what?" Hannah asked.

"I've been hearing and seeing a lot about growing unrest around the country over different issues, and I've been at a loss about what to make of them," Suresh said.

"Do you have specific events in mind, Suresh?" Angelo asked. He wondered if he and Suresh were concerned about the same things.

"I do," Suresh said. "I'm thinking about the protests around the country over injustice, government corruption, and the struggles of many in the lower economic classes."

"We can certainly try," Zach said. "There may not always be something in the reading that applies directly to what's going on in the country, but I can see how several topics we'll address do apply."

"I just want to avoid making our discussions each week so abstract that they don't have any bearing on our day-to-day life," Suresh said. "The reading this week talks about the idea that philosophy is an activity that addresses real life."

"That's a great point," Angelo agreed. "I'd also like to see how the readings and our conversations help us think correctly about life."

Everyone opened their books as Zach began the discussion. "Why don't we start with the topic of epistemology, or the theory of knowledge. As a scientist, I believe that science is the surest path to knowledge. The scientific method has proven to be reliable for centuries and has produced many results that have benefited humankind. When we extend the method to soft sciences like psychology, anthropology, and sociology, we see that we can discover reliable truth through almost any field using the scientific method."

Hannah looked down at her notebook, where she had jotted down some thoughts. "While I appreciate all that science has done for humanity, I'm cautious about singing its praises without serious reservations." Hannah's eyes darkened a bit as she thought about the harm some had done in the name of science. "That's why I place more stock in human experience. I know some things to be true because of the emotional satisfaction I receive from them and because they provide meaning for me. In some ways, I believe we make our own truth—because there may not be a reality out there to discover. I don't deny the importance of rationality and the need to make sure I'm not delusional in my beliefs, but I think there are many more paths to knowledge than just the scientific method."

"I agree, at least with your last point," Zach said. "I would just place more emphasis on the method and consider it the final arbiter of truth."

Angelo tapped his thumb against the table. "I think both empirical research and experience can show us the truth," he said. "However, I would add God's revelation to that. I believe that we can know some things only as God reveals them to us, because he has infinite knowledge and we don't. God has designed us to know him and our world, and he made our minds and senses to know truth when our faculties are functioning correctly. We *are* finite though, and our thinking is sometimes flawed, so sometimes we believe things that aren't true. Our subjective experience and our desires often get in the way of our ability to see and know things as they truly are. For me, the Bible is the ultimate arbiter of truth."

"I'm torn on this issue," Suresh chimed in. "My education here seems to conflict with my Eastern upbringing, which taught me that truth is found within and isn't a singular thing. I understand Hannah's emphasis on the personal, experiential nature of knowledge. I know that science has brought us so many benefits, but I believe truth is more personal than simply scientific knowledge. I have confidence that I know something only if it strikes a deep connection within me."

"Wow!" Zach said. "We have some seriously different views on epistemology!" He was pleased by the variety of thought processes in the group.

"And yet we all seem to have a basic appreciation for the role that empirical observations and research have in knowledge formation."

"I can't help wondering," Hannah said, "if we'd find this variety in views among our coworkers and friends—the people we interact with on a daily basis—if we actually talked about these things."

"That's a great question," Angelo said. "I guess I often assume that people mostly think the same way as I do on core issues."

Zach set his coffee cup down. "Why don't we talk about a couple more topics from the reading and then try to apply these questions to the protests," he said.

The group looked back at their books.

"*Metaphysics* is the study of reality. It asks questions like, 'What is reality?' and 'Is there anything beyond material reality, such as spirit or soul?' and 'What are people?' Does anyone have thoughts on this?"

"I'll share," Suresh said. "My friend Disha, at the restaurant, is helping me reclaim some of my Eastern ways of thinking. We've been talking about this a lot lately. One of the most important principles of Buddhism is that nothing is permanent and everything is constantly changing. In reality, nothing exists—because every nanosecond, everything changes. What we think of as becoming, enduring, and ceasing is an illusion. At the core of our suffering is the mistaken belief that there is a self that exists independently of everything else." Suresh looked around the table. "Buddhism says that all is one, so the way to peace is to escape the illusion that I exist separately from everything else in the universe."

"Wow," Hannah said. "That's a lot to wrap my mind around."

"Yeah, I know," Suresh said. "I'm not sure *I* understand it entirely myself. I do understand the attraction though. I have become more peaceful since trying to see all things as one."

Zach set his book down. "That is fascinating. And it's so foreign to everything I've ever thought. My understanding of reality is pretty simple—everything that exists is material reality. I don't believe in metaphysical realities like God, the soul, or anything else like that. What we mean when we say *soul* or *spirit* is simply the firing of the synapses in our brain that make us think and act the way we do. I find this perspective helpful because then I don't have to try to figure out the immaterial concepts of soul or spirit. For me, it's better to stick with empirical reality that can be studied objectively by the scientific method."

"If there's no such things as soul or spirit, are our choices really free?" Angelo asked. "Wouldn't that make us robots, completely controlled by unconscious forces? And what about abstract concepts like love, justice, beauty, and virtue? If there are no immaterial realities, then what do *those* words mean?"

"Well, no . . ." Zach stammered a bit. "I mean, I still believe we have free will and are more than robots, but . . . I guess I'm trying to stick with things we can *really* know and avoid the speculation that so often comes with religion."

"It seems that takes you back to epistemology, doesn't it?" Suresh asked.

Zach thought for a moment and then nodded. "I guess it does. I never noticed that. My conception of metaphysical reality seems to be predetermined by my epistemology." He shook his head as if to clear his thoughts. "Regardless, I still think I can explain everything with a materialistic metaphysic even if there are some conundrums."

"This is what I was hoping would happen in this group," Hannah said, "that we would challenge each other so we can refine our beliefs and view of the world. My view is that there is no givenness to reality. While people can make things like tools or works of art that have a purpose, we ourselves have no purpose. We are simply raw material. We can and must decide what we are. This quote from Jean-Paul Sartre sums it up for me: 'Man is nothing else but that which he makes of himself.' Every person must decide at some point what to do with the fact that they exist."

Suresh scratched his head. "Wow, Hannah. I have a hard time wrapping my head around this. Do you find this perspective hopeful or depressing? It feels like it could go both ways."

"It really could . . ." Hannah said. "I sometimes do feel anxious or cynical, but this viewpoint often fills me with hope that I can pursue a purpose of my own choosing, that I can strive to make something significant of myself."

Everyone pondered that for a moment.

"This is so interesting," Angelo said. "I believe that reality starts with God, who has existed eternally. I also believe that God is triune. That means that he is one in essence and three in person—Father, Son, and Spirit."

Suresh lifted a hand in question. "I'm sorry, but how is that possible? One essence but three people?"

Angelo smiled. "I know the Trinity sounds contradictory, but I would call it a paradox rather than a contradiction."

"What's the difference?" Suresh asked.

"If I understand the terminology correctly, a paradox is an *apparent* contradiction, not an actual contradiction. When I say God is one, I mean that he is one being, but within the being of God are three persons who are distinct from each other, but each is God."

"I'm not sure I understand that."

"I don't completely understand it either," Angelo said, "but Christians have always believed in the Trinity because the Bible reveals that this is God's nature. Besides, if God is infinite, there will be things about God we don't fully understand."

"I guess that makes sense," Suresh said. "I'm sorry I interrupted. You were just starting to tell us your view of metaphysics."

"No problem!" Angelo said. "My understanding is that a Christian view of metaphysics begins with the eternally existing triune God. Humans are unique because they are made in God's image, so our givenness relates directly to God."

Angelo then shared about what Christians refer to as the Fall. "When the first humans disobeyed God, sin was introduced and a curse fell on the world. Because of this, I believe that sin and evil are real things. The focus of the Christian faith is on the life, death, and resurrection of Jesus, who bridges the gap between the eternal, infinite God and creation." Angelo spoke with great enthusiasm. "Everything in creation is longing for and anticipating the restoration of all things to a perfect state when Jesus returns to judge the world. So this present, imperfect reality is anticipating a future, perfect reality."

"I grew up in a Christian home and church," Hannah said, "but I've never heard this explained so clearly."

"Should we move on to the subject of ethics?" Zach asked the group.

Zach then explained atheism and how it grounds ethics on the basic drive of natural selection—survival. Whatever promotes survival is ethical and whatever diminishes the possibility of survival is unethical. Survival for humans is best encapsulated in the phrase *human flourishing*—that humans don't simply seek to survive by the skin of their teeth in minimal conditions but rather pursue the healthiest life possible, with protection and comfort that keeps them from having to spend so much time trying to meet basic needs.

"This pursuit of flourishing is best accomplished by what some call 'enlightened self-interest,'" Zach said, "meaning actions that lead to flourishing not only for yourself but also for all of humanity—and even for all of life in the universe—are ethical actions."

"Couldn't you also say that a society that normalizes complete sexual freedom might be one that diminishes flourishing," Angelo asked, "especially in light of the known sociological consequences of infidelity, children born out of wedlock, broken families, and more?"

"I wouldn't deny that," Zach said. "I just don't think we need to see sexual activity in moral terms but rather as something that can contribute to or detract from flourishing. Sex wouldn't be associated with guilt and would instead be viewed in the realm of social good."

Angelo brought up his struggle with this perspective. "What is and isn't considered good in society seems to be too vague to be useful in real life."

"I'm also struggling to reconcile what you're saying," Hannah said. "I agree about the need for people to work together for the flourishing of society, but it seems that people could legitimately disagree on how to achieve flourishing. You make it sound cut-and-dried, but I don't believe life is quite that neat."

Hannah shared her perspective on ethics—that they are more subjective and individualistic. When humans ask if something is good or bad, we are asking the wrong question. Existentialism rejects an external source and standard of morality. It is concerned first with personal freedom and then with the freedom of others.

"For me, any action that conflicts with the value of freedom is unethical," Hannah said. "My fear with Zach's proposal is that some people's freedom could be denied in order to create flourishing for others."

"That's a fair concern," Zach said, "but I think your view may be unrealistic. Preserving the freedom of someone who is destructive to others presents its own conflict."

Suresh jumped in. "I was wondering the same thing. If there is no external morality besides preserving freedom, wouldn't that potentially lead to conflict between freedom and flourishing?"

"I guess that's possible," Hannah said. "I'll have to consider that. I really appreciate the feedback."

"I have never been able to talk so openly about these things," Suresh said. "I'm really enjoying the dialogue."

"I second that," Angelo said, raising his coffee cup in a faux toast. "I'm learning so much from all of you!"

Hannah asked Suresh to tell the group more about his understanding of Eastern ethics.

"Buddhism and Hinduism share core ethical commitments. Because there are different branches of both religions, there is some difference. They center on the principle of doing no harm to others and respecting all life. In some ways, they sound a lot like Christian ethics."

Suresh shared the five central ethical principles of Hinduism: non-injury, non-fornication, non-stealing, non-lying, and non-possessiveness. Other writings add principles such as steadfastness, uprightness, compassion, moderation, purity, patience, self-control, and absence of pride. Buddhism has similar principles known as the Six Perfections and the Ten Bad Courses of Action, which also forbid divisive and harsh speech and command wisdom and generosity.

"That is a serious call to morality," Zach said. "What's interesting to me is that I appreciate so many of those virtues and strive to practice them despite the general nature of my ethics. I guess I would say that I see those as things that lead to human flourishing even though atheism doesn't specifically demand them."

"I know I want neighbors who live this way. Don't you?" Angelo said.

"Totally!" Hannah exclaimed. "I guess that's what I think everyone should aspire to as they exercise their freedom. However, in my belief system, people could choose otherwise."

Angelo nodded. "Or even the opposite."

Hannah thought for a moment. "I suppose you're right. I'd like to think people are basically good and will naturally choose these virtues, but I have to admit that not everyone does."

"How well do you think you live up to these ethics, Suresh?" Zach asked. "They seem very demanding."

"I try hard to live up to these principles, but I often fail. Like Angelo said, I want other people to live this way so that my life will be good. Who wouldn't want to be surrounded by others who are seeking to live this way? The problem comes when I can't live up to them myself. What do I do with my own failures?"

"Can *anyone* live up to them?" Zach asked.

"Yes, I think so," Suresh said. "In these religions, those who keep these ethics obtain enlightenment, so we do believe it is possible. But it takes many lives, hence the belief in reincarnation."

Angelo thumbed at the pages on his book. "You're right that many of these values are shared with Christianity. In my faith, ethics begins with the character of God."

Angelo shared more about his understanding of God, that God is infinitely loving, righteous, holy, merciful, just, and good. The commandments God gives in the Bible find their origin in God himself. Since God has revealed himself in creation, religions share many of the same values because they can see that such behaviors lead to human flourishing, as God designed them to. One difference is that in the Christian faith the purpose of ethical living is primarily to please God and only secondarily for human good. So, there is a personal aspect to it.

"We are commanded to be like God morally," Angelo continued, "which means we strive for something we can never fully attain on our own. Christians believe that apart from God's transformation, we wouldn't want to be like God. So, ethics begins with the need for God to change our inner being, because otherwise we wouldn't even want to keep his commands. This is where the need for Jesus enters. Jesus is the only one who perfectly kept the law of God, and he did it on our behalf. The Bible says that for our sake God made Jesus to be sin, even though he knew no sin, so that in him we might become the righteousness of God. That means the innocence of Jesus was credited to our account, and our sin was what put Jesus on the cross. This is important because when we fail to live up to God's standards, forgiveness is available through Jesus."

Suresh nodded thoughtfully. "That would be a major difference between

Christianity and Eastern religion. We don't have the concept of forgiveness from a god, but rather debt to the impersonal principle of karma. So, rather than forgiveness, we seek to pay off karma. Once again, that requires many lives through reincarnation."

Hannah spoke up. "Since we covered most of the chapter, should we discuss how we each view the protests around the country, as Suresh suggested?"

"I'd love to," Suresh said. "I've been watching coverage of the protests over injustice, housing shortages, labor disputes, and environmental causes. My coworkers and I have been sharing our concerns. Many of us come from countries that have seen violent coups and a breakdown of law and order that drove them to the US for safety and a better life. Now we're seeing similar events here and wondering if it'll get as bad as it was in our home countries."

Suresh looked around the table. "What do each of you think is the cause of this growing unrest? And how will our worldviews inform our actions if things get worse?"

"I have really mixed feelings," Angelo said. "But I share your concern. I think some of the destruction from the protests could be avoided if protestors respected the law and authorities enforced it. Plenty of peaceful protests over very serious injustices have happened over the years without the violence we're seeing today. Think of the civil rights movement and pro-life rallies that have been almost entirely free of destruction. As a Christian, I don't believe violence and destruction are justified simply because we believe we have been wronged."

"I agree that the looting and destruction of property in some protests is unfortunate." Hannah's voice was measured, but there was a flash of fire in her eyes. "But I think you may underestimate the rage people feel when they take to the streets. They may feel that no one will notice or act unless the protest is disruptive. And the effects of protests have been clearly proven. Laws have been changed. Corporations and political leaders have felt pressure to act. In most cases, I personally think the damage done is worth it because of the ultimate outcome. I'd be happier if every protest was peaceful, but I don't know if the results would be the same. I see all this as a struggle for freedom."

Zach nodded. "While I wouldn't put it in the same terms, I agree with

Hannah for the most part. I'd lay more blame on the part of religion. Sorry, Angelo and Suresh."

"How so?" Suresh asked.

"I don't want to blame religion for everything, but I agree with Karl Marx that religion is 'the opiate of the people.' Religion teaches people to be content in the face of injustice, poverty, and mistreatment. Just think about Jesus' command to 'turn the other cheek' when someone strikes you or the command to servants to obey their masters. Marx believed that this teaching is exactly what prevented people from rising up and throwing off the abusive authority of their leaders. As a result, common people just endured and never fought back. Only when Marx and others encouraged people to rise up and revolt did they develop the strength to refuse to live with injustice anymore."

"How did that work out for the Russian people?" Angelo asked with a slight smile.

Zach laughed. "Okay, okay, so it didn't work so well for the countries of the Soviet Union. No doubt about that. I'd argue, however, that the principle still stands and that a Marxist worldview could help provide the environment for human flourishing. Evolution in nature must be helped by our efforts in the social sphere, and fighting against injustice and inequality is one way that can happen. I'm for the protests, but I agree that protestors should minimize destruction and violence."

Suresh had been hesitant to share his thoughts on the conversation. He was hesitant to verbalize a view that might be radically different. But seeing how respectful everyone was of each other's views emboldened him to share his own.

"I know I might be an outlier, but I feel very differently about the protests. I have seen how these types of demonstrations have the potential to overturn governments or lead to anarchy. Americans have such a high standard of living and the blessing of democracy, however flawed it may be. While I believe in justice and think we should advocate for it, compared to many parts of the world, we have a very high quality of life here. When I think about the underlying causes of the protests, riots, looting, and violence, I feel like the root problem is desire."

Suresh looked around the table, trying to gauge how this was being received. "Buddhism offers a lot of help here. One of the goals of Buddhism is to rid yourself of desires because they are the root of our illusions. To me, it seems that what drives much of this unrest is a refusal to be content."

"That is a whole new perspective," Angelo murmured. "I certainly agree with many of your points. The Bible warns about discontent, lust, greed, and the conflict they can bring. I share your fear that things may get much, much worse in this country. I'm hoping our discussions will help us understand different viewpoints better so we can help bring peace."

"Ditto to what Angelo said," Zach said.

Hannah looked across the table. "You've given me a lot to think about, Suresh."

Just then, phones throughout the coffee shop began dinging. People were digging through backpacks and pockets to see what was causing so many notifications to go off at once. Zach was the only member of the group whose phone was on the table. He glanced at his phone and drew in a sharp breath.

"Oh no."

THEORY

The Nature of Philosophy

In chapter 1 we learned about worldviews, those ubiquitous sets of beliefs about the nature of reality that guide how we interpret our experiences. The chapter ended by posing some questions that it said would be addressed in chapter 2: Does everyone have a worldview? How do we get our worldviews? Can I change my worldview? And what's the value of a worldview, anyway? Let's address these.

Starting with the first question, most people have a worldview, although some people don't. Since a worldview is comprised of various beliefs about the fundamental nature of reality, anyone who is not able to have such beliefs wouldn't have a worldview. Hence newborns, for example, don't have worldviews. Similarly, people with severe intellectual disabilities may not have a worldview simply because they may not have the requisite kind of beliefs. Most people do have a worldview, though.

Your worldview is formed as you grow up. Your parents, your friends, your teachers, the shows and movies you watch, the books you read, and numerous other factors affect what you believe and therefore influence how you think about reality. And while you can certainly reflect on your worldview and make changes to it as you see fit, many people simply absorb a worldview from their environment without even being aware of it.

What is the value of having a worldview? Well, that question is perhaps a bit malformed, since it seems to imply that having a worldview is optional. It may not be possible for a thinking person to be completely "worldview free." But to answer the question: There are benefits to having a coherent set of beliefs about the fundamental nature of reality. For one thing, it frees you from feelings of inconsistency and self-contradiction that come from holding conflicting beliefs, and it can spare you the embarrassment of someone challenging you on the inconsistency of your beliefs when they contradict one another. There's even more value to having a worldview that accurately corresponds to the way things are, for that will provide a sound basis for interpreting experiences and making decisions. But since nearly everyone has a worldview, perhaps the better question is whether it can be changed, and if it can, how.

This is where **philosophy** comes in. Philosophy is "the critical examination of our foundational beliefs concerning the nature of reality, knowledge and truth, and our personal and social values."[1] Look carefully at this definition and you'll notice that philosophy is not a set of beliefs, doctrines, or positions. What is it, then? Philosophy is an *activity*. It is the activity of thinking carefully about what you believe and why you believe it. That's something that anyone can do, regardless of what you believe. Atheists and theists can philosophize, as can communists and capitalists, Republicans, Democrats, and Libertarians, young people, middle-aged people, and senior citizens, and people of all races and nationalities. Everyone who is able to think can critically examine their fundamental beliefs and try to have a more coherent and accurate worldview, and that's what philosophy is all about.

The English word *philosophy* comes from the Greek word φιλοσοφία (*philosophia*). The Greek word is composed of two root words: *philos*, which means friend, and *sophia*, which means wisdom: "the friendship of

---

1. Mark Foreman, *Prelude to Philosophy: An Introduction for Christians* (IVP Academic, 2014), 24.

wisdom." Those people who were passionate about understanding things on a deeper level were called philosophers, the friends of wisdom. Notably, this was true regardless of their religious or political views: Atheists like Epicurus, as well as very religious thinkers like Pythagoras, were considered philosophers.

The answer to the question about whether your worldview can be changed is "yes." In fact, it's common for a person's worldview to change gradually over time. Occasionally worldviews change quickly and radically, sometimes as the result of a major life event, like moving to another part of the world, having a near-death experience, or undergoing a religious conversion. And occasionally a person consciously undertakes an evaluation of his or her worldview and in the process makes intentional changes to it.

This often happens when we study philosophy: We ask ourselves why we believe what we believe and whether it's really best to believe those things. If we find that it is, then we come away with greater assurance and understanding of the justification of our beliefs. If we find that it's not, then we adjust our beliefs to better fit the evidence and to better cohere with each other. This can be an exciting process. You get to determine your own beliefs! It can also be a bit intimidating, as you call into question things that you've always accepted without questioning. Don't be put off by this: Surely it's better to form your own worldview than to let your culture dictate what you believe, isn't it?

An inspirational story about someone committed to examining his beliefs comes from the trial and death of **Socrates**, who is sometimes called the grandfather of Western philosophy. Socrates was the teacher of Plato, who was the teacher of Aristotle, who was the teacher of Alexander the Great. Hence, he had a big impact on the development of the Western intellectual tradition.

Socrates questioned everything. He was extremely curious and wanted to understand everything around him, but because Athens was in a frequent state of war with neighboring cities, his questioning didn't sit well with the Athenian leaders. Eventually they arrested him for disturbing the peace and corrupting the youth. He was tried and then given an ultimatum: either cease questioning everything, or die. Socrates famously responded, "The unexamined life is not fit for a man to live."[2] In other words, he'd rather die than reduce himself to the level of an unthinking beast. He was executed accordingly.

What's inspiring in this sad tale is Socrates' devotion to the pursuit of wisdom. From his day to ours, a constant stream of people have contemplated, studied, and researched life's most fundamental questions. Some of them have been philosophers; others have been theologians, scientists, scholars of various sorts, and thoughtful laypeople. These 2,400 years of work have yielded much insight: Our grasp of logic has advanced considerably, and so has our understanding of how truth is grasped. This has enabled us to set aside some beliefs as clearly mistaken. However, many debates continue.

In this book we'll examine a wide range of ongoing philosophical debates, looking at the positions that people take on foundational issues and the arguments they use to support their positions. We'll also look at ways to objectively evaluate the strength of those arguments. We won't tell you what to believe, but we will help you develop your skills at deciding for yourself where the truth lies.

Philosophical Topics

Since evaluating the strength of the arguments and evidence that support a belief requires careful thinking, and since careful thinking requires the skillful use of logic, we'll begin our exploration of philosophy with a study of logic. Then we'll take our sharpened reasoning skills and apply them to a series of philosophical issues that will be grouped into six categories: epistemology, metaphysics, religion, ethics, jurisprudence, and philosophical anthropology. We believe these are the most important categories of problems studied in philosophy.

Epistemology is the technical term for what's sometimes called the **theory of knowledge**. In the study of epistemology, we investigate the relationship between belief and knowledge, what it means for a belief to

---

2. Plato, *Euthyphro. Apology. Crito. Phaedo*, ed. Christopher Emlyn-Jones and William Preddy, *Loeb Classical Library* 36 (Harvard University Press, 2017): 181. The more traditional translation is "The unexamined life is not worth living."

be true, and various ways that we can tell whether a belief actually is true. Since one goal of philosophy is to develop a worldview composed of true beliefs, it's important to study epistemology early on in our philosophizing so that we understand exactly what constitutes a true belief. Once we've determined that, it can serve as a standard for our subsequent philosophical investigations.

Metaphysics is the study of the ultimate nature of reality. People generally assume that they know what the nature of reality is, or at least they do until they begin studying it. Then they find that there is an array of possible positions on this issue. Is reality physical? Or is reality fundamentally spiritual? What is spirit? What is matter, for that matter? Is matter reducible to energy? If it is, is that different from being reducible to spirit? And what are humans—material, mental, spiritual, all three, or something else entirely? The various possible positions that people take on these issues have implications that make them important questions for us to answer.

Philosophy of religion is the application of the tools of philosophical analysis to the sometimes perplexing questions that arise in the context of religious belief. It addresses interesting questions such as how we can know about things that are not experienced with the senses, whether gods and/or angels exist, and if they do, what they are like. In some ways it's similar to theology, but it relies on logical reasoning from human experiences rather than divine revelation.

Ethics is the study of what is morally right and wrong and how we can know which is which. Ethics can be studied in religion classes and is sometimes studied in psychology, sociology, and anthropology classes. However, many professional ethicists are trained as philosophers because the critical thinking skills acquired through studying philosophy are a significant benefit to the study of ethics.

Jurisprudence, or philosophy of law, is the study of the presuppositions that underlie the legal system of any given society and the logical outworking of those presuppositions within that legal system. For example, the American legal system presupposes that all humans have intrinsic rights, but that is an assumption that has not been shared by very many cultures in recorded history. In the study of jurisprudence we can ask whether this assumption is justified, and if it is, then how.

Philosophical anthropology is the study of humanity that is conducted using the tools of philosophical investigation. In this unit we ask ourselves what human nature is, whether humanity is unique, why we are here, and what happens when we die. These are really big questions that people have been wrestling with from Socrates up through the existentialists, phenomenologists, and today's post-humanists.

As we study each of these areas of philosophy, you'll discover new ways of looking at reality. Some of these new ways will seem intriguing, like they might make good sense, while others will seem too strange to possibly be true. It can be helpful to postpone judgment about the plausibility of a view until after you've come to fully understand it. We're all prone to jumping to conclusions before we have sufficient data and understanding to be justified in making a judgment about something.

Philosophy's Importance

There are a number of reasons why studying philosophy is beneficial—and even *important*. One reason is that philosophy emphasizes the development and use of critical thinking skills. For some reason, courses on logic and critical thinking are entirely absent from most elementary and secondary school curricula. It's as if we expect students to know how to think logically without ever being taught logic. We don't have that attitude toward math, reading, writing, or any other subject. It's odd that we have it toward logic. Clearly, people can figure out some basic critical thinking skills without a teacher or textbook—just as they can figure out some of the basics of addition and subtraction simply through life experiences. But just as it would be unrealistic to expect many people to advance beyond the basics of mathematics without the help of a teacher, it's unrealistic to expect the untrained to figure out informal and formal fallacies; deductive, inductive, and abductive logic; and the various other skills of critical thinking without instruction. Philosophy is essential to instill critical thinking skills.

Philosophy is also important because it addresses important issues that no other method of research addresses. In fact, some issues cannot be addressed by other approaches: The proper tools for investigating them belong specifically to philosophy. For example, normative ethics cannot be addressed by science, mathematics, history, psychology, anthropology, or sociology. Some of these disciplines can tell us some things about some aspects of an ethical problem, but they cannot tell us what makes an act moral or immoral. That's a specifically philosophical issue that must be addressed using philosophical tools.[3] Similar things can be said about epistemological and metaphysical problems that are susceptible to philosophical analysis but cannot be analyzed using the tools of science, mathematics, history, psychology, and the like.

An example of this comes from the perennial debate on the morality of abortion. Many who oppose abortion do so because they believe that a fetus is a person who has not done anything worthy of death. Therefore, they believe that an abortion is an unjust killing of a person and, hence, is immoral. In contrast, many who support abortion believe that a fetus, at least up to a certain point in its development (and for some people, all the way up to birth), is *not* a person and therefore aborting it is not immoral. So the key disagreement between these people is about the personhood of a fetus: Is a fetus a person? When does that which is developing in the womb become an actual person?

This is a tricky question to answer. Many people mistakenly assume that it's a medical question, one for scientists and physicians to answer. But while such experts can tell us a lot about the development of the body in the womb, they can tell us neither what constitutes personhood nor when personhood begins, for those questions involve more than bodily development. Historians, on the other hand, can tell us that ancient Greeks and Romans generally did not consider it immoral to abandon infants, allowing them to die. Historians can tell us that even though there was disagreement in early Christianity about the ontological status of a fetus before it has "formed" or "quickened," the early church was unanimous in considering abortion a sin.[4] However, while historians can tell us what others have believed, they cannot tell us whether a fetus is a person, nor whether abortion is moral or immoral. For this, we need philosophy.

3. Issues of normative ethics can be addressed by theology, but when theology addresses such issues, it is able to do so because it is incorporating the tools of philosophy.
4. The term "formed" refers to taking on human appearance, while "quicken" refers to a fetus moving on its own.

A final reason that philosophy is important is that it affects how we live our lives. What you believe directly impacts what you do. If you believe that eating carrots is good for your eyes, then you're likely to eat carrots. If you believe that global warming is a threat to humanity, you're likely to favor environmentalism. If you believe that animals have feelings and value their lives, you're likely to consider vegetarianism. If you believe in God, you're likely to pray. That carrots have health benefits is not very controversial, but the other three examples certainly are (to varying degrees). Philosophy can help you think through these issues so that you can make an informed decision about what to believe and how to live in a reasonable and responsible way.

Zach, Hannah, Angelo, and Suresh will help each other gain clarity on their beliefs and their implications as they talk. How would our culture be improved if we spent more time talking graciously and constructively about our philosophical differences? Maybe we could help each other refine what we think and believe.

QUESTIONS TO PONDER

- If philosophy began in antiquity, how can it be of any use in modernity?
- What exactly did Socrates mean by "the unexamined life"? Was he right that the unexamined life is not worthy of human beings? What does this mean?
- Do you think it's necessary to be taught how to think logically, or does it just come naturally to most people?
- It's not just logic that is absent from most elementary and secondary curricula—so is philosophy in general. Why do you think this is? Would it be good to add some philosophy classes to the curriculum?

TERMS TO KNOW

- philosophy
- Socrates
- epistemology
- theory of knowledge
- metaphysics
- philosophy of religion
- ethics
- jurisprudence
- philosophical anthropology

FOR FURTHER READING

Kenny, Anthony. *A New History of Western Philosophy*. Clarendon, 2010. This is a one-thousand-page survey of the history of Western philosophy. There are both shorter and longer histories of philosophy; this book represents a fairly complete history in one volume.

Miller, Ed L. and John Jensen. *Questions that Matter: An Invitation to Philosophy*. 6th ed. McGraw-Hill, 2008. This, as a survey of the issues, ideas, and the history of philosophy, has become a standard university textbook. It is very fair in its presentations and contains excerpts from the most important thinkers in the Western tradition.

Moreland, J. P. and William Lane Craig. *Philosophical Foundations for a Christian Worldview*. 2nd ed. IVP Academic, 2017. This text intentionally approaches philosophies as worldviews and makes direct comparisons between rival worldviews and their supporting arguments. It is, as the title indicates, written from a Christian perspective.

Morris, Tom. *Philosophy for Dummies*. 2nd ed. John Wiley & Sons, 2022. Don't let the title fool you: This is a very good (while very readable) introduction to philosophy.

LOGIC

3

LOGICAL FALLACIES

SYNOPSIS

This chapter addresses the need for correct thinking by considering various fallacies that commonly occur in argumentation. Learning to spot such fallacies will enable us to avoid them and will assist us in developing sound arguments, the conclusions of which can be trusted.

DIALOGUE

As Suresh entered the café, his three new philosophical friends were already seated at the group's preferred table, reserved for them by the friendly staff at Brews Brothers. Their meeting the week before had been interrupted by a disturbing news alert about what was now being called a domestic terror incident. As he got to the table with his latte, he wasn't surprised to discover that the group was talking about it.

"I still can't believe it!" Hannah said. "How was someone able to plant explosives on such a busy bridge?"

Zach shook his head. "No one has figured that out yet. I read that a train crosses Chesterton Bridge an average of every six minutes, carrying both freight cars and passenger trains. If all the bombs had detonated, a lot of people would have been killed."

Angelo looked up from his phone, "It says here that 150,000 to 200,000 people cross that bridge every day! Whoever is responsible set out to murder a lot of innocent people."[1]

"Thank goodness only one of the bombs triggered," Hannah said.

The FTA and Amtrak had announced that repairs to the damaged section of the bridge would begin that week to limit potential economic damage to businesses in the area and to avoid inconveniencing commuters. Given how slowly projects like this generally get completed, it was almost more amazing how swiftly they were beginning repairs, never mind that somebody had been able to plant bombs on the bridge unobserved.

Suresh settled in and joined the conversation. "The five other bombs had the capacity to destroy the entire bridge. What a horribly heinous act."

Angelo took a sip of his drink. "I think it's interesting that no one has publicly taken credit. Usually terrorists want credit for this sort of thing."

Zach agreed and added, "Perhaps the terrorists didn't come forward because it failed and they don't want to give themselves away before trying something else."

Everyone shuddered at that thought.

"A lack of information sure hasn't prevented people from having opinions about it," Angelo said.

Suresh nodded. "News shows and editorials are full of speculation, much of it seemingly pulled out of thin air."

"This is actually a great opportunity," Zach said. "I think we should do some study on logic and arguments before we get into the rest of our conversations. If we don't reason correctly, we won't progress very effectively."

"Are you suggesting," Hannah asked, "that we won't *naturally* be logical?"

Everyone at the table laughed.

"You'd be surprised!" Zach said, laughing as well. "But seriously, it's easy to slip into sloppy reasoning. I'm sure we all do it occasionally. And while we're trying to work out our worldviews, I think careful and accurate reasoning is crucial and is worth exploring."

"What are you thinking?" Suresh asked.

---

1. This bridge is fictional, but railway bridges with this level of activity exist.

"I purchased several copies of a short book on critical thinking."[2] Zach passed the books around to each member of the group.

He explained a little more about the book. After laying some foundations in basic logic, the book would cover some of the informal argumentation fallacies people are prone to ("informal" in the sense that they don't violate strict logic but are constructed in such a way that they mislead).

"I was thinking we could do two things over the next week: One, read the book, or at least the section on argument fallacies, and two, catch the news and other discussions about the railway attack to see how logical people's argumentation is. It could be instructive."

* * *

A week later, the group was eager to share and compare the results of their investigations. Everyone settled into their customary spots with beverages in hand.

"It's interesting," Angelo said, "that no one has claimed responsibility and also that the authorities aren't saying if they know who did it. But it sure hasn't prevented people from having opinions."

"No kidding," Suresh said. "Another chef at work decided to explain his theory to the entire kitchen staff. I can't remember all the details, but it involved the Chinese, the North Vietnamese, Swiss explosives manufacturers, and some kind of conspiracy with the governor of Pennsylvania, where the bridge is located."

"Did anyone challenge his theory?" Angelo asked.

"Of course. I asked how he knew he was right. He said it 'just made sense,' and when people pushed back, he said we couldn't prove he was wrong."

"Ah!" Hannah said. "That's one of the argument fallacies we read about this week, the argument from ignorance: My theory is true because you haven't yet proved it false."

"Using that reasoning," Angelo said, "the more complicated a theory is, the more likely it would be to be true. But it seems obvious to me that lack of evidence against something doesn't equal evidence *for* it."

---

2. See the end of the chapter for recommended resources on critical thinking.

Zach nodded. “That’s a great example.”

Suresh spoke up. “You know, as I read that section in the book, I didn’t expect to see or hear most of the fallacies in real life. But when you’re looking for them, it’s amazing how many pop up!”

“What’d you hear?” Zach asked.

“This one is funny, although I suppose it’s not as funny when you realize that people take it seriously. You know the famous Western actor Clint Wayne? He’s getting up in years now, but he put out a statement explaining the political situation and why people might feel forced to make this kind of attempt. He got some airtime, and people seemed to think his explanation was plausible.”

“Why would this be an example of an argument fallacy?” Hannah asked. “He’s a famous actor. Hasn’t he earned the right to express his opinion?”

“How does being a successful actor qualify someone to explain a political situation or to claim to be able to get inside the head of terrorists, given that he has the same information we all have?”

“I think Suresh’s point,” Zach said, “is that an authority in one area is not automatically an authority in other areas.”

“Okay, I can see that,” Hannah said. “If someone accepted Mr. Wayne’s explanation simply because he is a famous actor, that person would be appealing to authority, which is a fallacy.”

“I can see how easy it would be to do,” Angelo jumped in, “especially if you respect or admire the authority figure. We all accept the word of authorities in various areas of our lives. Most of what we know about the bridge incident has come from news outlets or pundits. Why should we believe them, but not Mr. Wayne?”

“The credibility of any authority depends on their access to privileged information,” Zach said. “If I had a question about cooking, I’d ask Suresh. If you wanted to know about chemistry, I might be a good source of information. It’d be reasonable to believe Suresh or me in our areas of expertise until contrary information surfaced. The appeal to authority is a fallacy when the authorities in question have no expertise in that arena and yet set themselves up as having the right to pontificate, as Mr. Wayne seems to have done.”

Zach excused himself for a moment to refill his coffee and stretch his legs. Suresh took the opportunity to grab some food and brought something back for everyone to share.

"I'd love to add an example," Hannah said as they all took their seats again. "An online editorial argued that the bombers were either domestic terrorists or Islamic jihadists. The writer went on to give arguments against the bombers being domestic, leading to the conclusion that we're once again facing Islamist terror like America experienced in 2001."

"Why do you think this is a fallacy?" Zach prompted.

"It seems like a false dilemma to me," Hannah said. "What if the terrorists aren't domestic or Islamist? His whole case for the bombers being Muslim was that he tried to rule out the only other option, but it seems like there could be other alternatives."

"Absolutely," Zach said. "Another fallacy is *amphiboly*, where ambiguous language is used in order to leave various interpretations open."

"Can you give an example?" Hannah asked.

"Sure. This statement for example, 'The politician gravely assured his constituents that he would accept no bribes that would affect his judgment.' Is he promising to accept no bribes or to accept only bribes that would affect his judgment?"

The group laughed.

"I can see how amphiboly could be useful for politicians," Hannah said, eating the last of the pastries Suresh had provided. "Should I get us something else to eat?"

Everyone agreed that they had eaten enough.

Suresh set down his coffee. "I was amazed at how certain explanations for the bombing picked up steam even though no new evidence came to light. Early in the week, an analyst suggested that the bombing was a deliberate attempt to disrupt the economy in view of the upcoming midterm elections. By the middle of the week, that conversation was everywhere."

"That's a great example of the bandwagon fallacy," Zach said. "We tend to think an explanation has more merit as more people embrace it. But it's unwarranted to believe something simply because several people claim that it's true—unless you know *why* they believe it's true."

Angelo nodded. "It's easy to see how a large number of people accepting something makes it attractive for me to accept as well," he said. "But I wonder—are we denying the value of tradition? Wouldn't tradition also be considered the acceptance of something by many people over a span of time? As a Christian, tradition is important to me. But it would make sense that each of you leans on various traditions, even a chemist like you, right, Zach?"

"That's a great distinction," Zach said. "Tradition has a role in all worldviews, I suppose, but the bandwagon fallacy seems to come down to this: Is the main reason you're holding to a certain belief because other people are holding it too? You wouldn't say that about Christianity, right?"

"Definitely not!"

Suresh jumped in. "The book also talks about *question begging*, or arguing in a circle. Did anyone see an example of that this week?"

"Not related to the bridge," Hannah said, "but I heard someone arguing that marijuana should be banned in his state because it's harmful. When someone asked how he knew it was harmful, he said it must be since it's illegal in some states."

"Oh wow!" Zach said. "That's definitely circular."

Suresh shared something he had heard relative to identifying the bombers that sounded like a fallacy. "A woman who had called in to a radio show said she's nervous anytime she sees Muslims at the mall or in other public places. She's afraid they'll be bombers. It seemed like a leap to assume that all Muslims are dangerous because one or a few *may* have planted a bomb. We don't even know if Muslims were involved."

Angelo pointed out that even if the bombing could be traced back to Islamist terrorists, that doesn't mean most, or even many, Muslims are terrorists.

"Exactly," Suresh said. "Generalizations like this can so easily lead to prejudice. Such sweeping conclusions from a small sample set are dangerous."

"Two other fallacies relate to this," Zach said. "*Division* is the fallacy of assuming that characteristics of the whole automatically also apply to the parts—like assuming that an Italian person must like spaghetti. Most Italians probably like pasta dishes, but we can't know for sure if that's true of any one Italian person.

"*Composition* is almost the reverse of this," he continued. "It's the fallacy of assuming that the characteristics of the parts automatically apply to the whole. For example, the fact that many Hindus live in poverty does not mean that Hinduism is a 'poor' religion—Hindu temples are often lavish and beautiful."

Suresh nodded. "It's interesting that the same mentality seems to drive this set of fallacies. No one wants to be assessed based solely on whatever group they belong to."

"This makes me think of the Golden Rule," Angelo said. "'Do unto others as you would have them do to you' is one of the central teachings of Jesus and is the principal guide to Christian behavior. I want people to treat me as an individual, listening to my specific arguments and assessing me based on who I really am. I don't want them to dismiss me or make assumptions because I'm Christian or white or male or Italian or whatever. So I should extend the same consideration to others. In that sense, critical thinking ends up being charitable."

After a moment of thought, Zach said, "Obviously I'm not a follower of Jesus, but that seems like a very reasonable way to carry on a debate. That approach would certainly result in more civility and fewer sloppy arguments."

"That sentiment isn't unique to Jesus," Suresh said. "Versions of this 'rule' are scattered throughout many religions and philosophies." He looked around the table. "The four of us may not agree on our worldviews, but hopefully we can agree on this idea."

After a few moments, Zach shifted the conversation yet again. "I think I can illustrate how the Golden Rule often *isn't* followed. I'm not on social media much—no judgment; it's just not my thing—but spending time on several platforms this week was eye-opening. I can't count how many times someone would make an argument about the event, and others would respond by calling the person an idiot or some other name."

"*Ad hominem*, right?" Suresh said.

"Yes! Attacking the person rather than responding to their arguments."

"It's a shortcut," Hannah said, "and I'm realizing that most shortcuts are sloppy reasoning. It's easy to attack people; it's more difficult to deal with arguments."

Suresh lifted a hand slightly. "Here's an example that's similar to *ad hominem* but I think illustrates another fallacy. One of the tabloids printed a wild theory about the bombing, as you might expect. An 'expert' on such incidents was hosting a blog about the bombing, and someone asked him to respond to the tabloid's theory. He basically said, 'Why should I waste my time responding to something from such an unreputable source?'"

"So he dismissed the theory based on its origin?" Angelo asked.

Suresh nodded.

"That's an excellent example of the *genetic fallacy*," Zach said, "where something is rejected based on its 'bad genes.' Does anyone remember why the book said this is a fallacy?"

"I do!" Hannah replied. "Two reasons, if I recall. First, lots of helpful and interesting things have been produced by bad or seemingly insignificant people. Also, like I said a few minutes ago, it's a shortcut. The theory itself still needs to be addressed."

"Does that mean I'd be using sloppy reasoning if I didn't respond in detail to every argument posed by kindergarteners?" Angelo asked.

Zach laughed. "Most arguments posed by kindergarteners wouldn't require detailed refutation, right? The fact that a kindergartener might have a good idea means we should be slow to dismiss them just because of their age and inexperience. We wouldn't want the kindergartner to reject our reasoning because we're 'old' and don't know our way around the playroom, would we?"

"Touché," Angelo said. "I've been guilty of dismissing some arguments because of my lack of respect for the arguer, but doing so breaks the Golden Rule *and* takes another of Hannah's shortcuts."

"How about this one?" Zach said. "We've all seen gas prices go up in the last couple weeks. They're the highest they've been this year."

Everyone nodded.

"Why does that matter?" Angelo asked.

"Some people are saying that the bombing is what drove prices up, which they then tied to the idea of nations in OPEC being behind it."

"That seems like a shaky argument, but why do you think it's a fallacy?" Hannah asked.

"In my work in the lab, I must be constantly alert to this concept. One thing will happen, and then another thing will happen at the same time or shortly thereafter—they'll be correlated in time, if you will. It is easy to jump to the conclusion that one of them is causing the other. But correlation does not prove causation. Gas prices go up all the time; without extensive knowledge of all the factors that lead to price increases, it's invalid to assume that the bombing caused it."

Zach explained that this is the *post hoc* fallacy—that since one thing follows another, it is assumed to be caused by it. "Of course, they then compounded their bad argument by tracing the bombing to evil intentions of OPEC countries without any evidence at all."

"If the bombing turns out to be unrelated to Islam, a lot of people are going to end up looking bad," Angelo said.

"Even if it turns out that Islamist terrorists are responsible, it still doesn't justify all this bad reasoning," Zach said. "Just because a conclusion turns out to be correct, that doesn't validate the arguments. In logic, as in other things, ends don't justify means."

Zach set his book on the table. "Of course, this book doesn't claim to list all the possible argumentation fallacies, just the major ones. Why don't we take a quick break and then talk about a few more?"

The group broke for a few minutes to visit the bathroom, check their phones, and refill their drinks.

As everyone settled back in, Suresh kicked off the conversation. "During a press interview with an FBI spokesperson, the reporters were able to determine that the FBI had some suspects. They started asking questions to try to uncover information about potential suspects. When one reporter asked about a specific terrorist organization, the spokesperson refused to comment. In his article the next day, the reporter declared that the spokesperson's failure to deny the organization's involvement was evidence that the organization is involved in some way. That's using the absence of evidence as evidence, right?"

"Sounds like an *argument from silence*," Angelo said, taking a sip of his topped-off coffee. "It doesn't seem like you could draw any valid conclusions from the spokesperson's refusal to answer."

"Not in this situation," Zach said. "FBI spokespeople are often evasive. Their silence should probably never be considered positive evidence."

"You're being specific though," Hannah said. "Can silence ever be interpreted as evidence?"

"I think so," Zach said. "Let's say I step away from the table after setting down my fresh coffee. When I return, the cup is empty. If I asked you guys who drank my coffee, and you and Suresh said you didn't, it might be reasonable for me to draw conclusions from Angelo's silence." Zach's eyes twinkled a bit.

"I'd never drink your coffee!" Angelo said. "You drink dark roast, and I like my coffee lighter."

Everyone laughed.

"I'm glad my coffee is safe—at least from Angelo—but you see my point, right?"

"In some contexts, silence may point to a reasonable conclusion, but for the most part, we should be cautious about interpreting the lack of evidence as evidence, right?" Suresh said.

"Yes!" Zach looked around the table. "Any other fallacies you'd like to discuss?"

Hannah set down her cup. "I've been thinking about this example ever since I read the chapter. My dad grew up in New York City and is a big New York Knicks fan. Are any of you NBA fans?"

"Not closely, but I'm sure we can follow this illustration," Angelo said.

"Suppose I was trying to prove that the Knicks are the best team in the league. To make my argument, I make the following points: New York City is the largest city in the country; the Knicks play in Madison Square Garden, the most famous sports venue in America; the team has wealthy and stable ownership; and one or two Knicks players almost always make the All-Star team. What would you think of my argument?"

"You gave an interesting assortment of arguments," Angelo said, a smile on his face, "but you left out one important thing—that they haven't won a championship in more than fifty years and only occasionally make the playoffs, even though they're in a league where almost everyone makes the playoffs."

Suresh and Zach chuckled.

"Your proofs were red herrings!" Angelo said.

"Exactly!" Hannah said. "I was trying to distract you from the main issues, which would have undermined my thesis, by using secondary ideas that can't actually establish it."

"That's a great example, Hannah," Zach said. "It also brings up an interesting point about red herrings. If people see through them, you've weakened your case. An unbiased person would hear your argument and conclude that the Knicks must be pretty bad if that's all you can come up with to prove they're the best."

"Well, don't tell my dad about this example. He's not unbiased!"

Everyone laughed.

"How about this?" Suresh said. "Let's say I was trying to refute Christianity—no offense, Angelo, just an example—and I argued that Christianity can't be the true religion because it produced the Inquisition, the Crusades, and televangelists who only want money. What kind of argument would that be?"

"Even as an atheist," Zach said, "I recognize that as a straw man. Describing Christianity in terms of some of its worst features and ignoring its strengths and most attractive features is an unfair way to refute it. I wouldn't want you to attack atheism by saying that atheists are automatically immoral or irrational."

The group talked for a bit about the idea of *critical thinking*—or engaging positions at their strongest, presenting their case as their followers would, and answering them at the highest level.

"How about this?" Angelo said. "We should believe the Knicks are the best NBA team because Hannah and her dad will be really sad if we don't, and as her friends, we have grown to care about Hannah."

Hannah laughed. "That's very kind, Angelo, but it's a *terrible* argument. You are appealing to pity rather than facts."

Suresh was laughing as well. "A person shouldn't believe an argument because it feels right or moves their emotions. Emotions aren't intended to assess reason."

Zach looked around the table and started to collect his things. "This was a very productive evening! As we keep studying and discussing, I hope we'll all be more aware of avoiding these flawed ways of reasoning."

The other three agreed.

"And let's hope and pray that the bombers are caught before they can do any more damage or threaten anyone's life . . ." Angelo said, his voice trailing off.

THEORY

The above dialogue explored, in an informal way, several argument fallacies, using speculation about a bridge bombing as the context. The purpose was to show how readily argument fallacies can occur in normal life. Now we'll give you formal definitions and explanations of these fallacies—plus a few others.

Some things seem to come naturally to humans: All of us can do them without needing to take lessons or get any sort of special training. For example, everyone (with the exception of those who are deaf or mute) learns how to speak. Nearly every child figures out how to run without the need of a running coach, and most people can sing to one degree or another, even though few people take singing lessons. Nonetheless, having an English teacher is almost essential to learning to speak with proper grammar, having a good running coach is essential to learn to run your fastest, and studying vocal technique can improve singing, even for someone with a beautiful voice.

The same thing is true about thinking logically. Most people figure out on their own that you should have good reasons for what you believe and that it's not good to contradict yourself. Most people have some basic sense of logic. However, there's a big difference between the basic awareness of the need to be logical that most of us have and the ability to think logically that comes from actually studying logic. Formal training in logic would be extremely useful while we're trying to think logically about issues relating to our worldview. Therefore, we're going to study a little logic before moving any further in our investigation of worldviews. This is just an introduction, though. If you want to go further—something we encourage with enthusiasm!—there are helpful books recommended at the end of this chapter.

Informal Fallacies

People unintentionally make mistakes when trying to think logically. For example, earlier in this chapter the friends discussed the phenomenon of an actor making authoritative pronouncements about a terrorist attack even though the actor had no special qualifications for doing so. Admirers of the actor might be inclined to trust his opinion, but, as the friends realized, that would be an appeal to authority, an argument fallacy—indeed, a fallacy that all of us can be prone to.

A **fallacy** is simply a mistake that ruins the logic of an argument. There are many ways that an argument can be ruined, and the most common fallacies have been given specific names (like "appeal to authority"). Learning to identify and avoid fallacies is a very good way to begin the study of logic. If we can avoid making these all-too-common mistakes, we've made a good start toward thinking more logically. So let's take a look at some common fallacies.

The **appeal to authority** fallacy occurs when someone tries to defend his or her belief by citing the favorable opinion of someone who is not actually an expert in the relevant field. For example, Bill Gates is a successful businessman, but he is not an environmental scientist, a geotechnical engineer, or any other type of expert related to coal energy. Hence, his opinion on the subject is not a reliable indication of the truth on that subject.

A fallacy that is nearly the opposite of this is known by the Latin name ***argumentum ad hominem***. *Ad hominem* literally means "at the man." This is the fallacy of attacking your opponent rather than your opponent's position or argument. This can be abusive, like calling your opponent an idiot, a fool, or ignorant, rather than pointing out why his or her opinion is factually incorrect. Alternately, it can simply be pointing out some irrelevant circumstance about your opponent that distracts everyone from the real issue, as when a politician jokes about his opponent's looks or age rather than addressing their practical and ideological differences. In either case, the underlying problem is the same: You aren't talking about the real issue but instead are talking about the person.

Another fallacy that has to do with focusing on people rather than facts is the **bandwagon fallacy**. This happens when you argue that everyone else believes X (or is doing X) and therefore you are justified in believing (or doing) X. Of course, that everyone believes X does not guarantee that X is true, so the mistake here is pretty obvious.

There are at least two other fallacies that involve focusing on a person. The first of these is the **straw man** fallacy. This involves describing the opposing position in such a way that it is easy to refute. It's called "straw man" because just as it would be very easy to beat a scarecrow (a straw man) in a fight, it's easy to defeat those with whom you disagree if you misrepresent their position so that their position appears as if it is based on poor reasoning or clearly mistaken facts.

The second of these is the **appeal to pity** fallacy. This is committed when someone tries to convince you of something by arousing your sympathy rather than using facts and argumentation. There's nothing wrong with sympathy, of course, but appealing to emotions is a strategy often resorted to when compelling facts and reasoning are not available. Feelings are not a reliable indicator of truth.

The fallacy of **begging the question** occurs when, in the attempt to prove his or her position, a person's argument presumes the very thing that he or she is attempting to prove. Sometimes this involves blatantly circular reasoning, such as if a paleontologist were to use the age of fossils to date the layer of earth in which they are found and the age of the strata to date the fossils it contains. At other times it's much more subtle.

The fallacy of the **complex question** (or loaded question) occurs when someone asks a question that presumes an answer to another, unexpressed question. For example, let's say that you meet someone for the first time, and you're trying to make conversation with her, so you ask her what her favorite kind of music is. That question would assume that she has a favorite kind of music, but perhaps she doesn't. It would be more logical to begin by asking if she likes music; then, if she does, you can ask her if she has a favorite kind and what it is. If she doesn't like music, then you can ask her if she likes sports, movies, the outdoors, or something else. This way you avoid making a mistaken assumption and you spare the other person the awkwardness of having to explain why she doesn't have a favorite type of music.

The **false cause** fallacy, also known as *post hoc, ergo propter hoc* ("after this, therefore because of this") or simply **the *post hoc* fallacy**, results from mistakenly attributing causality to something that is not the cause. In the dialogue above, the friends noted that some people assumed an Islamist terror attack because OPEC raised gas prices shortly after the bombing. Correlation of events cannot prove causation, and we must be very careful in drawing conclusions not warranted by the facts.

One of the most common fallacies is the **false dilemma**. This results from posing a question in such a way that the response is limited to fewer options than are really possible or so that one must choose between options rather than embracing multiple compatible possibilities. Consider, for example, the following questions: Are you a Democrat or a Republican? Do you believe in God or science? Do you live by faith or by reason?

The **appeal to ignorance** fallacy argues that something is true because it hasn't been proven to be false (or vice versa). Since something that hasn't yet been shown to be false could possibly be shown to be false sometime in the future, this is a fallacious line of reasoning.

An **argument from silence** treats the absence of evidence as evidence of absence. In other words, it takes the lack of evidence for X as evidence that X is false (or that X doesn't exist). For example, the current lack of evidence of life in other solar systems does not prove that there isn't life in other solar systems; in fact, given how little information we have about other solar systems, it's not surprising that we don't have evidence of life in them. Perhaps when we have more data about other solar systems, we'll have data supporting the existence of life in some of them—who knows?

A caveat must be inserted here. There are contexts in which a lack of evidence is evidence of lack; there are contexts in which an argument from silence is not fallacious. In a context where the existence of something should result in strong evidence of that thing, the lack of evidence strongly suggests the nonexistence of that thing. Recall that Zach believed Angelo's silence about drinking Zach's coffee could, in fact, have been strong evidence that Angelo was guilty. But silence as an argument must be used with great care.

The **genetic fallacy** is committed when someone argues that a position is false because of some detail of its origin (its genesis). Reasoning that belief X must be false because it comes from someone you don't like, some political party other than your own, someone who has sometimes made false statements in the past, etc., commits this fallacy. Even liars tell the truth sometimes, and thoughtless people often stumble upon the truth almost in spite of themselves. Pointing out the source of some belief is rarely, if ever, sufficient to show that it is false.

The **red herring** fallacy involves introducing some extraneous issue into a discussion in order to draw attention away from the real issue. In effect, you're using a decoy to distract people. This happens quite often, especially when someone senses that the argument isn't going in his or her favor. In that situation, people frequently try to change the subject—sometimes subtly, sometimes blatantly—instead of admitting that they are wrong, and that's a form of the red herring fallacy.

The fallacy of **composition** is committed when you attribute the characteristics of the parts to the whole. For example, if you think that having all the best players on a team will automatically result in that team being the best team, you are probably committing the fallacy of composition. Great players don't automatically make a great team, for there is much more to functioning well as a team than simply having highly skilled players.

The fallacy of **division** is committed when you attribute the characteristics of the whole to its parts. It's the opposite of the fallacy of composition. Thus, if you think that having the best team means that you also have the best player at each position, you are probably committing the fallacy of division. Sometimes the best team doesn't have any superstars on it, but it's still the best team, because good players who work well together often outperform superstars who hog the ball and don't get along.

Equivocation is a fallacy that stems from misuse of language. Equivocation results from using a word in more than one way in an argument without acknowledging the change in meaning. For example, the Declaration of Independence states that all men are created equal. However, it could be argued that since women aren't men, not all women are created equal. (In this argument the word "men" is used in two different ways while seeming to be used in the same way throughout.)

Amphiboly is another fallacy stemming from misuse of language. The term amphiboly refers to grammatical ambiguity that leaves a phrase open to more than one legitimate interpretation. While equivocation has to do with a change in the meaning of a word, amphiboly has to do with poor grammar. Zach's example of a politician saying that he would accept no bribes that would affect his judgment shows how this fallacy might occur. A similar but even better example might be the following statement made by a political candidate: "I am opposed to taxes that slow economic growth." It's not clear whether the candidate opposes all taxes because he thinks that all taxes slow economic growth, or whether he only opposes some taxes, because only some taxes slow economic growth. Either interpretation seems possible, and the candidate may have intentionally let this ambiguity exist in order to appeal to two different kinds of voters. That's rather deceptive, of course.

The final fallacy that we will mention here is **self-referential incoherence**. This fallacy occurs when a statement fails to live up to its own standard. In essence, the statement contradicts itself. An example of this would be the statement that one occasionally hears that "only scientific statements are true." The problem here is that this statement is not itself a scientific statement: It's not a statement that results from a scientific investigation. If anything, it's a philosophical statement. Thus, if it's true that only scientific statements are true, then the statement that only scientific statements are true cannot be true. Hence, it's self-contradictory, and it's self-contradictory precisely because it fails to live up to its own standard.

We could list many other fallacies. However, since this is not a logic textbook, for now we'll content ourselves with these, which are among the most common and most important. The student who understands (and avoids) these fallacies will be off to a very good start in the study of logic.

Zach, Hannah, Angelo, and Suresh are going to be chatting about philosophy throughout this book. They are going to try to avoid logical fallacies, but they're only human. You should listen carefully to their discussions and see if you can spot times when they make arguments that commit one or more of these fallacies.

QUESTIONS TO PONDER

- How important is it to be able to think logically?
- Is there an alternative to thinking logically?
- Do you ever commit these fallacies when you are thinking about an issue or arguing with someone? Would you know if you did?
- When you disagree with someone's argument, how useful would it be to be able to tell him or her what is wrong with it? Would you be able to?

TERMS TO KNOW

- fallacy
- appeal to authority
- *argumentum ad hominem*
- bandwagon fallacy
- straw man
- appeal to pity
- begging the question
- complex question
- false cause
- *post hoc* fallacy
- false dilemma
- appeal to ignorance
- argument from silence
- genetic fallacy
- red herring
- composition
- division
- equivocation
- amphiboly
- self-referential incoherence

FOR FURTHER READING

Arp, Robert, Steven Barbone, and Michael Bruce. *Bad Arguments: 100 of the Most Important Fallacies in Western Philosophy.* Wiley-Blackwell, 2019. This book explains a large collection of logical fallacies.

Bluedorn, Nathaniel, Hans Bluedorn, Rob Corley, and Tim Hodge. *The Fallacy Detective: Thirty-Eight Lessons on How to Recognize Bad Reasoning.* 4th ed. Christian Logic, 2015. This one is filled with fun exercises for identifying fallacies. Although written for children, it's excellent practice for everyone.

Withey, Michael. *Mastering Logical Fallacies: The Definitive Guide to Flawless Rhetoric and Bulletproof Logic.* Zephyros Press, 2016. This is a practical introduction to logic that focuses on fallacies.

Zegarelli, Mark. *Logic for Dummies.* John Wiley & Sons, 2007. This is a much more insightful book than the title suggests. It is by no means for dummies! In fact, it is more advanced than Withey's book (above) but with less focus on fallacies and more focus on logical theory.

4

FORMING STRONG ARGUMENTS

SYNOPSIS

At the heart of philosophical reasoning is the formulation of arguments to support conclusions. This chapter will discuss how strong arguments of varying types are formulated and how the various forms of argumentation differ from one another.

DIALOGUE

Despite all the turmoil going on, Hannah had worked hard to do her philosophy reading and spend time thinking about the portion of the logic chapter Zach had assigned her. Before they departed last time, he had given each of them a different part of the chapter to focus on so they could learn about the rest from each other at their next meeting. Suresh and Angelo read the portion of the book that dealt with deductive logic; Zach and Hannah read about inductive logic.

The unsettling events happening in America, including the bridge bombing a few weeks prior, had Hannah on edge. The FBI had announced arrests this week, but information about motives was only slowly coming out. It appeared that the perpetrators weren't terrorists in the ideological sense. They were simply well-financed operatives who had sabotaged the bridge for someone who hoped to benefit from the massive shutdown.

Meanwhile, there were always people who used disruption as an excuse to do illegal things themselves. People were talking about the demonstrators in Greenfield who had started out peacefully protesting what they saw as government conspiracies and had devolved into breaking into stores and setting fires. Although Hannah generally approved of peaceful demonstrations, she wasn't happy about the violence. Hannah had been concerned about Angelo, who worked downtown. A closeness was developing in their little philosophy group. When she called to make sure he was okay, Angelo thanked her and said how kind it was that she, Zach, and Suresh had all checked on him.

The logic homework was refreshing compared to all this drama, so Hannah decided to investigate *analogy*, something she believed she'd been doing instinctively for most of her life. Analogy, the book said, was a form of inductive logic in which a person draws a conclusion about one thing by comparing it to another.

Hannah had a very practical way of using this approach. She started most mornings at Brews Brothers because her job was on that side of Greenfield and she could stop for coffee on the way to work. Getting to the coffee shop before work involved going through downtown, however, and some of the streets were still blocked off after the riots. Luckily there was another coffee shop on her side of town owned by the same people with the not-so-creative name—Brews Brothers Too. She had looked at the menu online, and it was the same as what she was used to. The coffee shop's exterior even looked similar. She had decided that there were enough points of similarity to draw the reasonable conclusion that the coffee would be just as good. If she went to Brews Brothers Too, she could then catch the bus to work and avoid driving through downtown.

The coffee was just as good! But something caught her by surprise. Hannah had also assumed that the prices would be the same. Surely the analogy would hold in that area as well. Turns out, Brews Brothers Too was in a posher neighborhood, and every drink was nearly a dollar more than at the original coffee shop. Although she didn't like spending the extra money,

Hannah was pleased that her little induction experiment had demonstrated both the value and limitations of reasoning by analogy.

* * *

Angelo had gotten permission to go to work a little late that morning and was just starting his day as Hannah was boarding the bus after grabbing coffee. Angelo had been through something frightening during the previous day's riots, so his boss had told him to take some time that morning.

At his station guarding the courthouse yesterday afternoon, Angelo had an excellent view of a crowd that had gathered just a few blocks down Capitol Avenue. The demonstrators' signs contained general rebukes of the government for alleged corruption, cover-ups, and abuse of power, but it was hard to determine what specifically they were upset about. He saw a lot of laughter, as well as liquor bottles being passed around, which didn't seem like the stuff of serious protest.

Before long, the demonstrators had shattered the window of an electronics store, vandalized cars parked on the avenue, and blocked traffic. Greenfield's small police force began to arrive, but the situation had already gotten out of hand.

The disruption was still a few blocks away, so Angelo decided to mind his own business.

But then a gun fired.

Angelo heard not only the report of the weapon but also the impact of the bullet as it smashed through a first-floor window in the courthouse behind him. He threw himself to the ground. If the bullet had come from the crowd, it couldn't have missed him by more than a dozen feet. Angelo's weapons instructor's wry comment that "people only dodge bullets in movies" rushed to his mind.

Angelo peered around from his spot on the ground. *Is anyone in the building hurt?* he wondered.

Police responded quickly, and fortunately, the bullet had entered an empty room and embedded itself in a wall. The shooter was drunk and seemingly fired at random. The police arrested him and removed him from the scene.

As he prepared for work the next day, Angelo thought about some of the reading for the week and how it might be a helpful way to process what had happened the day before. He had learned that a *syllogism* is a type of logical argument that uses deductive reasoning—a major premise and a minor premise—to arrive at a necessary conclusion. He liked the examples of hypothetical syllogisms he had found in the reading; they used a conditional in at least one of the premises.

As he sat at the table with his coffee, he jotted down this premise: *If an armed rioter gets drunk, he becomes dangerous.* His second premise was that the armed rioter got drunk. The conclusion was obviously that the armed rioter became dangerous. Angelo was satisfied that this was a valid argument—one constructed to preserve truth. If his premises were true, the conclusion would accurately reflect that.

Of course, not all drunk rioters get dangerous, so his first premise was questionable. But that didn't make the argument invalid. It simply wasn't sound. Angelo had highlighted in his reading that a sound argument requires both a 1) valid argument form and 2) true premises.

What other valid argument can I form with the same initial premise? he wondered. If his minor premise was that the armed rioter did not become dangerous (even though drunk armed rioters do become dangerous), it was clear to Angelo that the armed rioter must not be drunk. As the book instructed, Angelo wrote out the two forms of argument he was considering:

> If an armed rioter gets drunk, he is dangerous.
> An armed rioter gets drunk.
> Therefore, he is dangerous.

> If an armed rioter gets drunk, he is dangerous.
> An armed rioter is not dangerous.
> Therefore, he is not drunk.

The reading had warned against two common fallacies that would result if you didn't construct your argument correctly, so Angelo decided to try to construct those too. The examples were clear enough that it was easy to apply them to this argument:

If an armed rioter gets drunk, he is dangerous.
An armed rioter does not get drunk.
Therefore, he is not dangerous.

Why is this invalid reasoning? Angelo thought. The first premise says what will happen if an armed rioter gets drunk, but what does it reveal about the situation where the armed rioter does not get drunk? Nothing as far as Angelo could tell. The reading called this the fallacy of *denying the antecedent.* (The antecedent is the first part of the conditional in his first premise; the second part of the conditional is called the consequent.)

But there was a second related fallacy. Angelo flipped through the book to remind himself of the form and wrote his example:

If an armed rioter gets drunk, he is dangerous.
The armed rioter is dangerous.
Therefore, the armed rioter got drunk.

Aha! Angelo thought. The major premise reveals what will happen when an armed rioter gets drunk, but it does not communicate all the conditions under which a rioter might become dangerous. So a minor premise that says the rioter does become dangerous cannot logically lead to the conclusion that the rioter got drunk.

Angelo looked at the clock. He needed to grab some lunch before heading to the courthouse for his shift. He put the book and his paper away and finished getting ready. Putting that terrifying experience the previous day into this framework was a helpful way to think through what had happened, even if he was still rattled.

* * *

Zach worked with induction constantly. He ran controlled experiments in the lab at the pharmaceutical company, gathered data from the repeated experiments, and then theorized about the expected results from the data.

He was familiar with one famous example of induction going very wrong—the turkey who gets fed every day for months and reasonably concludes from that data that he will also be fed on the day when they come to wring his neck and make Thanksgiving dinner out of him. There can always be variables we're not aware of (for the turkey, not realizing the purpose of the daily feeding) that will cause the conclusion to diverge from where the data seems to be taking it. Zach and his colleagues were constantly on the lookout for such data-skewing factors. But in the meantime, he trusted the experimentation process.

The book they were reading had thrown a new term at him though. Zach couldn't remember ever studying *abduction*, and he found the idea fascinating. During his teenage years, he had read all Sir Arthur Conan Doyle's Sherlock Holmes stories. Holmes spoke of making deductions, but even as a teen, Zach had been suspicious that the great detective wasn't actually using deductive logic. The data Holmes was basing his conclusions on didn't look like syllogistic premises.

In *The Hound of the Baskervilles*, Doyle's great novel about Holmes, a character used a portion of *The London Times* to send a cryptic message. Holmes took this as proof that the person was educated, since the *Times* "is seldom found in any hands but those of the highly educated."[1] *But unless only educated people read the* Times, Zach thought, *this couldn't be a sound deduction.*[2] *What kind of reasoning was Holmes using?*

Zach now believed the great detective used abduction.[3]

Based on the reading, abduction involves gathering data from observation, just like induction, but it doesn't require repeated data points over time. Instead, the data are the points of observation at a given time, and abduction seeks the best explanation for what is observed. Zach decided that's what Holmes usually did. He would look at a person or a situation,

1. A. Conan Doyle, *The Hound of the Baskervilles*, in The Original Illustrated Sherlock Holmes (1902; repr., Castle, n.d.), 361.
2. The syllogism that would presumably lie behind Holmes' conclusion would be the following: Major premise: If a person reads the London Times, he is highly educated. Minor premise: The person reads the London Times. Conclusion: Therefore, he is highly educated. This argument is valid in form, of course, but the truth of the major premise is quite doubtful, making the argument likely unsound.
3. For the use of Sherlock Holmes as an example of abduction, see Louis Pojman, *Philosophy: The Quest for Truth* (Oxford University Press, 2002), 34–36.

observe several features, and then draw a conclusion that seemed like the best fit to the data.

Zach decided he'd look for a way to try abduction after work, and he got his chance on the drive home. He had heard about the riots, but he wasn't thinking about them as he drove home. Suddenly he found himself caught in a traffic snarl, and across from him was a convenience store that looked worse for wear. Pretending to be an amateur Sherlock Holmes, Zach sat in traffic analyzing the scene. The front door was hanging loosely on its frame; both windows on either side of the door had been smashed in; the entire storefront was blackened by fire, with piles of ash and soot on the pavement in front of the structure. The shelves inside appeared to be ransacked and broken.

Suppose I had no knowledge of the riot. What would I conclude from the observable data? Zach asked himself. Could it have been a natural disaster? A fire would damage the interior, but it wouldn't ransack the shelves. This didn't look like the work of a tornado. If it was caused by humans, he thought he could rule out robbery. Thieves would rarely cause such noticeable destruction. Perhaps vandals had defaced, ransacked, and burned the building while it was unoccupied. When Zach looked further, he saw that the buildings adjacent to the store were also damaged. The destruction seemed to go up the road as far as Zach could see. Vandalism on this scale suggested a riot. The freshness of the evidence of fire and looting suggested that the event had occurred recently.

Zach believed that abduction might have led him to conclude that a riot had occurred and had spread several blocks—even if he hadn't learned about it on the news. It was simply the best explanation for the available observable data.

Of course, it was sad to think of the people who had lost their businesses, and he hoped no one had been seriously hurt. But the process of abduction was pretty cool, and he determined to practice evaluating situations, formulating hypotheses, drawing conclusions, and testing them as often as possible.

* * *

Reconnecting with his Eastern roots had given Suresh something of a lifeline as he struggled in the highly competitive world of high-level chefs. He enjoyed conversations with Disha during breaks from their grueling shifts at Studio 31, the high-end steak restaurant where both sought to perfect their culinary skills. The riots had been far from the upscale section of town where their restaurant was located, but they were disconcerting all the same. Suresh was struggling with Disha's unwillingness to categorically condemn them.

"They clearly weren't motivated by ideology," Suresh said. "The alcohol, the reckless destruction of property, the seeming purposelessness of it all—one guy even fired a gun that came dangerously close to a friend of mine! How can we not call this evil?"

"Fine," Disha conceded, "I'm not saying there was no evil involved. I'm just saying that the Buddha teaches us to beware of basing our thinking on antitheses like good and evil, as though we're the good guys and they're the bad guys. Greed, passion, and selfishness were certainly part of the riots, but those things are also present in our kitchen—and in our own lives."

Suresh was listening.

"Rather than comparing ourselves against the rioters because they supposedly did evil, we should embrace whatever good was in them as being part of the One that underlies everything, and we should banish the passion that may have been present in them but is surely present in us. Make sense?"

"I guess," Suresh answered hesitantly. "I'm reading a logic book right now, so this has been on my mind a lot."

Disha raised her eyebrows but didn't interrupt.

"Suppose I framed our discussion in the following way," Suresh said. "It is wrong to loot and burn other people's property. Wrong behavior should be condemned. The rioters looted and burned other people's property. Therefore, the rioters did wrong, and they should be condemned. You seem to want me not to condemn the rioters, but where is the flaw in my argument?"[4]

"The flaw," Disha said, "is in framing the situation using Western logic. Does my owning property exclude all others from using it? Can *wrong* be defined as clearly as your argument implies? As fellow sufferers, should we

---

4. One might structure this in the following way: Premise 1: If one loots and burns other's property, he or she is doing wrong behavior. Premise 2: If one does wrong behavior, he or she should be condemned. Conclusion: Therefore, if he or she is looting and burning other's property, he or she should be condemned.

condemn others? Western logic often expresses clarity where we should have humility."

"Is it humility to not be sure of anything?" Suresh asked. "Forgive me, my friend. I find your insights enormously helpful, but I could restate what you just said as the following: Western logic uses precise language; precise language implies arrogance; therefore, Western logic is rooted in arrogance."

Disha laughed. "I see what you just did there. You accused me of using Western logic to say we shouldn't use Western logic. Eastern thinking doesn't deny all antitheses, especially on the surface of things. But the oneness of all reality means that antitheses will dissolve the more deeply we go into things. As long as we frame life as a battle between good and evil, we will be consumed by desire, which will lead to pain. Buddha recommended a better way."

"This is a lot to think about," Suresh said, getting up to head back to the kitchen. "But let me ask a question: How would our conversation be different if the rioters had burned down our restaurant and you and I were out of work?"

Disha gave what looked like a cross between a smile and a wince, but she didn't respond as they put on their aprons to return to the kitchen.

* * *

Thursday night couldn't come soon enough for the four friends. Everyone first wanted to hear from Angelo about what had happened at the courthouse. He tried to reassure them that he was fine, adding that he felt ready to die in any event.

It didn't take long to dive back into their discussions on philosophy, in particular on formal logic, their current topic. They began with deduction, the more mathematical form of logic, or so said the book. Suresh got the ball rolling.

"It struck me that deduction doesn't add any new information," he said. "Whatever truth is contained in the premises is preserved in the conclusion if the argument is in valid form."

"Can you illustrate this?" Zach asked.

"Suppose I say, 'All border collies are dogs, and all dogs are mammals,' you would draw an obvious conclusion, right?"

"All border collies are mammals," the group said in unison.

"But our conclusion didn't go beyond the premises, did it?" asked Suresh. "That border collies are mammals was necessitated by the premises. In fact, that's the exact word to use: The conclusion is a *necessary* inference from the premises."

"I'm not sure I understand why this is important," Hannah said.

"If a person can construct a valid argument," Suresh said, "then the conclusion is quite powerful. It *must* be true."

"Hold up," Angelo interjected. "You mean it must *follow*. You're forgetting an important ingredient. For the conclusion to be true, the premises must also be true."

"Yes, of course," Suresh said. "I got ahead of myself and wasn't careful with my language. A valid argument preserves the content of the premises, but it doesn't make false premises true."

Zach again asked for more clarification.

"Okay, here's another one," Suresh said. "All rioters are sober. The man who fired his gun at the courthouse was a rioter. Therefore, the man who fired his gun at the courthouse was sober. This is a valid argument, but the first premise is obviously false, which means the argument is not sound."

"*Soundness* meaning the quality of being both valid and true, right?" Angelo added.

"Your examples of deductive arguments seem to take various forms. We read about these, but could you elaborate?" Hannah asked.

Angelo grabbed his notebook. "I've got this. First, these forms are known as *syllogisms*, which comes from a Greek word that means 'reason with.' The book discusses three ways in which a person can syllogize: categorical, disjunctive, and hypothetical forms. If you don't mind my being a little silly, I'll illustrate each one," he said, looking around the table for nods.

"Categorical syllogisms employ categories, as you might expect. For instance, all near-death experiences are terrifying occurrences; all encounters with drunken rioters are near-death experiences; therefore, all encounters with drunken rioters are terrifying occurrences. Make sense?"

His three friends looked a little stricken.

"Too soon?"

"Yeah . . ." Hannah said. "I appreciate your lightheartedness, but given what you went through this week, let's find different examples. For what it's worth, I do see how a categorical syllogism works."

"Okay. A disjunctive syllogism relates things using either-or language. Either I dodged the bullet, or I got shot. I didn't get shot. So I must have dodged the bullet."

"Angelo!" they all yelled. "Seriously?"

"Okay. Okay!" he raised his hands in surrender. "Either buffalo wings are the best appetizer or chicken tenders are the best appetizer. Chicken tenders are not the best appetizer. Conclusion: Buffalo wings are."

"But what about onion rings or nachos with guacamole?" Suresh asked, laughing.

"My premise is that one or the other is the best. If neither is the best, then the argument is unsound. But if we premise that one or the other is best, ruling out one necessitates the other. It's a valid argument," Angelo said.

"If we change your example a bit," Zach said, "we can illustrate a fallacy associated with that. Suppose we make the major premise this: Buffalo wings are an appetizer, or chicken tenders are an appetizer. If we now say, buffalo wings are not an appetizer, we could validly conclude that chicken tenders are. But suppose our second premise is this: Buffalo wings are an appetizer. Could we then conclude that chicken tenders are not?"

"No," Angelo said. "Because in logic, the word *or* does not rule out the idea that both could be appetizers. If we have A or B, then saying we don't have A proves that we have B. But saying that we *do* have A doesn't rule out B. Both may be true."

Suresh was shaking his head, clearly confused. "I might need you to illustrate the last type of syllogism, Angelo—but no lethal language."

"Sure, no problem. Hypothetical syllogisms use a conditional statement in one or both of the premises. If I use a socially awkward example, you guys will be upset with me. You aren't upset with me. Therefore, I did not use a socially awkward example. Does that make sense?" he said. "I played around with these this week. They're quite interesting, and I think people can stumble into faulty reasoning with them."

"I'm not sure I'm following," Hannah said.

"Okay, let's say a coach made this announcement: 'If rain is forecast on Saturday, the game will be canceled.' A player receives a notification that the game is canceled and draws this conclusion: Rain must be forecast for Saturday. Is he being logical?"

"No," Suresh said. "That is a fallacy. The major premise says the game will be canceled if it rains, but it doesn't say that's the only reason the game might be canceled. Maybe the other team couldn't make it. There are many possibilities."

"Exactly," Angelo said, looking at his notes. "This is an example of *the fallacy of affirming the consequent.*"

"The way I see it, a deductive argument can fail in two ways. One, it can have invalid form (it can be illogical), or two, it can have untrue premises. If the premises aren't true, the validity of the argument won't guarantee soundness. And sound arguments are ultimately the goal, right?"

Zach rubbed his chin. "Indeed."

"I think that mostly sums up what Suresh and I learned about deductive logic this week," Angelo said, raising his eyebrows at Suresh to see if he had any additional input. "Do you guys have any questions?"

"Why don't we shift gears and talk for a few minutes about induction," Zach said, looking around the table. Seeing the nods from his friends, he continued. "If deduction is mathematical, induction is more typical of what scientists like me do—although everyone does induction whether they know it or not."

"Can you illustrate this?" Hannah asked, imitating Zach's voice.

Everyone laughed, including Zach.

"Okay, okay," he said, laughing. "Here's one. Why do people pick the restaurants that they go to?" He looked around the table. "Generally, they try a restaurant—perhaps someone suggested it or they noticed it while they were out, or maybe they saw an ad. If they like it, they go again. After they've eaten there three or four times, if all the experiences have been positive, they'll probably recommend it to their friends. Most of us have learned not to recommend a place after eating there just once. Small sample sizes yield dubious results. Whereas the more times we have a positive experience, the surer we become that the restaurant is in fact good and that the good experiences weren't anomalies or accidents. This is a simple form of induction: *learning by experience.* And we do it all the time, in many areas of our lives."

Angelo tapped the rim of his cup. "Hmm. Based on that example, the induction process seems much less certain, less absolute, than the deduction process. You could never go to a restaurant enough times to be *sure* the next visit would be good."

"That's true," Zach said. "But everyday life doesn't usually require that level of certainty. If I get a bad meal on the tenth visit, I'll probably think it was the exception. When it comes to eating out, 90 percent success is probably considered successful."

"Not at Studio 31!" Suresh said. "A perfect meal. Every time." He tapped his hand against the tabletop for emphasis.

"Okay . . ." Zach said. "The point is that an inductive argument isn't evaluated on validity or soundness. An inductive argument is strong if it has enough evidence to strongly warrant the conclusion, or it is weak if it doesn't."

"So how might induction go bad?" Angelo asked.

"Well, I've already suggested one way—people can make what are called *hasty inductions*. If we stay with the restaurant illustration, let's say a person eats at a restaurant twice and has negative experiences. They might conclude that the restaurant is bad. The restaurant may be fifteen years old, serve hundreds of customers per week, and have positive ratings on various websites. But in their mind, it was bad twice, so it's a poor restaurant."

"I would call that jumping to a conclusion," Hannah said.

Zach nodded and pointed a finger at Hannah. "Exactly! Now, you have the right not to go back to a restaurant that failed twice. There are plenty of options in most towns. But the conclusion that the restaurant is bad from such a small sample size isn't logically tenable."

"Okay, that makes sense," Angelo said. "Any other ways to do induction poorly?"

Suresh jumped in, "What if a person went to the restaurant fifty times, was disappointed every time, and then recommended the restaurant to a friend anyway? That would seem to be poor induction."

"That's called *lazy induction*," Zach said, "not drawing an appropriate conclusion despite abundant evidence."

"What if someone intentionally included some of the data but ignored the rest?" Angelo asked. "That would skew the induction, wouldn't it?"

"Yes! Using data selectively—picking the parts that confirm your ideas and ignoring parts that don't—is called *forgetful induction*."

Hannah cleared her throat. "One thing I found interesting is that induction doesn't always follow the straightforward pattern of repeated experiences. We can't always perform multiple experiments to gather data from which to draw our conclusion. Sometimes a conclusion must be drawn from a single experience. There are a couple key ways this can be done inductively. I focused on one of them this week, and Zach worked on the other."

Zach and Hannah then explained to Angelo and Suresh their efforts at understanding and applying reasoning by analogy and abduction, sharing some of the examples they'd individually explored. The group went back and forth with questions.

Suresh scratched his head and then laid his hand on the table. "I've got a long day at the kitchen tomorrow. I'd better call it a night."

"Sounds good," Zach said. "Now that we've addressed some of the formal reasoning needed in order to do philosophy well, maybe we can dive into some of the topics everyone wants to discuss."

"And let's hope the world calms down a bit this week," Hannah added.

THEORY

The above dialogue illustrates how important it is to use sound arguments if one wishes to arrive at correct conclusions. Let's look at how you, too, can build strong arguments. By **argument** we do not mean a quarrel or fight. We mean a group of propositions (statements) in logical sequence that lead, step by logical step, to the conclusion you are trying to prove.

Typically, an argument contains three components. First, every argument has evidence that it uses to support its conclusion. When the evidence is expressed propositionally, these statements are called **premises**. Second, every argument has a conclusion. The **conclusion** is what the argument is trying to prove; it's the part of the argument that is supported by the premises (the evidence).

The third component of an argument is typically the most difficult for a beginner to detect. It is the logical relationship between the premises and the conclusion by which the conclusion can be said to follow from the premises. This relationship will be entailment in a deductive argument and inference in an inductive argument. It's a bit difficult to detect because it's not written out: To see it you have to read between the lines, so to speak. That takes practice—but it's an important skill to acquire!

Deductive Arguments

Deduction is a form of argument wherein the premises logically entail the conclusion. To **entail** something is to make it necessarily follow. In a properly constructed deductive argument, if the premises are true, then the conclusion is necessarily also true. A properly constructed deductive argument wherein the conclusion is entailed by the premises is **valid**. A deductive argument wherein the conclusion is not entailed by the premises is **invalid**.

A valid deductive argument is a very strong argument. Even stronger, though, would be a **sound** deductive argument. A sound deductive argument is a valid deductive argument that has true premises. Soundness involves two things: valid deductive logic and true premises. Naturally, if the premises are true and the logic is valid, then since the premises entail the conclusion, the conclusion is true.

The classical form for a deductive argument is called a **syllogism**. A syllogism is an argument that has a major premise, a minor premise, and a conclusion. These are frequently written out on three lines like this:

- Major premise: All college students are intelligent people.
- Minor premise: All of you are college students.
- Conclusion: Therefore, all of you are intelligent people.

There are three types of syllogisms: categorical, disjunctive, and hypothetical. Let's talk about them in this order.

A categorical statement expresses things in terms of categories, like "all college students are intelligent people." Both "college students" and "intelligent people" are categories. A **categorical syllogism** is an argument wherein all the propositions are categorical statements. The syllogism given above is a categorical syllogism. A generic categorical syllogism can be created using letters as variables: All Y are Z; all X are Y; therefore, all

X are Z. If you follow this pattern faithfully when constructing categorical syllogisms, you will have logically valid arguments. However, if you change things up, your arguments are likely to be invalid.

A **disjunctive syllogism** is an argument wherein the premises contain a disjunctive ("either . . . or") statement. Here's an example:

- Major premise: Either you are a high school student or you are a college student.
- Minor premise: You are not a high school student.
- Conclusion: Therefore, you are a college student.

This sort of argument works via the process of elimination. If you know that one or the other of the options is true, and if you can show that one of them is false, then you know that the remaining option must be true. There's a fallacy to beware here, though: the fallacy of **affirming a disjunct**. If you argue that either person X is a high school student or she is a college student, and you can prove that she is a college student, you are not justified in concluding that she is therefore not a high school student. This is because she could be dual-enrolled. Remember: Disjunctive syllogisms work via a process of elimination. You must eliminate one of the options. Affirming that one of the options is true does not always prove that the other one is false, so affirming an option (a disjunct) is not a reliable way to argue.

A **hypothetical syllogism** is an argument wherein at least one of the premises contains a conditional ("if . . . then") statement. Here's an example:

- Major premise: If you want to get better at logic, then you need to practice.
- Minor premise: If you need to practice, then you need some practice problems to work on.
- Conclusion: Therefore, if you want to get better at logic, then you need some practice problems to work on.

This is called a **pure hypothetical syllogism** because all the statements are conditional. The statements in a pure hypothetical syllogism, just like the statements in a categorical syllogism, need to follow each other in a logical succession: They link together like a chain. The order must be like this: If X, then Y; if Y, then Z; therefore, if X, then Z.

This is not the only form that a hypothetical syllogism can take. The other form is the **mixed hypothetical syllogism**, wherein the major premise is a conditional statement, but the minor premise and the conclusion are not. Here's an example of a mixed hypothetical syllogism:

- Major premise: If you're reading this book, then you must be an intelligent person.
- Minor premise: You are reading this book.
- Conclusion: Therefore, you must be an intelligent person.

Here the major premise is a hypothetical statement, but the minor premise and the conclusion aren't, and this mixture is why it's called a mixed hypothetical syllogism.

There are two logically valid ways to order the propositions in a mixed hypothetical syllogism: "affirming the antecedent" and "denying the consequent."

Affirming the Antecedent (*modus ponens*)[5]

- Major premise: If you really want to get better at logic, then you will practice.
- Minor premise: You really want to get better at logic.
- Conclusion: Therefore, you will practice.

The first half of the major premise of this argument, "If you really want to get better at logic," is called the antecedent. "Ante" means *before*, and the statement "If you really want to get better at logic" comes before the logical operator in the argument ("then"). The second half of the major premise, "you will practice," is called the consequent because what it states is a consequence of what the antecedent states. "You will practice" is a consequence of your desire to get better at logic. This form is called affirming the antecedent because the minor premise affirms the truthfulness of the antecedent of the major

5. *Modus ponens* means "the way of affirmation."

premise (while the conclusion affirms the truthfulness of the consequent). You can probably see that if the major and minor premises are true, then the conclusion necessarily follows. That's what makes this a valid argument form. Any mixed hypothetical syllogism that has this form is logically valid.

Denying the Consequent (*modus tollens*)[6]

- Major premise: If you really wanted to get better at logic, then you would have practiced.
- Minor premise: You didn't practice.
- Conclusion: Therefore, you must not have really wanted to get better at logic.

In this argument, the minor premise denies the truthfulness of the consequent of the major premise, which is why this argument form is called "denying the consequent." Then the conclusion denies the antecedent. In the example we see that if the major premise and the minor premise are both true, then the conclusion logically follows. Every syllogism that has this form is logically valid.

Of course, one could attempt to affirm the consequent or deny the antecedent instead of affirming the antecedent or denying the consequent. Sometimes when you do that, the result looks like a valid argument. However, upon closer inspection it turns out that such arguments are always invalid. Consider the following examples.

Affirming the Consequent

- Major premise: If you really wanted to get better at logic, then you would have practiced.
- Minor premise: You did practice.
- Conclusion: Therefore, you must have really wanted to get better at logic.

This seems logical. However, does the fact that you practiced actually prove that you want to get better at logic, or are there other possible motives

---

6. *Modus tollens* means "the way of negation."

that could explain why you practiced? For example, perhaps you wanted to hang out with your friends, and they were working on logic, so you worked on logic along with them. You cannot infer that you wanted to get better at logic from the fact that you practiced, since practicing could result from other motives altogether.

Denying the Antecedent

- Major premise: If you really wanted to get better at logic, then you would have practiced.
- Minor premise: You didn't really want to get better at logic.
- Conclusion: Therefore, you didn't practice.

This seems like a logical argument, but examination shows that it isn't. The fact that you don't really want to get better at logic does not entail the conclusion that you won't practice, since you could practice for other reasons. Disproving the antecedent does not disprove the consequent.

It's easy to confuse the two valid forms with the two invalid ones. You should find a dependable way of remembering which forms are valid so that you can avoid this problem.

Inductive Arguments

Induction is a form of reasoning wherein the premises (the evidence) support and make probable the conclusion. Several interrelated factors distinguish induction from deduction, and these are implied right in their definitions. The most significant difference between them is that while the premises of a valid deductive argument logically entail the conclusion, the premises of a strong inductive argument only support and make probable the conclusion; they do not entail it. Therefore, it's possible for an inductive argument to show that some conclusion is highly probable but for the conclusion to turn out to be false anyway. That's because while the conclusions of sound deductive arguments are absolutely guaranteed, the conclusions of strong inductive arguments never are. That's just the nature of induction.

This structural difference between deduction and induction has a parallel terminological difference. While a well-formed deductive argument is called "valid," a well-formed inductive argument, one in which the evidence succeeds in showing that the conclusion is probable, is called "strong." Rather than calling an unsuccessful inductive argument "invalid," an unsuccessful inductive argument is simply called "weak."

Three of the most common forms of induction are generalization, analogy, and abduction. **Generalization** works by observing many examples of some kind of object or event and then drawing a conclusion that seems likely to be true of every such object or event. For example, if you're travelling across the United States and, while passing through the Midwest, you meet a string of unusually nice and polite people—first at a gas station in Ohio, then at a restaurant in Indiana, and this goes on through Illinois, Wisconsin, Minnesota, and South Dakota—you're likely to come away thinking something like, "Wow, Midwesterners are really nice people!"[7] This impression is a generalization that you've made based upon your experiences with Midwesterners. It's induction.

Analogous induction works by comparing two objects or events that are similar in many respects and concluding that, since they are similar in so many other relevant ways, they are likely to be similar in some additional respect as well. For example, let's say that you are a college student and you are shopping for a good used car. Being a student, you want a car that's inexpensive but also reliable, and it needs to be good on gas. Your last car was a Honda Accord, and it had fit that bill perfectly: It was old enough (and plain enough) to be very inexpensive, it was the four-cylinder model so it got good gas mileage, and it had the reliability that Honda is known for. Your search turns up several cars that seem promising, including another Honda Accord that is nearly as old as your previous one but with much lower mileage. It's similarly equipped to your old car. The advertisement lists a price that is within your budget, so you are very interested, but the ad doesn't say what gas mileage the car gets. You figure, though, that since it's basically the same car, with the same engine and everything else, that it will probably get about the same gas mileage as your previous one did.

That's an example of analogous induction: You're comparing the new Accord with your old one and noticing that they're similar—that is, that

7. For the record, although all three co-authors of this book have lived in the Midwest, none of us are Midwesterners.

they're analogous—in many ways, and then you're inferring that they're likely to be similar in other ways too. Our minds do this almost instinctively. We also generalize automatically. Somehow we are able to reason inductively without even being trained how to do so.

Abduction is a form of induction that argues for the truth of a theory by showing that it is the best explanation of the known data. It is also called "inference to the best explanation." Abduction is used in many fields, including science, medicine, and law, among others. In medicine, when a patient describes her symptoms to her doctor, the doctor attempts to diagnose her illness by comparing her symptoms to a list of maladies that cause exactly those symptoms. The malady that best accounts for the exact combination of symptoms and circumstances that the patient has is the one that is most likely correct. This is abduction in action.

In all three of these forms of inductive reasoning, the conclusion is supported by the premises but not guaranteed by them. The conclusion is, therefore, probable but not certain. Inductive reasoning suffers from an inherent limitation: No inductive argument is 100 percent conclusive. Nonetheless, inductive reasoning is a useful and very important tool in our logical toolbox.

Since induction is both important and fallible, the right thing to do is strengthen our skill of inductive reasoning. We must learn the common mistakes (fallacies) of inductive reasoning so we can avoid them. You've already learned a lengthy list of inductive fallacies. However, the most common ones were not on that list. They are the following:

1. **Hasty induction** involves basing a conclusion on an insufficient amount of data. In layperson's terms, it's "jumping to a conclusion." Let's return to the earlier example of traveling through the Midwest, meeting a series of nice and polite people, and drawing the conclusion that Midwesterners are really nice. If you've only met six out of the 65 million or so people who live in the Midwest, drawing any sort of conclusion about Midwesterners on the basis of those six would be very hasty. You'd need a much larger data sample to justify your conclusion.
2. **Lazy induction** involves drawing a conclusion that is weaker than

the evidence suggests. If, after examining the evidence, you draw the conclusion that "it is possible that X," but the evidence actually shows that it is *probable* that X, then you're guilty of lazy induction. For example, if a pharmaceutical company reports that debilitating migraines are a *possible* side effect of a medication that the company has developed, but the evidence shows that such migraines are a *probable* side effect of the medication, while it's true that migraines are a possible side effect, the company has seriously understated the findings, hasn't it?

3. **Forgetful induction** involves neglecting some relevant data that could alter the conclusion. This can involve "cherry picking" the data, using only the data that supports the conclusion that you prefer. For example, if the above-mentioned pharmaceutical firm has lots of data that supports the effectiveness of its new medication, but a small number of studies also show that it has significant side effects, the firm is morally and legally obligated to publish the results of those few studies in addition to the studies that show it to be effective. To publish only the favorable studies would be to fail to be completely truthful about the evidence: It would be dishonest, and logically speaking, it would be embracing a conclusion that does not follow from the data.

In the first portion of this chapter, the four friends tried to work out different forms of argumentation in dialogue with one another. It might be a good exercise for you to formulate arguments and try them out on a friend. But beware of argument fallacies!

QUESTIONS TO PONDER

- Can you explain to a younger sibling the difference between deduction and induction?

- Do you understand why induction is also an important way of reasoning, despite the fact that its conclusions are not 100 percent certain?

- We use generalization and analogous induction throughout the day, every day. Can you think of examples of this?

- What are some real-life examples of abductive reasoning?

TERMS TO KNOW

- argument
- premise
- conclusion
- deduction
- entail
- valid
- sound
- syllogism
- categorical syllogism
- disjunctive syllogism
- affirming a disjunct
- pure hypothetical syllogism
- mixed hypothetical syllogism
- affirming the antecedent
- denying the consequent
- affirming the consequent
- denying the antecedent
- induction
- generalization
- analogous induction
- abduction
- hasty induction
- lazy induction
- forgetful induction

FOR FURTHER READING

Holland, Richard A., Jr. and Benjamin K. Forrest. *Good Arguments: Making Your Case in Writing and Public Speaking*. Baker Academic, 2017. This is a concise and practical introduction to reasoning logically.

Hurley, Patrick J. *A Concise Introduction to Logic*. 14th ed. Cengage Learning, 2023. This is a much more thorough treatment, sufficient for two or more semesters of logic classes.

THE NATURE AND SOURCE OF LOGIC

SYNOPSIS

Having approached the subject of logic primarily by investigating fallacies and argumentation, this third and final chapter on logic looks at what logic is and where it comes from. These more fundamental questions raise significant challenges for the four friends.

DIALOGUE

The following week, Suresh found himself obsessed with the subject of formal logic. He tried to come up with syllogisms that would explain or illustrate what was happening in a variety of situations. One of his fellow chefs got in trouble for leaving a key ingredient out of a dish that went out to a discerning diner. Suresh amused himself: *If Louie leaves out the lemon zest, the summer chowder will displease the customer. Louie left out the lemon zest. Therefore, the chowder displeased the customer.*

He knew it was silly, but these examples helped Suresh remember the various deductive forms.

Constructing *valid* arguments was much easier than forming *sound* arguments. It was often difficult to come up with premises that he was certain were true and accurate. Even the soundness of his playful lemon zest syllogism depended on a customer having a discerning palate. His major premise might prove untrue if a customer failed to detect the missing ingredient or enjoyed the dish regardless. In real life, it seemed challenging to come up with deductive arguments that were entirely or obviously sound.

If sound deductive arguments were that hard to formulate, perhaps they were optional. Perhaps reasoning could take place without recourse to deduction at all. It seemed like inductive and abductive arguments in real life were everywhere. Suresh was constantly drawing conclusions from repeated experiments or comprehensive investigations, and he knew that these conclusions were only *probably* correct. But such probabilities were the stuff of daily life. He found such arguments more practical but less interesting than deduction. Even though sound arguments were challenging to produce, the foundations of deductive logic—the Law of Non-contradiction and the Law of Excluded Middle—seemed indisputable.[1]

Suresh felt a strange tension between his attempts to reconnect with his Eastern heritage and his newfound love of formal logic. Disha believed that reality was too complex to be reduced to logical formulas and regarded syllogisms as straitjackets that stifled creativity and individuality. Of course, not all Easterners reject logic; the number of brilliant mathematicians and scientists from India and the Far East disproves such a conclusion. Whatever these mathematicians and scientists think about the Eastern religions of their cultures, in the labs, they function much like their Western counterparts.

Suresh began to wonder where formal logic came from. Was it a Western development, suitable only for certain cultural contexts? Could a different culture simply disregard formal logic and arrive at truthful and valid conclusions by some other route?

Suresh decided he'd ask the group what they thought.

* * *

1. These two laws are often viewed as the foundations of Aristotelian logic. The Law of Non-contradiction says that contradictory propositions cannot both be true at the same time and in the same sense. The Law of Excluded Middle says that for every proposition, either the proposition or its negative must be true.

On Thursday night, Suresh, Zach, and Angelo gathered at Brews Brothers. Hannah was with a family that had been traumatized by the downtown riots. The family's business had been burned down, and they had asked social services for counseling for their two teenage children, one of whom was struggling with intense anger and the other with debilitating fear. Hannah spent the evening trying to comfort them.

The men sat down with their coffees. Before they could dive into a new subject (Zach had hinted that they'd be exploring the relations between belief, truth, and knowledge), Suresh jumped in. "I've been thinking a lot about logic this week. Where did it come from? And could we just forgo logic and come to truthful conclusions in some other way?"

"I've thought about that too," Zach said. "So far, the book hasn't said anything about that. The authors seem to assume that logic is an integral part of life and thought and don't attempt to justify or explain its existence."

Suresh was relieved that he wasn't the only person wrestling with the idea.

"As a scientist, I can't imagine a world without logic. Induction is my bread and butter; the scientific method requires a certain stability in reality. If two different things could also be the same, or if a thesis could be both true and not true at the same time and in the same sense, no certain results could be achieved in the laboratory. So I think logic is a necessary part of the world."

"You don't think it evolved?" Suresh asked.

"People's awareness of logic must have evolved," Zach said. "But I don't see how humans could have invented it."

"Why not?" Suresh asked.

"Someone must have been the first person to think, *This is either an apple or an orange; it's not an orange, so it must be an apple*. But did that person cause that relationship to exist?" Zach asked. "If a stegosaurus happened upon a piece of fruit that could be either an apple or an orange, as soon as the stegosaurus sensed that it was not an apple, it would have known what it was about to eat. It didn't have to know it was performing formal logic for the logic to apply and be true."

Angelo spoke up. "But doesn't this somewhat undercut your materialistic philosophy, Zach? How could logic emerge from purely material processes?"

"It's definitely a difficulty, but I'm inclined to say that logic isn't a thing that exists. Reality consists entirely of matter and energy, but logic is simply the way material things relate to one another. Logic isn't an object in itself."[2]

"Do you believe material objects must relate to one another in this way?" Suresh asked. "Why couldn't nature have organized herself in some different way that didn't entail logic?"

"I do think logic is necessary. But I don't know the answer to your second question," Zach said, taking a sip of his coffee. "But I'll give it more thought. I haven't been wrestling with all this for very long—really only since we've been meeting. But it seems to me that we couldn't have an orderly universe without logic. Logic must be the language that connects things together. Organization and evolution wouldn't be possible if something could be both different from and the same as something else at the same time, if two plus three equaled five at one time but equaled seven at a different time, and so forth. But I don't currently see a reason for that necessity."

"Fair enough," Suresh said. "I appreciate your honesty in not trying to spin some kind of answer. There are some things we clearly can't get to the bottom of and just have to accept."

Zach nodded.

"Some of my Eastern friends would say that your inability to prove that logic is necessary leaves the door open to the possibility that Western logic isn't as fundamental to the universe as you think, that maybe reality isn't bound to the Law of Non-contradiction. The Buddha developed the 'four corners,' which theorize the possibility of direct contradiction within reality.[3] I pointed out to a friend that she seems to be using logic to say that logic isn't necessary. She seems to be saying that Western logic is either fundamental to reality or not, but it can't be both."

Angelo laughed. "How did your friend respond?"

"Well, since she doesn't believe that logic is always binding, she doesn't mind being caught in a contradiction," Suresh said. "She thought my observation confirmed one of the Buddha's four corners. But I'm not really satis-

---

2. See chapter 9 for a discussion of abstract objects.
3. See Graham Priest, "Beyond True and False," in *Aeon*, May 5, 2014, https://aeon.co/essays/the-logic-of-buddhist-philosophy-goes-beyond-simple-truth, for an interesting attempt to show that Buddha's affirmation of contradiction is consistent with developments in modern mathematics.

fied with that line of reasoning. It feels like saying you can keep the rules or break them whenever you want. I agree with Zach that no alternative to logic seems available for arriving at conclusions that match reality.[4] But I'm a little troubled that there's no apparent answer to how logic arose in the first place."

"I don't say this arrogantly," Angelo said, "but Christians have wrestled with this question, and many think the necessity of logic is integral to our theistic way of viewing the universe. God is a logical being, always acting in accordance with what we know as logic, and therefore, when he created the universe, he imprinted logic on it that is unavoidable."

Zach shook his head. "I thought you believe that God is an ultimate sovereign being, not constrained by anything. If he must follow the laws of logic, wouldn't that place him under logic—logic being even more ultimate than he is?"

"That's a great question. I did some reading about it. Your concern is similar to one raised by Socrates in one of Plato's dialogues"—Angelo flipped through his notebook and tapped one of the pages—"that the gods are either good because their actions perfectly conform to some external standard of morality, in which case this external standard is a higher moral authority than the gods themselves, or the gods are the highest moral authority and can declare anything to be moral or immoral according to their whims. This is the Euthyphro Dilemma you mentioned a couple of weeks ago, Zach.[5] Both sides seem undesirable to me."

Angelo continued. "Similarly, a person could say that God is perfectly logical because he perfectly conforms to some external standard of rationality, which seems to make this external standard a higher authority than God himself, or that God is the highest authority on rationality and can declare anything logical or illogical according to his whims. Historically, most Christians have been uncomfortable with either option. But is there a third option? The solution posed by most Christians to both the Euthyphro Dilemma and the similar problem with logic is that goodness and logic

---

4. For the remainder of the chapter, when "logic" is not modified, it refers to Western, Aristotelian logic. Buddhists refer to Buddha's four corners as a form of logic, but one of the corners directly affirms the possibility of contradiction in reality.
5. Plato's Euthyphro is available online at https://classics.mit.edu/Plato/euthyfro.html.

describe God's essential nature. He is logical, and he is good. Logic and goodness are not over him, controlling him, but neither are they arbitrarily created by him. God has to act logically, and his actions must be good because he is a logical and good being. Logic and goodness are grounded in and flow from the nature of God himself. They describe part of what it means to be God. If we're right about that, it would explain why he created a universe in which it is impossible to evade logic and, by the way, in which right and wrong can be clearly distinguished by permanent, transcultural principles."

"If theism is true, that is a satisfying solution," responded Suresh. "Of course, that's a big *if.* I don't presume that you think someone has to be a theist to believe in logic or morality."

"Of course not," Angelo answered. "I just think theism is the best explanation for how logic and morality arose in our universe. Zach is entitled to think that logic is simply a necessary corollary of the evolutionary organization of matter and energy, but a logical God creating a logical world makes more sense to me."

Zach looked thoughtful and said, "I see your point and appreciate the clarity and charity with which you've expressed it."

* * *

They didn't realize how long they'd been talking until they saw that Brews Brothers was about to close. Then Hannah suddenly appeared.

"What did I miss?" she asked, not even bothering to buy a drink.

"Hannah! Great to see you!" Suresh said. He gave a brief summary of the conversation. "We seem to agree that logic is necessary and unavoidable for accurate depictions of reality and drawing dependable conclusions."

The men quickly shared the key difference between Zach and Angelo's beliefs: for Zach, that logic is simply the way the universe must work, and for Angelo, who attributes logic to God the Creator. Suresh admitted that Angelo's account had more explanatory power, but it entailed accepting Angelo's theistic worldview. Zach didn't try to explain why the universe is logical, but he was confident that it is.

"I would have accepted your explanation when I was younger," Hannah said, looking at Angelo, "but my existentialist explorations push me more toward Zach's. Existentialist teachers assert our right to define right and wrong for ourselves. But I don't think they've typically said the same about logic. Even though existentialists reject the idea that we have an inner nature that determines our choices, they accept that we are born into circumstances that constrain us, and logic is one of those. So I generally agree with you guys. I even used some logical arguments in my counseling tonight."

"Really? Tell us about it," Angelo said.

Hannah looked over at the employees cleaning behind the counter. "I'll be quick," she said. "I was trying to help these teens release their anger and fear over the riots. I told them that these were the first destructive riots in Greenfield in more than eighty years. There's a very low chance that they'll experience something like this again. Principles of induction would suggest they have nothing to worry about."

Zach smiled. "Of course, the reliability of the induction depends on the stability of the surrounding circumstances. Those eighty years of peace were the result of certain conditions, and the riots arose in very different conditions. Can we really be sure things will calm down?"

"I'm glad you weren't at my counseling session!"

"Logic isn't always convenient, I'm afraid," he said.

THEORY

As the four friends wrestled with this topic, their conversations may have raised questions for you. The remainder of the chapter will address the nature and source of logic more systematically.

The Nature of Logic

At this point you have read two chapters on logic, studying the fallacies that render someone's thinking illogical and the principles that are necessary to think logically. You can probably see the importance and usefulness of these "laws of logic." But have you ever stopped to question the nature of these laws? Have you asked yourself where they come from or wondered if they apply equally across all cultures? Could different cultures have different rules of logic? Are the laws of logic a product of society, such that each society creates its own logic just like each society creates its own rules of etiquette, traffic laws, and tax regulations?

These are interesting and important questions. If humans created the laws of logic, then one society could reject another society's rules and create its own. Some society could, for whatever reason, become convinced that affirming the antecedent and denying the consequent are bad ways to think, or that they're impractical or distasteful ways to think, or something along those lines. As a result, that society might decide that affirming the consequent and denying the antecedent are better. This would certainly result in an approach to reasoning that is very different from ours—and that would lead to drawing very different conclusions when faced with the same data!

Similarly, a society could decide that citing the support of people who are not experts on the topic being discussed is actually better than citing the authority of experts. In such a society, people could believe that attacking your opponent really is better than attacking your opponent's position. They could be convinced that jumping on the bandwagon is the best path toward finding truth.[6] In short, they could reject all the logic taught in the preceding two chapters and replace it with something else—even something that is the complete opposite of traditional logic.[7]

But could they really? If the goal of studying logic is to become better at reasoning *in order to increase the likelihood of arriving at conclusions that are true*, would it be beneficial to replace the traditional logic found in the preceding chapters with some alternative? Let's give it a try so that we can see if rejecting the laws of logic helps us arrive at the truth. We'll begin with an argument that affirms the consequent rather than the antecedent:

1. If you do all the homework for Dr. Banyacski's class, then you'll get a good grade.
2. You got a good grade.
3. Therefore, we know that you did all the homework.

---

6. The fallacies being alluded to here are, in order, appeal to authority, *ad hominem*, and the bandwagon fallacy. These were introduced in chapter 3.
7. The logical principles taught in the preceding chapters date all the way back to Aristotle (fourth century BC) and as a result are often called "Aristotelian logic." This approach to logic, with minor modifications, has been the standard in the Western world since Aristotle's time.

Does this conclusion seem true? Is it true that we know that you did all your homework since we know that you got a good grade in the class? At first, the fact that you got a good grade in the class does seem to suggest that you did your homework. But is doing your homework the only way to get a good grade in class? The major premise tells us that doing your homework is *one* way to get a good grade, but it does not tell us that it's the *only* way to get a good grade. Perhaps you can also get a good grade by doing well on the exams and completing the extra credit assignment. Or perhaps you can get a good grade simply by having perfect attendance. The fact that one option works does not mean that no other options work. And if it's true that there's more than one way to get a good grade, then it's possible to get a good grade without doing all the homework. So, then, it's possible for it to be false that you did all your homework in spite of the fact that you got a good grade in the class. Oh no! That means that our non-traditional logic has led us to a false conclusion! It appears that affirming the consequent doesn't work after all.

Let's try again. This time we'll try affirming one side of a disjunctive statement in a disjunctive syllogism instead of going the traditional route, which is to deny one side of the disjunction.

1. Your mom said that you can have pancakes or eggs for breakfast.
2. We know that you had eggs.
3. Therefore, we know that you didn't have pancakes.

In this case the argument really seems to work, doesn't it? If Mom said you have to choose between eggs and pancakes, and we know you chose eggs, then we know that you didn't choose pancakes, right?

The apparent success of this non-traditional argument form is a result of ambiguity in the English language. In English, if Mom says that you can have eggs or pancakes, she could mean that you have to choose one or the other but that you can't have both. However, "Do you want eggs or pancakes?" can also mean that both options are available and you can choose to have both if you'd like. Mom could even say something like: "Do you want pancakes, waffles, toast, biscuits, or grits for breakfast? The Claghorns are coming to breakfast, so I made a variety of options." It's likely that Mom is not intending to imply that you must limit yourself to only one of these options: She probably intends simply to inform you of what is available so that you can choose one or more options as it strikes your fancy.

The moral of this little story about Mom and breakfast is that since it's sometimes logically possible to affirm both sides of a disjunction, affirming one side does not disaffirm the other. Concordantly, knowing that one side has been affirmed does not result in knowing that the other has been disaffirmed. In contrast, traditional logic says that knowing that one side of a disjunctive syllogism has been denied entails that the other side has been affirmed. That does, in fact, work all the time, for if you are faced with a choice between two options and you know that at least one of them is true, then knowing that the first one is false guarantees the truthfulness of the second. Therefore, we see once again that traditional logic works and rejecting traditional logic does not.

We could give countless more examples of this sort, but we'll content ourselves with these two. Those who need further convincing can look in the books listed at the end of this chapter. We do want to mention, though, that there are logical systems that are compatible with traditional logic but are developed along different lines.[8] These include Boolean logic, polyvalent logic, modal logic, deontic logic, and others. We should also point out that embracing logic does not imply that all of reality is reducible to easily grasped and obviously coherent beliefs. The world is a complex place, and many aspects of it—from the riddles of ancient Greek metaphysicians to the puzzles of modern quantum mechanics, not to mention the mysteries of poets and mystics—are difficult to wrap our minds around.

The Source of Logic

We've considered and rejected the possibility that logic is a cultural creation that can legitimately vary from one society to another. It seems much more

8. The view that there is only one valid system of logic is called logical monism. The view that multiple incommensurable but equally valid systems of logic are possible is called logical pluralism. Logical monism is advocated in this book. Logical pluralism is explained and defended in J. C. Beall and Greg Restall, *Logical Pluralism* (Clarendon, 2006), and Stewart Shapiro, *Varieties of Logic* (Oxford University Press, 2014).

likely that the rules of logic are universal: that they are equally true regardless of time, place, or any other factor. This leads us to a question about the source of logic: Where does it come from? If logic isn't a cultural creation, who or what created it? Or is it uncreated—an eternal, unchanging feature of reality?

The latter seems like a strong possibility. If logic was created, that implies that it had a beginning. If it had a beginning, then it follows that there once was a time when logic didn't exist. If logic didn't exist, then during that time it wasn't fallacious to set up a straw man or to settle a disagreement by appealing to authority, and it was fine to affirm a consequent or a disjunction. In short, if logic had a beginning, then there was a time before its beginning when none of the laws of logic were in effect.[9] Outright contradictions would not have been problematic. In fact, they could have been commonplace. Perhaps it would have been possible for things that exist to also not exist at the same time; perhaps things that were true were also false.

However, such a reality would be completely chaotic; it would be incoherent and incomprehensible. It seems more likely that the laws of logic are eternal, that it has always been true that affirming the consequent was an unreliable way to arrive at a conclusion, even back when humans and other forms of biological life didn't exist.[10] If that's the case, then there's no point in asking where logic came from: It didn't "come" but instead was always here. But why? Why would a material universe be permeated by or characterized by what seem to be immaterial intellectual principles? If the

9. Some might argue that logic didn't exist before the creation of the time-space continuum that we call the universe. This seems to presume that there was a time before time existed—which is an interesting but possibly incoherent theory. It is a very interesting topic, but unfortunately a lengthy discussion of this isn't appropriate for this chapter.
10. This way of stating things could be accused of "reifying" the laws of logic, of viewing descriptions of the way that things work as if they are objects that actually exist (somehow, somewhere). While there are people who view the laws of logic as actually existing objects, this may not be the only coherent way to view logic. Another possibility could be to think that the laws of logic are real, eternal, and immutable without thinking that they are physical or even that they exist in some incorporeal fashion like spirits and other immaterial entities do. We'll discuss this more in a later chapter.

common view that mental things are essentially different from material things is correct, it seems a bit odd that the material universe would be pervaded by such mental laws.[11]

There are at least two ways to explain the eternal presence of logic. Interestingly, one of them is common among naturalists and the other is common among people who affirm some sort of supernaturalism (such as theism). The first of these sees the laws of logic as "brute facts" about the nature of reality that simply couldn't be any other way. This view holds that whenever there is a universe, that universe will necessarily be a place where things happen in logical patterns and where, if there are reasoning beings, they will need to affirm the antecedent rather than the consequent, avoid setting up straw men, and the like. In short, every possible world is a world in which the traditional laws of logic necessarily obtain.[12]

This view does little to explain why the laws of logic exist in every possible world other than to point out that it would be incoherent for things to be otherwise. That assertion seems plausible, but it does not shed any light on the peculiar situation of a material universe being characterized by, permeated by, and/or governed by immaterial laws. The theistic response takes explaining this at least one step further.

According to classical theism, the universe was created by a supremely intelligent spirit being who is not physical but nonetheless is present everywhere throughout the physical universe.[13] As the clay pot reflects the hands of the potter, so the universe reflects the intelligent and logical nature of its creator. Thus, it is to be expected that the universe will be an ordered place where things happen in a logical fashion. On this view, since this supreme intelligence is eternal, so is logic, and whenever the supreme spirit creates a universe, the universe will reflect that logic.[14]

---

11. This view will be examined in a later chapter.
12. For a survey of realist approaches to understanding the metaphysical nature of logic, see Tuomas E. Tahko, "A Survey of Logical Realism," *Syntheses* 198 (2021): 4775–90, https://doi.org/10.1007/s11229-019-02369-5.
13. Classical theism is the view that a God exists who is of maximal greatness in every possible way: omniscience, omnipotence, omnipresence, omnisapience, omnibenevolence, etc.
14. For an example of this view, see James C. McGlothlin, *The Logiphro Dilemma: An Examination of the Relationship between God and Logic* (Pickwick, 2017).

This view explains the source of the logic that we see in our world and why logical rules are universal rather than varying from society to society. It also explains the consistency of logic over time: If God is eternal and immutable, and if logic is an aspect of the nature of God, then it seems to follow that logic will also be eternal and immutable. The naturalist could press back against this view, pointing out that it doesn't explain why God has the exact logical attributes that we see reflected in the world around us. Why does God have the logical nature that he does rather than some other logical nature?

In truth, while the theistic view does seem to have provided more of an answer to the difficult question of the origin of logic, the theist may have to admit that she is not able to answer this question fully. Nonetheless, she might reply, at least she has provided an intellectual basis for the existence of the laws of logic rather than merely asserting that they are necessary characteristics of an otherwise material universe or reducing them to constructs of transient human minds.

QUESTIONS TO PONDER

- What is the nature of the laws of logic? Are they physical or mental? Are they eternal or created? Are they universal, or does each culture create its own logic?
- Is it possible for a world without logic to exist?
- If you believe in God, do you think that God is constrained by logic, or is he above logic?
- If you believe in God, do you believe that he created logic? If he did, what guided his thought before logic existed?

TERMS TO KNOW

- laws of logic
- traditional logic
- Aristotelean logic
- classical theism

FOR FURTHER READING

Few books deal with the question of the nature of logic in a way that is accessible to the beginning student. All the books below are fairly advanced for undergraduate readers, but they are among the best resources available.

Gould, Paul M., ed. *Beyond the Control of God? Six Views on the Problem of God and Abstract Objects*. Bloomsbury Academic, 2016. This book examines the relationship between belief in an incorporeal God and belief in other immaterial entities that may exist, such as the laws of logic, the laws of nature, moral truths, human rights, etc.

Kahane, Howard, Alan Hausman, and Frank Boardman. *Logic and Philosophy: A Modern Introduction*. 13th ed. Hackett, 2021. This book discusses many issues on the nature of logic and various alternatives to traditional logic.

McGlothlin, James C. *The Logiphro Dilemma: An Examination of the Relationship Between God and Logic*. Pickwick, 2017. This book shows how theism accounts for the eternal existence of unchanging laws of logic without impinging upon the sovereignty of God.

Shapiro, Stewart, ed. *The Oxford Handbook of Philosophy of Mathematics and Logic*. Oxford University Press, 2007. This is a wide-ranging collection of fairly advanced and technical essays on the nature and possible sources of logic.

EPISTEMOLOGY

6

BELIEF, TRUTH, AND KNOWLEDGE

SYNOPSIS

This chapter will begin to explore epistemology, the study of how humans know things. Epistemology is fundamental to the rest of philosophy since we cannot move forward confidently unless we have some basis for distinguishing truth from error. The four friends will grapple with this issue before the second half of the chapter, which argues for clear definitions of belief, truth, and knowledge.

DIALOGUE

Zach read the headline with dismay. Mayor Lancaster had been arrested the night before on charges of embezzlement, corruption, and bribery. His long tenure had been marked by widespread support from both political parties, and his record for improving life for residents was unparalleled. The downtown area had attracted new restaurants, a performing arts center, popular bookstores, and specialty shops that attracted people from far and wide.

Yet there he was in the photo, cuffed and being taken to jail by the sheriff's deputies.

Zach had grown up with the mayor's son, Tristan, and had eaten dinner with the family many times when he was in high school. He had always admired Richard Lancaster for his friendliness, kindness, and seemingly straightforward views on how to govern. The mayor had treated his own children—and Zach—like adults and shared plans for the city with them, sometimes even before they'd been announced to the public. Zach often watched press conferences online to see which of the ideas discussed over the dinner table had made it to the public. When Zach turned eighteen, he voted enthusiastically for Tristan's father and encouraged his friends and family to do the same. If Zach knew anyone who was a person of integrity and could be trusted, it was Mayor Lancaster.

But this evidence seemed damning.

The attorney general had spearheaded the nine-month-long investigation. According to the news report, Mayor Lancaster was photographed multiple times in parking garages around the city accepting envelopes of cash. Alongside the FBI, the Department of Justice had recorded more than forty hours of conversations between the mayor and various elements of organized crime. In these wiretaps, the mayor was heard threatening business owners, promising contracts to companies who were willing to contribute to his campaign, and accepting luxury cars and expensive vacations in exchange for granting permits for work that never would have passed inspection otherwise.

The man Zach thought he knew was someone he didn't know at all.

To say that Zach was shaken would be a significant understatement. As he began to read the assigned chapter for the week—on belief, truth, knowledge, and justification—he began to realize how pertinent it was. What Zach would have said he *knew* to be true about Mayor Lancaster turned out not to be true at all. It seemed that his trust in the mayor's integrity was a belief but not knowledge.

What other beliefs have I held that weren't true and, therefore, were not knowledge? he wondered.

Zach would ask the group. Their collective wisdom was often helpful despite their differences.

* * *

As everyone settled in around the table, they caught up on each other's lives over the last week. Within a few minutes, Suresh mentioned the news about the mayor.

"That is some story," Hannah said. "I don't follow local politics much, but there is no denying that the city has seen tremendous improvement and revitalization under the mayor's leadership. The indictment seems so serious. I wonder how many of the accusations are true—and what will be left of his legacy if he's convicted."

Angelo remembered a comment Zach had made once. "Zach, don't you know his family?"

Zach nodded, glancing down at his hands. "If you had asked me a week ago if I knew of any politicians who were above corruption, I would have pointed to Mayor Lancaster as a shining example. I'm questioning everything I thought I knew."

"Wait," Suresh said, seeming to realize the connection between the week's reading and their conversation. "What you just said is a perfect example of our reading about belief and knowledge. What do we believe, and what do we actually *know*? How can we have certainty concerning the things we believe?"

"I thought the same thing when I saw the headlines," Zach said. "It turns out that my belief did not line up with reality."

"That seems to confirm that the correspondence theory of truth is . . ." Hannah's statement trailed off as she searched for the right word. "True? Is that what I am trying to say?"

Angelo nodded. "I think we'd say that the way we test our beliefs is to put them in the form of a statement and see if they correspond with reality. So yes, I believe the correspondence theory of truth is true."

"Isn't that assuming too much though?" Suresh wasn't convinced. "This assumes that language is adequate to describe realities outside ourselves. What if our language only *approximates* reality, meaning that our statements are only loosely connected to reality?"

The group fell silent for a moment.

Hannah was the first to speak. "I guess it's possible if we're talking about a statement like 'God is holy,' but I'm not sure how that could be true of a statement like 'It is raining.' We might differ on our descriptions of the rain—whether it's 'pouring' or 'sprinkling'—but if water was falling from the sky, I don't know how we'd get around the fact that the statement truthfully described reality."

"I was thinking more about a statement related to God's nature rather than empirical statements about the weather," Suresh said. "Honestly, I'm not sure how I would distinguish between types of propositions about truth. But it seems that some beliefs can't be verified in any way, yet we believe them to be true. If that's the case, then the *correspondence theory of truth*, the idea that a statement is true if it accurately describes the reality, wouldn't be sufficient. For that reason, I probably lean more toward a *coherence theory of truth*, that a proposition is true if it fits with other beliefs, and that belief systems, not individual beliefs, are true if they all correspond."

"I think you're partially correct," Angelo said. "Coherence is an important aspect of true beliefs, but it seems there must be more than coherence in a system to judge the beliefs as true. I can imagine a paranoid person believing that everyone and everything is against him and plotting to destroy him in a way that seems coherent to him—even though none of it might be true. What would disrupt that coherent belief system would be the truth that no one is out to get him. We wouldn't want to affirm that person's delusional beliefs, even though he seemed coherent. We'd want him to believe the truth that he was safe from people with evil intent."

"Maybe that's what I was trying to emphasize," Suresh said, tapping his pen against the table. "It seems that coherence in our beliefs is crucial if we want to avoid contradiction."

Angelo nodded. "I can certainly agree with that. In the correspondence theory of truth, beliefs stand in relation to one another, often without our conscious realization. When I see rain coming down, hear the sound of it hitting pavement, and feel it on my face, my subconscious beliefs in the reliability of my senses and my previous experiences of rain, combined with my limited understanding of the science of rain, contribute to my belief that what I'm experiencing is in fact rain. My beliefs cohere with one another and correspond to reality."

"Suresh does raise a good question," Hannah said. "How do we evaluate beliefs that can't be empirically verified, such as belief in a higher power or the nature of immaterial realities such as virtues?"

Angelo thought for a moment. "Maybe the problem is in limiting verification of truth to the empirical—in other words, the assumption that the only way a truth claim can be proven true is through the senses or the scientific method. While we do test many truth claims that way, if we believe that immaterial realities like God exist, then we shouldn't expect that they can be proven the same way that material realities are demonstrated."

Suresh's eyes brightened. "Ah yes! That makes sense. I definitely believe there are immaterial realities, so I shouldn't expect that they can be proven in the same way as material ones."

"Christians believe that God has revealed himself objectively," Angelo said, "primarily in the incarnation of Jesus Christ and in Scripture. We consider the clear statements of Scripture to be adequate verification of a truth that might not be verifiable any other way, such as the character of God. Do other religions consider their sacred writings to be proof of their claims?"

Zach had been quiet for a while. "I wonder if it's better to be skeptical of everything since we can't truly know anything with certainty." The disillusionment in his voice was clear.

Hannah could feel Zach's sorrow. "I understand why you might feel that way, Zach. What a blow to your confidence in a person you trusted."

Zach nodded.

"Surely you still feel confident about your work as a scientist, right? At least in science and mathematics you can test claims against their correspondence with reality."

"True," Zach said, "but I'd like to believe we can know some things about the people around us with some level of certainty. Otherwise, how do we avoid becoming cynical? How do we live in society, or even have friends, if we can never know if other people are trustworthy?"

"It's a great question," Hannah said. "I personally think the only way we can trust other people is by looking for evidence of their trustworthiness, even while knowing that it can be faked. I guess another part of it is intuition. I meet people in my field who immediately set off alarms in my head even if they haven't done anything I can definitively point to as wrong. I've learned to trust my gut, while also knowing that I could be wrong. So far, I've rarely been proven wrong."

"Wow . . . I wish I had that ability," Angelo said. "That would certainly help in my job. I guess I do trust my gut some in security work, but sometimes I end up being very wrong about someone."

"Would you say that's an example of *evidentialism in justification of belief* or *fideism*?" Zach was always bringing the group back to the reading.

"Remind me again what fideism is," Suresh said.

"It's the belief that you do not need to present arguments for that which you claim is true. People believe what they believe and aren't required to present arguments or evidence for their beliefs."

"That doesn't seem wise," Suresh said. "Doesn't that mean everyone could believe contradictory beliefs just because it's intuitive to that particular person? And wouldn't that leave us unable as a society to share beliefs, since people could accept beliefs based on their own perceptions, regardless of whether they line up with reality?"

"It definitely seems like an inescapable outcome," Zach said, nodding. "I think that's kind of what I was wondering. Does intuition count as evidence for belief or not? I could see it as a nonempirical way to justify a belief such as, 'This person isn't trustworthy.' But I could also see trusting intuition as a fideistic approach because it doesn't depend on an argument or on evidence."

"That's a tough one," Hannah said. "I feel like intuition straddles evidential and fideistic—when I trust my intuition, I do so because the feeling is real and has proven to be reliable. Yet I often can't communicate good reasons for why I distrust someone. It probably comes across as fideistic, even though it doesn't feel to me like it is."

"Oof," Angelo said. "This is bending my brain. Should we try applying this to real life and see how it could help us day to day?"

"That's a good idea," Zach said. "How could we look at this in relation to how we know if the people we believe are good actually *are* good? The news about Mayor Lancaster has me doubting the character of everyone in my life."

"Including us?" Suresh said, elbowing Zach a bit.

"Not you." Zach laughed. "I never thought much of you to begin with anyway."

Everyone laughed.

"So if knowledge is belief based on good reasons that turns out to be true," Hannah said, "and you believed in the mayor's integrity based on your experience with him, hence possessing justification for your belief, how is it then not true that he had integrity?"

Zach pondered this for a moment. "I don't want to think I was simply naïve and easily fooled by the mayor's kindness and hospitality, but I guess I have to accept that possibility. I'm sure many corrupt people maintain a façade of character while covering up immorality or dishonesty."

"I'm sure any of us would have been fooled if we'd been treated so kindly by someone like him," Suresh said. "It seems to me that an optimistic person who thinks well of others and believes in the basic goodness of humanity wants to give people the benefit of the doubt."

"That's where Christianity may help us to be more realistic about humanity," Hannah said. "I know I'm not a Christian anymore, but Christianity does have the advantage of teaching that people aren't basically good but instead are sinful and flawed."

"But isn't that a bit cynical and pessimistic?" Suresh asked.

"It can be," Hannah said, "but it doesn't have to be. This is one belief from Christianity that I've held on to. And it has been confirmed repeatedly in my job. It also fits well with my beliefs as an existentialist. Although unlike Christians, I don't believe that people are made in God's image, which means everyone has to decide who and what they are. For some, this is hopeful and liberating, but it also means that not everyone will make good choices. Some people make bad choices or reject traditional morals and adopt their own morality that others consider to be wrong or distasteful. I've seen this repeatedly with people who neglect and abuse children.

"People have the freedom to choose to be good parents, but instead they make selfish choices that harm their children. And yet these same people can be charming and friendly. Sometimes they pass a social worker's inspection, and the next week, their child ends up dead by their hands. I've become very wary of overly charming people because so many of them behave that way to cover up their real character and actions."

"That is incredibly sad," Zach said. "I have great respect for the work you do."

"Thank you," Hannah answered, her face grim. "I'm sorry to bring such a dark cloud over the conversation. I just wanted to affirm that you might not have been able to see through the mayor's public image simply because he hid his true nature so well. Some people are very good at image management. They spend a lot of time carefully crafting their persona to conceal their true selves."

"Maybe that should be a part of your consideration, Zach," Angelo suggested. "Despite your positive experience with him, perhaps the fact that the mayor is a politician should have factored more significantly into your estimation of him."

"There is that negative perception of people in Christianity," Suresh said.

"I wouldn't call it a negative perception," Angelo said. "Christianity holds a high view of humanity because it believes that people are made in God's image and therefore possess inherent dignity. But we also take seriously the impact of sin and corruption in the human heart. We don't expect that people will inherently possess character—except on rare occasions. We believe that apart from God's power, anyone is capable of corruption and great evil. Yet because people are made in God's image, they are also capable of living moral lives and contributing to the good in the world. I like the way Hannah said it—not a negative view of people but a realistic one."

Angelo continued. "In addition, because of the corruption of the human heart, we know that power can easily intensify character flaws. I agree with the famous saying that power corrupts, and absolute power corrupts absolutely—at least when we're referring to people."

"I agree with that," Suresh said. "I wonder how many people in politics are able to maintain their integrity. It seems like the whole environment is ripe for bribes, payoffs, favors, and corruption."

Hannah nodded. "Something else to consider, Zach, is that the mayor is genuinely a kind person to his family and close friends and a loving husband and good father. Maybe his lack of integrity is limited to his political office."

Zach's eyes widened a bit.

"Did you ever get a sense of the mayor's dishonesty in your friendship with his son?" she asked.

"No, I can't think of anything Tristan said or did that hinted that his father wasn't who he claimed to be. I wonder if this has all been as big of a shock to Tristan as it is to me." Zach shook his head. "Maybe he knew that some things weren't what they seemed but never shared it with me."

"The grim fact is that some things we are certain about turn out not to be true," Hannah said in a way that was both clear and comforting. "I sure don't like that realization, but it's hard to deny."

"I agree," Angelo said soberly. "The same kind of façade has been exposed in people I was sure were godly Christian leaders, and it's devastating."

"I guess it's part of the human experience," Zach said. "Some of the most accomplished scientists whose works I've read later turned out to be frauds. I don't know if there's any demographic immune from corruption."

"Well, I can assure you that no chef has *ever* substituted an inferior ingredient when a high-quality one was called for," Suresh said with a smirk.

"Maybe this is one of the purposes of philosophy," Angelo said. "It challenges our beliefs so we consider different viewpoints, which helps us work through our differences." He paused. "I don't think this exercise in examining what we think is true has to result in a loss of belief or abandoning certainty, but it could definitely reduce the number of things we're certain about."

"Or perhaps we'd limit our dogmatism to certain kinds of beliefs," Suresh added.

"That wouldn't be a bad thing, would it?" Hannah asked.

"Not necessarily," Zach said.

Suresh glanced at his phone.

"Maybe that's enough for today," Zach said.

"Sounds good," Angelo said. "My brain hurts a bit."

"Thanks for the conversation, everyone," Zach said. "I think I'll make a few calls and send some texts. Whether I need to or not, I think I'll feel better if I reach out to some of the people who know how much I endorsed Mayor Lancaster. I may even reach out to Tristan to see how he's doing. I can't imagine how wrecked he must be by these revelations."

"That's a great idea," Hannah said. "This must be so disorienting. If he didn't know these things, he's probably really hurting."

"I know one thing with certainty," Suresh said as he gathered his things.

"Yeah, what's that?" Angelo asked with a smile.

"We need to sit somewhere more comfortable next time," he said, eyeing the hard wooden chair as he rose to his feet.

THEORY

Our four philosophy friends have just wrestled with issues fundamental to philosophy—what are belief, truth, and knowledge, and how do they relate to one another? The key to this topic, perhaps, is clear definition. The following will clarify some of the issues raised in the dialogue.

Epistemology (from the Greek *epistemē*, "knowledge") is the study of human cognition. It's the study of how we gain knowledge, how reliable human beliefs are, what the nature of truth is, and related issues. Another term for epistemology is the **theory of knowledge**.

Belief

When someone says, "It is my belief that the Green Bay Packers are the greatest football team of all time," what does the phrase "my belief" mean? Analyzing the phrase logically, "my belief" seems to indicate that the person speaking accepts the phrase that follows it ("the Green Bay Packers are the greatest football team of all time") as true. Believing something seems to mean accepting it as being true. The phrase "my belief" uses *belief* as a noun: It views a belief as something we possess. The phrase "I believe" expresses an activity: the activity of believing something. Regardless of whether we're dealing with a noun or a verb, the underlying concept has to do with accepting something as true.

Truth

But what does it mean for something to be true? The Bible famously records that Pontius Pilate asked Jesus, "What is truth?" (John 18:38). Unfortunately, neither Pilate nor Jesus answered the question. The most common view among epistemologists is that when we say a statement or a belief is true, we are asserting that it corresponds to the way that things actually are. If I say that the Packers are the greatest football team, my statement is true only if the Packers actually are the greatest football team. This is called the **correspondence theory**

"To say of what is that it is not, or of what is not that it is, is false, while to say of what is that it is, and of what is not that it is not, is true."
–Aristotle

of truth. According to this theory, a proposition is true if and only if it corresponds with reality.

Some have objected to the correspondence theory. For example, some object that when I say, "It's true that the Packers are the best," that's not stating anything more than that I believe that they're the best, so the correspondence theory reduces truth to belief. This is an insightful criticism: When I assert something, I am stating what I believe. But if someone says that I'm wrong, I might respond with something like, "No, it's true! The Packers have won more national titles than any other team!" In doing so, I'm providing evidence that shows that my belief corresponds to reality, but it's still my belief.

"If names be not correct, language is not in accordance with the truth of things. If language be not in accordance with the truth of things, affairs cannot be carried on to success."
–Confucius

Nonetheless, "truth" and "belief" are not synonyms. Since it's possible for beliefs to be false but impossible for truth to be false, "belief" and "truth" cannot mean the same thing. The correspondence theory accommodates this nicely. It provides a criterion for differentiating between beliefs that are true and those that are false: correspondence with reality.

Another objection to the correspondence theory is that when someone claims that a proposition is true, she is making this claim based on how well that proposition fits with the body of other propositions that she holds to be true. If a proposition contradicts the other things that someone thinks are true, then that proposition will be rejected as false, but if it coheres with the other things that she considers to be true, then it will be accepted. Thus truth, some say, has more to do with coherence with one's other beliefs than with correspondence with reality. This is called the **coherence theory of truth**.

An implication of this theory is that true beliefs do not necessarily correspond to reality. As long as a proposition coheres with your other beliefs, you will accept it as true, regardless of whether it corresponds to reality. It may even be possible for a person to have an entire belief system that is internally consistent but completely divorced from reality. Movies like *The Matrix*, *The Thirteenth Floor*, and *Inception* come very close to illustrating such belief systems.

However, epistemologists have criticized coherence as a theory of truth. Even if someone's belief that a proposition is true is the result of its coherence with her other beliefs, that does not entail that if she says it's true, what she means is merely that it coheres with her other beliefs rather than that it corresponds to reality. Correspondence with reality seems to be the root meaning of truth. Perhaps coherence serves some other goal; we'll return to that shortly.

An argument against the coherence theory of truth is that if it's true, it's not because it coheres with universal beliefs about the nature of truth, since many people hold to other theories of truth. Instead, if it's true, it's true because it corresponds to reality. But that means that if the coherence theory is true, it's true because the correspondence theory is true. But if the correspondence theory is true, then the coherence theory is false. Thus, if the coherence theory is true, then the coherence theory is false. Ironically, this shows the coherence theory of truth to be incoherent.

Knowledge

Now let's define knowledge. Beliefs can be true or false, but that does not appear to be the case with knowledge. If I say that I *know* something, I'm implying that it is true. This seems to be a very important difference between beliefs and knowledge: The former can be mistaken while the latter cannot.

If knowledge cannot be mistaken, then truth is a necessary attribute of knowledge. Likewise, knowledge presupposes belief. You cannot have the former without the latter. I can't both know something and not believe it—at least, not in the ordinary sense of these terms.[1] So knowledge involves believing something that is true. If you know proposition X, then two things are true about proposition X: You believe it, and it corresponds to reality.

1. Someone might say something like, "I know that's true, but I'm having a hard time believing it." That person probably means that he knows X is true, but he's having a hard time accepting X, like when a person says, "I know that summer break is over, but it's hard to believe that the new school year is here already."

In addition to belief and truth, knowledge has traditionally been thought to have one more necessary attribute: justification. That's why the traditional definition of knowledge is often abbreviated **JTB**: **justified true belief**. Here we should note that the phrase "true belief" does not mean "genuine belief" or anything like that. It denotes a belief that corresponds to reality. But what does "justified" mean? Let's talk briefly about belief justification.

Justification

Epistemic justification is what entitles us to accept something as being true. Intelligent people hold widely differing views regarding this rather controversial subject. Broadly speaking, there are two main types of approaches to belief justification: those that see beliefs as justified by evidence and those that do not involve evidence. The former are referred to as "evidentialism" or evidentialist approaches to justification. The latter are called, as a group, non-evidentialist approaches to justification, or sometimes fideistic approaches to justification (although that term does not apply equally well to all non-evidentialist approaches).

The discussion of evidentialist and non-evidentialist approaches to belief justification is so important that we're going to devote a whole chapter to it. How beliefs are justified has been one of the main issues explored in epistemology, and there is much to discuss on this topic.

Objections to JTB

Epistemologists have criticized the JTB analysis of the nature of knowledge on several points. One criticism is that two of the necessary conditions for a belief to constitute knowledge cannot be fulfilled. The three necessary conditions are belief, truth, and justification. It's easy to have beliefs, but it's probably impossible to know with 100 percent certainty that your beliefs are true because it's possible to conceive of some scenario in which even your most justified beliefs turn out to be false.

Take, for instance, René Descartes' famous *cogito ergo sum* ("I think, therefore I am"). To Descartes, this seemed to be obviously true: If he's thinking, then he must exist, for it's impossible to think if you don't exist. Descartes' argument is completely dependent on logic. Thus, while his conclusion seems airtight, it works only if we assume the validity of human logic. As unlikely as it might seem, it is at least conceivable that human logic is significantly flawed, or at least incomplete. Perhaps human logic falls as far short of being a comprehensive system of logic as the logic of ants falls short of human logic. Perhaps God has a system of logic that exceeds our logic as far as ours exceeds the logic of ants. And perhaps in God's logic, thinking can exist without beings who think—even though this seems unimaginable to us.

Therefore, it's possible that we cannot be certain that our beliefs correspond to reality, and so it's possible that we can't be certain that our beliefs are true. This is a form of **skepticism**, the belief that humans cannot know truth.[2] If skepticism is true, it undermines one of the necessary conditions of JTB. However, it's possible to respond to this skeptical challenge, since it points out that we can't be *certain* our beliefs are true, not that our beliefs *cannot* be true. Since JTB does not require us to be certain that our beliefs are true but instead merely requires that they be true, this skeptical challenge to JTB seems unsuccessful.

Another skeptical challenge to JTB argues that it's impossible for beliefs to correspond to reality. Often this argument points out that human concepts fall short of grasping the actual nature of things and therefore at best they approximate the nature of reality. For example, even my rather simple belief that there are still some Earl Grey tea bags left in the kitchen, which seems to be accurate (because I just checked and indeed there are some left), involves simplistic understandings of the nature of physical matter (I never have understood string theory), spatial location, and other complexities of existence. In short, my grasp of the nature of reality is on an infantile level in comparison to the actual complexity of reality.

There may be some truth to this argument: Perhaps many, most, or maybe even all my beliefs fail to actually correspond to reality. If that's the case, though, then it's true that at least this skeptical belief corresponds to

2. There are varying degrees of skepticism. One can be skeptical about the supernatural, or about the possibility of life on Mars, or about the possibility of the Dallas Cowboys ever winning another Super Bowl, without being skeptical about all knowledge whatsoever. The latter form of skepticism is what we're talking about here. It is sometimes called "global skepticism."

reality, and that's rather strange. It's odd that the very belief that my beliefs don't correspond to reality would be an exception to the rule.

Nonetheless it could be true. What should we make of this? Perhaps when someone says something like "My belief about Earl Grey tea is true," what is meant is that the belief is true in a general sense: It's not intended to capture all the scientific complexity of the situation but rather to accurately reflect some general facts about it. Perhaps it is possible to be epistemically modest while also affirming that beliefs can capture general truths about the world. And maybe this is the best balance: modesty and humility in the face of the complexity of the world around us combined with a positive attitude about our ability to recognize some truths about that world.[3] Such a position is compatible with the JTB analysis of knowledge.

Both of these challenges to JTB are motivated by skepticism. A challenge *not* motivated by skepticism is the **Gettier problem**. In 1963 Edmund Gettier published an article titled "Is Justified True Belief Knowledge?"[4] It gives examples of beliefs that are true and that seem to be justified but that don't appear to be knowledge. Here's one of them: Smith has a justified belief that "Jones owns a Ford." He therefore logically concludes that either "Jones owns a Ford, or Brown is in Barcelona." Smith can do this without having any information on Brown's location because if it's true that "Jones owns a Ford," then it's true that either Jones owns a Ford or anything else whatsoever—it doesn't matter what the other option is, since we already know it's true that Jones owns a Ford.[5] However, it turns out that, in spite of Smith's justified belief that Jones owns a Ford, Jones actually doesn't. Conversely, by sheer coincidence, Brown really is in Barcelona. So Smith's belief that "either Jones owns a Ford or Brown is in Barcelona" is both true and logically justified.[6] The problem is that, even though Smith's belief

---

3. **Epistemic modesty** is the recognition that human cognitive ability is finite and fallible and that there may be things that surpass our ability to comprehend. **Cognitive humility** is an attitude of modesty that stems from the awareness of epistemic modesty and results in willingness to accept that one might be mistaken about one's beliefs.
4. Edmund L. Gettier, "Is Justified True Belief Knowledge?," *Analysis* 23 (1963): 121–23, https://doi.org/10.1093%2Fanalys%2F23.6.121.
5. If X is true, then "either X or Y" is also true, regardless of the truth value of Y.
6. If "either X or Y" is true, and if it's false that X is true, then Y is necessarily true.

that either Jones owns a Ford or Brown is in Barcelona is both justified and true, very few would think that Smith's belief constitutes knowledge, and it probably doesn't.

Some epistemologists wrestling with the Gettier problem have argued that Smith wasn't actually justified in believing that Jones owns a Ford. Others have argued that Smith's belief that "either Jones owns a Ford or Brown is in Barcelona" does not constitute knowledge. Many have argued that the Gettier problem shows that we need to either replace or modify JTB. Perhaps the requirements for justification need to be strengthened. Perhaps JTB is a necessary, but not a sufficient, condition for knowledge. In any case, while JTB does seem to be in the ballpark, there also seems to be more work to be done to refine it.

Epistemology and Worldviews

When it comes to epistemology, there are few differences between most worldviews. A naturalist, a monotheist, and a polytheist (to name three prominent worldviews) all have beliefs that they think are justified and true. Some philosophical traditions are characterized by skepticism, such as Pyrrhonism[7] (in ancient Greece) and **postmodernism**. The latter is a twentieth- and twenty-first century current, the members of which argue, among other things, that since all believing occurs within historical contexts outside which any belief would not make sense, the coherence and justification of beliefs are historically and socially conditioned to an extent that renders all beliefs subjective. Consequently, postmodernists are usually skeptical that beliefs correspond to reality and of JTB as an explanation of knowledge.[8]

Postmodernism is not without merit: It can be praised for its sensitivity to cultural contexts, its epistemic modesty, and its cognitive humility.

7. See Harald Thorsrud, "Ancient Greek Skepticism," in *Internet Encyclopedia of Philosophy*, https://iep.utm.edu/ancient-greek-skepticism/#H3.
8. For an understandable, popular-level introduction to postmodernism, see Matthew Van Cleave, Paul Jurczak, Christopher Schneck, and Douglas Sjoquist, "What Is Postmodernism?," in *Introduction to Philosophy* (Central Florida University Press, 2020). The entire book can be read online or downloaded without charge from https://pressbooks.online.ucf.edu/introductiontophilosophy.

However, postmodernism is not itself a worldview. In fact, postmodern thinkers typically eschew attempts to construct such comprehensive accounts of reality ("totalizing metanarratives," as the French postmodernist Jean-François Lyotard called them[9]).

However, some worldviews intersect with epistemology in specific ways. For instance, some naturalists believe that science is the only reliable way to know reality. Similarly, some theists argue that the existence of God is necessary for an adequate explanation of how humans can know truth. We'll discuss these views—scientism and reliabilism—in the next chapter.

9. See Jean-François Lyotard, *The Postmodern Condition: A Report on Knowledge*, trans. Geoff Bennington and Brain Massuni (University of Minnesota Press, 1984).

QUESTIONS TO PONDER

- Can you think of anything that you believe but that you don't think is true?
- Can you think of anything that is true that you don't believe?
- Which do you think is better, the correspondence theory of truth or the coherence theory of truth? Why?
- Do you think JTB is a good explanation of what we mean by the word "knowledge"? If not, how would you improve it—or with what would you replace it?
- How does epistemology impact your worldview?

TERMS TO KNOW

- epistemology
- theory of knowledge
- belief
- truth
- correspondence theory of truth
- coherence theory of truth
- knowledge
- justified true belief (JTB)
- belief justification
- skepticism
- epistemic modesty
- cognitive humility
- Gettier problem
- postmodernism

FOR FURTHER READING

Audi, Robert. *Epistemology: A Contemporary Introduction to the Theory of Knowledge*. 3rd ed. Routledge, 2011. This is an advanced introduction.

Bernecker, Sven and Duncan Pritchard, eds. *The Routledge Companion to Epistemology*. Routledge, 2011. With seventy-eight different entries, this is a very useful collection of articles and a veritable encyclopedia of epistemology.

Dew, James K., Jr. and Mark W. Foreman. *How Do We Know? An Introduction to Epistemology*. 2nd ed. IVP Academic, 2020. This is an accurate and approachable introduction to epistemology.

7

JUSTIFICATION OF BELIEF

SYNOPSIS

Chapter 6 discussed the important concepts of belief, truth, knowledge, and justification. This chapter zeroes in on justification and analyzes how beliefs are justified.

DIALOGUE

Zach had always relied on the scientific method—both in the laboratory and in life. If empirical data could be gathered to prove something, he believed it; otherwise, he didn't. This was a major reason he had adopted atheism. Religious claims never seemed verifiable, and he wasn't inclined to believe things that lacked evidence. He believed that his recent philosophical investigations had identified his approach as *scientism*. And he had been quite comfortable with that position—until last night.

He had explained this viewpoint as they sat at the café together. It had thrown Zach when Suresh almost offhandedly asked how Zach knew scientism was true. He was suddenly struck by the difficulty of proving scientism scientifically.

Drinking his morning coffee and planning his workday, Zach mulled over the implications of this discovery. Apparently he believed in scientism for reasons not directly tied to the scientific method. Was he being self-referentially incoherent?

Zach didn't want to abandon ship though. After all, it would be unreasonable and irresponsible to believe things without sufficient proof, wouldn't it? But what kind of evidence could prove that a person must not believe anything without sufficient evidence? He wasn't sure, but as he headed for the door to leave for work, Zach realized it was all giving him a headache.

* * *

Hannah had adopted *voluntarism* for intensely personal reasons. Almost daily, she saw the pain and suffering of people broken by difficult circumstances, by wrongs perpetrated against them by others, and by systemic societal evils. All of it seemed out of control and without meaning or purpose. But rather than lie down, give up, or escape into nihilism, Hannah had decided to follow the advice of the French existentialist Jean Paul Sartre to create her own meaning. She would make a difference! Choosing social work as the avenue for helping others (she didn't care for politics and didn't think she could handle law enforcement) had allowed her to care for crushed people.

She had recently discovered—mostly due to her new philosophy friends—that her view of truth was known as voluntarism. Part of voluntarism involves exercising one's right to believe whatever one regards as the truth. The night before, as her friends had discussed ways to justify their beliefs or be certain that their beliefs were true, Hannah realized they were speaking a different language. Voluntarists don't have to justify their beliefs. They just need the courage to believe what they will, and they are automatically justified in doing so.

Her friends called her position *fideism*—believing without requiring evidence for belief. The root of *fideism* was a word that meant "faith," and Hannah was okay with that.

This morning, though, an annoying thought nagged at her. Zach had planted it when he pointedly asked if she believed multiplication tables. Of course she did. Then he asked if the multiplication tables would be true if she chose not to believe them. Try as she might, she couldn't think of how she would exercise her personal freedom to redefine multiplication. Whether she believed them or not, it seemed like math needed to be true for her to balance her checkbook.

She left for work feeling a little unsettled.

* * *

Since Suresh had begun reconnecting with his Eastern roots, he had started noticing how ordered, logical, and sometimes boring so many everyday aspects of Western life seemed. Westerners seemed trapped by cause-and-effect reasoning, with expectations that the physical world, as well as the moral and intellectual worlds, would follow rules and make sense.

Suresh was exhilarated by the freshness and depth of Eastern thinking. And although not all Easterners thought the same way about categories of truth, Suresh was gravitating toward *irrationality*, the idea that our categories can never plumb the depths of any real thing. The more a person tries to say true things about "reality," the more they will discover that reality defies analysis.

Truth, instead, is affectional or intuitive, a matter of feelings and passions. He had recently seen a quote by someone named Pascal to the effect of "The heart has its reasons, which reason does not know." He didn't know who Pascal was,[1] but that quote resonated with him. Suresh trusted his heart more than his reason, and as the group chatted about the idea of truth verification, he felt strangely satisfied that he was apparently more humble than they were about the limits of reason.

Suresh had tried explaining it when they met last night, but he got a little frustrated that Hannah and Zach didn't seem to understand. Angelo had missed the meeting because he had to work. Suresh was trying to make his perspective as clear as possible when Hannah said, "Suresh, if you're right about reality and the nature of truth, won't your case get weaker the clearer your explanation is?" He didn't know how to respond to that.

---

1. Blaise Pascal (1623–1662) was a French mathematician and philosopher. Pascal was not advancing irrationalism in this quotation. The quote is found in *Pensees*, IV: Of the Means of Belief. A copy can be found here: https://www.gutenberg.org/files/18269/18269-h/18269-h.htm.

He was struggling this morning. Part of him wanted to frame his theory of truth in such clear, well-organized, and convincing arguments that his friends would understand and find it compelling. But another part of him believed that his theory of truth could never be reduced to mere logical expressions and that if they didn't feel the way he did, they'd probably never get it.

But the problem was worse than that. He had a new thought (or feeling—he couldn't tell): What if his theory of truth was itself irrational? It should be, right? It should be too deep to comprehend and put into words. Where would that leave him?

Suresh was so distracted as he left for work that he tripped on a piece of furniture and jammed the big toe on his left foot. That felt stupid, but not necessarily irrational; the pain, on the other hand, seemed like a cold, hard truth. *The furniture is hard, and my toe hurts—and my theory of truth seems to have a hard time handling either one.*

* * *

Things at the courthouse had been crazy since the story about the mayor's criminal activities broke. For the first time since the group had begun meeting, Angelo had to miss because he had taken on extra shifts. There hadn't been any signs of violence, so he wasn't really nervous, but the security company he worked for wasn't taking any chances. They had assigned two guards for every shift that had previously required only one, and Angelo was getting a lot of overtime. The extra income was nice, but he hoped things would calm down soon.

During one of the breaks, he FaceTimed with the group. They were beginning a discussion of truth claims and how to justify them. Angelo regarded truth as a crucial part of his Christian worldview, so he was excited that they were tackling this issue. He didn't expect that his thinking would be challenged much, but he hoped he could add to the conversation.

Today he was reviewing some of the language used in this discussion and discovered it was a little more complicated than he had assumed. The main issue was that Angelo regarded certainty as an important part of genuine knowledge. The article he was reading referred to this as *apodictic certainty*,

100 percent certainty that a claim is true. The author seemed to think that such certainty was rare outside a small scope of ideas, namely facts of current experience (such as, *I can be sure I'm thinking about philosophy right now*) and undeniable facts (such as three plus two equals five). The article called these latter facts "incorrigible," meaning one must believe them.

Angelo felt sure about a lot of things beyond those two narrow categories. He was sure that God exists; he was sure that the Bible is true; he was sure that he was going to go to heaven when he died. He didn't think he could be satisfied with 95 percent certainty on any of these issues, or any percentage short of 100. But could he show that he had apodictic certainty about these things? Could he gather sufficient evidence for these claims?

Angelo believed that God revealed himself in nature, but he didn't see how he could've figured out who God is only through nature. To understand who the Christian God is, you need the Bible. The Bible says a great deal about God, so assuming the Bible is true, he could have genuine knowledge of God. But on what basis did he believe the Bible was true? After a few minutes, Angelo realized that he believed the Bible is true because the Bible says it came from God, and he trusts God.

His palms were getting a bit sweaty.

If he believed the Bible because he believed in God, and he believed in God because he believed the Bible, was he trapped in a vicious circle? If the evidence he thought he was basing his beliefs on wasn't rooted in anything, was he believing just because he wanted to? Was his faith actually fideism?

As Angelo drifted off to sleep, trying to catch a few hours before heading in for another long shift, he decided he was in no position to correct the "wrong" views of his friends. Maybe they would even end up helping him.

* * *

The following Thursday, Zach, Suresh, and Hannah met up at Brews Brothers, hoping Angelo would be able to make it. When Zach texted him, Angelo had said he wasn't sure when his shift would end. They went ahead and launched into their discussion.

Suresh began. "I was doing some more work on the subject of truth verification—"

"I've been thinking about it a lot too! Oh, I'm sorry, for interrupting," Hannah said, putting her hand up to her mouth. "My existentialist view of truth is bothering me a bit, but I didn't mean to interrupt."

"That's okay!" Suresh said as he continued his train of thought. "I was comfortable with irrationality until I realized how unsatisfying it is to have a view of truth that never seems to rest on anything. So I feel your pain." Suresh took a sip of his coffee. "I found an interesting article by William James, a philosopher who helped develop pragmatism, an alternative theory of knowledge,[2] that I find appealing."

"It seems reasonable to assume that pragmatism has to do with things working," Zach said. "Is there more to it than that?"

"That's certainly the heart, but yes, there is some additional complexity," Suresh answered, checking his notes. "James argues that people should accept conclusions as true only if they can 'assimilate, validate, corroborate, and verify' them, meaning propositions become true as they are proven true by outcomes. If people are arguing about the truth or falseness of an idea, they are wasting time, James says, unless the topic of discussion makes a difference."

"That makes sense," Hannah said. "People do argue about a lot of obscure things that don't really matter."

"And James says that the thing that makes arguments matter is their outcome or results. Obviously some facts can't be personally verified—historical facts, for instance, or some fact on the other side of the world, where I may never visit—but we are justified in accepting these as true if they are vouched for by someone who has verified them. For James, this verification process is truth. If an idea can be tested, works with all our other beliefs, and helps us move forward individually or as a species, then it is true."

Suresh placed his hand on his notebook. "I have to say, I found this very satisfying. It seems practical rather than theoretical, flexible rather than rigid, and progressive in the sense of charting a way forward in epistemology. Surely we can all agree that truth should work."

---

2. For James' famous lecture series on pragmatism, see William James, *Pragmatism: A Series of Lectures by William James, 1906–1907* (Arc Manor, 2008).

* * *

As Suresh was wrapping up, Angelo walked into the coffee shop. He waved at the group as he stopped at the counter to order. He was still wearing his uniform and had obviously come straight from the courthouse.

"Angelo!" Hannah exclaimed. "I'm so glad you're back. You've been working so much."

"I know," Angelo said, grabbing a chair and settling in. "Hopefully things will slow down soon." He took a welcome sip of his coffee. "It sure is good to be back with you guys. I've missed our conversations."

He asked what they'd been discussing. The group was still wrestling with belief justification, or how people can know that their beliefs are true. Angelo said he'd been giving that same topic a lot of thought during his long shifts and briefly shared the concerns he had about his own belief system. Was he a fideist, a coherentist, or just a wishful thinker? "I'm hoping you can help me sort it out," he said.

"Definitely," Zach said, "but first you need to hear what Suresh was sharing with us."

Suresh explained pragmatism again, a little more efficiently this time.

"That was really helpful, Suresh," Angelo said. "In this vein, I have a hypothetical scenario I've been wrestling with. A doctor determines that a patient needs surgery. Unfortunately, the patient has a weak heart in addition to the issue requiring surgery. The doctor talks to a colleague. Without the surgery, the patient will die, but the surgery is incredibly risky and odds of success aren't high. If they can keep the patient calm, the chance of heart issues would decrease and the patient's chances would improve."

Hannah interjected. "If the doctors tell the patient that the surgery is routine and that he'll be fine, that would seem to provide the best chance for success, right?"

Angelo nodded.

"I think I see what you're getting at," Suresh said. "By telling the patient something the medical team doesn't really believe, they improve the chance of a good outcome. Pragmatism would seem to say that the statement that the procedure is routine is true because it works."

"The statement would be true if the sole condition of a statement being true is that it works," Angelo said. "Right? In this scenario, what we might classify as a lie would be truth, and what most people consider candor, or truth, might in fact accelerate the man's death."

"I can't believe how quickly you came up with that story," Zach said.

"I've had a lot of time to think during these extra shifts. I'm so glad I could come tonight to talk about some of my concerns. I think pragmatism may have other problems as well."

"Like what?" Suresh asked. "It makes a lot of sense to me."

"If pragmatism is true," Angelo said, "how can someone know when he makes a statement that he's telling the truth? Wouldn't everyone involved have to wait and see the consequences to determine if it's true or not? And how long should people wait? Let's say pragmatism works in ten minutes, or an hour, or in two days, or how about in two years? What if the statement lacks any useful properties a week later—and so is false—but then eventually pays off and therefore becomes true? Was it true and then false and then true again?"

Angelo was met with a lot of blank stares, but he kept going. "Furthermore, isn't there something self-defeating about saying an idea is true only when it is verified? How do we act on the basis of an idea if we don't know that it's true? But how can we find out if it's true without assuming and going forward on the basis of it? To me, it looks like pragmatists have to borrow from other bases of truth to make their theory work, which is ironic."

"You're really pummeling my view, dude," Suresh said. "Isn't it compelling to argue that truth will generally succeed more than falsehood? James repeatedly tries to make the discussion practical. If a so-called truth doesn't do anybody any good, who cares?" Suresh was clearly exasperated. "I'm not sure how to respond to your concerns. They do seem valid, but I can't deny feeling like usefulness is a good way to assess truth."

"Maybe truth is usually useful, but usefulness can't define truth." Hannah said, looking around at the group members. "Some things that seem like facts don't appear to have practical value in the moment."

"Interestingly, James says that the true being useful and the useful being true mean the same thing," Suresh said. "I did feel uneasy about that statement, and your comment has me wondering if they could be two different ideas altogether."

"I find it interesting," Zach said, looking at Angelo, "that you're having misgivings about your faith framework."

"Well, I'm not considering giving up my religious beliefs," Angelo said. "I hold them very deeply. I've just been disconcerted thinking about the epistemology involved. I seem stuck in the apparent circle of believing in God because of the Bible and believing in the Bible because of God, which troubles me."

Hannah looked at her notes. "One of the concepts I ran across is *foundationalism*, the idea that all our beliefs can be traced back to foundational ideas called presuppositions."

Zach nodded. "I was initially very uncomfortable with the idea that I'd believe anything without sufficient proof, but I'm coming to see that it's unavoidable. Even the idea that I need to have sufficient proof for any proposition is itself seemingly impervious to proof."

"The guy I was reading pointed out obvious things like the fact that the world has existed for more than five minutes," Hannah said. "We all believe that, of course, but how would we go about proving it? If a person doubted that the world existed five minutes ago, we'd think they were certifiable. So maybe *some* things can be accepted as true without proof?"

"That would be encouraging," Angelo said. "Maybe that's how my belief system is functioning. Maybe God or the Scriptures, or both, are part of the foundation of my belief system and don't require proof."

"That seems like a big step," Suresh said. "Those are pretty big beliefs to hold without proof, don't you think?"

"I don't know," Angelo said, shrugging a bit. "The Bible doesn't prove God's existence. It affirms that he is and demands obedience to him. Requiring evidence before I believe in him could be dishonoring him. Maybe accepting that God is and then reasoning from there is part of what the Bible calls faith."

"You're certainly welcome to believe that," Hannah said, "but to me it seems like a wide foundation to build a person's beliefs on. Maybe you've landed in fideism after all."

"It's possible. I'm still working this out obviously," Angelo said. "But all acceptance of presuppositions can't be fideism. That would mean everyone is a fideist. If I can show coherence between the presupposition of God with my other beliefs, then accepting God as a presupposition wouldn't be irrational, would it?"

Zach had been quiet. "I'm willing to concede that we all have presuppositions. It was hard for me to get there, but it seems unavoidable. But I'm keeping my list as short as possible—maybe only facts of immediate experience and things that are undeniable. I think I could construct a belief system from there: a few obvious presuppositions and lots of evidence."

Hannah nodded. "I came across one more idea this week that I want to explore. Some philosophers talk about *reliabilism*—the idea that beliefs are justified if they're based on a reliable process of getting to them."

"How would a person determine whether a process is reliable?" Suresh asked. "Do we see if it works—pragmatism—or if it works with our other beliefs—coherentism—or if it is supported by our presuppositions—foundationalism? Is reliabilism different from all of them? It's attractive, but I don't see quite how it works."

"I don't think I can fully explain it, but it seems promising," Hannah said. "I'm going to keep exploring the idea."

"I guess we should call it a night," Zach said.

He shared with the group what he had read about Socrates' trial before the men of Athens. "He said that the unexamined life is not worth living. Until recently, I assumed that knowledge was straightforward, but examining epistemology has been very eye-opening. How do we show that our beliefs are justified? There doesn't seem to be any consensus among philosophers about how to justify them."

"And yet all of us want to know things—and know that we know them," Hannah said.

Everyone around the table nodded. This was a lot to think about.

THEORY

The four friends found themselves in deeper water than they expected as they tried to sort out how to justify their beliefs. This chapter will explain in more detail what they were trying to do.

In the previous chapter we learned that epistemic justification is what entitles us to accept some belief. In other words, you are justified in believing something if you have good reason to think it's true. Just what counts as "good reason" is controversial, though. Evidentialists think it involves having good evidence that the belief is true. Others suggest a variety of alternative theories. We'll look at several forms of evidentialism first, and then we'll look at several forms of non-evidentialism.

Evidentialism

Evidentialist approaches to belief justification view a person as justified in believing something if he or she has sufficient evidence that the belief is true. For example, I'm justified in believing that there's milk in my refrigerator because I remember seeing it in the refrigerator this morning and I have good reasons to believe that no one's been home all day to drink it. Belief-justifying evidence comes in many forms. There's sensory evidence: evidence obtained through seeing, hearing, smelling, tasting, and touching. There's also experiential evidence that does not come through those five senses, like feeling hungry, cold, or happy. These are experiences of ourselves and give us information about ourselves, but sometimes they give us information about the world around us, too, like the information about the temperature of our environment that we can get through feeling cold or hot.[3] And then there are even more subtle experiences, such as the mental experience of sensing a logical connection between two facts or making an inference from one fact to another. Similar to those are mathematical intuitions, such as the sense that if I have five of something and four are taken away, only one is left.[4]

These are fairly simple and direct forms of evidential justification, but there are more complex forms. The most famous of these is called **foundationalism** and can be traced back to the French philosopher, scientist, and mathematician René Descartes.[5] Descartes sought to overcome skepticism by finding something that he could know with absolute certainty and then

---

3. The view in epistemology that says that all knowledge can be traced back to sensory experiences is called empiricism. Famous empiricists include Aristotle, Francis Bacon, George Berkeley, and David Hume.
4. The view in epistemology that says that at least some knowledge can come through reason rather than sensory experience and that this knowledge plays an important role in human cognition is called rationalism. Famous rationalists include Plato, Descartes, Leibniz, and Spinoza.
5. Descartes (pronounced Deh-cart) lived from 1596 to 1650 and is considered by many to be the first modern philosopher.

using that belief as the foundation on which to build all his other beliefs. His most foundational belief was that he himself exists, since in order to be thinking about beliefs he must exist. This is his famous ***cogito ergo sum*** ("I think, therefore I am"). Since this is self-evidently true, anything that he could validly deduce from this truth must also be true. This, he believed, gave him the ability to be certain about a great many beliefs, thus defeating skepticism.

As brilliant as this strategy is, not everyone finds it convincing. One potential problem is that for Descartes' approach to succeed, it must not depend on hidden, unjustified assumptions. However, it does in fact have at least one such assumption: the validity of logic. "I think, therefore I exist" involves a logical inference from thinking to existence. However, he just assumes that logic can be trusted rather than proving it. Furthermore, it doesn't seem likely that he could prove logic without using logic in his proof, which would beg the question. Because of this, Descartes' strategy may not be as successful as he thought it was.

Descartes' strategy for overcoming skepticism may not have been completely successful, but he did succeed in drawing our attention to a useful strategy for justifying beliefs. If we have good reason for believing X, and we can validly deduce beliefs Y and Z from X, then we have good reason to believe Y and Z. In this case, X forms the foundation for Y and Z, so to speak, which is why this strategy is called foundationalism.

An alternative to foundationalism is coherentism, this time used as an evidentialist strategy for justifying beliefs rather than as a theory of truth. The **coherentist** approach to justification views a person's belief system like a web or network of interrelated beliefs that support each other. For example, my belief (1) that today is Sunday is related to and supported by my beliefs that (2) yesterday was Saturday, (3) I went to church this morning, (4) church takes place on Sundays, (5) I didn't go to work today, and (6) Saturday and Sunday are the days that I usually don't go to work. Beliefs (2) through (6) support belief (1). Additionally, beliefs (3) and (4) support each other and beliefs (2), (5), and (6) support each other. Together they form a coherent network of beliefs.

In this illustration, if beliefs (2) through (6) are true, then it's very likely that belief (1) is also true. Of course, if beliefs (2), (3), and (5) are false, then even if beliefs (4) and (6) are true, belief (1) may well be false even though it coheres perfectly well with all the other beliefs listed. So coherentism has this inherent weakness: A system that contains false beliefs may cause me to believe that I'm evidentially justified in accepting other false beliefs. But if most of your beliefs are true, then new beliefs that cohere with them are also likely to be true. Therefore, if you have good reasons for most of your beliefs, then you can utilize coherentism as a strategy to justify other beliefs that cohere with them. It should be noted, though, that when seeking evidential justification for your belief system as a whole, the coherence of your system of beliefs is not sufficient evidence to prove the system true, since a coherent system of false but complementary beliefs is possible.

Another alternative to foundationalism is **pragmatism**, which is the view that beliefs that work when put into practice are justified by their success. In short, if it works, it's probably true. William James, a nineteenth-century American philosopher and psychologist, was one of the seminal figures of pragmatism as a school of philosophy. According to James, a belief is shown to be true when it enables someone to perform some task. James expressed the view concisely: "You can say of it then either that 'it is useful because it is true' or that 'it is true because it is useful.' Both these phrases mean the same thing."[6]

Pragmatism is easy to illustrate. Caleb drives an old truck with a broken gas gauge. Other than that, the truck is generally reliable. However, one day it stops running. He isn't sure how many miles have passed since he last bought gas, but he suspects that it has run out. There are at least two ways he could test his belief that it is out of gas. He could disconnect the fuel lines, lower the gas tank to the ground, and peer inside to see if it is empty. That's a lot of work, but it would tell him via empirical observation whether his belief corresponds with reality. However, an easier approach would be to simply add a few gallons of gas to the tank and then try to restart the truck. If it starts, then it's very likely that his belief that the truck is out of gas is true.

6. William James, *Pragmatism: A New Name for Some Old Ways of Thinking* (Longmans, Green & Co., 1907), 204.

This "experimental" approach to justifying beliefs is an example of pragmatic justification. Caleb's theory worked, showing that it was probably correct.[7]

Direct experience, foundationalism, coherentism, and pragmatism are versions of evidentialism. Each uses some kind of evidence to justify beliefs. There have sometimes been disputes between the advocates of these various strategies, but they need not be viewed as mutually exclusive. Someone might have some beliefs that are based on direct experiences, some that are inferred from more foundational beliefs that are based on direct experience, some that are justified because of how they are supported by other elements of her belief system, and some beliefs that are held only because they've been shown to work in the past. These types of evidentialism can complement each other.

There's one last version of evidentialism that needs to be mentioned: scientism, the view that the scientific method is the only reliable way to justify beliefs. The scientific method involves collecting empirical data, formulating a hypothesis that explains the data, and carefully designing and implementing an experiment to test the hypothesis. The scientific method is a powerful research strategy that has resulted in great leaps in understanding our world.

However, there are two convincing arguments against scientism. One is that science is not the only way to gain knowledge, particularly knowledge in fields outside the natural sciences. For example, if you wanted to know about the history of some lost city from the ancient Near East, you would use historiographical methods rather than the scientific method. If you wanted to solve some problem in mathematics, you would use mathematical techniques rather than the scientific method. If you wanted to solve metaphysical or moral problems, you would use philosophical analysis rather than the scientific method. Each domain of study has methodologies

---

7. Unfortunately, sometimes a theory works even though it's not correct. Thus, pragmatic justification can be risky, for it may sometimes justify believing something that's actually false. Perhaps while Caleb was filling his gas can and then adding the gas to the truck, the hot engine cooled down, and that's why it restarted after he added gas to it. In that case, his belief seemed to be pragmatically justified even though it's false.

appropriate to that domain. There is no one-size-fits-all methodology, not even the scientific method.

The second argument is that scientism is self-referentially incoherent. A belief or an argument is self-referentially incoherent if it fails to live up to its own standard. Scientism says that science is the only reliable way to know anything. However, this belief is not a result of the scientific method; it's a philosophical conclusion rather than a scientific one. So whoever makes this claim is claiming something that is known through a method other than the scientific method, which seems like a clear self-contradiction.

This should not be viewed as a criticism of science, of course. Science is great, but scientism is not. It's important to keep the two distinct in our thinking.

Alternatives to Evidentialism

None of these evidentialist methods of justification can give us 100 percent certainty about the truthfulness of our beliefs—what epistemologists call "apodictic certainty."[8] Most of the time—perhaps all of the time—we settle for sufficient justification rather than apodictic certainty. But this raises a good question: How much justification is sufficient for my belief to qualify as knowledge? Is it sufficient for the belief simply to be more likely true than false? Or do I need to meet a higher standard? If so, then what is that standard, why do I have to meet it, and how do I know when I have?

The underlying problem brought to light by these questions about evidentialist justification is that we are rarely if ever in a position to know whether, all things considered, a belief is justified because we rarely ever know if all things really have been considered. After examining one hundred considerations relevant to the truthfulness of some belief, we may think

---

8. "Apodictic certainty" is the kind of certainty that is beyond any possibility of being mistaken. This is what Descartes thought he had about his own existence (*cogito ergo sum*, remember?). Whether mere mortals can have apodictic certainty is debatable. On the other hand, the term "psychological certainty" refers to the feeling of certainty that we all experience from time to time. This feeling can turn out to be mistaken, so it is not apodictic. There's also a third option: reasonable certainty. Something is reasonably certain if you have justification for believing it even though this justification falls short of 100 percent.

we've thought of every relevant consideration. But there could be another one hundred considerations we haven't even thought of. Although it will seem to us that we are justified in holding to that belief, we could still be wrong.

This concern and others like it have led some epistemologists to reject evidentialism and offer alternatives. One has already been mentioned: **skepticism**. The view that none of our beliefs are sufficiently justified to qualify as knowledge has a history stretching back to the ancient Greek Pyrrhonians (and perhaps further). However, saying that I'm justified in believing that none of my beliefs are justified seems self-referentially incoherent. Furthermore, most epistemologists think we have a great many justified beliefs, even if we don't have any that are apodictically certain. These range from analytic truths like "1+2=3" and "all triangles have three sides" to more sophisticated ones like Descartes' *cogito ergo sum*. It seems virtually impossible for these beliefs to be false: They're about as close to apodictic as a belief can be. So skepticism seems unlikely to be correct.

"We no longer believe in the power of reason over life. We feel that it is life which dominates reason."
—Oswald Spengler

A more common alternative to evidentialism is an approach that we can call **fideism**. The Latin word *fides* is sometimes translated "faith." Fideism is based on this word: It's the view that some beliefs are justified simply by our choice to believe them rather than by supporting evidence. Fideism comes in various forms. Religious people ("people of faith") sometimes have beliefs that are based on the trust that they place in God or in their religious tradition. In such cases, they may not have any evidence supporting the belief itself, but they trust that, if God said it (or if their religion teaches it, or anything like that), then it must be true.

A secular version of fideism is sometimes called **existentialism**.[9] A strong belief in free will permeates the worldview of existentialists like Jean-Paul Sartre and Albert Camus. They see this freedom as an attribute of genuine humanness, as one of the chief things that set us apart from brute

9. There are both religious and secular existentialists. Here we're focusing on secular existentialism.

beasts. In epistemology, this leads existentialists to hold that we have the right—and even the responsibility—to base our beliefs on free exercise of the will. Consequently, existentialists believe we are justified in believing whatever we willingly choose to believe. According to existentialism, justification isn't about having evidence for a belief but rather one's right to believe. That's using "justified" in a different sense from how evidentialists use it.

Another option is **irrationalism**, the view that objective, rational thought is not the best way to gain knowledge. There are several different versions of irrationalism. One holds that instinct and emotion are superior to reason as guides to knowledge. Many laypeople seem to give at least some credence to this view, as is shown by the frequently heard exhortations to "follow your heart" and "go with your gut."

A more metaphysical[10] form of irrationalism holds that reality is beyond the grasp of human reason. Many people assume that if we study something long and hard enough, we'll be able to figure it out. Metaphysical irrationalists disagree, either because they believe that reality does not have a coherent order and therefore cannot be understood by using reason or because they believe the order of the universe is beyond human comprehension.

A very different alternative to evidentialism is **reliabilism**. Reliabilists hold that a belief is justified if it is the product of a generally reliable process of belief formation. Thus, if someone is drunk and believes that he is seeing a pink elephant, his experience of seeing this elephant does not justify the belief that a pink elephant actually exists, since his senses (and his reasoning) could have been significantly distorted by alcohol. On the other hand, if a person is not drunk and does not have his senses impaired in any other way, then seeing a pink elephant would in fact justify his belief that such an elephant exists. (That, of course, would probably lead to further investigation of this unusual creature, but that's beside the point.)

This illustration of reliabilism makes it seem compatible with evidentialism, since the belief is based on reliably acquired sensory evidence. However, other examples show instances wherein a belief is justified although no evidence is involved. For instance, if an omniscient

10. Metaphysics is the study of the ultimate nature of reality. There are several chapters on metaphysics coming up soon in this book.

and veracious (truthful) God were to create humanity with a set of innate beliefs, then since a veracious God would only instill beliefs that are true in humanity, such a God instilling such beliefs would be a reliable belief-forming process. Hence, on reliabilism such beliefs would be justified, even if the humans have no evidence in support of them. However, on reliabilism it may not always be possible to know if a belief is justified. Consider this: If a veracious God implants a veridical belief in someone, she may not know whether the belief came from God or from some less veracious source. Therefore, she may not know whether the belief-formation process is reliable. Thus, she won't know if the belief is justified, and consequently she won't know whether she knows it. That seems a bit odd.

Each of these alternatives to evidentialism seems to have some truth and some value. Fideists don't generally want to do away with evidentialism entirely but instead want to say that while some beliefs can be justified evidentially, other beliefs cannot be justified by evidence that is justified another way: via "faith." Evidentialists may respond that faith is usually based on evidence that is simply less proximal to the belief than most. We'll talk more about the nature of faith in a future chapter on philosophy of religion.

Existentialists rightly point out that many beliefs involve a choice. However, this is not incompatible with evidentialism. Evidentialists are not by any means required to reject belief in free will. They just believe that taking into consideration the available evidence increases the likelihood of making the right choice.

Irrationalism reminds us that it is difficult to be fully objective about our beliefs: We frequently have biases and preferences, plus gaps in our understanding and our information, that skew our reasoning and throw off our conclusions. And sometimes emotions and instincts can be a very useful guide, though the evidentialist might argue that instincts form over time based upon our experiences and thus are not completely divorced from evidence. Metaphysical irrationalism may be correct that there are aspects of reality that transcend human comprehension. However, that does not mean that no aspect of reality is comprehensible to humans. In fact, the assertion that the universe contains things that transcend us is itself a statement about the nature of reality that the irrationalist deems true. The irrationalist must be careful to avoid self-referential incoherence here.

Finally, the argument for reliabilism seems strong. However, weighing the evidence for a given belief is one reliable way of belief justification, so reliabilism does not exclude evidentialism.

CONCLUSION

Inasmuch as worldviews are constructed of beliefs, and we want our beliefs to be true, the question of whether and how our beliefs are justified is directly relevant to the study of worldviews. Most of the strategies for justifying beliefs that we've discussed are compatible with naturalism, theism, and various other worldviews. It's a good idea for students of philosophy and worldviews to give these strategies careful consideration and decide what they think are the best ways to go about forming and justifying their beliefs. Doing so has great potential for strengthening the accuracy of your belief system.

QUESTIONS TO PONDER

- What do you think is the best approach to justifying your beliefs?
- Do you have any beliefs that are unjustified that you think should be modified or abandoned?
- Do you have any beliefs that are unjustified that you think you should retain? Why?
- Is irrationalism compatible with theism? Is it compatible with naturalism? Why or why not?

TERMS TO KNOW

- justification
- evidentialism
- foundationalism
- René Descartes
- *cogito ergo sum*
- coherentism
- pragmatism
- scientism
- fideism
- existentialism
- irrationalism
- metaphysics
- reliabilism

FOR FURTHER READING

All the books recommended in the previous chapter discuss epistemic justification. The following focus specifically on this issue.

Alston, William P. *Epistemic Justification: Essays in the Theory of Knowledge*. Cornell University Press, 1989.

Steup, Matthias, ed. *Knowledge, Truth, and Duty: Essays on Epistemic Justification, Responsibility, and Virtue*. Oxford University Press, 2001.

Swinburne, Richard. *Epistemic Justification*. Clarendon, 2001.

METAPHYSICS

8

MONISM VS. PLURALISM

SYNOPSIS

This chapter begins a section of four chapters on metaphysics, the investigation of the true nature of reality. A fundamental question in metaphysics is: Is reality a single substance, a unified whole, or does it consist of many different substances? The philosophy friends discover this question to be more challenging than it first appears. The discussion that follows seeks clarity through definition and alignment with one's worldview.

DIALOGUE

God, help me!

Zach found himself praying involuntarily as the disheveled man pressed a large blade against his abdomen.

"Give me your wallet now!"

The crazed look on the man's face made it clear that he would not be reasoned with. Zach slowly reached for his wallet and handed it over. The thief grabbed it and was gone in a flash, turning a corner and disappearing into the night.

Zach breathed a sigh of relief. *Why did I take a shortcut down this alley to save a few seconds getting to my car?* It was after midnight. He had been downtown with some friends celebrating a birthday. He had parked a few blocks from the restaurant and didn't think twice about walking back to his car.

Heart racing, Zach made it to his car, got in, locked the doors, and drove to a well-lit location. He quickly dialed 911 and reported the crime.

As he finally drove home, a powerful wave of unease washed over him. The annoyance of having to cancel his credit cards and get a new driver's license wasn't what bothered him. In the moment, he had reacted to the surprise and fear with a spontaneous prayer. Why did he do that? He didn't believe in God, or in anything immaterial for that matter. The thought continued to bother him as the adrenaline wore off and he collapsed into a fitful sleep.

* * *

When the four friends gathered at Brews Brothers the next day, Zach shared about the mugging.

Hannah gasped.

"I worry about this when I leave the restaurant late at night," Suresh said. "Some scary-looking people often hang around the back of the restaurant. Depending on who it is, I sometimes don't feel safe out there on my own."

"I believe petty crime is increasing," Angelo said. "We've been encouraged to be more vigilant on the job."

Hannah reached out to touch Zach's hand. "I can't imagine how terrified you must have been! That's one of the reasons I don't stay out late in the city. It's safer to leave with friends, but it's still scary."

"It was definitely scary, but I could sense that if I cooperated, he wouldn't hurt me. I could be wrong, but it looked like he might be hopped up on something and might be looking for drug money." Zach sighed deeply. "It was unnerving to have a knife held to my gut. I could feel the point through my shirt and knew it wouldn't take much force for him to jam it into my stomach."

"Ugh." Hannah shuddered. "It's so terrifying to think of what could have happened."

"The most surprising thing about the encounter"—Zach gulped—"was that, without thinking, I asked God to help me."

"Wait," Angelo said. "What do you mean?"

"I don't know. In my head, I just said, 'God, help me!'"

Zach was met with wide eyes from around the table.

"I don't know why I did it. And I've been turning it over in my head since last night."

"I have an idea why!" said Angelo with a smile, thankful for the opportunity to bring some levity into the heavy conversation.

"I think I know what you're going to say, Angelo," Zach said.

"Try me."

"You're going to say that I asked God for help because, deep in my heart, I know God exists, that when push comes to shove and I'm absolutely helpless, I can't help but acknowledge that something or someone is out there."

"That's pretty close!" Angelo laughed. "Not to make light of your fear in that moment, of course."

"Oh, I know," Zach said. "Of course, I disagree with you, but I'm still wondering why I did it. The best I can come up with is that belief in God or in anything immaterial is leftover superstition from a premodern age that we haven't yet shed. Since American culture has had a religious flavor from the beginning, this idea is naturally implanted in our thinking. Even when we consciously reject belief in God, at certain times it seeps out unconsciously, especially in moments of stress or fear of death."

"That's an interesting theory," Suresh said. "I'm not sure it would make sense in much of the world, where belief in some kind of deity is considered common sense. Maybe it makes sense in a Western culture though."

"I know we've talked about this before, Zach, but do you believe in anything outside the natural world, or is the physical universe all there is?" Hannah asked.

"I'd call myself a materialist," Zach said, "in the sense that the only thing that exists is the natural world, the universe. I don't believe in a spiritual world, or more accurately, an immaterial world. I'd argue that everything that exists is one, in that it is all material. What we call immaterial entities like logic, virtue, morals, or the soul are just terms we give to natural phenomena. In reality, though, they don't *exist*. They're just the names we assign actions to in order to explain simple, material causes."

"I guess that simplifies your worldview," Angelo said. "If everything is material, then there's no need for debate about ultimate realities or immaterial realities."

"Exactly," Zach said. "Everything can be explained in material terms because that's all that exists. We know reality through the senses and our increasingly accurate scientific method. It means we don't have to speculate about an immaterial world that can't be tested."

Suresh had been listening intently. "In some ways I agree with you," he said, "but the way I see it is exactly the opposite. I'd say I only believe in one reality as well, but that it is really a spiritual reality with the material world as an illusion. So everything is one and unified—and our primary problem is our tendency to believe that separate entities exist. The one reality that does exist is eternal and unchanging, but the appearances we encounter change over time."

Zach nodded thoughtfully. "So all is one, but it is all immaterial?" he asked. "How can it be immaterial when it is obviously material?"

"I wouldn't say all is immaterial but rather spiritual with material manifestations."

Hannah shook her head. "My head is spinning trying to comprehend this. It seems to me that the material and spiritual are two *separate* realities. How can they be one?"

"I'm not sure how to make it sound logical and make sense," Suresh said. "I'm still trying to grasp the concepts myself. Disha has been explaining it. She says I struggle with the concept because I was raised in a Western culture and therefore naturally find these ideas difficult to comprehend. I suppose she could be right about that."

"Maybe part of the problem is that we're confusing categories," Angelo said. "It seems to me that material and immaterial go together, and spiritual and physical go together. When we throw natural and supernatural into the mix, it gets confusing. Suresh, you said that you see everything as spiritual but not necessarily immaterial. Can you explain that distinction?"

Suresh thought for a moment. "I'd say that all is spiritual in that the essence of existence is spiritual, even though something might have a physical embodiment."

"But wouldn't that mean there are two realities, the spiritual and the physical?" Hannah asked.

"No . . ." Suresh said, seeming a bit flustered. "There's still only one reality—that which exists—and it's spiritual, but physical entities partake in that spiritual reality."

"Okay, I think I'm starting to understand," Zach said. "Angelo, your distinction of categories is helpful. I've always thought that only materialists believe in one reality and that it had to be the physical world since it's most obviously real and true. But I'm starting to see that although something can't be both material and immaterial, reality may be a combination of things from different categories, like Suresh is saying, both material and spiritual and yet still one."

Angelo rubbed the side of his temple. "My brain hurts."

Everyone laughed.

"Metaphysics has always been so fuzzy," Angelo said. "I can understand epistemology more easily because it's about knowing. We've all experienced learning certain things in a number of different ways. I can know something through experience, through instruction, through reasoning, and through intuition. That seems obvious to me. But metaphysics is so much more abstract. When we start talking about the nature of reality, everything gets blurry."

"Agreed," Zach said. "I'm used to concrete facts and data in my work, but these philosophical considerations are hard to grab onto. My family used to play this game at family reunions. Someone would grease a watermelon with Crisco and throw it in the lake, and all the cousins would compete to see who could carry the watermelon to shore. The watermelon was so slippery that even when you were sure you had it, it would slip right out."

"Your family reunions sound more exciting than mine!" Hannah said, laughing. "But it's a great analogy. Talking about metaphysics *is* slippery."

"What about you, Hannah?" Angelo asked. "Do you think all is one, or are there different realities?"

"Ooh, that's a tough one. One famous existentialist, Martin Heidegger, would say that all is one. I think he wrote that what we call 'the self' is merely the action of existing and is therefore part of our physical body, specifically the brain. In many ways, I'd agree with Zach that only the material world exists, and yet we act like the immaterial world is real in the way we describe its effects. I can't escape the sneaking suspicion," she said, shaking her head, "that there may be more than the material world . . . We can't seem to stop referring to immaterial realities in our thoughts and conversations. If they didn't exist, wouldn't we have moved on from talking about them as if they are real? Even ardent materialists I know at work will talk about their souls, about virtue and justice, and about meaning. They don't actually believe that such things are real, but they can't help talking as if they are real in everyday life."

"I've noticed that as well," Angelo said. "People may say that immaterial labels are just names we apply to physical objects or processes, but they seem to treat them as real things. Take justice, for instance. If justice is just a label we apply to physical realities, but there's no actual *metaphysical reality* of justice, couldn't people claim that each person or society is justified in applying the label of justice to whatever physical function they want? Wouldn't we end up with societies defining morality differently?"

"That's what we have now, isn't it?" Zach asked. "Doesn't each culture define morality its own way? For example, what is considered the proper way to treat women is vastly different around the world, which would make sense if morality were only a label applied to actions. Each society and culture could call their customs moral, regardless of how they treat women."

Angelo nodded thoughtfully. "Yet we tend to view some cultures as morally better than others, don't we? That would seem to indicate either that there is some ultimate standard of justice by which we judge all human actions or that we are cultural imperialists by nature, thinking that our own ideas of justice are better and imposing them on other cultures."

"I think Angelo has a point," Suresh said. "If all that exists is material, where do we get our sense of morality? Or any other immaterial reality for that matter? Are they just labels, or is there more to it? I want to say there's more to it, which may support my belief that all is one and spiritual. The spiritual provides the basis for the sense of morality."

"But are we straying from the question of reality to the question of morality?" Hannah asked.

"I think it's easy to because they're related and are difficult to keep separate," Angelo said. "Should we go back to Zach's ordeal and his prayer?"

Zach had been listening and looked up from his drink.

"If we can figure out why people tend to cry out to God—or gods—in moments of desperation, it might shed light on the nature of reality," Angelo said.

Hannah suddenly remembered the beginning of this long and winding conversation. "What did Zach say earlier about how you would explain his impromptu prayer, Angelo?"

Angelo laughed. "He was rightly guessing that I believe people pray in moments of desperation because they intuitively know that God exists. Sometimes we can't deny it even when we want to—which leads to my view about reality. I believe in a duality of realities."

"Can you explain?" Hannah asked.

"There is God and then there is everything else. God is eternal and uncreated, and everything else is temporal and created. Christians call this the Creator-Creature Distinction. God exists in an entirely different reality than creation, even immaterial things, such as angels and demons. He is infinite, divine, and independent of anything outside himself, while everything in creation is finite, creaturely, and dependent on God."

"How did you rattle off all those terms so easily?" Hannah asked.

"We've been studying the nature of God at church for the last few months, and the pastor has covered the Creator-Creature Distinction several times to help us really grasp it. Before learning some of this, I probably would have believed in one reality, like Zach or Suresh, without realizing the significance of the question. But I've come to see the importance of recognizing that God's reality is separate from ours."

"Why is it important that God has a separate reality? I am not sure I understand," Suresh said. "I'm thinking about this in relation to my beliefs."

"That's a good question. I guess it's important because it answers the question of the first cause of everything that exists," Angelo said. "God's eternal nature means we have an explanation for why there is something rather than nothing."

Angelo shared more of what he had learned about how God exists in a timeless reality and has no beginning. God freely created a new reality, the universe, that is very different from his own existence. All ultimate questions about existence would then go back to this eternal God who created everything that exists. He also shared about the moral aspect of the two realities: God and creatures. While God created humans innocent, at some point they fell into moral corruption. In addition to the other distinctions between God and creation, in Angelo's framework, God is holy, and people are fallen.

"I think that's why I have a hard time thinking about reality apart from morality," Angelo said. "For Christians, differences in reality imply a difference in morality, at least since the fall."

"I have a question," Hannah said. "If God exists in a reality distinct from creation, how can he interact with it? How does the infinite relate to the finite?"

"That's a good question, and it gets to the heart of the Christian worldview. Because the nature of creation is finite and dependent, we couldn't know anything about the infinite God if he didn't reveal himself to us."

Angelo shared more of his understanding of the Christian worldview—that the reason people can know anything is because God made everything in the world to be revelational, that is, to reveal truth about God and his glory. Christians believe that the central message of the Bible is that God came down to his creation to reveal himself to us for the purpose of relationship, which culminates in the infinite God assuming a human nature and entering the human experience for the purpose of saving people from their guilt before a holy God.

"So by his incarnation, meaning he was born as a man and lived a perfect life before being crucified, Jesus is the one who bridges the gap between the divine and the created. Jesus' death reconciled God and humans, and his resurrection secures eternal life."

"Interesting," Suresh said. "I never knew that the story of Jesus was about bridging the gap between two realities. We think of Jesus as enlightened and a moral teacher, but what you said is a different concept altogether."

"I think my view of Jesus is different because the two realities, God and humans, are personal beings. God speaks, loves, comforts, and saves. It seems that some other conceptions of God tend to view him as an impersonal force."

"That's true," Suresh said. "In one form of Buddhism that argues for multiple realities, what a Westerner might call 'the divine' is really just emptiness. The divine isn't a personal being like how you're describing the Christian God."

"So where does that leave us in terms of Zach's situation?"

"I'm not sure," Zach said. He had scribbled down some notes as everyone talked. "I may need more time to figure this out."

"I agree," Hannah said. "I haven't been able to make sense of it yet."

The friends gathered up their things and headed for the door, each deep in thought over the ideas they had discussed.

THEORY

Like Angelo, your brain may hurt from thinking about things you've never previously considered. In the remainder of the chapter, we will seek to bring clarity to this subject through careful definition, and you will see how this question of monism and pluralism closely aligns with one's worldview.

We have now begun our study of **metaphysics**, the study of the ultimate nature of reality. It is the attempt to answer questions such as, "What is real? What does it mean to be real? Are all real things physical? Do any *non-physical* things exist? Do any *physical* things exist?" We'll explore these and similar questions in this chapter and the next three.[1]

This chapter discusses the monism vs. pluralism debate. **Monism** is the view that, in some sense, only one thing exists. Monism can take various forms. For example, the ancient Greek philosopher Thales of Miletus held that all of reality is composed of water. This may have made sense to Thales for several reasons. For one thing, Miletus was on the Mediterranean Sea and had a humid climate and a high water table. Thales could not help but notice that there was water all around him—in the sea, in the air, and even in the ground. Furthermore, water can be a liquid, a solid (ice), or a gas (steam), so it can have a form that corresponds to every kind of object that we experience. Additionally, many of the objects of our world either contain a watery liquid (animals contain blood, trees contain sap, fruits contain juice, etc.) or can be transformed into a liquid (either through condensation or melting). So while it may not actually be the case that all is water, it's not such a crazy idea given Thales' context.

Another form of monism comes from the classical Hindu school of

---

1. A good general introduction to metaphysics is Anna Marmodoro and Erasmus Mayr, *Metaphysics: An Introduction to Contemporary Debates and Their History* (Oxford University Press, 2019).

thought called Advaita Vedanta, which means "non-dualism." Hindus from this school of thought believe that there is only one god (whom some call Brahman), that Brahman is omnipresent, and therefore, that all that exists is Brahman. Hinduism is usually viewed as a polytheistic religion, but according to Advaita, all the gods of the Hindu pantheon are simply different appearances of Brahman. Likewise, everything else that exists is an aspect of Brahman. This in effect makes Advaita Hinduism both monotheistic and monistic. Note that on this view, reality isn't one only in the sense of being made up of one kind of underlying substance (i.e., water); reality is one thing, one entity: Brahman.

A third form of monism is **idealism**, the view that reality is fundamentally mental rather than physical. This surprising view is called "idealism" because its adherents believe that reality is composed of ideas rather than physical objects. Even objects are ideas; they're not physical in the way we usually assume they are.

The most famous idealist in the Western intellectual tradition is the bishop George Berkeley. He believed that everything that exists is spiritual or intellectual, since everything is either God, who is a spirit rather than physical, or a creation of God that reflects the nature of its creator. Berkeley grounds his position in sophisticated arguments and should not be dismissed too hastily, but we needn't go into those here. It suffices to point out that in his version of idealism, monism is true in both ways mentioned above: Everything that exists is composed of one type of substance (mental; ideas) and, after a fashion, all of it forms one contiguous entity (God and his creation).[2]

In contrast, **pluralism** is the view that more than one thing (or more than one type of thing) exists. Just as we can find examples of monism from the ancient world as well as today, there are examples of pluralism back then and now. Empedocles was an ancient Greek philosopher who famously argued that reality is comprised of four elements (earth, air, water, and fire) and that these are governed by two forces: love and strife. Since on this view reality can be reduced to six constituents rather than one, this

2. While metaphysical idealism is a fascinating possibility, such a small number of people in the Western intellectual tradition have held to it that we're not going to discuss it at length in this book.

is a pluralist metaphysic. Like Thales' view, we might be tempted to hastily dismiss Empedocles' view as implausible, but on closer analysis it may have some merit. If we translate his ideas into twenty-first-century terminology, he could be interpreted as saying that reality is comprised of solids, gases, liquids, and energy, and that these are regulated by the laws of attraction and repulsion. That's not that crazy of an analysis for someone who lived before the invention of indoor plumbing!

Another noteworthy ancient pluralist is Anaxagoras, who recognized that the big objects in the world around us are composed of smaller things. He proposed, perhaps metaphorically, that the smallest particles that make up reality be called "seeds" and that the ways in which these seeds combine to form larger objects is governed or directed by a force that he called the "cosmic mind." Anaxagoras appears to be a pluralist in two different ways: First, he argues that there is a variety of different kinds of "seeds." Second, the cosmic mind is of a completely different nature than the seeds. The former are physical, while the latter seems to be incorporeal and therefore non-physical.

Contemporary with Anaxagoras was another Greek philosopher named Leucippus. He and his famous pupil Democritus proposed naming the tiny particles that make up the larger objects in the universe "atoms." Our English word "atom" actually comes from the Greek word *atomos*, which means "undivided." This was a fitting name because Leucippus and Democritus believed that atoms are indivisible.

These ancient Greek philosophers were perhaps the very first atomists. On their view, atoms are the smallest things in existence, there are many different kinds of them, and combinations of them account for the existence of everything else. This is a pluralistic metaphysic because there are many different kinds of atoms. However, this pluralistic metaphysic is also materialistic: It does not propose the existence of anything other than the physical atoms that compose the physical universe.

Today, of course, we know that atoms are themselves composed of smaller, sub-atomic particles. Scientists have known about protons and electrons for over a hundred years and about neutrons for almost as long. So atoms are not the smallest particles that make up the universe. However, if we replace atoms with protons, neutrons, and electrons as the constituent elements of reality, we still have a pluralist metaphysic, for we still have at least three different kinds of things that make up reality. But we wouldn't do that, because we know that even protons, neutrons, and electrons are made up of even smaller elements such as quarks, leptons, and bosons. Some of these are thought to be indivisible and therefore could be the smallest components of which the universe is constructed. If that's correct, then we still have a pluralistic metaphysic, because reality is composed of several kinds of elementary particles (quarks, leptons, and several kinds of bosons). All these are physical, but they are so small that they are characterized as being one-dimensional.

In addition to the question of whether the physical world is reducible to a single kind of underlying particle or substance, there's also the question of whether there's more to existence than just the physical world. Both the monist Berkeley and the pluralist Anaxagoras affirmed that there is. In fact, Berkeley argued that there is no physical world as we usually understand it: There's only immaterial thought. That's why he's a monist. Anaxagoras affirmed the existence of a physical world and of an immaterial intelligence that pervades or overlays the physical world, which makes him a pluralist. Anyone who affirms both that there is a material world and something else—anything else whatsoever—is a pluralist. So if you believe in incorporeal ghosts, gods, angels, the force, or anything else that's not physical, it's very likely that you are a metaphysical pluralist.[3]

Examples

Let's talk about some contrasting examples of monism and pluralism. Naturalism and supernaturalism provide one such example that relates directly to worldviews. Naturalism is the view that nothing exists except the natural world. Although it's theoretically possible to be a naturalist and to affirm that the natural world contains both material and immaterial objects, it's much more common for naturalists to be physicalists. That is, naturalists usually deny the existence of incorporeal entities. One reason for that comes

---

3. Ed Miller does a good job introducing monism and pluralism and the ancient Greek monists and pluralists in his book *Questions that Matter: An Invitation to Philosophy*, 5th ed. (McGraw-Hill, 2004), 57–67.

from Big Bang cosmology, which affirms that the universe and all it contains are a result of a giant explosion that sent matter flying in every direction, giving birth to the universe. If the universe includes everything that exists, and if the universe was birthed by matter flying in every direction, then it seems to follow that everything that exists is composed of matter. Hence, physicalism seems to follow from the Big Bang. Many people think that naturalism fits well with Big Bang cosmology because neither involves any sort of creator that transcends the physical realm.

Supernaturalism is the view that there is both a natural world and also something that transcends the natural world, something that is *super* (above) natural. That could be a god, a collection of gods, an invisible immaterial force, a set of timeless and immutable laws, or something else. The view that reality contains both natural elements and supernatural elements is inherently pluralistic, since it claims that reality includes at least two fundamentally different kinds of things. Naturalism, on the other hand, is monistic in the sense that it claims that only one thing exists: the natural world. In another sense, though, naturalism could be pluralistic if it sees the natural world as containing more than one type of naturally occurring object. For example, the current view that the natural world is comprised of quarks, leptons, and various kinds of bosons is pluralistic because these (supposed) fundamental building blocks of the natural world are distinct kinds that are neither reducible to each other nor to something else that's even more fundamental.

Another contrasting example of monism and pluralism is pantheism and panentheism, which we will talk about again in chapter 13. Both of these are religious worldviews, but they are fundamentally different from each other in a way that relates directly to monism and pluralism. Pantheism is the view that the physical universe is God. What pantheists mean by this is that the physical universe is all that exists, so it is necessarily omnipresent. Furthermore, being all that exists, it contains all the power that exists, so in that sense it's also omnipotent. Since it contains all the brains that exist, it also contains all the knowledge that exists, so it's omniscient. Thus, the universe possesses many of the classical divine attributes and can be considered an impersonal form of God. This is monistic because everything that exists is part of or comprises one entity.

Panentheism, on the other hand, is the view that the physical universe is the body of God but that God also has an immaterial, intelligent side that pervades the universe. In effect, the universe has a mind. This is similar to Anaxagoras' view. It differs from pantheism because it involves a unified intelligence that orchestrates (in some way and to some degree) what happens in the universe. This potentially enables the god of panentheism to be more personal than the god of pantheism. Panentheism is a pluralistic view since it involves both a material reality and an immaterial reality, though in a way it's monistic, since the two aspects of reality combine to make up one god. Hence, we could call panentheism a hybrid view (monistic in one way but pluralistic in another). Theism, deism, and polytheism are religious worldviews that are more purely pluralistic.

Another contrast comes from arguments about the nature of "abstract objects" (sometimes called "immaterial entities"). Abstract objects are things that appear real, despite the fact that they aren't physical. A good example of this is numbers: Certainly the number twelve is real, isn't it? I'm not asking about the numeral twelve—such as the ink on this page that is formed into the shape t-w-e-l-v-e. I'm talking about the abstract concept that this numeral symbolizes. Twelve, or twelve-ness, is something real that we talk about and use almost every day of the week. The same is true for one, two, three, etc.

The view that abstract objects are real though not physical is called Platonic realism or "realism about abstract objects." The view that abstract objects are not real is called "nominalism." Nominalists claim that "twelve" is simply a man-made label that we give to an idea in our minds. They argue that there is not a real but an immaterial "twelve." Similarly, they view all so-called abstract objects as merely ideas and the labels we give them. Nominalism complements physicalism and tends toward monism, while Platonic realism complements pluralism, since it believes that the category of things that are real includes both things that are physical and things that are immaterial. We'll discuss this in more depth in the next chapter.

One final example of the contrast between monism and pluralism comes from the study of human nature. Are humans 100 percent composed of the cells and substances that make up the human body, or is there, in addition to those physical substances, also an immaterial component? In philosophy this is called the mind-body problem. What is the nature of the human mind? Is it physical (the brain) or immaterial (the soul, the spirit, the mind, or something like that)? The former view is called "mind-body physicalism" and the latter "mind-body dualism." Mind-body dualism necessitates pluralism, since it posits the existence of two fundamentally different kinds of things: immaterial minds and material bodies. On the other hand, while mind-body physicalism does not require that monism is true, it is compatible with monism. If it is true, then monism might also be true, while if mind-body dualism is true, then monism cannot be.

Arguments

Monism and pluralism are abstract concepts. How could we go about proving either of them to be true? If we could prove that immaterial objects do not exist, that would support physicalism and hence lend at least some support to monism. However, it is difficult to prove that immaterial things do not exist, since such things could exist but not be detectable by the senses and hence would appear not to exist even if they are real.

On the other hand, it might be possible to prove that some sort of immaterial object does exist, and if we can do that—even if we succeed in proving the existence of only one such object—then we've succeeded in proving that physicalism (and hence the most prominent form of monism) is false. Some theologians think they can provide strong evidence for the existence of an incorporeal God;[4] many people think there are good reasons to affirm the reality of abstract objects like numbers, laws of logic, moral absolutes, universal human rights, etc.;[5] many mind-body dualists think there are powerful arguments for the existence of immaterial human minds.[6] If any of these arguments are successful, then physicalism is false and, if metaphysical idealism is also false, pluralism is likely to be true.

If the arguments for the existence of abstract objects fail, does that prove that there aren't any (and therefore, that physicalism is true)? Perhaps, but not necessarily. We must be careful to avoid the fallacy of the argument from silence. That we don't currently have evidence of the existence of something does not necessarily prove that no such evidence exists. Here the maxim

4. See the chapter in this book on theistic apologetics.
5. See the chapter in this book on abstract objects.
6. See the chapter in this book on the mind-body problem.

"the absence of evidence is not evidence of absence" seems applicable. But if the existence of abstract objects should result in abundant evidence of their existence, then the lack of evidence of their existence does suggest that they don't exist. This raises the question of whether the existence of abstract objects should be expected to result in abundant evidence of their existence as well as the question of whether abundant evidence in fact exists. There are philosophers on both sides of the debate over these questions.

Some physicalists argue that the (supposed) absence of clear evidence for or against the existence of abstract objects requires us to reject belief in them. This, they believe, follows from a principle called Ockham's razor.[7] William of Ockham was a medieval philosopher and theologian who argued that a theory or explanation that is both simple and able to adequately explain the phenomenon in question is preferable to a more complicated theory that doesn't explain that phenomenon any better. This is a better way of stating the KISS principle (Keep It Simple, Stupid). Some physicalists argue that, since the natural world can explain everything that we experience, there's no need to postulate the existence of anything supernatural. In essence, they see physicalism as the simpler theory since it doesn't require belief in the supernatural.

This application of Ockham's razor assumes that all of our experiences can be explained as natural, physical phenomena. If that assumption is correct, then this may be a very good argument. However, pluralists point out that there are many things that are difficult to explain naturally, and there are also things that seem real but are clearly not physical. Examples of the former include free will, moral responsibility, and universal human rights, while examples of the latter include numbers, the laws of logic, and timeless moral truths. Since the nature of such phenomena is part of the monism-dualism debate, assuming that such things are natural and/or physical amounts to begging the question. Conversely, some pluralists think that naturalism's inability to explain such human experiences as freedom and moral responsibility, as well as more esoteric phenomena like near death

7. See Sharon Kaye, "William of Ockham (Ockham, c. 1280—c. 1349)," in *Internet Encyclopedia of Philosophy*, https://iep.utm.edu/ockham/.

experiences and telepathy, show pluralism to be the stronger theory. These controversial topics will be discussed in future chapters.

CONCLUSION

As you can see, the monism vs. pluralism debate, abstract though it may seem, is very important to your worldview. Whether you believe in things like transcendent gods, immaterial souls, timeless moral truths, and universal human rights has a major impact on your worldview. This discussion of monism and pluralism lays a foundation for discussing these and other metaphysical issues that form your view of reality and in many ways determines how you live your life.

QUESTIONS TO PONDER

- How many ways can you list in which thinking about metaphysics would be at least a little helpful?
- Do you consider yourself a monist or a pluralist? Why?
- What do you consider to be the best argument for monism?
- What do you consider to be the best argument for pluralism?
- If any immaterial entity or entities exist, what are they made of?

TERMS TO KNOW

- metaphysics
- monism
- pluralism
- idealism
- naturalism
- supernaturalism
- abstract objects
- Platonic realism
- nominalism
- mind-body physicalism
- mind-body dualism

FOR FURTHER READING

Goldschmidt, Tyron. *The Puzzle of Existence: Why Is There Something Rather Than Nothing?* Routledge, 2013. This interesting book deals with some of the deepest of all metaphysical issues.

Hasker, William. *Metaphysics: Constructing a Worldview. Contours of Christian Philosophy*. IVP Academic, 1983. This older volume is a nice introduction to metaphysics from a theistic perspective.

Mumford, Stephen. *Metaphysics: A Very Short Introduction*. Oxford University Press, 2012. This is a concise (129 pages) and readable introduction to metaphysics. The authors are Aristotelian, but they present alternative positions fairly.

9

ABSTRACT OBJECTS

SYNOPSIS

This second chapter on metaphysics addresses the existence or non-existence of abstract objects—things that are, if they exist, non-material. Both the dialogue and the discussion that follows it demonstrate how closely one's view of abstract objects will align with his or her worldview.

DIALOGUE

That week, as the four friends contemplated the number of realities, each of them came to realize that one of the central questions was whether abstract objects like virtue, logic, and laws of nature actually exist. As usual, each person wrestled with this question differently.

Zach was in a training seminar at work during a presentation on the growing trend of fraud in the sciences. Zach was appalled when the speaker mentioned several articles in scientific journals that exposed the commonality of fraudulent scientific claims. He had been drawn to the sciences because of his belief in the "purity" of the scientific process as the most reliable way to arrive at knowledge. He considered his own integrity in research to be his most important commitment to science. As the seminar continued, he couldn't help thinking about the latest discussions in the philosophy group.

Is integrity a real thing? Is there a reality behind the word? Or is it just a label people give to behavior that follows a widely accepted set of procedures? The latter was more consistent with Zach's belief in only one reality—the physical world—but it didn't sit well with him. *Integrity has to be something real, doesn't it? If it's real, though, what is it? It certainly isn't an object with physical properties.*

Time and time again, Zach was driven back to the idea that integrity is nothing more than a label used to describe honesty, faithfulness to accepted practices, and courage to accept the results of one's work, whether desirable or undesirable, profitable or unprofitable.

Once the meeting came to an end, Zach joined his coworkers in a round of applause. As everyone moved to the exits, Zach caught Dr. Okafor's eye. Dr. Okafor was a team leader in his department, and Zach greatly admired him. Dr. Kwame Okafor had emigrated from Nigeria and had risen quickly through the ranks at Zach's company. His charm and quick wit made him popular. Not many top scientists Zach had met were as friendly and likable. Dr. Okafor had a sharp mind for solving research problems, so Zach and the other younger scientists had consulted him many times when their work hit a dead end. His willingness to help and encourage them further endeared him to them. To Zach, he had become "Dr. O."

"A very troubling lecture, wasn't it, Zachary?" Dr. O commented as he and Zach converged at the back door on their way out.

"Yes, so disappointing. I hate to think of scientists getting ahead, even if only temporarily, based on dishonest work. Honesty is the cornerstone of good science. What good is getting a grant or a promotion only to later be discredited?" Zach shook his head. "I can't relate to someone who thinks that getting ahead by deceit is worth the risk and just hopes no one will find out. Something will fail eventually and expose them."

Dr. O nodded gravely yet still had a trace of a smile on his face.

How does he do that? Zach wondered.

"It reminds me of something Jesus said."

Zach had heard this line from Dr. O many times before, and even though he did not usually enjoy it when his religious coworkers brought up religion, he didn't seem to mind it as much when it came from this man.

"'What does it profit a man if he gains the whole world and, in the process, loses his own soul?'" Dr. O smiled widely.

Dr. O loved dispensing wisdom, and Zach had grown to appreciate it. He suddenly realized this was a good opportunity to bounce his ideas off someone who wouldn't dismiss his questions. "Can I ask you a question?"

"Of course, Zachary."

Dr. O always used Zach's full name, something he wouldn't have appreciated from many people. From Dr. O, however, it came across as both a term of endearment and respect.

"Do you believe a soul is a real thing? Or is it simply a label we attach to what we perceive as our real selves as distinct from our bodies?"

Dr. O arched his left eyebrow—always his left—just as he did whenever someone said something particularly noteworthy or interesting.

"You got that out of the lecture?" Dr. O was genuinely intrigued now.

"No . . . well, kind of." Zach was struggling to articulate his thoughts without a complicated backstory. "The meeting got me thinking about fraud and integrity, which led to pondering abstract ideas and wondering if there is any reality to these terms or if they're just the names that we call certain behaviors. I think the concept of a soul would fit in this category as well. My intuition is that such concepts have some kind of reality to them beyond simply a label."

Again, Dr. O's left eyebrow perked up. He glanced at his watch. "That is a deep question, Zachary. How much time do you have? We could walk down to the café for a bit."

Zach nodded without even consulting the time. He had to get some answers.

"Let me text my department head and let him know I'm taking a short break."

They made their way to the stairs as the elevators were busy ferrying the hundred or so employees who had attended the meeting back to their various floors.

Once seated in a corner with hot drinks, Dr. O began. "What would the logical implications be for your theory if you're correct that abstract ideas such as the soul or integrity are merely labels we assign to certain actions or physical entities? And why do you care?"

Zach had a feeling that the conversation would start this way. Whenever he and his colleagues went to Dr. O with a problem, he would begin with a systematic examination of the situation by using questions. Zach had learned that this was called the Socratic method, named after the Greek philosopher of the fifth century BC who often grilled his conversation partners with questions to help them arrive at truth for themselves.

Zach paused for a few seconds to gather his thoughts. "I suppose one problem that might arise is that people could have widely divergent ideas about what constitutes what we call a soul or what we call integrity. If there's no reality behind the label, then who has the authority to define it and pass judgment on whether something qualifies to possess the label?"

"Good," Dr. O said. "Go on."

"Does every community get to use language its own way to make truth claims? If so, science can't be a universally practiced discipline because every community could claim its own concepts of truth, accuracy, measurement, and more."

"Unless . . ." Dr. O prompted.

Zach thought for a minute. "Unless some entity claims power and enforces a certain understanding of these concepts for anyone who wants to participate in an endeavor in that community."

"In some ways," Dr. O said, "that is what we have in Western science. Certain authorities such as scientific affiliations, universities, corporations, and governmental agencies establish principles by which scientific enterprise must be done if it is to be accepted in the mainstream."

"Aha! So my conclusion that these abstract ideas are simply labels *isn't* problematic!"

Zach suddenly felt better about being a materialist and rejecting the reality of abstract objects. But he quickly remembered who he was talking to, and a cloud of doubt emerged on the edges of his consciousness. "You're a Christian and believe that the soul is a real entity, don't you? Wouldn't that mean you believe that virtues such as justice, truth, integrity, and morality are somewhere in the mind of God or some such place?"

"Yes, something like that," Dr. O said with a smile.

"So how can you affirm that we have something like a materialist reality in Western science, where we label things, and the scientific community establishes and polices the use of these labels?"

"Do you know what a false dilemma is, Zachary?"

Dr. O was grinning from ear to ear, and Zach sensed his impending demise.

"I think so," Zach said.

"A false dilemma is when only two options are presented, and they're presented as if you must choose one or the other. But you want to choose both—or perhaps some third option. The way you describe a materialistic view of abstract concepts leaves materialism as the only viable option. I described the scientific community as one aspect of the picture but not the whole picture."

Dr. O peered at Zach. "You're right that I believe in the reality of the human soul and the reality of abstract objects like virtue, because something doesn't have to possess a physical reality to exist. It can exist in an immaterial form but still be very real. At the same time, the labels we assign to things can be established by the communities in which we live and work."

Zach chuckled. "Believe it or not, I just had this conversation about material and immaterial realities with some friends."

The eyebrow arched again. "Really? What kind of friends talk about material and immaterial reality when they get together?"

"I get together regularly with three other people who are all interested in philosophy. We are reading the same philosophy book and discussing the chapters when we meet."

"That's marvelous, Zachary! Improving your mind is a key to growing in scientific knowledge and skill. I prefer poetry to philosophy, but the principles are the same. Devoting your mind to something other than your work helps develop your critical and creative thinking ability."

It didn't surprise Zach that Dr. O liked poetry. In fact, it wouldn't have surprised him if Dr. O revealed that he had designed the Taj Mahal or written a symphony. The man was deep and seemingly had the capacity to do anything.

"So back to the point. Just because the scientific community in some way controls and serves as the gatekeeper to science, that doesn't mean that objects such as integrity, justice, or the science itself are merely labels. They are names that reflect a reality. The question is where we get these intuitions of how we should act and speak. The Bible speaks about the law of God written on the hearts of every person so that we know something of the character of a holy God, how he designed the world to work, and what he has commanded. Now, if you don't believe in God, the question is where to ground these intuitions."

"I certainly see the advantage of believing in a metaphysical reality like God," Zach said. "It neatly solves the problem of abstract objects: An immaterial God made real, immaterial things that we portray in language. So when we use words like *justice*, *honesty*, and *love*, there are realities behind the words that we know about naturally, having been, as you said, 'made in the image of God.' Is that right?"

"You explained my position beautifully. I appreciate people who fairly portray an opposing view."

Zach leaned forward. "This is my dilemma. My scientific bent encourages me to seek out neat and tidy answers to the complexity of the world, but I feel like going down the path of accepting an immaterial reality would undermine the work I'm trying to do as a scientist. I can't explore metaphysical or abstract realities using the scientific method."

"No, you cannot," Dr. O agreed. "This is the crux of the matter. You must accept that there are more realities besides the physical, or else you are stuck in the loop of believing that abstract things like justice, integrity, and love are simply labels we apply to actions we deem good for flourishing."

"I don't like the loop," Zach said with frustration.

"I don't imagine anyone does," Dr. O said. "That's why I would encourage you to seek a third way or consider a view that takes metaphysical reality seriously. I think many scientists struggle with this same issue but feel that accepting the reality of immaterial things would threaten their standing in the scientific community. Keep pressing this issue, maybe with your philosophy group, until you find a noncontradictory answer. I imagine it'll take a while, but a true scientist doesn't let a dead end keep him from pursuing an answer another way."

Dr. O looked at his watch and pushed back his chair.

"We shall talk again soon, Zachary."

Zach thrust out his hand. "Thank you, Dr. O. I appreciate the time and your challenge for me."

"When will you start calling me Kwame like most others do here?"
"Never, Dr. O," Zach said, grinning as they said goodbye.

* * *

Across town, in a security briefing, Angelo blanched as his captain briefed courthouse security on a message they'd received from the FBI that morning. A credible threat had been reported via a confidential informant that a drug cartel operating in the area had recently received a crate of stolen US Army–issued Squad Automatic Weapons (SAWs). The informant had hinted that the cartel was fanatical and included anti-American and anti-democracy elements. The FBI wasn't sure whether the cartel was one of the many South American organizations that plagued the United States or a new faction out of Albania. Either way, the thought of someone deploying such powerful weapons in Greenfield was terrifying.

Terrifying. That was a good word for it. The type of mass terror such weapons might wreak on the public was almost too awful to imagine.

Captain Lennox reassured the security squad that none of the intelligence suggested that the cartel had any intention of utilizing SAWs in the area. Law enforcement agencies believed the weapons were being hidden in the area until they could be moved to a big city on the West Coast, where they would offer the unknown cartel significant tactical advantage in a turf war.

The captain proceeded to provide the details of the weapon and reviewed the courthouse's heightened awareness protocols, particulars that Angelo knew by heart. He had always been fascinated by technical details and could have given most of the briefing himself. His mind began to wander to the subject of terrorism. What was it exactly? People often talked about terrorism as if it were some kind of biological reality. "Let's work to rid the world of terrorism!" It made terrorism seem like a virus that could be eliminated through public health efforts.

These attempts seemed to misunderstand terrorism's nature and had failed to end it. *Is terrorism purely an ideological entity, or are there more complicated explanations? Is it culturally driven?* Maybe there was a physiological connection to brain function.

Just then Captain Lennox was interrupted by a staffer and left the room for a few minutes, giving all those present a chance to talk about what they had heard.

Angelo pulled out his phone and searched for a definition online. The FBI's website defined *terrorism* as "Violent, criminal acts committed by individuals and/or groups who are inspired by, or associated with, designated foreign terrorist organizations or nations (state-sponsored)." An accompanying definition of *domestic terrorism* said, "Violent, criminal acts committed by individuals and/or groups to further ideological goals stemming from domestic influences, such as those of a political, religious, social, racial, or environmental nature."

The first definition seemed to follow the thinking of Aristotle, who said that there is no reality "out there," just instances of a reality in the physical world. The first definition didn't really explain the origin of terrorist acts or their essence, just the physical acts themselves. The definition of *domestic terrorism*, however, traced violent acts back to ideology. *How interesting*, Angelo thought. *Surely, the FBI didn't mean to imply that international terrorism isn't influenced by ideology.* He wondered if the FBI had considered how differently the two sources had defined *terrorism*.

Was terrorism only the violent acts that are carried out, or does it include the beliefs, attitudes, ideas, and culture that are nurtured in the organizations that carry out the attacks? To Angelo, both elements needed to be included, the ideas and the acts. Before an attack is ever carried out, hatred and plans to harm other people exist, for whatever reason. Isn't that the essence of terrorism?

Angelo was leaning more toward Plato's idea that a reality exists outside the physical world, what Plato called the "forms" or perfections of existence. Any act of terrorism, then, reflects the heart of terrorism to one degree or another. In other words, there's a nonphysical reality of terrorism.

There has to be, he thought.

But in a flash, he wasn't sure. Maybe everything leading up to an act of terrorism is something else. Maybe hatred, cruelty, and even evil plans are just that, and terrorism proper is simply the label applied to an act of violence that causes terror.

Why is abstract thought so difficult?

The captain returned and waved his hand, signaling the end of the briefing. "Alright, everyone. That is all for now. Back to your posts!" Captain Lennox's booming voice interrupted Angelo's thoughts.

Angelo hustled to his post on the west side of the courthouse grounds. He hated the thought of another act of mass violence in America, or anywhere for that matter. It grieved him to read of ethnic cleansing, the persecution of Christians and other religious groups, and the neglect and abuse of minors.

What exactly is evil? he wondered.

Angelo remembered asking this question in a Bible study at church a few years before. People argued that evil was a real entity—until someone asked when it came into existence. The group struggled to come to a confident answer. Was evil eternal like God? Has it always existed?

It wasn't until the leader mentioned St. Augustine's conclusion about evil that Angelo felt like a plausible answer was possible. Evil isn't a thing in itself. If it was, it would either have to be eternal like God or something that God created. Rather, evil is a lack of good, just as sickness is a lack of health and darkness is a lack of light.

This way of thinking about evil was helpful for Angelo. He understood it to mean that evil is a real thing but that it owes its essence to good. Good is grounded in the being of God, which means evil is anything that lacks or deviates from God's character. We use labels like *evil* and *terrorism* to describe actions that fall short of or deviate from those values. So it was a question of both/and, not either/or. Abstract objects are labeled by humans, but they have their reality established in transcendent truth.

Angelo wondered what the discussion group would think of his conclusion. He was no longer too timid to share his ideas. His friends had shown themselves to be charitable to ideas they didn't agree with. Would his conclusions withstand their scrutiny? He looked forward to finding out.

THEORY

Zach's and Angelo's conversations wrestled with the nature of abstract objects. The following discussion will clarify what abstract objects are and the various philosophical attempts to make sense of them.

Examples of Abstract Objects

The chapter on monism and pluralism briefly touched on the debate over the existence of **abstract objects**,[1] "non-physical, non-mental object(s) that exists outside of space and time."[2] Quite a few philosophers see good reason for thinking that abstract objects exist, while others do not. Let's take a look at this controversy.

Previously we used numbers as an example of abstract objects. People generally assume that numbers are real. "One," "ten," and "one hundred" are not merely conventions: They refer to very real quantities. However, "ten" isn't a physical object, is it? While you can have ten physical objects—ten tennis balls, for example—and although the numeral that represents the number ten will consist of physical ink, marker, paint, or whatever, "ten" itself isn't physical. But if it isn't physical, can it be real?

Perhaps it can. Perhaps being physical isn't a **necessary condition** of being real.[3] After all, gods, angels, souls, minds, spirits, thoughts, feelings, and forces of nature such as gravity, electromagnetism, and the weak and strong atomic forces arguably are not physical. If any of these things are real, then being physical is not a necessary condition for being real. Therefore, belief in any of these things makes accepting the existence of other immaterial entities, including various abstract objects, more reasonable.

There are other possible abstract objects in addition to numbers. Timeless moral truths are another example. Most people can list a number of actions they believe are always moral or always immoral regardless of circumstance. For instance, it's hard to imagine any circumstance wherein it would be moral to torture other people simply for fun. We might be able

---

1. Abstract objects are also called abstract entities, ideal objects, or abstract ideas.
2. Mark Balaguer, "Abstract Objects," in *Oxford Bibliographies*, January 15, 2019, https://doi.org/10.1093/obo/9780195396577-0384.
3. A **necessary condition** is anything that is absolutely required for something else to exist, take place, or be true. For example, having three sides is a necessary condition for any polygon to be a triangle. In contrast, a **sufficient condition** is anything that, by itself, is all that is needed for something else to exist, take place, or be true. For example, if you know that a certain polygon has exactly three angles, you don't need to know anything else in order to know that it's a triangle. Some conditions are both necessary and sufficient, and conditions that are neither necessary nor sufficient can still be contributory.

to imagine people enjoying torturing others, but it's hard to imagine the act actually being moral. On the other hand, it's almost equally hard to imagine a circumstance in which it would be immoral to help people in need when it lies within your ability to do so without causing any offsetting loss or harm. The principles of nonmaleficence and beneficence that underlie these moral intuitions may be timeless moral truths that are, in some very important sense, real.

Another possible example of an abstract object comes from universal human rights. Human rights are the liberties and benefits that are thought to be due to every human being, regardless of age, sex, race, nationality, or any other characteristic. According to the Universal Declaration of Human Rights, adopted by the United Nations in 1948, there are about thirty universal human rights, including the rights to life, liberty, and security of person.[4] Such rights do not appear to be physical objects, but nonetheless they do seem to be real.

The laws of logic are yet another example of abstract objects. The law of identity, the law of noncontradiction, the law of excluded middle, and the others seem to pertain all the time and everywhere, regardless of culture and perhaps even regardless of whether people exist to think them. They seem to be much more than merely human inventions: They seem to be timeless, necessary truths. But they clearly aren't physical.

We could add other examples of abstract objects. Colors are a common example, along with geometric shapes and perhaps the laws of nature. Rather than trying to amass an exhaustive list, let's move on to examining the ways various philosophical schools have interpreted abstract objects.

Realism, Nominalism, and Conceptualism

The view that abstract objects are real though not physical is often called **Platonic realism** (or simply "realism about abstract objects"). The name is derived from the ancient Greek philosopher Plato, who believed that everything that exists in our world is an imperfect instantiation of a perfect

---

4. United Nations, "Universal Declaration of Human Rights," https://www.un.org/en/about-us/universal-declaration-of-human-rights.

archetype that he named a **Form**.[5] According to Plato, these Forms exist in another realm, called "the world of the Forms." The Forms are not physical but ideal, and there is an ideal Form for everything that exists in our world, whether the earthly instantiation is physical or immaterial. If there are imperfect trees on earth, it's because there are one or more perfect trees in the world of the Forms. Likewise, if there is imperfect justice on earth, it's because there is perfect justice in the world of the Forms; if there is imperfect love on earth, there is perfect love in the world of the Forms; if there are imperfectly understood numbers, laws of logic, and timeless moral truths on earth, it's because archetypical numbers, laws of logic, and moral truths exist in the world of the Forms.

Since theists generally believe in heaven, they may have little difficulty accepting the idea that something like a heavenly world of ideal Forms exists. Naturalists may find this idea peculiar, for the idea of a heavenly realm might seem old-fashioned to them, and they might wonder what reason there is to believe in such a place. Additionally, they might wonder what evidence there is for the existence of archetypical Forms.

Realists after Plato have further developed his theory in response to such concerns. For example, if abstract objects aren't physical, then they don't exist in any one place, for spatiality only applies to physical objects. Therefore, we probably shouldn't picture the "world of the Forms" as a literal place within this universe or any other; perhaps it's more like an alternate dimension. In fact, Plato seems to leave this possibility open. But perhaps even an alternate dimension is insufficient. Maybe we should view abstract objects as necessary truths in any world like ours. It does seem hard to imagine a world like ours wherein it's moral to torture people just for fun, or wherein the number ten doesn't exist, or wherein the law of non-contradiction is false. If this is the correct view of abstract objects, then abstract objects are real in some sense, but it's far from the physical sense of reality that we're used to.

Interestingly, Plato's star pupil, Aristotle, was among those who thought that Plato's theory of Forms was problematic. He argued that "form" is simply an aspect of any physical object. Every object is a collection of matter

5. Plato, *The Phaedo*, in *Plato: Complete Works*, ed. J. M. Cooper (Hackett, 1997), 49–100; idem, *The Parmenides*, in Cooper, *Plato*, 359–97.

that is in a specific form.[6] For example, this book that you are reading is a collection of atoms that are in the form of a book. Obviously, this changes Plato's idea of Forms significantly: It reduces form to nothing more than the characteristics of any specific collection of matter.

The view that transcendent Forms and other abstract objects are not real is called **nominalism**. Nominalists claim that "ten" is simply a man-made label that we give to an idea in our minds. They argue that there is not a real but an immaterial "ten." Similarly, they view all so-called abstract objects as merely ideas and the names that we give to them. In fact, the term "nominalism" comes from the Latin word *nomen*, which means "name." Aristotle's revision of Plato's idea of Forms is moving toward nominalism.

There is a possible third position that one can take on the nature of abstract objects. **Conceptualism** is sort of a compromise between Platonic realism and nominalism. It affirms that abstract objects are real and at the same time that they are nothing but ideas. Conceptualists point out that ideas really do exist but only in minds, as thoughts. They don't have mind-independent existence. Numbers, the laws of logic, moral truths, and the like are real thoughts that we have, but when we talk about thoughts being real, we're using "real" in a slightly different way than when we talk about trees, boulders, and buildings being real. The latter are real and physical while the former are real and mental.[7]

Perhaps most laypeople wouldn't hesitate to accept that abstract objects can be real even though they are only mental. They're real thoughts. However, the same logic could be used to prove that unicorns, leprechauns, and the tooth fairy are also real. After all, the idea "unicorn" is a real thought in your mind, isn't it? Does that mean that unicorns are real?

In a sense it does. According to conceptualism, there's a sense in which unicorns are real. Fictional characters are real, too, in this manner. We know that they are made up and that they don't exist in the physical world. But why

6. The difference between the Platonic and Aristotelean views on forms is concisely explained in Bryan Duignan, "Plato and Aristotle: How Do They Differ?," *Encyclopedia Britannica*, February 14, 2018, https://www.britannica.com/story/plato-and-aristotle-how-do-they-differ.
7. This way of describing it may assume mind-body dualism, which will be discussed in the next chapter.

should existence in the physical world be a necessary condition to qualify as real? Surely our thoughts exist—somewhere—and therefore are real.

Regardless of what you think about conceptualism and unicorns, there is another potential problem with conceptualism. If abstract objects are real because they exist as ideas in human minds, that seems to imply that they weren't real—and didn't exist—until humans were around to think them. That might be acceptable regarding some abstract objects. For example, moral truths might have been entirely unnecessary until people existed to be guided and governed by them, so it might not be a big problem for moral truths to not exist prior to humanity. But for other abstract objects this could be highly problematic. Is there any possible world that could exist without the law of identity? Is it possible, anywhere, anytime, for the law of noncontradiction to not be true?

It seems that in order for conceptualism to work, it would be necessary for an eternal mind to exist in which these concepts could reside at all times. Such a mind would enable the existence of unchanging, universal abstract objects. But if no such mind exists, then conceptualism does not differ significantly from nominalism.

Worldviews and Abstract Objects

In this book we've been contrasting various worldviews, most frequently naturalism and theism. When it comes to the existence of abstract objects, the worldview alignments are pretty clear. Naturalism fits well with physicalism, the view that reality is entirely composed of material components. Since abstract objects, if they were to exist, would not be material, a physicalist cannot hold that they exist. Therefore, abstract objects are a poor fit with naturalism. In order to be consistent with the naturalistic worldview, a naturalist will view abstract objects as nothing more than ideas in our minds (or as the labels that we give to such ideas). This is nominalism. Naturalism and nominalism go well together. Conversely, Platonic realism is a poor fit for naturalism.

On the other hand, worldviews that are friendly to the existence of incorporeal things like gods, angels, spirits, and so forth can easily accommodate the existence of abstract objects. Hence, both Platonic realism and conceptualism are, at least *prima facie*, viable options for theists, deists, polytheists, and panentheists. Adherents to these worldviews would have little motivation to embrace nominalism, since they already accept the existence of other immaterial things. Furthermore, they are likely to find appealing the idea that abstract objects like numbers, the laws of logic, human rights, and timeless moral truths are human *discoveries* rather than human *inventions*.

Arguments

Two interrelated arguments for nominalism flow from **Ockham's razor**, which states that "entities should not be multiplied beyond necessity."[8] One is the argument from ontological parsimony, which reasons that a theory that involves postulating the existence of various things that have never actually been observed is less likely to be true than a theory that does not involve such postulates. The other is the argument from theoretical simplicity, which reasons that all other things being equal, a less complex explanation is preferable to a more complex one, since the more complicated an explanation is, the greater chance there is of human error. Since Platonic realism involves postulating the existence of things that have never actually been observed, and since nominalism requires no such postulation, nominalism is the more parsimonious theory. And since realism's explanation of math, logic, morality, and other such things involves entities that exist outside of the mind (abstract objects) in addition to entities that exist within the mind (ideas about those objects), realism is a more complicated theory than nominalism, which only involves entities that exist in the mind (ideas). Thus, nominalism is the simpler theory.

To be fair, Ockham's razor doesn't say that the more parsimonious or simpler theory is *automatically* better. It says that the more parsimonious or simpler theory is better if, but only if, it can adequately explain the phenomena in question. In other words, a theory so simple that it fails to explain the thing it's supposed to explain is not a good theory. Some theories need to be complex because they are attempting to explain complicated phenomena. So if Platonic realism better explains the existence of the rules of math, the laws of logic, timeless moral truths, etc. than nominalism does, then

8. See Kaye, "William of Ockham."

realism is the better theory even though it is less parsimonious and more complicated than nominalism.

Some people adopt nominalism because it is necessitated by their worldview. Naturalism says that all that exists is the natural world. This is generally interpreted to mean that everything that exists is composed of matter and energy, which are viewed as interchangeable, two sides of a coin (so to speak). Hence naturalism, as the term is generally used, entails physicalism, the view that everything is physical. If everything is physical, then immaterial things like abstract objects cannot exist. Naturalists are therefore logically motivated to embrace nominalism so that their views on the nature of reality and of abstract objects are not at odds with each other.

Logically, this argument can be viewed as a *pure hypothetical syllogism* (see chapter 4):

1. If naturalism is true, then physicalism is true.
2. If physicalism is true, then nominalism is true.
3. Therefore, if naturalism is true, then nominalism is true.

Since a pure hypothetical syllogism is a valid argument form, this is a valid argument. If the antecedent of the major premise is true, then the consequent of the conclusion is true. Thus, if naturalism is true, then nominalism is true. Of course, a naturalist cannot simply assume that naturalism is true and then claim that this argument is sound. The question of the soundness of this argument cannot be answered until we know whether naturalism is true.

Moving on to the arguments for Platonic realism, one of the more powerful arguments for that view takes the form of a *reductio ad absurdum*: If nominalism is true, then that implies that certain other things are true, but it seems likely that those other things are false, so it's likely that nominalism is also false.[9] What are these other things that are implied by nominalism

9. *Reductio ad absurdum* is an argument form that proceeds by showing that if you hold to some position consistently, it will lead you to an absurd or highly improbable conclusion. It is an effective way to show that some positions are wrong. The logical form of a *reductio* argument is *modus tollens*.

but are likely to be false? One would be that the laws of logic are simply ideas in our minds rather than being real principles that exist independently of our minds. But if the laws of logic are only ideas in the minds of human beings, then before humans existed, the laws of logic didn't exist. If that's the case, then it seems to follow that before human beings existed, it was possible for something to both be the case and not be the case at the same time, since there would not have been any law of noncontradiction. And since that's about as unlikely as anything ever could be, it's unlikely that the laws of logic exist only in human minds. Similar *reductio* arguments against nominalism can be formulated using moral truths, mathematical principles, universal human rights, and the other abstract objects that have been mentioned in this chapter.

Some think that Platonic realism falls afoul of Ockham's razor, but we have seen that's not necessarily the case. Others object to it because it's not compatible with a naturalistic worldview or because abstract objects cannot be empirically experienced. Of course, if you aren't committed to a naturalistic worldview, then you won't share that first concern, and assuming that everything that exists must be experienceable through the senses begs the question.

Another objection to realism comes from the theistic perspective. In classical theism, God is the only eternal existent. God wasn't created; he has always been, but everything else is created by him. However, Platonic realism holds that abstract objects are eternal: There was never a time when the laws of logic were not in place, that numbers didn't exist, etc. Thus, Platonic realism seems to set up rivals to God for the claim to eternality. Furthermore, when realists assert that there are eternal and unchanging moral truths, they set up a situation wherein there is a moral authority equal to or higher than God, which seems to impugn God's sovereignty. We'll say more about that in the chapters on ethics.

Nominalism and realism have strengths and weaknesses. Wouldn't it be nice if there was a theory that preserves their strengths while eliminating their weaknesses? This is exactly how some people see conceptualism. Like nominalism, conceptualism says that abstract objects exist only in the mind. Like realism, conceptualism says that abstract objects are unchanging, eternal truths. It succeeds in combining these two positions, which otherwise might be irreconcilable, by locating abstract objects in the mind of an eternal and unchanging God rather than in human minds. In this view, abstract objects exist or apply everywhere and at all times because they are in the mind of a God who exists everywhere and at all times.

The chief objection to conceptualism is that it requires the existence of God. For naturalists and others who don't believe in God, conceptualism isn't an option. Otherwise, it seems to offer a viable solution to the nominalism-realism dilemma.

CONCLUSION

The debate about abstract objects requires careful thought, but it's worth it, for it's a debate with practical implications. Furthermore, the various options align closely with different worldviews. People sometimes hold positions that don't fit well with their overall worldview. This may be simply because they haven't noticed the misalignment. Our goal in this book is to describe what naturalists and theists ought to believe if they want to be consistent with their worldview so that our readers can be consistent in their own beliefs.

QUESTIONS TO PONDER

- Do you think abstract objects are real? Why or why not?
- What are some practical implications of nominalism?
- What are some practical implications of Platonic realism?
- Does conceptualism succeed as a middle ground between nominalism and realism?

TERMS TO KNOW

- abstract objects
- necessary condition
- sufficient condition
- Platonic realism
- nominalism
- conceptualism
- Forms
- Ockham's razor

FOR FURTHER READING

Gould, Paul, ed. *Beyond the Control of God? Six Views on the Problem of God and Abstract Objects*. Bloomsbury Academic, 2016. This book is especially for theists and features seven philosophers defending six different theistic views on the existence of abstract objects.

Liggins, David. *Abstract Objects*. Cambridge University Press, 2024. This is a concise (68 pages) and readable introduction to the issue.

van Inwagen, Peter and William Lane Craig. *Do Numbers Exist? A Debate About Abstract Objects*. Rutledge, 2024. This book is a debate between two contemporary philosophers who take different sides on the existence of abstract objects.

10

THE MIND-BODY PROBLEM

SYNOPSIS

A key aspect of the monism-dualism debate is known as the mind-body problem. Suresh and Hannah will discover the challenging nature of this problem, and the discussion that follows will seek to clarify the major positions and their relationship to one's worldview.

DIALOGUE

Suresh put the finishing touches on another dish and called out for a waiter to take the order to the table. His satisfaction at completing yet another perfect dish was immense.

This was what drove a chef—knowing that the diner couldn't possibly find a flaw in the meal because every attention to detail had been paid and every single bite was a mind-blowing culinary delight. He wished he could witness their first bites.

The kitchen was a hive of activity: staff moving constantly, vigilant over pots and pans to ensure the perfect temperature and time, seasonings carefully measured or eyeballed to ensure maximal harmony of flavors. Suresh had made some of these dishes so many times that his body functioned automatically. He could think about something for hours that had nothing to do with what his body was doing. It made his shift fly by. The only indication that the evening was winding down was a slight shift in pace, usually around 9 p.m. (or 10 p.m. on weekends). The digital ordering system would slow down and the screen would be blank for longer, until the orders stopped altogether. Finally, someone announced that the kitchen was closed for the night, and cleanup began.

After three hours of prep work and five hours of nonstop action that flooded his system with adrenaline, Suresh welcomed the slower pace of cleanup. He needed this time to wind down, or else he'd lie in bed for hours before he could fall asleep. As he fell into his rhythm, his mind returned to the discussion at Brews Brothers the other night. Or was it day? Working the shifts he did usually resulted in an off-kilter internal clock, and he often found himself oblivious to time.

One of the newer kitchen staff, who worked with uncanny speed, had finished his tasks and had taken up residence with a book in a beat-up folding chair in the corner while he waited for a friend to pick him up. Will had begun two months before with almost no experience and had proved himself to be a quick learner.

"What are you reading?" Suresh asked.

Will looked up and took a moment to focus. "It's a fascinating book about the relationship between the brain and the mind."

"Come on," Suresh said in disbelief. "You are not serious!"

Will looked a bit taken aback by Suresh's response.

"I was thinking about that very idea all night!"

Will's face flushed. Suresh must be making fun of him. He hadn't gotten the impression that Suresh was a jerk in these last two months.

Suresh could see the anxiety on Will's reddened face. "I'm serious! I have been turning that very idea over and over in my mind."

Will's face cooled a bit.

"I'm not mocking you! I'm part of a philosophy discussion group, and this is one of the subjects that came up recently."

"You were really thinking about this while you worked?"

"Yes, I was struck by the way my body can carry out the complex tasks of making the roast duck with blackberry-orange sauce while my mind is somewhere else entirely. I've made the dish so many times that I don't have to think about it while I'm doing it. It's like my body goes into automatic mode while my mind isn't even paying attention, which made me think about the relationship between the mind and body, or more specifically the mind and the brain."

"I definitely can't do that! I still have to read my notes and concentrate on every step of the process for even basic recipes."

"You can't do it *yet*. You'll get there," Suresh said. "So what does your book say about it?"

Will shared Nobel Prize–winning scientist Francis Crick's ideas, who said that "you"—your joys and your sorrows, your memories and your ambitions, your sense of personal identity and free will—are no more than the behavior of a vast assembly of nerve cells and their associated molecules.

"Lewis Carroll," he continued, "might have phrased it, 'You're nothing but a pack of neurons.'"

"Wow. That seems so stark and impersonal." Suresh had heard this view before and hated how it reduced people to nothing more than biological functions. "Do you agree with that idea?"

"I'm not sure." Will thought for a moment. "It certainly sounds true as far as it goes. I don't think I could argue the science with a Nobel Prize winner, but it feels like there is more to us than simply our bodies and brains. How can the mind be reduced to the brain and its biological functions?"

"I'd even go further and question the reality of the body."

"What?" Will looked confused. "How can you doubt the body? I think the body would be a certainty, while the mind might be a hypothesis of some kind. I know what my body is," he said, pinching his arm, "but I'm not quite sure what my mind is—even if I believe it's real and distinct from my body."

"That's a very Western way of thinking," Suresh said. "What we can perceive through our senses is certainly real, but everything else is questionable. I lean more toward an Eastern way of thinking, which believes in spiritual reality as foundational. Everything physical, like our bodies, is a manifestation of the spiritual."

"How would you explain it then?"

Suresh tried to remember what Disha had taught him but wasn't sure he was getting it entirely correct. "I think the body is simply the label we give to the collected members of the body, so the body itself does not exist."

"Huh?"

"Think about it," Suresh said. "If you lose a finger or a foot, you don't stop having a body. In fact, you could lose body parts or functions and still perceive yourself to have a body. So the body or the self is really in the mind and not in the physical object of the body."

"Whoa." Will got up and walked over to where Suresh was finishing his cleaning. "That is heavy. I see what you're saying about the body not being gone if you lose parts of it, but isn't the body diminished by losing parts?"

"I guess that's true, but the body itself, whether complete or even missing several parts, is still in contrast to the mind, isn't it?"

"Maybe you're right," Will said, looking down at his hands. "I wonder if the focus is actually the difference between the brain and the mind. We can't think without a brain, but are the mind and the brain the same thing? And by *mind*, do we mean consciousness? A person in a coma or under anesthesia has a functioning brain, but does he have consciousness?"

"That's where Eastern thought might help. It views all of reality as a part of universal consciousness, which consists of all minds together," Suresh said. "So ultimately, the mind and body are inseparable and cannot be distinguished from one another."

Suresh shared more about this view—that the conscious human mind, not the physical world, is primary. When people start with the assumption that reality is only the physical world, they limit their options for arriving at the truth because maybe the truth is that the mind is primary. When people do that, however, the physical, instead of the spiritual or cognitive, controls their lives. Eastern thought believes that the nonmaterial is actually what provides happiness, which can be seen in the contrast between billionaires who are deeply unhappy and poverty-stricken people who exhibit genuine joy.

"The key," Suresh said, "is to cultivate the mind and seek enlightenment so we can be freed from the craving desires of the body that never seem to end."

"I can agree with a lot of that," Will said. "My family isn't wealthy, but my parents always emphasized gratitude and contentment. I'm amazed when I meet someone who has a lot but is miserable."

"The final step to understanding doesn't stop there. Only when you stop trying to maintain a distinction between the body and the mind and instead see them both as one spiritual reality participating in consciousness do you truly get close to enlightenment," Suresh looked up from what he was scrubbing. "I'm still learning this myself, so I may have gotten some of the details wrong, but overall, I think I have that right."

The kitchen was almost empty now, with the last of the staff preparing to leave. A wave of weariness washed over Suresh. He could see that Will was equally spent.

"Let's talk again when Disha gets back next week," he said. "She's better at explaining these concepts. In the meantime, I find comfort in growing in my connection with the consciousness of the universe. I like the idea that some of the physical realities of my world—how much is in my bank account, the size of my apartment, my old car—can be minimized in importance."

"It's a lot to think about," Will said. "I'm not sure I believe that the physical world is an illusion, but I like the idea of being part of a global consciousness. It makes me feel like I'm significant in some small way."

Suresh laughed. "Without you, there wouldn't be any blackberry-orange sauce for the roast duck!"

* * *

Hannah looked down at the pitiful figure standing in front of her. The girl had just been rescued by a police task force running a sting operation that targeted human trafficking. She couldn't weigh more than seventy-five pounds and probably wasn't even fourteen years old. She stood in dirty clothes near the bed while a medic checked her for critical wounds. In the next room, her abuser cursed loudly at the officers who had raided his room in this seedy motel.

The task force had burst through the door as soon as the hidden cameras made it clear that he intended to harm the girl. Hannah, who had been watching the screens with the officers, swept into the room as soon as it was secure and the man was in handcuffs. Her job was to help the victim, and victims were often as terrified by the rush of armed officers as they were of their abusers.

Hannah had done this several times in her three years moonlighting with the task force, but never had the victim been so heartbreaking. *I don't know how long I can do this*, Hannah thought as she looked at the girl.

Self-pity wasn't called for. How could she think about the emotional toll this was taking on her when who knows what this child had been through?

"What's your name, honey?"

The girl didn't answer. She just looked down at the floor as if she was too ashamed or terrified to see who was talking to her.

Hannah guided her to the bed and helped the girl sit while she pulled up a chair. "My name is Hannah, and I'm here to help you. That man won't harm you anymore. No one else will either. I'm going to make sure you get taken care of."

No reply. Then a sniffle.

"Can you tell me your name?"

Through cracked lips and stringy hair covering half her face, the girl croaked, "Candy."

Hannah had seen this before. Trafficked girls were often given a name that evoked sweetness or innocence and then beaten and interrogated until they had all but forgotten their real names.

"Is that your real name? Do you remember your real name?" Depending on how long this girl had been used and abused, her brain may have shut down details of her real identity to help her survive.

The girl cleared her throat and lifted her eyes a little, almost making eye contact. "It's Lauren . . . Lauren Bray." And then the tears began. The child began to sob and heave and vomit all at once.

Hannah quickly reached out and drew her into a hug.

The girl hugged back, clinging to Hannah as if she were being held over a precipice. A sound rose out of her that was unearthly and animal all at once, a gasping, moaning roar of terror, anguish, and grief. Hannah knew her clothing was being soaked in spit, snot, and vomit, but she didn't care. She had heard this pent-up howl once before from a person who had been horribly tortured and finally had the freedom to lament the horrors she had endured.

Lauren—that's who she was now, not just "the girl" but a name and a person—eventually began to loosen her grip on Hannah. Her body began to relax, and soon she let go of Hannah and sat on the bed with her head down, still staring at the floor. By this time the police had hauled the perpetrator away and had cleared all the camera equipment from the adjoining room. One officer remained by the door, waiting to transport the victim and Hannah to the hospital. A quiet settled over the room.

Hannah prepared to begin a speech she'd given before. She would tell Lauren what was going to happen next and reassure her that she'd stay with her until she was safely in the care of Hannah's coworker Sharon the next morning. In the meantime, Lauren would be transported to a local hospital, where she would be examined by a female doctor. In other cases like this, girls were often given an IV with antibiotics to treat any sexually transmitted diseases, as well as a sedative, if necessary, to calm them.

In the morning, Lauren would be cleaned up and given new clothes. Hannah would introduce Lauren to Sharon, who would spend the day with her, transferring Lauren's trust in Hannah to Sharon. Sharon would take her to a carefully screened family who had been trained in trauma recovery so Lauren could be cared for, fed, and given a place to sleep.

The family taking Lauren in had a daughter in high school who would be good company for Lauren in this unfamiliar setting. From there, Hannah and Sharon would supervise therapy and rehabilitation that could last from months to several years. Hannah had seen dozens of rescued teen girls and young women go through this process. Many found new life . . . but not all.

"All I am is a body for men." Lauren's words, mumbled barely above a whisper, brought Hannah back to the moment.

"Why do you say that?" Hannah couldn't believe she was saying this just minutes after being freed from a captor.

"That's what they told me," she said, wiping her nose on her sleeve. "I'm just a body. Something to be used for someone else's pleasure. It's all I'm good for."

Hannah sat stunned. This poor girl's body had been horribly mistreated, but so had her mind. If she had been told that, the damage to her soul was almost worse than the damage to her body.

Hannah wanted to grab Lauren by the shoulders and tell her this wasn't true! *You're a person and you're valuable and worthy of protection and being treated with dignity.* Lauren needed to know that.

Before she spoke, Hannah caught herself. Five years ago, she would have said these things to Lauren, but could she really say them now and mean it? Hannah had stopped believing in the inherent dignity of all people or the idea that all people are made in the image of God. From her time working with people in the worst imaginable conditions, she didn't feel that she could believe in a God who cared or in the Christian account of creation, which included God-given value in every person.

Hannah's recently adopted existentialism told her that there is no given dignity or worth. Rather, we find ourselves existing and must decide our essence, that is, who or what we are. Identity, or nature, is an act of will. Every person has to decide who or what he is. No one can decide that for anyone else.

Existentialism was at once an exhilarating and challenging belief. It seemingly opened the world to those who believe it. *I have no given identity? Great! I can be whatever I want to be. I don't have to conform to what anyone else says I am, not even God. I have no assigned purpose in life? Wonderful! I can choose my own purpose and live for whatever I decide is worth my efforts.* For many, this philosophy was liberation from a world dominated by those who sought to exercise power over others.

But as Hannah looked at this broken girl in front of her, she doubted. She hated doubting. Doubt had been the beginning of her walk away from her Pentecostal roots as a teenager. It had been an unnerving time in her life, not a happy liberation of a previously constricted soul. This time, the doubt was whether existentialism was what Lauren needed to hear. She had been treated as a purely physical being, a body, with no reality beyond that. And that had resulted in her dehumanization.

Existentialism might feel more like a burden than a release for Lauren. How could this broken shell of a person will herself to become something? She'd been beaten and abused out of the ability to will anything. She had been convinced there was no self to nurture or protect, just a body to be handled.

Existentialism seemed to work fine when a person had agency—the ability to make choices freely and live how she wanted. Hannah had never noticed this distinction before. What could be said to someone who had been enslaved? Could someone voluntarily turn over her will to another to create her essence for her? That didn't seem healthy, but what could she say to someone who insisted that it was her choice? Studies showed that abused children and trafficked people are so conditioned through fear and pain that they often won't even try to escape their abusers and captors when given the chance.

Against what she knew to be consistent, Hannah touched Lauren's arm and spoke firmly and compassionately. "That's not true, Lauren. You aren't just a body. You are a person, and you matter. What these men did to you was evil. But you are safe now, and I won't let them hurt you anymore."

"And women," Lauren said.

"What?" Hannah wasn't sure what she meant.

"Women hurt me too . . ." Lauren teared up again. "A girl just a few years older than me tricked me into going to a hotel room and introduced me to a pretty lady who seemed nice and said I could leave whenever I wanted."

Hannah realized tears were welling up in her eyes. *How could a woman do this?* She couldn't imagine the sense of betrayal Lauren must have felt. Hannah was confronted again with the inconsistency of her position. If there is no transcendent reality and we are just our DNA and brain function and people have to choose their essence and purpose, how could she argue against the choices these sex traffickers had made?

She shook her head to clear her thoughts. She had to focus on Lauren and the process of helping to restore her. Regardless of her inability to reconcile her own thoughts and intuitions, she knew they had stopped something evil and rescued a valuable life. When she had time to think about this later, she hoped she could solve the puzzle, maybe with the philosophy group. She knew she had to figure it out—for her own sanity if for no other reason.

THEORY

Philosophy can be hard, especially in the realm of metaphysics, which we have been investigating for the last few chapters. In chapter 8 we contrasted monism, the view that all of reality is in some sense one, and pluralism, the view that reality is in some sense more than one. One type of monism is physicalism, the view that reality is entirely physical. One type of pluralism is metaphysical dualism, the view that there are two different types of things that make up reality: the material and the mental (or spiritual). In chapter 9 we discussed abstract objects. Platonic realists believe that abstract objects really exist but aren't physical. Therefore, realists are metaphysical dualists. Nominalists, on the other hand, don't believe that abstract objects exist except as ideas in our minds. It follows that nominalists are likely to be physicalists and therefore are also likely to be monists.[1]

Another aspect of the monism-dualism debate is the mind-body problem. This is a debate over the constitution of human beings. Many believe that in addition to having a physical body, humans have an immaterial side. This has been called the mind, the soul, the spirit, and various other things. The view that humans are completely physical is monistic, while the view that humans have both a body and an immaterial mind is dualistic. The latter view is called mind-body dualism or substance dualism. The former view has been called materialism and physicalism, relying on context to indicate that we're talking about the nature of human beings rather than the nature of all reality.

There is a third possibility in addition to physicalism and dualism. Idealism was explained in chapter 8 as the view that reality is fundamentally mental rather than physical. If idealism is true, then humans are completely mental and lack any physical aspect. However, so few people hold to idealism that we're not going to consider it a live option.

Here we must pause to explain a minor semantic issue. English lacks a dedicated term to refer to the immaterial side of a person (if such a side exists). When referring to the material side, we can use the term "body" to refer to the bones, muscles, blood, nerves, skin, and everything else that makes up the body. However, there isn't an umbrella term for the immaterial side. If the mind does the thinking, the heart does the feeling, the memory does the remembering, the will does the choosing, the spirit does the relating, and the soul does the animating, what term do we use to represent all these at once? Philosophers tend to call this the mind, while theologians tend to call it the soul or the spirit, but that's like using the term "muscle" or "bone"

---

1. A person could hold that abstract objects exist only in the mind and at the same time believe in gods, angels, human souls, or some other kind of immaterial thing(s). Such a person would be a nominalist but not a physicalist and therefore not a monist.

to refer to the whole body. It's really not ideal, but for some reason English doesn't have a dedicated term for this. Since this is a philosophy text, we'll use the term "mind."

Historically, the mind-body problem arose as dualists attempted to figure out how the physical body and the immaterial mind relate to each other. Descartes advocated what has become known as **mind-body interactionism**, which is the view that the mind and the body are distinct substances that have two-way interaction, the body affecting the mind and the mind affecting the body. Since Descartes is the thinker most commonly associated with this view, it's sometimes called **Cartesian dualism**. It has become the most common way of conceiving the relationship between the mind and the body, but Descartes struggled to explain how something that is immaterial would communicate with something that is material and vice versa. If we suppose that the mind sends messages to the brain and the body via nerves, then we have to explain how an immaterial mind can send messages to physical nerves. If we postulate some other physical means of communication, we face the same problem. If, on the other hand, we postulate some unknown immaterial mediator, such as telepathy, then we need to explain how that immaterial means would succeed in hooking up to the physical nerves. This has become known as dualism's interaction problem.

The interaction problem is one of the main concerns that motivates mind-body physicalism: If we adopt physicalism, the mind-body problem vanishes. That's because according to physicalism, all our thinking, feeling, remembering, choosing, and so forth is done by the central nervous system. In essence, the mind is replaced by the brain. Since the brain is physical, it has no difficulty communicating with physical nerves and, via nerves, with the rest of the body.

Versions of Dualism and Physicalism

Interactionism isn't the only version of dualism. Prior to Descartes, the medieval theologian Thomas Aquinas used ideas from Aristotle to postulate that the relationship of the mind to the body is the relationship of form to substance. Just as every object is a substance with a specific form, a human is a substance (the body) that has a form (the mind). This is called **hylomorphism**. Subsequent to Descartes, some scholars argued for

epiphenomenalism, the view that the mind is a byproduct of the brain and that the causal relationship between the brain and the mind is one-way, the brain causing mental states without the mind influencing the brain in any way. The mind is sort of like a hologram that reflects what is going on in the brain. The German philosopher Gottfried Wilhelm Leibniz argued for **parallelism**, the view that God set up the mind and the brain in such a way that they function parallel with each other. Whatever goes on in one is automatically reflected in the other. A contemporary philosopher, William Hasker, has argued for **emergentism**, the view that the mind is produced by the brain but is not the same as the brain, rather like computer programs are written by humans but are not the same as humans. Because of the causal relationship between the brain and the mind, it's not surprising that they influence and affect each other.[2]

Turning to versions of physicalism, **eliminative materialism** sees talk of an immaterial mind, soul, or spirit as completely mistaken and therefore in need of elimination. The American philosopher Richard Rorty and others who hold to eliminative materialism view the idea that we have an immaterial side as "folk psychology" inherited from times when our ideas about human nature were not based on science. **Reductive materialism** holds that there's no harm in continuing the popular talk about minds and the mental as long as we recognize that, in the final analysis, the term "mind" refers to nothing more than the central nervous system and its activities. **Functionalism** argues that the mind isn't the brain, it's the *activities* of the brain. It distinguishes between the physical brain and the mind, using the latter term to refer to the activities of the former. That's not substance dualism, but it's closer to dualism than eliminative and reductive materialism are. Hilary Putnam was a well-known advocate of functionalism. **Property Dualism** is the view that mentality is a property of the physical brain. All objects have various properties—shape, size, color, etc. Thoughts, feelings, beliefs, and memories are subjective properties of the physical brain. "Mind" is just a convenient term for referring to these properties collectively. John Searle has defended this view.

---

2. Hasker succinctly explains emergentism in William Hasker, *Metaphysics: Constructing a World View* (IVP Academic, 1983), 73–76.

Arguments for Dualism

Since the purpose of this book is to explore philosophical issues in order to gain a deeper understanding of competing worldviews, we are not going to try to figure out which of the finely nuanced versions of dualism and physicalism is most likely to be correct. What interests us the most is whether mind-body dualism, in some form, is true, or whether mind-body physicalism, in some form, is true. This is the issue that relates most directly to worldviews, for some worldviews (most versions of monotheism, polytheism, and panentheism, for example) explicitly endorse dualism, while other worldviews (most versions of naturalism and pantheism) explicitly endorse physicalism.

The way to determine which view is most likely to be correct is, of course, to look at the arguments for and against each side. There are many, but upon scrutiny, many of them seem to beg the question, to commit some other fallacy, or to be based on dubious premises. Here are some arguments that may succeed in avoiding blunders of this kind.

Free will: Events that take place in the physical world are entirely determined by the laws of nature.[3] If physicalism is true, then human choices are events that take place in the physical world. Therefore, if physicalism is true, then human choices are entirely determined by the laws of nature. But if human choices are entirely determined by the laws of nature, then humans don't have free will. Therefore, if physicalism is true, humans don't have free will. Concordantly, if humans do have free will, then physicalism is false.

This argument is a *reductio ad absurdum*. It points out that if we take physicalism to its logical conclusion, we'll have to accept that humans don't have free will. If we don't want to accept that conclusion, then we should reject physicalism. Of course, there are people who deny free will. This *reductio* assumes that humans do have free will and uses that assumption to support dualism. If you don't believe that humans have free will, then you can't use this argument, but you could have other reasons for rejecting

3. If there are events that take place in the physical world but are not a result of the laws of nature, they would qualify as supernatural events. Some people believe in supernatural events, but unless we want to classify human choices as supernatural events, granting the possibility of supernatural events does not exempt human choices from the jurisdiction of the laws of nature.

physicalism and embracing dualism. We'll discuss the question of free will and determinism in our next chapter.

Out-of-body and near-death experiences have been offered as evidence supporting dualism. That people actually have such experiences isn't particularly controversial, but how to interpret them is. Some argue that all such experiences are hallucinations. When accounts of OBEs and NDEs are reviewed, it does seem very likely that many of them are either hallucinations or some other type of non-veridical experience.[4] However, it would be very difficult to prove that absolutely none of them are veridical, since that would require either examining all such experiences or finding a non-question-begging reason for concluding that veridical OBEs and NDEs are impossible. We have not seen such a reason. Furthermore, some OBEs and NDEs do seem to be supported by strong evidence.[5]

If OBEs and NDEs occur, then we need to ask what is producing them and then evaluate the possible answers. This will involve abductive reasoning. To cut to the chase, the theory that they are produced by an immaterial mind seems like it would be a strong contender.

Personal identity: In a future chapter we'll discuss the nature of personal identity. What is it that makes you, you? In what sense is the current you the same person that was you ten years ago? On physicalism, you are your body, nothing more and nothing less. But since over the span of a decade nearly all the cells that make up your body are replaced by new cells, physicalism has a difficult time explaining how the current you is the same person as the you that existed ten years ago. Physicalists have tried various strategies to overcome this challenge, but it's not clear that any has been fully successful. Dualism, on the other hand, has no such problem, since classical dualism sees the soul as the nexus of personal identity, and the soul isn't composed of cells (or other components) that are continually changing.

Religion: Many of the world's major religions advocate mind-body

---

4. A veridical experience reflects reality: It's a truthful experience. A non-veridical experience does not reflect reality, as is generally the case with hallucinations.
5. See Gary Habermas, "Evidential Near-Death Experiences," in *The Blackwell Companion to Substance Dualism*, ed. Jonathan J. Loose, Angus J. L. Menuge, and J. P. Moreland (John Wiley & Sons, 2018), 231–36.

dualism.[6] If any of these religions are true, that provides a good reason for believing that dualism is true. The logical form of this argument is *modus ponens*:

1. If a dualistic religion is true, then mind-body dualism is true.
2. A dualistic religion is true.
3. Therefore, mind-body dualism is true.

This is a logically valid argument. Whether it is sound depends on the truthfulness of the premises. Clearly, the major premise is true. Some people believe that the minor premise is true, but others reject the minor premise. So some people will believe that this argument is sound while others will believe that it isn't.

Arguments for Physicalism

Dualism's **interaction problem** has already been mentioned as a prime motive for physicalism. The logic behind this is a disjunctive syllogism (see chapter 4). In a situation where there are only two options, and one of them can be shown to be unlikely, the other option is likely. Hence, since either physicalism (in some form) or dualism (of some sort) is likely to be true, if we can show dualism to be unlikely, we have shown physicalism to be likely. What makes dualism seem unlikely is that after centuries of trying to figure out how an immaterial mind and a material body interact, we're no closer to solving the problem. On the other hand, there's no such difficulty in explaining how a physical brain interacts with a physical body. So, if we must choose between dualism and physicalism, the latter seems preferable.

Here's the argument in logical form:

---

6. Some people within some of these religions have rejected dualism. A contemporary example is a multi-author work attempting to develop a Christian physicalism: Warren Shelburne Brown, Nancey Murphy, and H. Newton Malony, eds. *Whatever Happened to the Soul? Scientific and Theological Portraits of Human Nature* (Fortress Press, 1998). A rebuttal is provided by R. Keith Loftin and Joshua R. Farris, eds. *Christian Physicalism? Philosophical and Theological Criticisms* (Lexington Books, 2018).

1. Either physicalism is true or dualism is true.
2. Dualism is probably not true.
3. Therefore, physicalism is probably true.

Two things need to be mentioned here. First, the interaction problem is primarily an objection to one specific kind of dualism: interactionism. It may also be a problem for emergent dualism, but it's not a problem for hylomorphism and parallelism and perhaps not for epiphenomenalism, either. Interactionism is easily the most common form of dualism, though, so the interaction problem is an important issue.

Second, lacking answers to significant questions does not prove a theory wrong. Most theories have questions that they answer and questions that they are still working on. The latter enables the theory to serve as the basis for an ongoing research program, which is a good thing.

Ockham's razor, mentioned in the previous chapter, is often used to support physicalism. Ockham was a nominalist (see chapter 9) who was opposed to postulating the existence of things like Platonic forms that, in his view, only make theories and explanations unnecessarily complicated. When applied to the mind-body problem, Ockham's razor leads us to prefer physicalism over dualism if (but only if) physicalism can explain all the relevant phenomena. If it can't, and if dualism can, then dualism is preferable. Physicalists think that physicalism can explain all the relevant phenomena, and therefore they believe that physicalism is superior to dualism because it does not have to postulate the existence of extra entities whose existence is difficult to verify (i.e., immaterial minds, spirits, or souls).[7]

Causal closure is often cited as a strong argument for physicalism. Causal closure is the idea that physical events always have physical causes—it's a closed loop.[8] The argument from causal closure goes like this. Mental

7. Dualists think there is a whole range of phenomena that physicalism struggles to explain, such as free will and enduring personal identity, as mentioned above, as well as intentionality, rationality, qualia, and out-of-body experiences, among other things.
8. This premise seems to assume naturalism and therefore is likely to be rejected by people who are not naturalists. It does not, however, assume mind-body physicalism, so it is not guilty of begging the question.

events (such as thoughts) cause physical effects; thinking about raising your hand can result in your hand going up; thinking about sitting down can result in you physically sitting down. Such physical effects can be traced back to physical causes in the brain. Therefore, the mental events that cause these physical effects are the physical causes of these effects. It follows that these mental events are physical.

Progress in neuroscience is often cited as evidence for physicalism. Neuroscience has shown a significant correlation between mental phenomena (thoughts, feelings, etc.) and brain activity. Furthermore, mental illnesses that once were treated with counseling and therapy are now frequently (and effectively) treated with medication that corrects chemical imbalances in the brain. These and other neuroscientific developments support the conclusion that the brain is the source of our mental activity. In turn, this supports the conclusion that our mental activity is brain activity and thus physical.

Worldview Alignments

There are many other arguments for dualism and physicalism, but we want to end this chapter with one last argument that sort of cuts both ways: worldview alignment. Many people's view on the mind-body problem will be determined by their worldview.

Think about it: If naturalism is true, that pretty much rules out substance dualism, doesn't it? If naturalism is true, then nothing exists except the natural world composed of atoms and subatomic particles. Therefore, if naturalism is true, then there are no incorporeal things. And minds (as dualists use the term) are incorporeal. It follows, then, that if naturalism is true, incorporeal minds don't exist.[9] Here's the logic of this argument:

9. It should be mentioned that there are some naturalists who affirm dualism. A modest number of scholars who are naturalists find the arguments for dualism convincing, have adopted dualism, and have had to attempt to find a way to reconcile dualism to their otherwise physicalist view of reality. For a contemporary example, see Brie Gertler, "In Defense of Mind-Body Dualism," in *Reason and Responsibility: Readings in Some Basic Problems of Philosophy*, ed. Joel Feinberg and Russ Shafer-Landau (Cengage Learning, 2017), 359–72.

- Major premise: If naturalism is true, then there are no incorporeal things.
- Minor premise: If there are no incorporeal things, then there are no incorporeal minds.
- Conclusion: Therefore, if naturalism is true, then there are no incorporeal minds.

Since this is a pure hypothetical syllogism, it is logically valid. The antecedent of the major premise is contested by non-naturalists, naturally. (That's a pun!)

There's a logical connection between theism and dualism, too, but it's not as tight as the connection between naturalism and physicalism. If theism (or deism, polytheism, or panentheism) is true, then an incorporeal God (or gods) exists. If an incorporeal God exists, then incorporeal things are possible. And if incorporeal things are possible, then incorporeal minds are possible. This, too, is a valid pure hypothetical syllogism, and again the antecedent of the major premise is controversial. The point is that worldviews themselves are a form of argument for the specific positions on the mind-body problem that best complement those worldviews.

QUESTIONS TO PONDER

- Whichever view you hold to, what are your reasons for holding to it, and how strong do you think they are?
- What are the practical implications of the mind-body problem? Does it matter if we're only physical? If we have an immaterial side, would that change how you would live your life?
- Is it possible that nothing is physical? Could all our experiences be mental instead?

TERMS TO KNOW

- mind-body problem
- dualism
- physicalism
- substance dualism
- Cartesian dualism
- interactionism
- hylomorphism
- epiphenomenalism
- parallelism
- emergentism
- eliminative materialism
- reductive materialism
- functionalism
- property dualism
- interaction problem
- causal closure

FOR FURTHER READING

Goetz, Stewart and Charles Taliaferro. *A Brief History of the Soul*. Wiley-Blackwell, 2011. This is a history of the mind-body problem. It has a slant toward dualism but provides a useful survey of the issue from antiquity to the twenty-first century.

Loose, Jonathan, Angus J. L. Menuge, and James Porter Moreland, eds. *The Blackwell Companion to Substance Dualism*. Wiley-Blackwell, 2018. This is an excellent collection of essays on Cartesian dualism.

Rosenthal, David M., ed. *Materialism and the Mind-Body Problem*. 2nd ed. Hackett, 2000. This is an up-to-date collection of essays on physicalism.

van Inwagen, Peter. "Mind-Body Problem." *Encyclopedia Britannica*. October 10, 2023. https://www.britannica.com/topic/mind-body-problem. This is a good online introduction to the mind-body problem.

FREE WILL VS. DETERMINISM

SYNOPSIS

One of the vexing questions in metaphysics is how to relate free will to the fact that many things seem to be determined by forces exterior to the will. In this chapter the friends will wrestle with free will and determinism, and then the chapter will clarify the issues by explaining the key concepts involved.

DIALOGUE

Given the number of FBI and ATF agents scattered around Greenfield, Angelo was surprised when his boss said the feds had requested that they supplement the Greenfield police by providing eyes and ears throughout the city. *The threat posed by the arms dealers must be severe*, Angelo thought, *if we're being asked to help.*

On this night, Angelo was strolling through one of the wealthier parts of Greenfield, an area he seldom visited. He was supposed to be watching for suspicious activity, but he really wasn't sure what to look for. Things seemed normal at nine o'clock this Friday evening. Maybe he'd stop at Suresh's restaurant, which was nearby, and say hello. Angelo hadn't yet visited the restaurant. Truth be told, Studio 31 was considerably out of his price range. Suresh would probably be too busy to chat, but at least he could see his friend's restaurant.

His thoughts were interrupted by a white van attempting to speed past him. It had a flat tire and evidence of having been in a scrape. It wasn't going to get much farther on that tire. The vehicle ground to a halt, and two men jumped out and began walking rapidly up the sidewalk, not noticing Angelo behind them.

I guess this is suspicious activity, Angelo thought to himself. Suddenly another vehicle came into view from the same direction. The two men ducked into the nearest building—Studio 31.

The car pulled up behind the van, and three FBI agents jumped out. Angelo got their attention, flashed his badge, and told them there were two men, pointing to the restaurant. One of them asked Angelo to circle the building and watch the back door while they pursued the two men into the restaurant.

* * *

It had been a busy evening. Suresh was in the back of the kitchen near the rear exit, retrieving some ice cream from the walk-in, when he heard a commotion coming from the dining area. Given the beehive of activity in the kitchen, it must be significant if he could hear it all the way in the back. People were shouting, screaming . . . what was going on?

Suddenly two men waving guns rushed into the kitchen from the dining room, practically knocking one of the waitresses out of their way. Seeing the guns, the other staff started ducking and darting out of their path.

The men had no interest in the staff. They were trying to get to the back door, where Suresh was standing. When they were about halfway through the maze of stoves, prep stations, and sinks, three men wearing FBI gear burst through the door.

Suresh couldn't believe what he was seeing.

Things happened with terrifying rapidity. As the men neared the back door—within just a few feet of Suresh—they turned and opened fire on the men pursuing them. One agent was hit, and the other two returned fire. Suresh dove out of the way, and in a matter of moments, both intruders were down, practically at Suresh's feet. When it was clear that they were no longer a threat, the agents ordered Suresh to remain still, approached slowly, and checked the bodies. One of the men was dead. The other was seriously wounded. Within just a few minutes, an ambulance arrived and took him away. Suresh later heard that he died en route to the hospital. Fortunately, the agent who had been shot suffered only a minor wound.

Suresh had never experienced violence like this. He'd certainly never witnessed a man die. He was deeply shaken. It was even more disconcerting when he learned that the gun battle had involved men believed to be linked to a criminal cartel suspected of moving weapons through Greenfield.

An agent pulled Suresh aside and took down a statement. Because Suresh had such a unique view of the event, the agent told him he'd likely be needed to provide testimony when authorities carried out an investigation of the shooting. He assured them that he would help however he could.

Suresh finally stepped out the back door to get some fresh air and try to stop shaking. Standing there, also looking rather pale, was Angelo.

Angelo ran up and gave Suresh a hug. "Are you okay?"

Suresh nodded, confused about why Angelo was there.

"I heard the gunshots and didn't know what had happened!" Angelo said. He told Suresh about his activities that night and that he'd had his weapon ready if the men escaped through the back of the restaurant. "I'm so glad I didn't have to get involved."

"I can't believe you're here," Suresh said.

"I was praying that you were safe."

Suresh was surprisingly comforted by this.

The restaurant closed for several days in the wake of the shooting. In some ways, the time off was difficult. Suresh kept reliving those terrifying moments and reliving the bullets flying around just feet from where he cowered.

* * *

Three days after the shooting, Suresh got a call from Hannah. Her agency had been tasked with providing support for everyone involved in the incident, and she'd volunteered to work with some of the restaurant's employees. She had already met with two of Suresh's colleagues, and now she was hoping to sit down with Suresh. They scheduled a time to meet later that day.

"I can't get the images out of my mind," Suresh confessed to Hannah a few minutes into their meeting. "I've seen plenty of violent movies, but in real life, it was so different."

He closed his eyes tightly.

"Hannah, some of the terrorists' blood splashed on my apron. I'm used to blood from cutting steaks, but this was so different. I don't understand why anyone would do this."

"Beyond the obvious factors like money and power, we probably won't ever know what motivated those men. People do amazingly destructive things to get rich or gain power," Hannah shook her head. "They may have been driven by some sort of ideology, but we don't know enough to be certain of that. The key point, I think, is to recognize that these men recklessly endangered others. They were willing to use guns against law enforcement in a crowded restaurant. Their deaths were tragic, but I think you can rest knowing that they were necessary. There was nothing you could have done to prevent this."

"I think I realize that, at least with my mind. My gut is still struggling to cope, but I appreciate the encouragement."

Suresh continued, "Is it possible that these men were fated to be this way? Sometimes things just seem to be the way they are no matter what. Were these men really free, or was the universe just arrayed against them?"

"What does your Eastern tradition tell you?"

"As I understand it, the Eastern tradition is quite diverse. Confucianism uses a lot of deterministic language, but that isn't the tradition I've been reconnecting with.[1] The Buddhist tradition emphasizes freedom. There is a concept of fate—I think Disha calls it *Niyati*—but Buddhists think it applies only to certain events that happen in one's environment. How a person responds is generally determined only by the person. Most Buddhists would

1. There is difference of opinion among scholars regarding Confucius's determinism. See, for instance, Fangqing Li, "A New Discussion of Confucius' Determinism," *Journal of Humanities, Arts and Social Science* 7 (2023): 342–47, for an argument that Confucius was a hard determinist. Kyung-Sig Hwang, on the other hand, argues that Confucius was a compatibilist in "Moral Luck, Self-cultivation, and Responsibility: The Confucian Conception of Free Will and Determinism," *Philosophy of East and West* 63 (2013): 4–16. Most agree that Confucius rejected libertarian free will.

argue that these two men made free choices and can't blame this outcome on anyone but themselves."

"My existentialist framework agrees with that," Hannah said. "No one can control everything going on around them, but people are free as they move through life to do what they think is best. For whatever reason, these men decided to do things that brought them to this tragic end."

"That's difficult though, isn't it? Saying there are things around us we can't control is an understatement. I was literally helpless when those men flew into our kitchen and then engaged in a firefight with FBI agents. What could I choose during those moments? I felt like a pawn of forces bigger than me," Suresh said, shuddering a bit. "Freedom isn't very reassuring when your actual choices are nearly eliminated by circumstances. What is free will when your only choice is to cower by a wall and hope no one shoots you?"

"I wish I had an answer," Hannah said. "Do you feel like you'll be up for attending our next meeting? Talking with friends can be a great way to process a traumatic situation."

"Yes, I think so," Suresh said. "I need friends right now."

* * *

Before Thursday night came, Suresh had a surprise meeting. On Wednesday morning, he was summoned to police headquarters, just a few blocks from the courthouse, to give a formal testimony about what he had seen the night of the shooting. As he walked into the lobby, he saw Angelo, presumably waiting for the same reason. He guessed that wasn't too surprising since he was at the restaurant as well.

Both men were shocked, however, when a few moments later, Zach walked in.

As the three friends said hello, none of them were sure what they were allowed to share with each other about why they were there. Zach knew the gun battle had taken place at Suresh's restaurant, so he surmised the reason for Suresh's presence. But he didn't know why Angelo was there and was reluctant to ask.

Zach had an unusual reason for being there. The initial FBI and ATF investigation had established that a cartel was moving Squad Automatic

Weapons (SAWs) through Greenfield. But a search of the white van had found evidence of chemical weapons. The Greenfield police didn't have much of a lab, so for initial assessment, the FBI contacted Zach's company and asked for qualified chemists to evaluate the evidence. (FBI laboratories would later confirm or correct their findings, but time was of the essence.) Zach had an excellent reputation at his company and had been chosen as part of the assigned team. What they found was disconcerting.

The terrorists were transporting what appeared to be a variant of sarin, a deadly nerve agent outlawed globally. The SAWs were a grave concern, but this discovery upped the ante considerably. Zach and other team members had been required to sign nondisclosure agreements, so he couldn't tell Suresh and Angelo why he and two colleagues were at police headquarters.

While the three friends sat together in the waiting area, they could see the same fundamental question in each other's eyes: Why would people get involved in such terrible activities with such disastrous results?

They gave testimony one by one. Zach and Suresh waited for Angelo, who was called back last, to return from his interview.

"That was more emotional than I expected," Angelo said. "Something like this really makes you ask a lot of questions about life." His friends nodded their agreement.

As they headed to their cars, Suresh verbalized what they were all thinking: "Tomorrow night can't come soon enough."

* * *

Zach opened their Thursday session with a suggestion. "I was looking at the table of contents in our book, and there's a chapter coming up about causation. Technically, it's about free will and what is called determinism. Given everything that has happened, it might be a good time for us to wrestle with this issue."

"What do you recommend?" Hannah asked.

"Well, we each seem to have some kind of involvement in the strange and unsettling events of this past week, but we can't and don't want to get into the details." Zach looked at Hannah. "Suresh told me he had a helpful session with you a few days ago. I don't mean to infringe on your professional life or ask you to work after hours, but . . ."

"Zach! I'd be happy to talk with you guys about this—or at least what you're feeling. It would be a privilege."

For the remainder of the evening, the four friends talked about fear; sudden, unexpected events; and the stable things in life, like friendship, each sharing insights from their own religious and philosophical views. As they said goodbye after a refreshing couple of hours, they agreed to read the chapter on causation before their next meeting.

* * *

Suresh returned to work at Studio 31, but it was strange to be back in the kitchen. Things were tense and a bit eerie, but business was business, and he found some relief in getting back to his routine. Angelo returned to his normal duty at the courthouse, but the entire security agency remained on high alert. The FBI and ATF believed those two men were just a small part of a much larger organization. Hannah continued to counsel people affected by the trauma of the shootout.

Zach easily had the strangest week of the four.

Despite being the second youngest member of the local team investigating this chemical weapon, Zach distinguished himself with keen insights and several breakthrough observations. But he was shocked when the senior FBI analyst asked Zach's boss to give him time off to work with the FBI chemical weapons team. He even hinted that Zach might be invited to come to the National Bioforensic Analysis Center in Frederick, Maryland, to lend his expertise to the continued study of the modified sarin compound. Zach barely found time to read the philosophy chapter. But he did read it, and his thoughts were unsettled leading into the Thursday night meeting.

When Zach arrived at Brews Brothers, he saw that his friends were already in their places around the usual table with their usual coffee preferences. It was almost like they were programmed to make those choices. How free were they really? Zach's mind went back to college and how most students chose the same seat for every class, despite the fact that few of the professors had seating charts. There was comfort in rhythm, repetition, and routine, but it was never clear to him what factors initially led to the seat choices. Were they free choices, or were they shaped by a bunch of influences, some obvious—Claire sits with Rebecca because they're close friends—and some not obvious—Jordan may sit toward the wall in the back because he had a terrible experience at the front of the class in fourth grade. Did we ever make choices free from external influences? And if we tried to say our choices emerged strictly from within, didn't a lifetime of influences tend to shape our inner nature?

The three friends hadn't yet begun discussing the night's topic. As he took his seat, Zach spilled all these thoughts to the group.

"Forgive me," Suresh said once Zach had finished, "but wouldn't your materialist worldview naturally—pardon the pun—lead to determinism? If the Big Bang released massive amounts of energy, and the whole of history consists of that energy organizing itself in various material ways, how would free will ever arise? To be consistent, wouldn't you embrace determinism as part of your worldview? Your questions, or at least your tone of voice, seem to indicate that you're troubled by this conclusion—yet it seems to fit with the rest of your beliefs."

"You're absolutely right," Zach said. "I depend on consistent causation as a scientist. If all the factors can be maintained with absolute consistency between the first test and a second, then the results should be the same. We call this consistency 'laws of nature,' although, of course, they aren't laws in the sense that they tell us what we can or should do. They're laws because they consistently describe how nature works. If nature includes everything, then the laws of nature govern everything, and nothing happens by chance or whim. That would obviously include us—when we think we're acting freely, we are simply doing what is natural for us in the strictest sense of the word *natural*. Our every thought, desire, and action are determined by the universe we live in."

Zach shook his head briefly. "But you're right. I do find this conclusion troubling. How can I blame the terrorists for smuggling arms, developing a new deadly chemical weapon—" Zach stopped himself midsentence.

The friends raised their eyebrows and glanced at each other.

"How can I blame them for smuggling arms and firing their guns in a crowded restaurant," Zach said, "if their actions were determined by natural forces released by the Big Bang? If the FBI agents were simply doing what they were programmed to do, why are they any more virtuous than the 'bad guys'? I'm frankly struggling with the implications of my worldview in this area."

"Thank you for being so transparent," Hannah said. "Surely there must be materialists who don't embrace determinism in the extreme sense in which you've presented it."

Zach recoiled a bit. "I don't think my presentation of determinism is extreme at all. No doubt some materialists claim that there is sufficient disorder in the universe to leave gaps for free will, but I don't see how they can reasonably substantiate that. If humans and other animals are strictly material just like rocks and comets, then why wouldn't they all follow natural law in the same way? It seems like special pleading to say that one set of material objects has the ability to act freely while another set doesn't. Something would have to be different about animals, including humans, that grants them a level of freedom that other objects don't possess. Presumably, that something different would have to be metaphysical to break out of the chain of causation, wouldn't it? It seems to me that free will, if it's as real as it feels like, would seriously undermine my materialistic worldview."

Zach took a breath and kept going.

"One more thing. I've run into a few materialists who call themselves *compatibilists*. They say that natural determinism is compatible with people making free choices, but they don't give an account of how this would work. The ones I've read say something like this: 'Because people feel like they are free when they make choices, we should call this genuine freedom, even though their choices are actually the result of material processes over which they have no control.' That seems like a word game to me, and I don't see any difference between that and regular determinism. The bottom line is that this isn't the first time I've been disconcerted by our discussions, but sorting out free will and determinism may be the most disturbing," Zach concluded.

Angelo finally spoke up. "If it's any consolation, I don't think any of us has a final answer on free will and determinism. This was the hardest chapter for me. I'm still wrestling with it."

"Here, here," Suresh said, and Hannah nodded her agreement.

Suresh and Hannah shared the gist of their conversation earlier in the week about their commitment to free will, what the book called *libertarian freedom*.

Zach and Angelo asked a few questions about the apparent power of external influences and how constrained choices sometimes seemed to be. But Suresh and Hannah refused to believe that external agents ever determined a choice in its entirety. They held firmly to free will. Even if someone holds a gun to your head and demands your wallet, you would be free to choose to yield to their demand or risk the bullet. It would be very rare for someone to take away a person's freedom in any ultimate, deterministic sense.[2]

"Not even being put in jail?" Angelo asked.

"Life circumstances obviously restrict the range of a person's possible choices, but being put in jail doesn't determine what you'll choose to do while there," Hannah responded.

The contrast between their view and Zach's view, if he was consistent with his materialistic worldview, couldn't be more striking.

By the time it was Angelo's turn to share, it had gotten late. All four had a busy Friday ahead, so they agreed to pick up the conversation the following week. Angelo was glad for the interruption. He had been given a lot of food for thought, and he wanted to do more research on the Christian view of these questions before speaking.

* * *

As the group settled in that next Thursday, Zach, Hannah, and Suresh asked Angelo to kick things off. He had read as much as he could about free will and determinism in Christian theology. He was amazed by the variety of views.

"I learned so much," Angelo began. "Christians have been all over the map on this question throughout the history of the church. Of course, most

---

2. Many philosophers who advocate for free will disagree with Suresh and Hannah on this. Death takes away a person's freedom, and it may someday be possible for one person to take over another person's mind via drugs or some machine such that that person can force another to do things that she wouldn't otherwise do. The view of freedom advocated by Suresh and Hannah is an imprecise view of the subject.

claim to be drawing their view from the Scriptures, but my understanding is that the Bible doesn't set out to solve this kind of philosophical problem. People find teachings in Scripture that point them in one direction or another, and once they settle the issue in their own minds, they tend to bring that perspective to the rest of the Bible.

"The least common position seems to be *direct theological determinism*, or as one key advocate called it, *occasionalism*.[3] In this view, God directly causes everything that happens in the universe. It's as deterministic as Zach's materialism, but instead of the Big Bang, God is the cause of everything."

"The way I've understood it," Hannah said, "is that Christianity says that one set of people—believers—are rewarded with heaven when they die, and another set—unbelievers—are punished with hell. That's right, isn't it?"

"Most Christians agree with that," Angelo said. "And I'm certain the Bible teaches those ideas, although I'd say heaven is a gift rather than a reward. I'd be happy to explain the theology behind salvation being a gift."

"I'd be happy to talk about that sometime," Hannah said. "My point, though, is that this theological determinism you're talking about seems in conflict with God assigning people eternal futures. How could he reward good people, or give them the gift, and punish bad people if he's causing people to be the way they are and they have no choice in it?"

"That's one of the reasons most Christians historically haven't held to this type of hard or absolute determinism. In addition, few Christians think the Bible presents God as the direct source of all the evil and bad in the world. In fact, some verses explicitly say that God doesn't cause people to sin,"[4] Angelo said. "I personally reject this account of how causation works."

"Where do most Christians stand?" asked Zach.

"They've historically been in two camps. I have no idea which is predominant. On the one hand, in order to safeguard human responsibility,

---

3. See Tad Schmaltz, "Nicolas Malebranche," in *The Stanford Encyclopedia of Philosophy*, ed. Edward N. Zalta (Spring 2022 ed.), https://plato.stanford.edu/archives/spr2022/entries/malebranche/ for an account of the occasionalism of Nicolas Malebranche.
4. The key verse on this topic is Jas 1:13: "Let no one say when he is tempted, 'I am being tempted by God,' for God cannot be tempted with evil, and he himself tempts no one" (ESV).

the legitimacy of reward and punishment, and, most importantly, God's character as a good, morally pure God, many Christians hold to libertarian freedom. This view says that God created free moral agents, those agents freely choose to sin and rebel against God, and God has acted to provide forgiveness and restoration. Proponents believe that all the promises and threats in Scripture, all the examples of people choosing to accept or reject God, the passages that refer to God's efforts to secure people's allegiance—not always successful—are a strong argument for humans being essentially free. If one of you stopped a random Christian on the street and asked them about free will, this is likely the account they'd give."

"I'm surprised there's an alternative view," Suresh said. "What is it?"

"The other view uses the same name Zach referred to last week: compatibilism. But Christian compatibilists don't typically describe their position as simply a language game to avoid the conclusion of hard determinism. They usually call their position 'soft determinism' and say that the key is how one defines *freedom*. A person is free if she acts without constraint—someone causing her to act—or restraint—someone preventing her from acting, if she could have done otherwise. They argue that God and glorified saints, for instance, don't have or won't have libertarian freedom. The Bible says that God cannot sin, cannot lie, cannot break his promises, etc., but these don't seem to be limitations on God's freedom. God is free to do whatever he wants, but he will never desire things contrary to his nature. Similarly, saints in heaven don't have the ability to sin, presumably, but they are freer than they were on earth.

"The other key feature of compatibilism, if I can reduce it to two main ideas, is that God's comprehensive plan, the determinism part, operates through many levels of secondary causation. They say, for instance, that Judas' betrayal of Christ was part of God's plan, but Judas himself acted viciously and traitorously and is blameworthy for being the immediate cause of his actions. Some of them divide God's plan into good actions of which God is the immediate cause and bad actions of which God is the final cause—the actions are part of the plan—but not the immediate cause. Agents freely doing what they want to do are, against their desires or knowledge, fulfilling God's ultimate plan.

"These advocates claim that God's determination of all things can be consistent with his creatures being responsible for their actions. Because God is loving and good, such soft determinism is far removed from cold, materialistic fate," Angelo said, letting out a sigh.

"One thought," Zach said. "It seems like compatibilism depends on people being responsible because they are doing what they want, even though people are not free to do otherwise. But what causes what people want? If everything is ultimately determined by God, which seems to be the case, then wouldn't people's desires also be determined? How has compatibilism gotten God off the hook, if you will? He still seems to be determining evil."

"Some compatibilists recognize this difficulty," Angelo answered, "but they typically respond that there is considerable mystery as to how a sovereign God can work through secondary causation. Their final appeal is to a lot of Scripture that seems to attribute evil actions both to evil human and angelic actors and to God's sovereign plan. In short, they don't really have a strong answer for that problem other than to say that the whole point of compatibilism is to believe that the Scriptures teach both a comprehensive divine plan and human responsibility. Their account is descriptive and doesn't claim to be able to untie all the resulting knots."

Hannah's brow was furrowed. "It seems like it would be simpler to simply believe in humankind's free will."

"Perhaps," Angelo responded, "but that would have many repercussions in how a person reads the Bible and constructs a theology. Most compatibilists believe that libertarian free will limits God's sovereignty and underestimates humankind's depravity."

"Wow," Zach said. "Christian theology is much more complex on this question than I thought. But I guess I shouldn't be surprised. None of us seems to have an answer for every question in this area. And the events of two weeks ago have raised a lot of hard questions."

THEORY

The friends' musings and conversations on free will and determinism have made clear how challenging these issues are. The remainder of the chapter will organize the topic and provide concrete definitions to help you further sort through the positions and arguments.

Logical Progression

There's a logical progression through the four chapters of this book that comprise the unit on metaphysics. The first chapter was on monism and pluralism, where we saw that naturalism is, after a fashion, a monistic view of reality, because it holds that everything that exists is physical. In contrast, theism (as well as deism, polytheism, and panentheism) is pluralistic because it embraces the existence of immaterial as well as material things.

The next chapter was about abstract objects. There we saw that because naturalism embraces this monistic view that everything is physical, the view on abstract objects that best aligns with naturalism is nominalism. In contrast, because theism has a pluralistic view of reality, it has the option of affirming that abstract objects exist even though they aren't physical.

In the third chapter we saw that because naturalism says that everything is physical, naturalism leads to a purely physical view of human beings and a denial of immaterial minds or souls. Theism, on the other hand, is dualistic about reality. It believes that an incorporeal God created a physical universe and therefore, that reality contains both physical and nonphysical entities. As a result, mind-body dualism is a live option for theists.

A clear pattern can be detected here: The foundational metaphysical views of naturalism and theism determine which positions on subsequent issues best fit each worldview. This is a matter of logical consistency. Since naturalism embraces metaphysical materialism, it would be inconsistent for a naturalist to believe in incorporeal gods, abstract objects, and immaterial minds. But because theists embrace a pluralistic metaphysic, it's perfectly consistent for a theist to affirm these things. And this pattern continues in our next issue, too: free will vs. determinism.

Determinism

Many people react negatively to ideas like fate, predestination, and determinism. Nonetheless, most people also believe that some things are predetermined. For instance, most would agree that, if two goats are mated, the offspring aren't going to be cows. Genetics dictates that the offspring will also be goats. However, that some things are predetermined does not entail that everything is. Could some things be determined while others aren't?

Determinism is the view that *everything* is predetermined. We'll call the view that nothing is predetermined "indeterminism." William James, a famous American philosopher, argued that there's enough play (slack, looseness) in the universe's causal nexus that events are not fully determined. This allows enough causal connection between events that the consequences of events can often be predicted but not so much that predicting them is easy. He thought this slack is what makes free choices possible.[5]

A more radical break from determinism is "chaos theory," which holds that there's genuine randomness in the universe that makes predicting the future impossible. This is a very controversial view. Although some things are notoriously difficult to predict, other things seem very predictable, such as the sun rising tomorrow and this year containing 365 days.

Returning to determinism: Determinism is widely held to be true of the physical universe. The natural world is governed by the laws of nature, which are consistent. There doesn't seem to be any play or slack in them. For example, in closed systems entropy always increases until the maximum is reached (the second law of thermodynamics), the pressure exerted by a gas is always inversely proportional to the volume it occupies (Boyle's law), every effect is equal to the sum of its causes (the law of cause and effect), and unless it is acted on by some external force, an object always remains in motion at a constant speed and in a straight line (Newton's first law of motion), etc. The physical universe is a giant causal nexus, an interconnected web of causality where every event is the result of preceding events that exactly determine what takes place.

This view is called **causal determinism**. While indeterminists deny that the physical universe is causally determined, everyone else accepts it, even those who believe that humans have free will. It's not all that controversial. Free will is controversial, though, and determinism teaches that human choices are just as determined as any other event.

This is where the logical connection to the mind-body problem can be seen. On naturalism, humans are physical bodies without any incorporeal element. Therefore, humans are caught up in the same causal nexus that

---

5. See William James, "The Dilemma of Determinism," in *The Will to Believe and Other Essays in Popular Philosophy* (Cambridge University Press, 2014), 145–83, https://doi.org/10.1017/CBO9781107360525.

governs everything else in the physical universe. Human choices and actions are just as determined by the laws of nature as is everything else in the universe. As the French philosopher Voltaire put it, "It would be very singular that all nature, all the planets, should obey eternal laws, and that there should be a little animal about five foot high, who in contempt of these laws, could act as he pleases, solely according to his caprice."[6]

Causal determinism is not the only form of determinism. Some theists are determinists who believe that in order for God to be truly sovereign, he must be controlling everything that happens. This is **theological determinism**, the view that God predetermines (predestines, foreordains) everything that ever happens.

There are at least two views on how theological determinism works. One view is that God directly predetermines everything. On this view, God is the immediate cause of everything that happens. The most extreme version of this was advocated by Nicholas Malebranche, a seventeenth-century Roman Catholic priest who argued that a logical implication of God being omnipotent is that God holds all power, and therefore only God has the power to cause things to happen. Hence, every event in history is occasioned by God. Malebranche called this view **occasionalism**.

More moderate theological determinism combines theological determinism with causal determinism. This view embraces the idea that all events are the results of antecedent causes that are themselves events resulting from antecedent causes. They reason that if you could trace the long histories of current events back through time, eventually you'd arrive at God's creation of the universe, which is the original event that set all these causal chains into motion. Because of God's great intelligence, he knew exactly how to set things up in order to bring about the results that he wanted at every step along history's long path. While on Malebranche's view God is the direct cause of everything that happens, on the more moderate view, there are some things that God causes directly, but he causes most things indirectly through causal chains.

6. Voltaire, *The Ignorant Philosopher*, trans. E. Haldeman-Julius (Haldeman-Julius, 1922), 15–16.

Libertarianism

The view that humans have free will is called **libertarianism**.[7] Just as there's more than one kind of determinism, there's more than one kind of libertarianism. William James' view that was mentioned earlier is known as indeterministic libertarianism (**indeterminism** for short). Indeterminism holds to a weak view of the cause-effect relationship, according to which a cause does not guarantee any specific effect. This rather loose view of causality is thought to leave more room for human freedom than does the more rigid view of causality that is common in the natural sciences. However, this is exactly the problem with this view: It's not in keeping with the scientific understanding of the world in which we live, which supports belief in a very tight connection between causes and the resulting effects.[8]

An alternative to indeterminism is **agency theory**. This is the view that people are agents of change: People can change the course of history by initiating new causal chains. Agency theory holds to roughly the same view of causality as do causal determinists, but instead of holding that all events have causes *and all causes are antecedent events*, agency theory holds that all events have causes, and sometimes those causes are antecedent events, but *sometimes those causes are agents* (people). People are not events, and they can initiate new causal chains. Agency theory views a choice as an event, the cause of which is an agent.

Agency theory is the form of libertarianism that seems most compatible with the modern scientific perspective on causality and the laws of nature. On agency theory, events that don't involve human choices are determined by the laws of nature, and events that do involve human choice are determined by people's choices. Furthermore, if there is an omnipotent God, agency theory does not contradict his ability to override human freedom.

---

7. In this context, the term "libertarianism" refers to the philosophical position that humans have free will. It does not refer to a political philosophy or party.
8. This is true on the macro level—the level of visible objects—but may not be true on the quantum level. The most common view of quantum physics holds that causality operates differently at the quantum level than it does at the macro level. However, this is a new area of scientific investigation and is still in the developmental stages.

Compatibilism

There is a third option in the determinism-free will debate: **compatibilism**. This is the view that determinism and free will are compatible with each other. On this view, all events are predetermined, even those that involve human choices.[9] At the same time, humans have the ability to freely choose. Since choices are events, on compatibilism, free human choices are determined, just like other events.[10] So how are they free?

This is a bit of a tricky business. It revolves around how "free" is defined. Determinists and libertarians generally agree that *a free choice is one wherein the agent is the cause of the choice and also has the ability to make a different choice*. For example, I have chosen to spend this afternoon writing, but I am fully able to choose to go to the gym instead. I chose writing, but nothing prevented me from choosing the gym. This is the kind of free choice that libertarians affirm, and determinists deny, that we can make. Compatibilists modify this definition and say that *a free choice is one wherein the agent is the cause of the choice and makes the choice that he or she wants to make*. Returning to the example, the compatibilist would say that I freely chose to write instead of going to the gym because writing is what I wanted to do, but I could no more have chosen to go to the gym instead than I could choose to ignore all the reasons and motives that caused me to prefer writing over working out. In theory, perhaps I could simply ignore all those preferences and motives, but in reality those preferences and motives precisely determine my choice. On compatibilism, a choice is an event the causes of which are internal to the one making the choice, things like the person's tastes, preferences, beliefs, values, etc. A "free" choice is a choice that's free from external constraints. Our choices are free because they are only subject to internal constraints.

Prima facia, this description of freedom may look more libertarian

9. Compatibilism is not saying that some things are determined while others are free, as libertarianism affirms. Compatibilism affirms that everything is determined, but it adds that choices can be determined without being coerced and therefore, such choices are freely made.
10. A seminal statement of compatibilism comes from the eighteenth-century Scottish philosopher David Hume in his essay "Of Liberty and Necessity," in *A Treatise of Human Nature*, ed. David Fate Norton and Mary J. Norton (Oxford University Press, 2007), 257–61.

than deterministic: We can choose anything we want within the limits of what our own tastes, beliefs, values, etc., permit. And since the only thing preventing us from choosing other than what we do is these aspects of our own nature, we're not being subjected to any external constraints. However, upon careful analysis, compatibilism turns out to be closer to determinism than libertarianism. That's why it's often called **soft determinism** (and regular determinism is often called **hard determinism**).

There are two ways in which compatibilism is closer to determinism. First, our tastes, values, beliefs, etc., are viewed as conclusively determining our choices. Second, they, too, have causes. If we were to carefully trace back the causal chains that lead up to and bring about our tastes, values, etc., we would find that they result from external factors over which we have little control. Factors such as upbringing, education, environment, the media we consume, and the like play a huge role in determining what we believe, like, and value. No one gets to choose where he is born or who her family is. Few have any say in where they go to school or if they attend religious services. During the most formative years of our lives, those decisions are made for us, and they mold who we become. Since, according to compatibilism, these factors determine our choices, an implication of compatibilism is that while you can do what you want, you have little control over what you actually want.

Arguments for Determinism

People think determinism is true for a variety of reasons. One argument for determinism is the **causality argument**, which is an inductive argument from the apparent universality of causal determinism in the natural world to the conclusion that since choices are made in the natural world, choices must also be causally determined. This argument envisions choices as the last event in a causal chain. If choices are events in the natural world, then we can infer that choices result from prior causes, and if the prior causes are also events in the natural world, then they are also the effects of prior causes, and so on. This causal chain stretches back through time all the way to the beginning of the universe (whether that's a naturalistic beginning, like the Big Bang, or a theistic one, like divine creation).

The causality argument is particularly convincing for those who, like naturalists, take a physicalist position on the mind-body problem. That's because the causality argument is an inference from something that we observe to be true in the physical universe (universal causality) to a conclusion about what's likely to be true regarding the will. If physicalism is true, then the will is a function of the central nervous system, and therefore, it is part of the physical universe.

Not surprisingly, advocates of free will have a response to this argument. As is often the case, unexamined assumptions play a pivotal role. The argument assumes that causality as we see it in the physical world is a good model for how causality works in the mental world. That's probably true if the mental world is physical, as mind-body physicalism holds. But if mind-body dualism is true, then the mental world is not physical, which calls this assumption into question.

Additionally, the argument seems to assume two more things: that all effects have causes and that all causes are themselves effects. The second assumption has received significant criticism. Agency theorists distinguish between non-sentient and sentient causes. A sentient cause is a cause that has intelligence and the ability to initiate new causal chains. A sentient cause may or may not be an effect. On classical theism, all persons are effects except for God, who is the only uncaused cause. On theism, both God and humans are sentient causes that can initiate new causal chains.

We've seen two significant caveats to the causality argument. First, it only seems cogent if physicalism is true and dualism is false. Second, it assumes that all causes are effects that form part of long causal chains; it requires that no causes be able to initiate new causal chains. Since these are very controversial assumptions, it's not clear that the causality argument succeeds.

Concerning theistic determinism, the **divine sovereignty argument** is based on the belief that God has power and authority over everything: He's the "King of kings."[11] If this belief is true, it implies that God is, in one sense or another, in control of everything. The argument is that if God is in control of everything, then he alone determines what will come to pass. If that's the case, then no human choice actually determines anything: God determines everything.

11. This title is used of God several times in the Bible (e.g., 1 Tim 6:15; Rev 19:16).

The basic argument here is a *modus ponens*, which is a valid argument form. Therefore, if the premises are true, then the conclusion stands. The minor premise seems to be at least provisionally true: If God exists, he would have to be sovereign, or he wouldn't be God. The major premise, though, is more debatable. A ruler who is an absolute dictator is sovereign within his kingdom, but that doesn't prevent him from delegating responsibilities to his subjects. If a king appoints a tax collector, for example, the tax collector will have the responsibility to levy taxes on the king's behalf, and he will probably also have the authority and power to impose punishment on those who fail to pay what they owe. In effect, the king has shared his power and authority with the tax collector. But the king is still sovereign: He voluntarily shared his power, and he can take it back at any time.

All this could be true of God too. God can delegate responsibility and share his authority and power and remain fully sovereign. And perhaps it's not necessary for God to relinquish his authority in order for us to be free—perhaps we are free because God has the authority to make us so. If either option is correct, then the major premise of the divine sovereignty argument is false; consequently, the argument isn't sound.

Another theistic argument for determinism is based upon the belief that God knows the future. This is called the **foreknowledge argument**.[12] Traditional theists hold that God knows everything that can be known, past, present, and future. If God knows the future, then all your future choices are already locked in. You can't change a single one. And that's true for every single aspect of all history: If from eternity past God has known everything that's ever going to happen, then nothing at all is open to change. No one is free to change his or her future.

Interestingly, if this is true of human choices, it's also true of God. Presumably God has known from eternity past every choice that he will ever make. Therefore, God cannot change a single one of his future choices: God's future, like yours and mine, is fully determined.

Notice that this argument is not saying that God has intentionally

12. Deists, some polytheists, and even some naturalists can use similar reasoning, since a naturalist could hold that someday it will be possible to predict all future events based upon very careful analyses of present causal conditions.

predestined anyone to do anything. It is not basing determinism on God's power, like the sovereignty argument does. It's basing determinism on God's knowledge. It's epistemological rather than metaphysical.

Arguments for Libertarianism

Let's look at some arguments for libertarianism. Perhaps the main reason most people believe they have free will is that this is our **ordinary intuition**. We've all experienced situations wherein we were faced with choosing between several options and we chose one without any sense of being coerced. In such situations, it feels like we have the ability to freely choose. The frequency of such experiences probably explains why belief in free will is so widespread. However, determinists can respond that if determinism is true, then we are predetermined to feel like we have free will and to feel like we are able to make free choices in such situations. Furthermore, they can argue that those who deny determinism are predestined to do so. On determinism, these things are out of our control, and we cannot help being blinded to the truth.

Such arguments don't sit well with theism. Classical theism holds that God is a morally perfect being. It doesn't seem likely that a morally perfect being would predestine people to believe something that's not true, so it doesn't seem likely that God would predestine billions of humans to believe that they are free when in fact they're not. Naturalism, though, may be compatible with the view that we are predestined to believe in free will even if we're not free. That's because belief in free will could have certain survival advantages over belief in determinism, so it could be argued that we have evolved to believe in free will because this belief has evolutionary benefits. For example, the belief that we can make up our own minds about things and thus make informed and advantageous decisions could lead us to be more thoughtful and intentional in our decision making, which would result in decisions that are more likely to be beneficial to our well-being. On the other hand, if we view our decisions as predestined, we may be inclined to think that it's not worth putting extra time, thought, and effort into making the best choice, since our choice is already predetermined.

Another argument for libertarianism is the **moral argument**. It is generally agreed that people are morally responsible for their actions only if they act freely. For example, if I am a cashier at the corner store and I voluntarily take all the money out of the drawer and give it to someone who isn't the owner of the store and who isn't buying anything, then I'm probably morally culpable for misappropriating (stealing) that money. If, on the other hand, I gave the money to that person because he was pointing a loaded gun at me and threatening to shoot me if I didn't give him the money, then, even though I did give him the money, people would consider me innocent of any wrongdoing. Freely choosing is important to moral culpability.

Now, if determinism is true, then people's actions are never free. Therefore, if determinism is true, then people should never be held morally responsible for their actions regardless of how heinous they are. But it seems absurd to say that no one should ever be held morally responsible for what they do. Hence, it seems unlikely that determinism is true.

This argument is a *reductio ad absurdum*. Its logical form is *modus tollens*:

1. If determinism is true, then people should not be held morally responsible for their actions.
2. It's not the case that people should not be held morally responsible for their actions.
3. Therefore, it's not the case that determinism is true.

This is a logically valid argument. We've already illustrated why we think the major premise is true, and the truthfulness of the minor premise seems obvious to most people, so this argument seems sound. However, while it may succeed in proving determinism false, it doesn't actually attempt to prove libertarianism true. Here's an argument that does.

1. Either determinism is true or libertarianism is.
2. Determinism has been shown not to be true.
3. Therefore, libertarianism is true.

This argument is a disjunctive syllogism, which is a valid argument form. If the premises are true, then the argument is sound. The minor premise was seen to be true. The major premise is more controversial, for it may be a false dilemma. It only presents two options: determinism and libertarianism. Some support compatibilism as a third option. But since determinism is a necessary condition for compatibilism, if determinism is false, so is compatibilism.

A third argument for libertarianism is theistic: the **theodical argument**. This argument is another *reductio ad absurdum*, this time reasoning that if determinism is true and if God exists, then God would be the cause of all the sin and evil in the world. It's called the "theodical" argument because theodicy is the term used to designate an attempt to reconcile the existence of an omnipotent (all powerful), omniscient (all knowing), and omnibenevolent (all good) God with the existence of evil. One way of doing this is by shifting the responsibility for evil off God and onto other beings who have free will but are morally imperfect.

If theological determinism is true, then it's impossible to shift responsibility in this way, since God is either the first cause or the direct cause of all actions, both good and evil. Philosophically, though, this is problematic, for God is perfectly holy and therefore cannot be the cause of all evil. It's theologically problematic, too, for God's opposition to evil is a major theme of monotheistic theology. Of course, one could postulate that God created evil so that he could then overcome it, but traditional theism holds that God allows evil rather than creates it—that he allows it only as a corollary to the free will of the lesser beings that he has created, and that he is engaged in overcoming it. None of this is consistent with the idea that God has predetermined every evil event that has ever and will ever occur.

This is another *reductio* argument and therefore another *modus tollens*:

1. If theological determinism is true, then God is the cause of all evil.
2. It's not the case that God is the cause of all evil.
3. Therefore, it's not the case that theological determinism is true.

Once again, if the premises are true, then this argument is sound. Like the moral argument for libertarianism, the theodical argument assumes that if determinism is false, then libertarianism is true. Again the compatibilist is likely to object that this is a false dilemma, and once again the libertarian is likely to respond that, since determinism is a necessary condition of compatibilism, the theodical argument is just as telling against compatibilism as it is against hard determinism.

Arguments for Compatibilism

The basic argument for compatibilism is straightforward: There are elements of truth in both determinism and libertarianism, and compatibilism combines these into a single view in a way that avoids internal inconsistency. It's the best of both worlds! More specifically, compatibilism is claimed to preserve the central role of causal sequences in producing choices and actions that is championed by determinism but undermined by indeterministic libertarianism, and it is claimed to do this in a way that preserves freedom of choice. For theists, compatibilism is also thought to preserve the sovereignty of God while shielding God from responsibility for evil.

Both determinists and libertarians reject the compatibilist attempt to redefine freedom as the ability to do what you want to do, since by that definition, a person whose desires have been entirely manipulated or even manufactured by someone else is still free. Furthermore, theistic libertarians argue that compatibilism is unsuccessful in shielding God from the accusation of causing all the evil in the world. They point out that compatibilism does not say that God predetermines some things and leaves others undetermined; that's libertarianism. Compatibilism says that God predetermines everything, but that he uses (predetermined) human choices to bring about some of the other things that he predetermines. That being the case, God is responsible for both the human desires and the resulting evils. Theistic libertarians find it difficult to reconcile such a view with the perfect holiness of God.

Worldviews

Interestingly, though, people's intuitions about the direction in which their worldview is leading them on this issue are sometimes not consistent with the actual logical implications of their worldviews. For example, naturalists, like most people, generally want to believe in free will. However, naturalism implicates metaphysical monism, which implicates metaphysical physicalism, which implicates mind-body physicalism, which implicates causal determinism.[13] Some naturalists have attempted to avoid this conclusion, but others have embraced it.

When we examine the views that theists hold on free will and determinism, we often find a similar tension. That's because theists are strongly inclined to view God as completely sovereign, and they assume that in order for God to be completely sovereign, he must be actively causing or controlling everything that happens. Thus, theists often think they must embrace determinism. But if we follow the logic of the theistic worldview, we see a dualist view of reality facilitating a dualist position on the mind-body problem, which enables theists to avoid embracing causal determinism. We also see in theism the view that God is completely holy and therefore neither the cause of sinful human desires nor the cause of evil. Hence, belief in free will seems essential to the classical theistic worldview.

13. This is nicely argued by Robert Sapolsky, a professor of neurology at Stanford University, in *Determined: A Science of Life Without Free Will* (Penguin, 2023).

QUESTIONS TO PONDER

- Can you think of additional arguments for free will or determinism?
- Can you think of additional arguments against free will or determinism?
- Can you think of any options besides determinism, libertarianism, and compatibilism?
- Which view on free will and determinism fits best with your worldview? Why?

TERMS TO KNOW

- determinism
- causal determinism
- theological determinism
- occasionalism
- libertarianism
- indeterminism
- agency theory
- compatibilism
- soft determinism
- hard determinism

FOR FURTHER READING

Campbell, Joseph K., Michael O'Rourke, and David Shier, eds. *Freedom and Determinism.* MIT Press, 2004. This is a recent collection of essays.

Dilman, Ilham. *Free Will: An Historical and Philosophical Introduction.* Routledge, 1999. This is a historical study of the debate.

Lehrer, Keith, ed. *Freedom and Determinism*. Random House, 1966. This is a nice collection of essays analyzing all three positions in the debate.

Timpe, Kevin and Daniel Speak, eds. *Free Will and Theism: Connections, Contingencies, and Concerns*. Oxford University Press, 2016. This is a theistic exploration of determinism.

RELIGION

RELIGIOUS EPISTEMOLOGY

SYNOPSIS

The next four chapters address the philosophy of religion. The starting point for the discussion is the question, "How is knowledge about religion acquired?" This and related questions constitute the subject of religious epistemology.

DIALOGUE

The weeks after the shooting were a blur, and the friends struggled to find time to meet. Zach was constantly away, working with the FBI in Maryland. He had spent two full weeks living there and lending his expertise to the specialists at the national lab.

In light of the continuing threat, Angelo found himself working long hours, feeling the exhaustion of not only the extra shifts but also the tension of imagining another confrontation with armed terrorists.

Suresh had expected the restaurant to struggle after someone had been killed there. To the contrary, people were coming from far and wide to see where it happened, and Suresh and his colleagues maintained a grueling schedule to keep up with the increased business.

Hannah had thought that a few sessions with people involved in the shooting would be sufficient. She tried to combine compassion with an optimistic message of believing in oneself, but she seemed unable to settle some of her clients' anxieties. They wanted to meet again and again to share their deep-seated fears—not only for their personal safety but also about what seemed to be a culture sinking into anarchy.

The friends texted each other periodically and fully intended to keep their study going, but this was an unusual season, so they agreed not to meet again until the time was right.

* * *

It had been almost three weeks since the shooting, and Hannah was in yet another conversation with Elle, a sweet and somewhat timid young waitress from Studio 31. She had been shoved aside by the first intruder the day of the shooting. She wouldn't normally have been in the path of the gunmen, but she had gone back to the kitchen to share a customer's compliment on a dish and ended up having the most harrowing experience of her young life. This was the fourth time Hannah had met with her. The City of Greenfield was generously funding social services for everyone involved who requested help, and a surprising number of people were asking for help.

"Thank you for coming again, Hannah," Elle said as Hannah entered her living room and took a seat on the sofa near the window. On her first visit, she had noticed the large painting of Jesus on the wall opposite the window and the metal crucifix on Elle's mantel.

"You've been so kind to help me cope with my fears," Elle said. "I finally returned to work this week, and even though my hands were shaking at first, I calmed down as the shift went on. It was almost like old times, except the restaurant is really busy right now."

"It's my pleasure," Hannah said. "I'm glad you found the strength to go back to work. Returning to normal life is an important stage in the healing process."

"That's actually why I wanted to meet again," Elle said. "I pulled back from my church after the trauma of the experience. I just couldn't bear to be around a lot of people. But on Sunday I finally went back to church."

"That's great," Hannah said. "Community is so important."

"I talked to my priest, and he said something that struck me. He said they'd been praying for me and asked if I'd felt upheld by my faith. I couldn't say anything back to him," Elle said. "I realized I'd barely thought about my faith since the shooting. I jumped at the chance for counseling. I thought counseling would show me how to navigate the fear and dread I was feeling."

Elle broke eye contact with Hannah and looked at her hands.

"Don't get me wrong, Hannah. You've been so sweet to listen to me and offer advice. But I forgot about Jesus and Mary and the church! Reconnecting with my faith has made a huge difference."

"That's wonderful," Hannah said. "Many people find religion helpful. I'm glad you have. Do you mind telling me why you believe that Jesus and Mary can help you?"

Elle looked a little puzzled. "What do you mean?"

"You said that remembering your faith in Jesus, Mary, and the church made a big difference. I'm just curious how that works. I know the church may do tangible things for you, but how do Jesus and Mary help? They've been gone for a long time."

"They aren't gone. They're still with me. I talk to both of them every day."

"How?" Hannah rarely asked counselees questions like this, but she was genuinely curious about Elle's thinking.

"Like I said, I reconnected with my faith. The church—Father Culbertson especially—teaches that Jesus and Mary help us when we're down, and I believe that."

"So you believe in Jesus and Mary because you believe Father Culbertson?"

"That makes it sound like my faith is in my priest rather than in Jesus and his Blessed Mother. I believe in Jesus and Mary because they help me."

The look on Hannah's face must have communicated skepticism without her saying a word.

"You seem to want reasons for my belief, but, like I said, it's faith," Elle said, her voice getting a little louder. "You don't have to have reasons if you believe. You just believe."

Hannah decided to let it go. She wasn't there to cause Elle to have *less* comfort. The young waitress's position struck Hannah as being faith in faith, believing in something—or someone—without having any rational basis for the faith. Hannah recalled her philosophy group's discussion of fideism. She began to think she'd just witnessed a good example of it.

* * *

Suresh clocked out after a grueling shift. He didn't think he'd ever seen the restaurant so busy. The pace gave him little time to reflect on how disconcerting the last few weeks had been. Something was bothering him, though, and he was determined to ask Disha about it before going home to collapse.

"I know you're probably as tired as I am," he said as he tracked Disha down in the kitchen. "So this can wait."

"I don't know what you're talking about, my friend, but I wouldn't mind winding down with a little conversation."

"Do you want to grab something to eat?"

They headed to a nearby diner and found a booth. Despite being in the kitchen for so many hours, both of them were starving.

"Do you ever experience doubts about your religious beliefs?" Suresh asked once they'd ordered. "Does anything ever come up that makes you wonder if you're on the right path?"

"Of course," Disha said. "I occasionally come across facts or ideas that are difficult to reconcile with the teachings of Buddha."

"Such as?"

"I'm not sure I can come up with an example off the top of my head tonight . . ." Disha paused for a minute. "Actually, when you challenged me some weeks ago about my seeming to use logic and deny logic at the same time, it bothered me. I tried not to show it at the time, but I was a little shaken by your observations. Later, I had to admit to myself that perhaps I was inconsistent, and it nagged at me for a while."

"My goal wasn't to unsettle you!" Suresh said. "I was simply pursuing truth the best I knew how. I do appreciate you sharing that though."

"Of course. As Buddha says in the Meghiya Sutta, 'Having good friends isn't half of the Holy Life. Having good friends is the whole of the Holy Life.'[1]

---

1. For discussion of the Meghiya Sutta, see John Haspel, *Becoming Buddha: A Buddha's Timeless Path of Meditation, Mindfulness and Profound Wisdom* (Simple

I knew you meant no harm. In fact, the conversation helped me sort it out. Buddhism doesn't deny that the Law of Noncontradiction, the idea that a proposition and its opposite cannot both be true at the same time in the same sense, can be a helpful way to sort out options. But it retains the possibility that contradictories may both be true in some deeper sense. I can reason for something as being a reasonable contrast with something else without thereby claiming that the Law of Noncontradiction is always binding."

A server brought their food to the table, and both friends happily dug in.

"That's interesting," Suresh said between bites. "But let's suppose, for argument's sake, you couldn't resolve the tension my questions created. What would you have done then?"

"A single matter of tension like that, even a big one, I suppose, wouldn't shake me from my overall commitment to Buddhism. Surely every worldview has something inexplicable in it, some tension it struggles to resolve. Only a naïve or boastful person would claim to be able explain everything."

"That's probably right. At some point, the weight of evidence might overthrow or seriously adjust someone's worldview, but I guess a person shouldn't abandon their worldview every time they run into something challenging."[2]

"Why is this on your mind?" Disha asked.

"My philosophy group has raised some hard questions. We haven't met in several weeks—for a lot of reasons—but we want to get back to it. In the meantime, I've been thinking about many of the issues that are coming up. Some gel with my Eastern thinking, but some have been very hard for me to digest and have caused me to wonder if my religious beliefs are true. It's helpful to be reminded that challenges to my worldview should be expected and that any major adjustments should be approached cautiously."

"Yes," Disha said, popping a fry into her mouth. "A person's worldview can't be granite—we must remain teachable—but it also shouldn't be JELL-O."

The two friends parted ways for the night.

Enlightenment Press, 2017). For discussion of suttas in general, see https://www.britannica.com/topic/Sutta-Pitaka.

2. Suresh is not familiar with the term, but he and his friend are expressing the Principle of Belief Conservation.

* * *

Angelo was driving home after a fascinating evening spent with his pastor and his family. He finally had an evening off, but rather than sitting at home reading or watching TV, he had called Pastor Lewis and asked if he had time to get together. Pastor Lewis generously offered to share dinner and to spend the evening together. Connie, the pastor's wife, had made a delicious lasagna, and he especially enjoyed spending time with their three kids, who were polite but rambunctious—in other words *fun*.

After a while, he and Pastor Lewis, who insisted that Angelo call him Jim, went to the den to talk. Angelo was wrestling with troubling thoughts that he hoped his pastor could help him with.

"God is transcendent, right?" Angelo began, somewhat abruptly.

Jim responded cautiously. "What do you mean by *transcendent*? I want to make sure we're defining it the same way."

"He's different from us. His power, love, and other characteristics are infinitely beyond ours. Right?"

"Yes indeed," Jim replied. "We call those his attributes, and they are beyond our ability to know completely."

"In that case, how can we have firm knowledge of him?"

"That seems like a strange question, Angelo," Pastor Jim said. "We point out virtually every Sunday that God reveals himself in Scripture."

"Yes, I understand. I'm thinking philosophically here—or trying to," Angelo said.

Pastor Jim nodded, urging Angelo to continue.

"So the Bible says that 'God is love' and 'God is holy,' right? If God's love and holiness are infinite, do we really know what those words mean? It seems to me like transcendence is a problem—my philosophy friends would say an epistemological problem. How can finite beings know infinite things or an infinite person like God?"

"Ah, I see what you mean," Pastor Jim said. "You're making a very good point about God—that God wouldn't be knowable at all unless he chose to reveal himself to us. All knowledge of a transcendent being would have to start with the being. That's the first thing to observe, I think."

"That makes sense."

"I also think we can agree that the revelation of an infinite being will be incomplete. God can't do anything that is logically contradictory, and it's a contradiction to say that an infinite being is exhaustively communicated through a finite medium like, say, a collection of writings."

Angelo nodded.

"Now the key question is this: Can a being like God reveal himself accurately even if the revelation isn't exhaustive? Can we get a true picture of him even if infinitely more could be said?"

"How do we answer that question?" Angelo asked.

"Christians believe that Jesus is the ultimate revelation of God. Jesus is, in fact, God in the flesh. This is the doctrine of incarnation. Jesus said to his disciples, 'Whoever has seen me has seen the Father.'[3] Do you see his point?" Pastor Jim asked. "Jesus is God, an invisible being, but Jesus united himself to humanity, thus making God visible. Therefore, Jesus portrays God to man by means of his humanity. But his humanity was and is finite. Therefore, it must be true that the finite can give true, if not exhaustive, knowledge of the infinite. If Jesus can reveal God through his humanity, then Scripture, though a human book, can also reveal God. In neither of these cases do we learn everything about God (or even everything about any of God's attributes), but what we do learn is genuine knowledge, true though not complete."

"So what you're saying is that we can know the transcendent without having knowledge that is itself transcendent," Angelo said. "We can have finite knowledge of the transcendent, and if that's what he wanted us to know, we'll be okay."

"Do you mind me asking what brought all this up, Angelo?"

"My philosophy friends and I—hopefully I'll get to introduce you to them sometime—have been wrestling with epistemological questions. At the heart of any worldview is the question: How do we know what we know? I've been trying to apply what I'm learning to my faith. And I appreciate you working through some of it with me. My friends are very helpful in sharpening my thinking, but they can't help me with questions that relate directly to Christianity the way you can."

"What an interesting journey you're on, Angelo," he said. "I find my

---

3. John 14:9 (ESV).

own thinking being sharpened by our conversation and hope we can do this again."

* * *

Despite the terrible circumstances that had brought about Zach's involvement with the FBI, he wasn't sure he'd ever enjoyed himself more than these last few weeks. Not only were the people at the FBI lab treating him like a respected colleague, which amazed him given his age, but one of these colleagues was becoming a friend. Her name was Samantha, and she was just a couple of years older than him. Her intelligence and expertise in chemical weapons analysis had led to her quick rise in the organization and had landed her a permanent position at the national lab. He'd spent many hours working with her and finally mustered the courage to ask her to coffee after work. Her enthusiastic acceptance made his heart skip a beat. They soon found themselves in Frederick at a small coffee shop called The Beanstalk.

For a while, they engaged in the kind of small talk that men and women who are trying to get to know each other make. Samantha was sharp and easy to talk to. Zach felt like he had known her for years.

The conversation shifted when Zach discovered that she wasn't an atheist. He had assumed that a young fellow scientist would share his worldview. She was one of the smartest people he'd ever met. He was quite surprised when she gently corrected him after he said something that implied a shared scientific and therefore atheistic perspective.

"I'm certainly scientific," Samanatha said, "but science points me to a divine designer rather than suggesting a universe determined by chance. I'm sorry if that disappoints you, but my commitment to God is quite strong, and I don't think it's at all irrational."

Zach was so surprised. "I'm not disappointed. Of course," he said. "I respect you and your beliefs; I just struggle with how religious people justify their faith. There seems so little evidence to support religious commitment."

"Are you familiar with the concept of abductive reasoning?"

"My philosophy group worked through the principles of formal logic a few months ago," he said. "I was already familiar with deductive logic from my studies in math, and inductive reasoning is my bread and butter. But abductive reasoning was relatively new to me, and I found it fascinating. It made me realize how often I use 'best-fit' analysis not only in my line of work but also in everyday life. I constantly draw conclusions based on what best explains all available data."

"I love that you're interested in this!" Samantha said. "I believe a powerful abductive argument for theism, and the Christian God in particular, can be formulated. Given the choice between the universe arising from an uncontrolled explosion and being designed by an infinite intelligence, I think the data strongly supports the latter."

Samantha definitely had Zach's attention. "But . . . if I recall correctly, abductive reasoning, like induction, can yield only probabilistic certainty. Would you say you have only a probable certainty that God exists?"

"Very perceptive," Samantha said, smiling. "I didn't say my faith rests entirely on abduction. I said I have a powerful abductive argument for God's existence. The truth is, the design I see in science simply corroborates the faith I have in God's revelation in the Bible. My studies in science didn't lead me to God—the Bible did."

Zach took a sip of his coffee. "You don't mind if I push back on that, do you?" He didn't want to offend his new friend.

"Not at all."

"I was willing to discuss the science with you and see which of us could come up with a better fit of our worldview to the data. Actually, I hope we still can. But when you say that the Bible is the real foundation for your belief in God, to me, it appears that you're being circular. Don't you believe the Bible because you think that, in some sense, God wrote it? If I don't think God wrote it, why would I believe its claims?" Zach asked.

"Defending the Bible's claim to be the written Word of God is a big subject to tackle, but I can tell you briefly how I'd proceed. First, I would note internal characteristics of Scripture that are hard to explain if the book isn't divinely inspired. Men, called prophets, predicted that certain things would happen, and centuries later, they did, sometimes in startling detail. For instance, we know that Isaiah predates Jesus by centuries because of the copies of his book found in the Dead Sea Scrolls. But Isaiah prophesies about a person like Jesus, who would be killed though innocent, would be buried in the tomb of a rich person, and would conquer death, among other things. That's one example of a widespread feature of Scripture that argues for divine authorship."

"The 'fulfillments' of those prophesies are also often contained in the Bible, right?" Zach asked. "Isn't it possible that people living later arranged things to match the earlier Scriptures and make it look like they were true prophecies?"

"If you're talking about the actual events, it seems quite unlikely. Would a man allow himself to be betrayed, mocked, and crucified in order to prove prophecies true? Perhaps, though, I guess you mean that the New Testament writers recorded the events to make it look like the prophecies were fulfilled. Is that right?" Samantha asked.

Zach nodded.

"It's difficult to prove that they didn't, but frankly that seems like a conspiracy theory to me. The simplest solution is that they told about something they witnessed, and it happened to match what prophets had predicted hundreds of years earlier," Samantha said. "The remarkable consistency of Scripture is another key feature when one considers that it was written over nearly fourteen hundred years by dozens of different authors."

"But don't skeptics claim that the Bible contains many contradictions?"

"Yes, of course," Samantha said, nodding. "Christian apologists spend a lot of time addressing such so-called discrepancies. There are large volumes on the subject. I could recommend some good books.[4]"

Zach was impressed by her knowledge base.

"My short answer," she continued, "is that Jesus Christ affirmed the trustworthiness of Scripture, and I trust him. I know that sounds viciously circular to you—that I trust Scripture because it records someone saying I should trust it. Nevertheless, the Bible makes claims about me, about my sinfulness, my insecurities, my needs, and it provides a solution to those problems through Jesus Christ. My experiences with him give me confidence

---

4. For instance, see Gleason L. Archer Jr., *New International Encyclopedia of Bible Difficulties* (Zondervan, 2001); Josh McDowell and Sean McDowell, *The Bible Handbook of Difficult Verses: A Complete Guide to Answering the Tough Questions* (Harvest House, 2013); and Norman L. Geisler and Thomas Howe, *The Big Book of Bible Difficulties: Clear and Concise Answers from Genesis to Revelation* (Baker, 2008).

that he is as he is presented in the Bible. So when I read him saying that the Scriptures 'cannot be broken,'[5] I believe him."

Zach nodded. Pushing back would be insensitive. It was difficult for him to find her inner experiences convincing, but he respected her and them.

"I also appeal to 'external' evidence," Samantha said. "The Bible contains a lot of historical information that spans centuries. While there are undeniable tensions between some of the Bible's claims and archaeological finds from the ancient Near East, hundreds of facts and stories in the Bible have been remarkably corroborated as historians learn more about the history of the region. The data is quite impressive."

"I don't know much about this part of history, so I'll take your word for it," Zach said. "But doesn't the Bible have extremely outmoded science? I hope I'm not offending you with all these questions."

"You're not. What about this: Is it a scientific error if a person says he saw the sun rise this morning?"

"Well, it isn't very precise."

"No, of course not, but scientific precision about things like the sun appearing on the horizon each morning would be excessive, wouldn't it?"

"I suppose so."

"Many of the so-called scientific errors in the Bible are just natural ways of expressing things in a pre-scientific age. If we don't demand scientific precision in a literary text—and we usually don't—there's no reason to view imprecision as error."

"Yes, but what about creation in six days just a few thousand years ago? Isn't that a radically different explanation for the origin of the universe?"

"Christians have differences on how to read Genesis. Some believe a literary reading of the text can accommodate many aspects of evolutionary theory and an old earth. Personally, I think the Scriptures teach a young earth, and I haven't entirely figured out how to deal with the preponderance of scientific evidence claimed against this view. Creation scientists make some good arguments, but I don't claim to be an expert on this," Samantha said. "Nevertheless, my confidence in the trustworthiness of the Bible remains unshaken."

---

5. John 10:35.

"It seems like you're appealing to two kinds of evidence," Zach said. "Evidence within Scripture, which you regard as decisive, and evidence from outside Scripture, which you take to be corroborative. Is that right?"

"It is. We call the first source 'special revelation,' God speaking to specific people at specific times. The extrabiblical evidence comes from what is known as 'general revelation.' Christians believe that the very existence of the universe argues for someone outside the universe having created it, that the design argues for a designer, and the existence of transcendentals, such as rationality, morality, and mathematics, argues for an eternal mind to think them. In other words, general revelation is very helpful in providing arguments in support of the Bible's authoritative claims."

Zach laid his hand on the table. "Wow. You've given me a lot to think about. Thank you for taking the time to explain some of your religious epistemology. I'm not convinced, but I find it more cogent than I expected."

"You're a great listener and ask good questions," Samantha said, laughing lightly. "It's important to know how and why we know. For me, even more important is *who* I know. Knowing Jesus has changed my life. Maybe sometime I can explain it to you."

"My friend Angelo has made the same offer. I'll let you know . . ." Zach replied. "I appreciate the offer."

THEORY

The experiences of our four friends demonstrate the importance of God and beliefs about God to a person's worldview. The remainder of this chapter will introduce philosophy of religion and dig more deeply into religious epistemology.

Philosophy of Religion

Many worldviews have prominent religious components. There are a variety of approaches to studying religion: anthropologically, historically, sociologically, theologically, philosophically, etc. Philosophy of religion is the study of religious beliefs and concepts using the tools of philosophy: careful observation, clarification of terms, and logical analysis.

Many topics can be explored in philosophy of religion. For example, one widely used textbook on the subject contains the following chapters:

1. Thinking About God: The Search for the Divine
2. The Nature of Religion: What Are Religious Beliefs About?
3. Religious Experience: What Does It Mean to Encounter the Divine?
4. Faith and Reason: How Are They Related?
5. Theistic Arguments: Is There Evidence for God's Existence?
6. Knowing God Without Arguments: Does Theism Need a Basis?
7. The Divine Attributes: What Is God Like?
8. Divine Action: How Does God Relate to the World?
9. The Problem of Evil: Is There Evidence Against God's Existence?
10. Miracles: Does God Intervene in Earthly Affairs?
11. Life After Death: Are There Reasons for Hope?
12. Religious Language: How Can We Speak Meaningfully of God?
13. Religion and Science: Are They Compatible or Incompatible?
14. Religious Diversity: How Can We Understand Differences Among Religions?
15. Religious Ethics: What Is God's Relation to Morality?
16. The Continuing Quest: God and the Human Venture[6]

We're going to explore only four of these issues: the nature of religious belief (religious epistemology), the nature of God (philosophical theology), arguments for God's existence (theistic apologetics), and arguments against God's existence (atheistic apologetics). However, more of these issues will arise and be discussed elsewhere in the book.

Religious Epistemology

In a sense, epistemology is context sensitive: How one gains knowledge varies from one context to another. For example, the way one gains knowledge of the past (historiography) is likely to be different from how one gains knowledge about the present, and it's likely that how one gains knowledge about scientific issues (for example, the composition of some unusual rock that you

6. Michael Peterson, William Hasker, Bruce Reichenbach, and David Basinger, *Reason & Religious Belief: An Introduction to the Philosophy of Religion*, 5th ed. (Oxford University Press, 2012), v–viii.

find while hiking) is different from how you would gain knowledge about things that transcend the physical world (such as gods and other immaterial entities). A book devoted entirely to epistemology could have chapters for each of these different epistemic contexts. Since the main focus of this book is the contrast between naturalism and supernaturalism, this chapter focuses on the religious context. This is called religious epistemology.

Naturalists have no need for religious epistemology, of course, since they don't believe in anything supernatural. Naturalism fits well with **empiricism**, the view that sensory experience is the wellspring of all knowledge. Although there have been many empiricists who were not naturalists, that empiricism complements naturalism is clear, since naturalism implies physicalism and what is physical is generally available to the senses. Supernaturalistic worldviews like theism, deism, and polytheism postulate the existence of immaterial things that cannot be known via the five senses. Accordingly, adherents to such worldviews frequently reject empiricism as inadequate.[7]

The Epistemological Problem of Transcendence

The biggest challenge here, epistemically speaking, is the problem of transcendence. To be **transcendent** means to be above or beyond the ordinary realm. God is thought to be so transcendent that he's beyond our wildest imaginations. But if that's the case, then we can't really know much about him, can we? All our finite, human ideas about God would be mere shadows of the real God, barely even reflecting the true nature of whatever it is that casts them.[8]

The problem of transcendence is more intense for some worldviews than others. Some versions of polytheism view the gods as having a physical form with supernatural abilities, including the ability to disappear from one

7. Some who believe in supernatural entities do embrace empiricism. Such people can argue that even if we cannot experience God (or other suprasensible entities) directly, we can experience his actions directly. Furthermore, they can argue that God sometimes appears in forms that can be experienced via the senses, such as appearing as a human, or as a dark cloud or a flash of lightning, or by speaking in a thunderous but disembodied voice.
8. This is an allusion to Plato's allegory of the cave, which is worth reading. Plato, *The Republic*, trans. Shawn Eyer (Plumbstone, 2016), 514–21, https://faculty.tamuc.edu/jherndon/documents/plato.pdf.

place and reappear in another. Other versions see the gods as incorporeal powers that have the ability to appear in physical form when and where they wish. The former are closer to physicalism than are the latter, and thus, the latter are more transcendent than the former. Classical theism sees God as both incorporeal and as able to appear physically. Thus, the God of theism is transcendent in his essence. The God of deism is incorporeal, and thus transcendent, and does not take on physical form and appear to humans; he is practically absent from his creation. Hence, the God of deism is the most transcendent of all. Therefore, the problem of transcendence is most acute for deism, but this in no way excuses polytheism and classical theism from having to deal with it.

Two Kinds of Revelation

The epistemic problem posed by divine transcendence affects theology as well as philosophy. Traditionally, theologians have responded to it by affirming the need for God to reveal himself to us. Here they make a useful distinction between general revelation and special revelation. **General revelation** is God's communication of basic truths to all people. These can include facts about his existence, his nature, and his activities and are communicated by things that are observable in nature. It is often said that just as you can discern certain things about an artist by looking at her artwork, you can discern some things about God by looking at his creation. By observing the immensity of the universe, we catch a glimpse of the enormity of God's power; by observing the complexity of the universe, we learn about God's amazing intelligence; and by observing the beauty that the universe contains, we begin to appreciate God's creativity.

Special revelation is God's communication of a specific message to a specific audience. This can take many different forms: God can assume a physical form and then speak, or he can speak without assuming a physical form, communicate through dreams and visions, and speak through prophets and inspired writings (Scripture). Christianity holds that God's most striking special revelation is the incarnation—when God was born as a human being and lived among us.

Naturalism has no need for revelation, of course. In fact, the idea of revelation is logically incompatible with naturalism, since revelation presupposes a supernatural being as its source. Pantheism, which holds that the physical universe is God (in a sense that we discussed earlier in this book), and panentheism, which holds that the universe is the body of God and is pervaded by a divine spirit or intelligence, have little need for revelation, since that would amount to God talking to himself. This is because in pantheism and panentheism, humans are part of God.

Versions of polytheism that lack a creator of the universe cannot make use of general revelation since there is no "artist" whose mark has been left on the cosmos. Polytheism is typically replete with divine-human interaction, though: The emphasis is on special revelation. Versions of polytheism that have an omnipotent creator who is sovereign over all other creatures, natural and supernatural, should perhaps be viewed as monotheistic religions that contain additional incorporeal beings (like the angels of Zoroastrianism, Christianity, and Islam). Theism can utilize both forms of revelation, though Scripture is often emphasized as the most readily available revelation. The major theistic religions—Zoroastrianism, Judaism, Christianity, and Islam—all emphasize the importance of their Scriptures.[9]

Since deism holds that God is not presently involved with his creation, there's no motive for deism to believe that God is currently revealing himself to humanity. However, since deism does believe that God created the universe, general revelation plays a role in deistic theology. Deists believe that you can discern God's existence, some of his attributes, and some aspects of his plan for his creation by looking at the world around us.

Faith

In addition to revelation, some people view faith as a source of religious knowledge. Some think that faith complements reason, while others think it can be a substitute for reason, and some think it is superior to reason. But

9. Although popular Hinduism is polytheistic, there are monotheistic strains of Hinduism that view all the Hindu gods as different appearances of the one God, who is often given the name Brahman. Advaita Hinduism is metaphysically monistic and could be interpreted as panentheistic.

faith is a tricky issue because the word is used in different ways by different people.[10] For example,

- Faith can refer to a set of beliefs that's central to a religion, as when people say "keep the faith" as an exhortation to stay true to your religious beliefs. Used this way, faith is not understood as the *source* of the beliefs but rather as the *body* of beliefs.
- Faith can be used as a fideistic, non-evidentialist way of justifying a belief (as discussed in chapter 7). Sometimes when you ask someone how he or she knows something, the answer given is "I know it by faith." Here the speaker probably isn't thinking of faith as the source of the belief. Instead, she is using it as a way of justifying the belief. In effect, the person is saying something like "I'm convinced it's true, and that's all the proof I need."[11]
- Faith can refer to commitment to a belief that you view as important but that you aren't presently able to defend rationally.[12] You have probably had the experience of someone presenting a good argument against something that you believe, but you feel like your belief is true anyway, even though at the time you don't know how to respond to the argument. Sometimes you later learn of a cogent response and are reassured that you were right.
- Faith can be an expression of trust. If I tell you that I have faith in you, I'm not saying that I believe you exist. I'm saying that I trust you (in whatever sense is appropriate to the occasion). For example,

---

10. See James Kellenberger, "Three Models of Religious Faith," in *Contemporary Perspectives on Religious Epistemology*, ed. R. Douglas Geivett and Brendan Sweetman (Oxford University Press, 1993), 320–35. Kellenberger discusses seven different understandings of faith.
11. A word of caution about this argument: A strong feeling that something is true is not always good evidence that it actually is true. Many people have had strong feelings about things and then later found out that they were mistaken.
12. This is an example of the Principle of Belief Conservation. Some epistemologists argue that we are justified in continuing to believe something that coheres with the rest of our beliefs despite arguments against it due to the support that belief has from the rest of our beliefs. This relates to coherentism, which was discussed in chapter 7.

> the Bible tells a story in which God commands Abraham to sacrifice his son Isaac on an altar. Abraham obeys, showing he trusts God not to tell him to do something he shouldn't. He trusts that God will make everything work out (and he does—God stops Abraham at the last minute). Subsequent biblical writers take this as a paradigm of faith. Abraham's faith wasn't his belief that God exists; it was his belief that God is trustworthy even when his commands don't make sense to us.

In the second of these four ways, faith is used in place of reason and evidence. This understanding of faith sees it as a "leap in the dark," as believing something based simply on willpower. Some people who view faith this way distrust reason and see faith as a better alternative. They may believe that faith is more intuitive and thus more directly in touch with reality, or they may view faith as coming directly from God. A problem with this view is that when two people with incommensurable beliefs both appeal to faith, there's no way to know who is right. Adjudication between competing beliefs requires the use of reason; any approach that disavows the use of reason is automatically at a disadvantage.

Faith does not have to be understood as being in opposition to reason. In the third understanding of faith, it is believing something in anticipation that good reasons are forthcoming. In the fourth way, faith is a type of trust rather than a type of belief, and reason and experience often lay the foundation for it. In Abraham's case, he trusted God due to his many past experiences in which God was found to be trustworthy.

In none of these uses of "faith" is it the source of our beliefs. It has more to do with justification of beliefs. Let's examine that next.

Justified, True Religious Beliefs

Let's reserve the term "religious belief" for beliefs involving the supernatural. Beliefs about where the nearest synagogue is, when the church services will be held, who the local imam is, and other beliefs that don't have a supernatural element aren't epistemically different from non-religious beliefs. On the other hand, beliefs that have a supernatural element are quite different from ordinary beliefs, for they are about something that transcends the natural world in a way that separates the object of belief from our sensory perceptions and frustrates inductive arguments based on our everyday experiences. Understood this way, religious beliefs are in a class of their own, and knowledge of their objects could involve a unique epistemology.

Traditionally, epistemologists have recognized two possible sources of beliefs: sensory experience and abstract reasoning. Through reason we can gain knowledge of the laws of logic, mathematical truths, geometric principles, and self-evident truths such as our own existence (remember Descartes' *cogito ergo sum*). Sensory experience is what gives us knowledge of the physical world.

Because religious beliefs are often about things that transcend the physical world, one might expect sensory experience to be ineffectual at producing religious knowledge. That could be a mistake, for the supernatural and natural may intersect. For example, it's common in polytheistic religions for the gods to appear in physical form and to speak to humans. In theistic religions, God created the world and sometimes intervenes in it. Theists typically hold that we can infer at least some things about God from examining his creation, and they believe that we can experience God's interventions as miracles and can at least sometimes recognize them as divine acts. If either of these points is correct, then the divide between the natural and the supernatural is not unbridgeable.

Returning to knowledge gained from pure reason, some theists believe that we can deduce God's existence and some truths about his nature without appealing to the senses. We'll discuss such *a priori* analyses of the nature of God in the next chapter, and we'll discuss an *a priori* argument for God's existence in the chapter on theistic apologetics.

A priori means "prior to experience." ***A priori*** knowledge does not come from our sensory experiences. In contrast, ***a posteriori*** knowledge is knowledge that follows from experiences. *A priori* beliefs can be justified by the thought process that produced them. *A posteriori* beliefs can be justified by the experiences that produced them. The thought process or the experience serves as the evidence that supports the belief.

You may be wondering whether all beliefs need to be supported by evidence. That's complicated, but the short answer is "maybe not, but it depends on what you mean by 'evidence.'" In a previous chapter we discussed foundationalism, coherentism, pragmatism, and reliabilism as strategies for justifying beliefs. These utilize evidence, each in a different way. Foundationalism begins with some basic, foundational belief and infers other beliefs from it. For example, let's say that I feel cold. That's a foundational belief or a **basic belief**, a belief that's not inferred from any other belief. What evidence do I have that it's true? Well, I don't really have any evidence: I just feel cold. Hence, this belief isn't supported by any evidence. That does not mean that it's not justified, though. It's sort of self-justifying, for it is the evidence of its own truthfulness.

This interesting observation leads us to ask what other sorts of beliefs can properly be considered basic. Immediately two types of beliefs come to mind: those that are a direct result of sensory experiences (such as feeling cold) and those that are self-evidently true (like the laws of logic and rules of math). Additionally, some people think that belief in God is properly basic. For example, the Protestant Reformer John Calvin believed that everyone is born with an innate sense that there is a God. He termed this the *sensus divinitatis* ("sense of the divine"). In recent decades a whole school of thought, called Reformed epistemology, has developed around this concept.[13]

Could belief in God be properly basic? Belief in God is not likely to be a direct result of sensory experience. It might be self-evidently true, though. We believe in the laws of logic and the rules of math because we intuitively sense that they are true, and Reformed epistemologists argue that some people may intuitively sense that God exists. They argue that God implanted awareness of his existence in the minds of at least some, and perhaps all, people. If we grant the existence of an omnipotent God, then it certainly seems possible that he could plant such an idea in people's minds. However, that he has actually done so may be called into question because many people around the world lack belief in God. Some Reformed

13. Leading figures in this movement include Alvin Plantinga, William Alston, and Nicholas Wolterstorff, among others.

epistemologists claim that such people are suppressing the belief, but skeptics reject this response as ***ad hoc***.[14]

In the end, although there are some differences, it seems that religious knowledge is generally similar to non-religious knowledge in many ways. In order to claim that you know something, you need to have a belief, it needs to be true, and you need good reason for believing that it's true. This is, to no small degree, one of the main motivations behind this book: the authors' desire to help the readers clarify their religious beliefs (and disbeliefs), evaluate the justification for them, and in doing so increase the likelihood that they are true, and as a result, increase the likelihood that they constitute actual knowledge.

14. *Ad hoc* is Latin for "for this purpose only." A theory is *ad hoc* if it seems to have been created merely to save some other theory from being disproved.

QUESTIONS TO PONDER

- Are there benefits to looking into religions using the tools of philosophy?
- If you believe in God, how transcendent do you think he is?
- What do you think faith is? Why do you see it that way?
- Do you think that people have an innate knowledge of God? If you do, how do you account for the fact that some people don't seem to?

TERMS TO KNOW

- empiricism
- transcendence
- general revelation
- special revelation
- faith
- fideism
- *a priori*
- *a posteriori*
- basic belief
- *ad hoc*

FOR FURTHER READING

DePoe, John M. and Tyler Dalton McNabb, eds. *Debating Christian Religious Epistemology: An Introduction to Five Views on the Knowledge of God.* Bloomsbury Academic, 2020. While not an introduction to religious epistemology, this is an interesting discussion of five different approaches as they are exemplified within Christianity.

Fuqua, Jonathan, John Greco, and Tyler McNabb, eds. *The Cambridge Handbook of Religious Epistemology*. Cambridge University Press, 2023. This is an advanced introduction to religious epistemology.

Lebens, Samuel. *Philosophy of Religion: The Basics*. Routledge, 2023. This is a very readable introduction to philosophy of religion.

Peterson, Michael, William Hasker, Bruce Reichenbach, and David Basinger, eds. *Philosophy of Religion: Selected Readings*. 5th ed. Oxford, 2014. This is an anthology of primary readings that complements the introductory text by the same authors.

Peterson, Michael, William Hasker, Bruce Reichenbach, and David Basinger. *Reason & Religious Belief: An Introduction to the Philosophy of Religion*. 5th ed. Oxford University Press, 2012. This is a more advanced and more comprehensive introduction to philosophy of religion.

Van Til, Cornelius. *A Christian Theory of Knowledge*. 2nd ed. Edited by K. Scott Oliphint. Westminster Seminary Press, 2023. This is Reformed epistemology.

13

THE NATURE OF GOD

SYNOPSIS

Once one determines if and how knowledge about God is achieved, the next key question in religious philosophy relates to what God is like. This chapter will explore God's nature and characteristics.

DIALOGUE

Zach missed his conversations with Samantha once he was back in Greenfield, but she'd made it clear that her religious convictions wouldn't allow her to develop a romantic relationship with an atheist. He wasn't sure he understood, but he respected her enough not to push. They could be friends, and she had certainly given him a lot to think about. In fact, her "God talk" had intrigued him, and he came home determined to take up the subject with his friends.

As he drove home from the lab, his phone rang. He was surprised to see Tristan Lancaster's name on the phone screen. When things had unraveled for Mayor Lancaster, Zach had considered reaching out to Tristan, but they hadn't been that close for a while, and he was afraid Tristan would think he was trying to get inside information.

"Zach! How are you, buddy?" Tristan asked, sounding surprisingly cheerful given the events of the past year. "It sounds like you're driving. Is this a bad time?"

"Not at all! Good to hear from you. What's up?"

"I heard a rumor that my old high school friend was getting into rarefied air," he said. "Is it true that you've been working with the FBI?"

How was his work with the FBI in the rumor mill? It was strange that someone he hadn't talked to in years would ask about it. "Where did you hear that? I'm just curious, you know . . ."

"Oh, I still have friends at the courthouse, and someone mentioned that a young chemist from Bradley Pharmaceuticals was helping the FBI national lab in Maryland. I just thought it might be you, and a friend in the FBI confirmed it," Tristan answered, nonchalant.

Zach was uncomfortable. He was under strict orders from the FBI not to talk about his work with them, and yet one of their agents had told a civilian with no apparent connection about it? But rather than be abrupt with an old friend, Zach decided to try a diversion.

"How have you been, Tristan? I thought about you a lot when, well, you know, when things went down. That had to be, uh, a tough time," Zach said somewhat clumsily.

"There are things about that situation the public doesn't know, Zach," his voice still light. "Dad's not the villain everyone is saying. I believe he'll be exonerated eventually. I've still got my insurance agency, and I haven't lost any business over the scandal."

Tristan's tone cooled a bit. "Anyway, I'm fine. But thank you for asking. And judging by your attempt to sidetrack me," Tristan went on, "I guess the FBI thing is true—but you don't have to say anything. I'm happy for you, man. That's a cool opportunity."

"I'm glad things are going well for you, Tristan. It's been good to hear from you," Zach said, but he wasn't quite sure that was an honest statement.

* * *

The philosophy group had to meet on a Friday night because Angelo was still working extra hours and was tied up Thursday night. Fortunately, Suresh had a rare Friday evening free. Zach had texted earlier in the week to arrange the meeting and asked everyone to give some thought to the general topic of God. *If there is a God, what is he like?* he texted the group. The others were shocked that Zach had brought this topic up, but they were eager to discuss.

After warm hugs all around, they took their usual seats and caught up a bit on life before Zach explained why he'd brought this topic up.

"During my time away, I met someone who challenged my thinking about the existence of a deity."

"Hmm," Angelo said. "I haven't been able to challenge your thinking about God all this time. She must be pretty."

Zach laughed. "As a matter of fact, she is."

The entire group laughed.

"But we're just friends. Our relationship is strictly platonic, which is ironic since we mostly spent our time discussing philosophy."

"Sure you did . . ." Angelo joked, but Hannah poked him and he quieted down.

Zach could take a little teasing.

"Did you guys have time to think through the questions I sent you earlier this week? If there were a God, what would he be like? Could there be more than one God? Is the idea of God coherent? So many people, including my new friend, Samantha, seem to find the idea compelling, and I'd like to learn more."

"How about this?" Hannah said, lifting her hand a little. "Have any of you been to the Carolyn Bradley Museum of Religious Antiquities in Coopersville?"

The men shook their heads.

"Carolyn Bradley was the wife of the founder of Zach's company."

Zach stuck his chin out in surprise. He didn't know anything about this.

"After her husband made a lot of money in business, she began collecting religious artifacts and eventually founded this museum. I've been told it's fantastic and read that it features information about world religions and their conceptions of deity. That could be a fun way to do our research."

"I could go tomorrow," Angelo said.

"So could I," Suresh said.

"If that works for you, Hannah, let's do it," Zach said.

Hannah checked the museum's hours on her phone. "It's open from ten to five. Want to meet here at nine to grab coffee and head over about nine thirty?"

"Sounds like a plan!" Zach said. "I'll drive."

* * *

The museum was in a converted Victorian mansion. After paying the entrance fee, the friends consulted the little map the attendant had provided. The museum was laid out to feature various religions and religious philosophies.

The first room had antiquities from various ancient civilizations that featured pantheons of gods and goddesses.

"I've read some of the Greek myths, and I've always found these gods and goddesses a bit amusing," Zach said as they looked at the displays. "They obviously aren't all-powerful or all-knowing, and often they aren't particularly moral. I don't suppose they have any relation to what you worship, do they, Angelo?"

Angelo laughed. "Definitely not. The Christian conception of God is different from these ancient superheroes in almost every conceivable way. These 'gods' seem to me like projections of human wishful thinking. The stories do make for fun literature though."

The next room they entered was dedicated to the Indian subcontinent. After reading a plaque that gave some basic information about Hinduism, they drifted around the room looking at statues, trinkets, and some beautiful artwork that portrayed various deities.

"So is Hinduism another example of polytheism?" Zach asked.

"I'm not sure . . ." Suresh said. "I think it's more complicated."

Hannah motioned to the guys. "Here's a table explaining the Hindu notion of deity."

As they peered at the table, Zach said, "Wow. It *is* complicated."

All around the room was evidence of popular polytheistic worship. Many Indian people seemed to function religiously as though they worshiped many different gods. But this display indicated that a philosophical Hinduism recognizes all the different gods and goddesses as manifestations of one all-powerful, all-knowing God called Brahman.

"In the philosophical sense, I guess Hinduism is monotheistic," Angelo said. "That surprises me. I wonder if most Hindus realize that. Do they worship Brahman as a personal God?"

Hannah was still reading. "Let's see . . . It looks like most do not. Most

Hindus view Brahman as something like unlimited energy, a supreme reality, but not a person."

The next room was devoted to Buddhism. Suresh was especially fascinated by the exhibits. He hadn't realized how diverse Buddhism was in different parts of Asia. They didn't linger in this room once they discovered that Buddhism doesn't officially endorse any god.

The next room was different from the previous ones. Rather than having a geographic identity, the room was devoted to philosophical views of God and religion. As they walked around the exhibits, electronic displays highlighted various religious philosophers with brief explanations of their thinking: Plato, Boethius, Anselm, Baruch Spinoza, John Locke, G. W. Leibniz, Ralph Waldo Emerson, Charles Hartshorne, and others.

The key religious options were deism (some of Locke's followers), pantheism (Spinoza and Emerson), and panentheism (Hartshorne). To maximize their time—and have a little fun—they decided to divvy up the options: Angelo looked for information on deism, Hannah pursued pantheism, and Suresh worked on panentheism, which he'd never heard of. Zach wandered around the room reading everything. After about forty-five minutes, they gathered in a common area and quietly debriefed about their observations.

"Deism has some things in common with my theistic tradition," Angelo began. "Deists' heyday was in the eighteenth century, and they were active during the Enlightenment. In Britain, many of them were followers of John Locke, although he doesn't fit neatly in their camp. Some of the French philosophers, like Voltaire, are probably best described as deists, and deism was influential in colonial America. Thomas Paine, who wrote *Common Sense*, as well as founders like Ben Franklin, Thomas Jefferson, and James Madison, were inclined to deism. Deism never became popular or captured any major organized religions."[1]

"Doesn't *deo* just mean 'god' in Latin?" Zach asked. "Do deists have specific views about the nature of God?"

"They view God as an infinite, sovereign being who created the world.

1. See https://moderndeist.org/ and https://www.deism.com/ for further information. The latter organization has as its motto: "God gave us reason, not religion."

But he made the world so perfect that he does not need to intervene in its workings. The world is governed by natural law. We shouldn't anticipate miracles or other divine interventions because such acts would imply that his creation project was flawed."

"Hmm. Otherwise, what is the deist God like?"

"He has many of the same attributes—that's what we generally call the characteristics of a divine being—as the Christian God. He is omnipotent, omnipresent, eternal, unchanging, and transcendent. He is personal in the sense that creation was a result of a decision on his part, but he doesn't exercise his personhood within creation, something theologians refer to as *immanence*. That's a significant difference from the God of theists," Angelo looked at the notes he'd taken in his small notebook. "If that seems like a minor difference, keep in mind that it entails the God of deism not revealing himself through Scripture, not entering the world through incarnation, not providing salvation from sin or sin's effects, and not desiring a relationship with his creatures. It's a massive difference."

"Why have a god at all if he's just going to sit on the sidelines and watch all the pain and suffering without getting involved?" Hannah asked, somewhat rhetorically.

Angelo turned to Hannah. "What can you tell us about pantheism?"

"*Pan* means 'all,'" Hannah said, "and that points toward pantheism's key idea: God is everything. He is comprised of all the matter and energy in the universe."

Zach cleared his throat. "My scientific naturalism believes that matter and energy are all that exist. For all we know, they have existed forever. So what's the difference between naturalism and pantheism?"

"Naturalists believe that the universe is made up of a huge number of distinct objects that are connected only by natural law. Pantheists believe that everything together makes up one massive entity, God. We are all connected in some kind of spiritual bond. It may sound like naturalism at first," Hannah said, "but from what I learned, it views the world in a very different way. The universe isn't just to be studied but to be worshiped."

Suresh said, "While we were in the Buddhist room, I ran across one of the exhibits about Vajrayana Buddhism, which departs from mainstream

Buddhist teaching. It says the world is spiritual, almost like a God. So it's yet another form of pantheism."[2]

"Why would I want to deify nature?" Zach asked.

"One of your problems with naturalism," Angelo said, "seems to be the fact that matter and energy is eternal, isn't it? Would it help if matter and energy formed an eternal being?"

"Hmm. I hadn't thought of that," Zach said, pondering this idea for a moment. "I'm not sure the mathematical problems of energy and matter being eternal are solved by putting a deity sticker on them. Something to think about though."

Zach asked Hannah if she had any other insights on pantheism to share.

"I guess it should be obvious, but the pantheist God isn't personal. In that sense, it's very different from the conception of God in deism and theism."

Everyone turned to Suresh.

"Let's hear about panentheism. I'd never heard of it," Zach said, "so I'm looking forward to your discoveries."

"I wasn't familiar with it either. A German scholar named Krause coined the term in 1828 while trying to reconcile monotheism and pantheism. If *pantheism* means all is God, *panentheism* means all is in God."

"What's the difference?" Angelo asked.

"In pantheism, as Hannah explained, the universe is God. But that approach doesn't allow God to be a personal spirit. Panentheists argue instead that the universe is God's body. In addition to this material body, God has a spiritual nature that pervades the universe. So everything is *in God* rather than everything being God."

"If this divine spirit is so closely identified with the universe, how is it a good being? As Hannah pointed out, there's a lot of bad stuff in the world. With pantheism, I guess bad stuff being part of God falls into the category of 'it is what it is'—there's no divine mind to be aware of it. But this panentheistic God seems to have bad stuff as part of him, and he doesn't do anything about it. Is that right?" Zach asked.

---

2. For an explanation of this variety of Buddhism, see D. T. Suzuki, *An Introduction to Zen Buddhism* (Lightning Source, 2013).

"That's one of the criticisms of this view," Suresh said. "I think proponents argue that God is growing and changing over time, so the problems you're pointing out are actually opportunities for improvement."

Zach looked down at the museum map. "It looks like there are three more large rooms: Judaism, Christianity, and Islam. We could spend quite a while going through them."

"The good news," Angelo said, "is that all three are monotheistic, or simply theistic. Christianity's God is Trinitarian, but we don't have to address that difference, even though it's very important to Christians."

"From my upbringing in Christianity, Christians say Jesus is God but still insist on one God, right?" Hannah said.

"Yes, exactly. Trinitarianism is crucial for us, but Jews and Muslims think it undermines monotheism. Christians are not arguing for three Gods though: We are firm monotheists. We believe that the Bible portrays the one God as existing in three persons, the Trinity. It's one of the deepest mysteries of our faith," Angelo said.

"I agree with your initial proposal," Zach said. "Let's not get that involved in Christian theology right now. I am interested in the fact that three of the most prominent world religions have opted for theism. What are its advantages?"

"Do you remember earlier when I mentioned the notion of attributes?" Angelo asked. "An attribute of God isn't any characteristic but rather something essential to God's being. For instance, the Christian God created the world, but most Christians don't believe that God *had to* create the world in order to be God. So creating isn't an attribute. It might be useful to come up with a list of attributes and see how the different options for the nature of God relate to them."

"How would we make that kind of list?" Suresh asked.

Hannah motioned to the other rooms they hadn't been to yet. "I bet divine attributes are addressed in the rooms devoted to the three great monotheisms," Hannah said. "Do you want to spread out, jot down the examples we find in the exhibits, and reconvene at the museum coffee shop to discuss?"

"Great plan!" Zach said. "Let's meet there in about an hour."

* * *

The four friends gathered in the museum coffee shop, called Sacred Grounds, purchased drinks, and began to compare notes. They came up with a list of attributes pulled from the theism exhibits. They then decided to test each version of deity for each attribute.

Hannah read the list. "Omnipotence, having all power; omniscience, having all knowledge; and omnipresence, being everywhere in space and time."

"Polytheism? No to all three," Zach said. "Pantheism and panentheism? Yes, since all power and knowledge would reside in the universe, right?"

The others agreed.

"Deism and theism? Yes. The omnis don't differentiate much, except to rule out polytheism."

"Transcendent, which means he surpasses the universe, existing beyond it," Hannah said.

"Polytheism?"

"They operate within the universe and are limited in power and knowledge. I think that would rule out transcendence," Suresh said.

"Pantheism? Clearly not," Zach answered himself. "But what about panentheism?"

"Even though panentheists believe that God has a spirit," Suresh said, "he doesn't transcend the universe because the universe is his body. So no, I don't think so."

"Deism and theism? Definitely." Zach was on a roll. "Let's just do a couple more. Obviously, we can each explore this more whenever we want."

"Immanent, which means present and active in the universe."

"Polytheism? Sure. Pantheism? Present, certainly. But active?" Zach asked.

"I think pantheists intend for their God to be immanent since everything that happens in the universe is God acting," Hannah said.

"Same deal with panentheism," Suresh said. "Immanence definitely applies."

"What about deism, Angelo?"

"As I understand it, that's tricky. The God of deism certainly could involve himself in the universe, but he chooses not to. So I'd say no to immanence. But theism is a definite yes. Theists believe that is a major advantage of monotheism over deism; the theistic God intervenes in a broken world to make things right."

Zach looked at his watch. The museum was closing soon. "I guess we should head out."

How interesting to spend almost an entire day learning and thinking about the nature of God.

THEORY

The museum excursion gave the four friends opportunity to investigate the nature of God. The remainder of this chapter will explore God's characteristics, called attributes, in a more systematic fashion.

In the preceding chapter we wrote about the use of reason and experience in gaining religious knowledge. Along the way, we introduced the terms "special revelation" and "general revelation." People have a lot of different ideas about what God is like, ideas inherited from their families, drawn from popular culture, absorbed from books, and so on. Some of these ideas are incompatible with each other. For example, Christians believe that Jesus is God incarnate, while Jews and Muslims reject this idea. Here's one place where it would be really useful to have a direct message from God (special revelation). And perhaps we do!

However, each major religion has its own claimant to the status of special revelation: Hinduism has the Vedas, Upanishads, and associated texts, Judaism has the Hebrew Bible, Christianity has its Bible (the Hebrew Bible plus the New Testament), Islam has the Koran, and so forth. Perhaps a careful, objective analysis of the arguments for and against each of these claimants would be able to uncover which is the true word of God. However, that would be a lengthy project. Therefore in this chapter, instead of appealing to special revelation, we are going to appeal to general revelation. In other words, we're going to use reason and the natural world to try to figure out what God (or the gods) is (or are) like.

When talking about God's attributes, we use specific terms that aren't commonly used in everyday speech. Let's list and define some of those up front.

- Aseity: the property of being self-existent (not being created by or dependent on anything else)
- Eternality: the property of existing at all times, past, present, and future
- Incorporeal: the property of not being physical
- Immanent: the property of being present and active in the universe
- Transcendent: the property of surpassing and being beyond everything else that exists
- Personal: the property of being a conscious individual with thoughts, feelings, and volition
- Immutable: the property of being unchangeable in essence
- Omniscient: the property of being all-knowing
- Omnisapient: the property of being all-wise
- Omnipotent: the property of being all-powerful
- Omnipresent: the property of being everywhere at all times
- Omnibenevolent: the property of always willing the good
- Holy: the property of having a perfect moral nature
- Free: the property of being self-directed

Polytheism

We'll work through the various understandings of God systematically, progressing from the more modest views to those that are more expansive. Some versions of polytheism include a pantheon of finite gods. For example, **henotheism** teaches that many gods exist, but each is limited to a specific geographical area. Another example is the Norse gods, with Odin as their powerful but not omnipotent king. In today's vernacular, we might term such beings "superheroes" rather than gods: They are much more powerful than humans, but they're not omnipotent, omniscient, and omnipresent. In ancient Greek polytheism, Zeus is the greatest of the Olympians, but even he is not omnipotent, nor did he create the other gods.

Inasmuch as theism generally understands God to be a perfect being who is sovereign over his creation and maximal in his attributes, polytheisms that see God as the most powerful god among many other gods but not maximal in his attributes are significantly different from theism. On the other hand, some versions of polytheism include a pantheon of gods that contains one god who is supreme over all the others. This form of polytheism can be similar to versions of theism that include beings that are more powerful than humans but less powerful than God, such as the angels and demons of Judaism and Christianity. However, if the lesser gods are viewed as co-eternal with God rather than being created by him, or if they are viewed as worthy of worship, that diminishes the similarity to classical theism.

Hinduism is a possible example of God-centered polytheism. While popular Hinduism is often genuinely polytheistic, philosophical Hinduism views all the gods of the Hindu pantheon as different appearances of Brahman, who is the source of everything that exists. Brahman is omniscient, omnipotent, and omnipresent.

Polytheism has certain strengths. For one, it is metaphysically dualistic, so it shares in the strengths of a dualistic worldview. These include facilitating belief in abstract objects and immaterial human minds. The latter facilitates explaining out-of-body experiences and some other parapsychic phenomena and facilitates belief in free will and life after the death of the body. None of these advantages will seem like strengths to a physicalist, of course.

Polytheism also faces challenges. For starters, if none of the gods is the creator of everything else, then the worldview fails to explain how the universe came into existence. If polytheism attempts to avoid that problem by asserting that the universe and all the gods are eternal, another problem arises: Things that are eternal are eternal because it's not possible for them to not exist (i.e., they have necessary existence). But neither the components that make up the universe nor the gods of polytheism seem to be things that must necessarily exist, since we can coherently conceive of them not existing.[3] So again we have a failure to explain their existence. If, on the other hand, polytheism says that one of the gods is an eternal, omnipotent being that exists necessarily and that created all the others, it is actually theism.

Another challenge for polytheism involves abstract objects. Since polytheism is a metaphysically dualistic worldview, it facilitates belief in

3. This argument utilizes the distinction between **necessary existents** and **contingent existents**. Contingent existents are things that exist but could conceivably not exist. Necessary existents are things that cannot not exist; they must exist. Possible examples of necessary existents include time and necessary truths like the principles of math and the laws of logic.

abstract objects. Therefore, polytheists do not have to make recourse to nominalism, as do naturalists. However, if polytheism does not believe in an eternal creator-god, then conceptualism is not an option. That leaves Platonic realism as the best option. However, realism asserts that there are eternal and unchanging moral truths, which sets up a situation wherein there is a moral authority higher than the gods. On the positive side, that provides an objective moral standard to guide the gods' behavior, but it also undermines their sovereignty, since it entails a moral authority higher than the gods.

Pantheism

Pantheism is a more exalted view of God that holds that there is only one God and he (or it) is maximal in all his attributes. That means that God is viewed as having all his attributes to the greatest extent possible. God is omnipotent, which means that he has the maximum amount of power possible. That could be an infinite amount of power, but it does not necessarily have to be infinite: The maximum amount of power possible could be less than infinite. Whatever the maximum possible is, that's what God has. The same thing is true about God's knowledge: It is maximal, which means that God knows everything that can possibly be known. If there is a very large but finite number of facts that can be known, then that's how much God knows; but if there is an infinite number of knowable facts, then God knows an infinite number of things.

Pantheism views God as the physical universe. The universe is God, and God is the universe. God is all that exists, and all the things that exist go together to make up God. This is a physicalist view of God and isn't all that different from naturalism. Both views see the physical universe as all that exists. The difference is that pantheism sees the universe as a single, maximal entity, while naturalism sees the universe as merely a collection of finite objects.

On pantheism, the universe contains all the energy that exists, and therefore, the universe is omnipotent. Similarly, it contains all the knowledge and wisdom that exists, and therefore, it is omniscient and omnisapient. Because the universe is all that exists, the universe is in every place that exists; therefore, it is omnipresent.

Working our way through the other attributes on our list, pantheism sees God as self-existent, immanent, and immutable in his essence. It does not see God as incorporeal, transcendent, or holy, since the universe is physical, immanent, and contains evil. If the universe is eternal, then God is eternal. The universe as a whole isn't personal, though it contains persons, so God has aspects of personality and impersonality. In the final analysis, pantheism is closer to naturalism than to the other views of God that we discuss in this chapter.

Important examples of pantheism include Orphism and Stoicism in ancient Greece, the seventeenth-century Jewish philosopher Baruch Spinoza in Holland, and a slew of nineteenth-century intellectuals such as Wordsworth and the early Coleridge in Britain; Fichte, Schelling, and Hegel in Germany; and Whitman, Emerson, and Thoreau in the United States. In the East, there are pantheistic (as well as non-pantheistic) versions of both Hinduism and Buddhism.

Deism

Deism is the view that a maximal and personal god exists and is the creator of all else, but he is completely transcendent and does not interact with his creation. Like polytheism, deism holds that God is distinct from the universe and is personal, able to think, feel, act, and have relationships with other sentient beings. Like pantheism, deism holds that God is self-existent, immutable, and maximal in his attributes. Therefore, he is omniscient, omnipotent, and omnisapient. He's also omnipresent, in a way, but that requires careful nuance.

Pantheism views God as physical, and it views God as omnipresent because he physically fills every space in the entire universe (after all, he *is* the universe). But deism views God as a spirit; hence, he's **incorporeal**.[4] Since he's incorporeal, he doesn't occupy *any* space in the universe. Therefore, we *could* say that, according to deism, God is *omniabsent*. And some deists would probably find that quite acceptable. However, when people talk about God being present somewhere—with the believers in their places of worship when they pray and celebrate his excellence, for example—they aren't saying that he's physically present, like some sort of invisible gas that fills the

---

4. *Incorporeal* means "without a body." *Corpus* is the Latin word for body; it's where we get the word *corpse* from.

room. They're saying that he is present with them in the sense that he sees their raised hands or their bowed heads, and he hears their words of praise, prayer, and rejoicing.[5] Hence, he's cognitively present with them: He knows everything that's going on in every part of the universe. Furthermore, it's not just his knowledge that extends everywhere—his power does too. God can "touch" anything, anywhere in the universe, at any time.

This sort of omnipresence is perfectly compatible with deism. Deists are sometimes accused of having an absentee God, but that's not completely fair, for the God of deism is epistemically and metaphysically present everywhere at all times. There's another sense in which the God of deism is absent, though. This is the main point that separates deism from classical theism. Even though deists view God as omnipotent, they do not believe that he actually intervenes in the universe. His power is present but inactive.

There are a number of factors that motivate deists to emphasize God's transcendence. Probably their most fundamental concern is that, if God needs to intervene in his creation, that suggests that there were flaws in his original plan for this world. They reason that since God is omniscient and omnisapient, he is able to design a world so well that it will run better than a clock: It will run perfectly and will never need a clockmaker to adjust, wind, lubricate, or repair it. And since God is omnipotent, he is able to execute that plan perfectly. Thus, if there really is an omniscient, omnisapient, omnipotent creator of this universe, then this universe must be running just how he wanted it to. Therefore, there's no need for God to intervene.

Skeptics of this line of reasoning might argue that creating free creatures (like humans) necessarily involves taking the risk that changes will be introduced into creation that will require or at least justify divine intervention. They could also argue that God designed a world in which it is necessary—or desirable—for him to intervene because he wants to have an ongoing relationship with his creation. Furthermore, one might look at all

5. This is anthropomorphic language. **Anthropomorphism** is when we use human terms to describe something that's not human. Here we're describing God's awareness of our actions and words as if it results from him having eyes that see and ears that hear, but since he's incorporeal, he doesn't, and yet he knows what we're doing anyway.

the problems in the world and wonder if they are even compatible with the idea of a flawless design perfectly executed.

But this brings up another possible motive for emphasizing God's transcendence: the problem of evil (POE). We'll talk more about the POE in the chapter on atheistic apologetics, so we'll keep it brief here. The basic issue is that if God is omniscient, omnipotent, omnibenevolent, and providentially active in this world, then there shouldn't be any evil in the world, since God would have the knowledge, power, and desire to do away with it. But then why is there evil in the world? Deism can respond to this by arguing that God has a policy of non-interference in creation: He is committed to letting us figure things out on our own.

Three more attributes complete the list. On deism, God is eternal, the creator of all else that exists, and free. Quite a few famous historical figures have embraced this understanding of the nature of God, such as Leonardo da Vinci; Benjamin Franklin; Adam Smith (the economist); Thomas Paine; Thomas Jefferson, James Madison, and James Monroe (founding fathers of the USA); Samuel Clemens (Mark Twain); and Neil Armstrong (the astronaut).

Theism

We'll follow the common practice of using "theism" as shorthand for **monotheism**, the belief that there is only one God. Most theists view God as the greatest possible being (GPB for short). St. Anselm, Archbishop of Canterbury, famously illustrated this when he characterized God as "something than which none greater can be thought."[6] This is called "classical theism."

If God exists, it's logical to suppose that he's the GPB. This is in part a semantic issue: When we use the word *God*, we could have in mind our creator without assuming that he is the GPB, but if there's another being who is more powerful, more knowledgeable, and wiser than our creator, shouldn't that being be called God instead? Likewise, if we use God to refer to a being who is the most intelligent but not the most powerful, or the most powerful

6. St. Anselm is one of the great medieval thinkers. This description of God can be found in Anselm, *Proslogion*, in *The Prayers and Meditations of Saint Anselm*, trans. Benedicta Ward (Penguin, 1986), 87.

but not the wisest, or the wisest but not the most holy, our preference for naming one of these God and not the others is arbitrary. The one choice that would not be arbitrary is if there is a being that is the greatest in all possible ways. Hence, it makes sense to reserve the term God for the GPB.

Returning to our list of divine attributes, theism affirms that God is self-existent, eternal, incorporeal, immanent and transcendent, personal, immutable, omniscient, omnisapient, omnipotent, omnipresent, omnibenevolent, holy, and free. There is discussion among theists about the correct understanding of some of these terms, though. For instance, while theists affirm that God is omnipotent, most also hold that there are some things that even God can't do. These fall into two categories: things that are logically impossible and things that go against God's nature. Examples of the former are making a square circle, creating a stone so heavy that he can't lift it, and creating a being more powerful than himself. Examples of the latter include sinning and ceasing to exist. The inability to do such things does not contravene God's omnipotence.

Similarly, there's discussion about whether God knows our choices before we make them, whether he exists within time or is atemporal, how an incorporeal God interacts with the physical world, and more. Such issues provide much for theists to think about.

Traditional Judaism, Christianity, and Islam are theistic religions. Important theists include Abraham (the Jewish patriarch), Jesus (the founder of Christianity), and Mohammed (the founder of Islam). Additionally, Zoroastrianism is a monotheistic religion (though there have been significant deviations from this throughout history); its founder was Zoroaster. As previously mentioned, philosophical Hinduism is also monotheistic, after a fashion. Hinduism doesn't have a founder, but Madhva is a very important advocate of monotheistic Hinduism.

Panentheism

Our final perspective on the nature of God is panentheism, which holds that the universe is the body of God and is infused by God's mind. This view is dualistic: It sees God as having both corporeal and incorporeal aspects. It can be viewed as combining theism and pantheism, theism contributing the incorporeal aspects and pantheism contributing the corporeal ones.

Panentheism is also like pantheism in that it views God as everything and everything as God. It differs from pantheism in that it does not subscribe to physicalism: Like theism, it is dualistic, affirming that reality contains both material and immaterial components. Consequently, it affirms that God contains both material and immaterial components. This sets it apart from pantheism and naturalism on the one hand and also from theism and deism on the other.

The God of panentheism is a maximal god. He is omniscient, omnisapient, omnipotent, and omnipresent. He is personal, unlike the god of pantheism. In a way, he is both immanent and transcendent. He is self-existent but not immutable, since the universe changes. Regarding eternality, God is as old as the universe—however old that is.

One strength of panentheism is that it clearly makes God omnipresent. Since the physical universe is the body of God, God is *physically* present everywhere. This is true for pantheism as well, but it's not true for polytheism, monotheism, or deism. Polytheism simply denies omnipresence, while theism and deism see God as non-physically omnipresent via his universal knowledge and power, which is a concept that's a little more difficult to grasp. Therefore, pantheism and panentheism have a simpler, more straightforward take on divine omnipresence.

On the other hand, on panentheism, God is not omnibenevolent, since he isn't working to overcome the evil in the world. Nor is he holy, since the world is God's body and includes much evil. Hence, while the God of panentheism possesses some features of the GPB, he lacks others.

Notable panentheists include the ancient Greek philosopher Heraclitus, possibly Baruch Spinoza (the Jewish philosopher), and the American philosopher Charles Hartshorne.

CONCLUSION

In this chapter we've examined the chief perspectives on the nature of God. We haven't been able to spend much time examining arguments for and against each perspective, but at least we've seen some of the strengths and weaknesses of each view. The question of the existence and nature of God is a foundational aspect of your worldview. What you believe about God will influence what you believe on many other topics. It's too important a question to leave up to your casual intuitions or the currents of the culture in which you live. Hence, we strongly recommend doing further reading in this area. As always, additional books are recommended below.

QUESTIONS TO PONDER

- What conception springs up in your mind when you hear the word "god"?
- Are you more inclined to think there is one god or many gods? Why?
- If you believe in one or more gods, do you think it makes the most sense to understand one of them as maximal, as a "greatest possible being"? Why, or why not?
- Which understanding of god—atheism, polytheism, monotheism, deism, pantheism, or panentheism—makes the most sense to you? Why?

TERMS TO KNOW

- henotheism
- aseity
- eternality
- incorporeal
- immanent
- transcendent
- personal
- immutable
- omniscience
- omnisapience
- omnipotence
- omnipresence
- omnibenevolence
- holy
- necessary existents
- contingent existents
- anthropomorphism
- theism
- polytheism
- monotheism
- deism
- pantheism
- panentheism

FOR FURTHER READING

McCall, Thomas H. *An Invitation to Analytic Christian Theology*. IVP Academic, 2015. This is an introductory text written from a Christian perspective.

Smart, Ninian. *Worldviews: Crosscultural Explorations of Human Beliefs*. 3rd ed. Prentice-Hall, 2000. This has become one of the standard texts on religious worldviews.

Taliaferro, Charles and Chad Meister. *Contemporary Philosophical Theology*. Routledge, 2016. This fairly advanced philosophical study discusses perspectives from many religions and takes a much closer look at the arguments than we were able to.

14

THEISTIC APOLOGETICS

SYNOPSIS

The next two chapters on philosophy of religion will make the cases for and against the nature of God. This involves both sides in a study known as apologetics. Chapter 14 will make a case for the existence of God, and chapter 15 will lay out a case against his existence.

DIALOGUE

Zach woke slowly. The disturbing dreams he'd had began to fade, and his brain started to register the date and time. It was Thursday morning around 5:30 a.m. At this time each morning, he pictured his body as a computer booting up after being in sleep mode overnight. He felt his mental processors kicking into high gear, and he half expected to hear the whirr of a computer cooling fan to dissipate the heat that he imagined his brain was radiating. Just then, the air conditioning kicked on. *Perfect*, he thought. A fitting ambient confirmation that he was a highly functioning computer gearing up for challenging computations.

Before he could set his feet on the floor, the memories of the past few weeks interrupted his robotic daydream. The train bombing, the political scandal, the human trafficking, and the specter of automatic and chemical weapons in their town. The world, and even the previously quiet hamlet of Greenfield, was increasingly troubling for Zach. He was committed to the idea that science and human evolution would eventually and inevitably bring progress, but he knew that such a vision of the future wasn't a linear ascent with no setbacks.

Dr. O and Samantha were confident that their belief in God was a better explanation of the world than natural selection. If he hadn't watched their behavior, had conversations with them, and seen how they grounded their work in the sciences in their belief in a personal and loving God who created the world and gave humans the commission to cultivate the world for his glory, he wouldn't give such beliefs much credence.

He'd read a quote by Thomas Nagel, an NYU law professor, who said about his fear of religion: "I speak from experience, being strongly subject to this fear myself: I want atheism to be true and am made uneasy by the fact that some of the most intelligent and well-informed people I know are religious believers."

It's not that Zach doubted his atheism per se. Rather, like Nagel, he was troubled that some very bright minds could still believe in God in the twenty-first century. He wanted to make sure he wasn't missing anything. Maybe there was an argument or piece of evidence he wasn't aware of. He'd always tried to give a fair hearing to alternative views, but he had to admit that his knowledge of Christianity and its main arguments for the truth were second-hand and not always from the most objective sources. How hadn't he searched for the best possible defense of the Christian faith up to this point? Was he afraid that Christianity might be true? No, of course not. But he couldn't be sure until he heard a quality defense of it by someone who knew what he was talking about. Maybe then he'd feel some peace of mind regarding his views.

* * *

When the four friends gathered again, Zach participated, but his attention was on the conclusion of their conversation. The group usually began to wind down after ninety minutes or so and almost always concluded before the two-hour mark. This evening was no different. As they began to discuss what they would cover at the next meeting, Zach jumped in.

"I know this will derail our schedule a bit, but something has been burning a hole in my mind."

"What are you thinking?" Hannah asked.

"Well, I've been thinking a lot about how you all have helped me sharpen my ideas about philosophy and in some cases have changed the way I think. One thing I haven't really contemplated completely, however, is the question of God. For many years, I was fine with simply leaving that question out of the picture, but I keep coming back to it over and over lately. I want to be sure I'm not overlooking any key arguments for the existence of God."

Zach nodded toward Angelo. "Some coworkers, as well as you, Angelo, have said things that have me thinking maybe I haven't heard the best arguments for or against God yet. I don't feel attracted to belief in God, but I also want to be sure that I don't reject belief in God without hearing a strong case for it. Angelo, I was hoping you'd be able to help me—and that Hannah and Suresh won't mind if we take some time to focus on this."

Zach's palms were sweaty. But he had no reason to be nervous.

"This is so surprising," Angelo said. "But I'd be happy to do this."

A thought struck Angelo. "Maybe after I present arguments for the existence of God, you could present an equally detailed case for atheism, just so we can all hear the best possible cases for both."

"I like that idea!" Suresh said. "I've never heard comprehensive arguments for either worldview."

"I'm all for it as well!" Hannah smiled brightly. "After all, what do we have to be afraid of? If we can't hear a strong case for either view without being bothered, can we really say we hold our beliefs firmly?"

Angelo was jotting down a few notes. "Can I have a couple weeks to prepare? I'll do a much better job if I have time to consult my pastor and some other Christians."

"Absolutely," Zach said. "And I'll do the same. I want to be sure we address the big questions fairly and intelligently."

"Okay then," Hannah said with smile. "This is going to be fun! See you all in two weeks."

* * *

Two weeks later, Angelo stood in line to get a coffee before heading to their table. He was excited and nervous at the same time. He would present a case for Christian theism, and Zach would present his defense of atheism the following week. Their friendship had grown so strong that the friends knew that the others would treat each other gently and with respect, even if they disagreed about a point.

Angelo settled in and pulled out his notes. "There are several ways to present an apologetic for the existence of a God."

Hannah interrupted. "What do you mean by *apologetic*? I'm guessing that doesn't mean apologizing for what you believe."

"No, not at all. *Apologetics* is taken from the Greek word *apologia*, which means 'a defense or a case for something.' Think of the arguments a defense attorney presents when his client has been charged with a crime."

"Ah, that's helpful."

"So, yes. There are several ways to argue for the existence of God. Some are more philosophical than others, but I'll try to present the major ways to do this. The five classical arguments for God go back to the Medieval period and are based purely on reason with no specific reference to the Bible. The idea is that anyone can arrive at the conclusion that God exists by applying rigorous reasoning. I'll mention just a couple of them and then talk about other ways to defend belief in the Christian God.

"The first argument basically says, 'Imagine the greatest possible being, greatest in every quality. That is God. If you can imagine anything greater, then your first thought wasn't great enough. God is that being about whom nothing greater can be conceived.'"

"Sorry to jump in so soon," Zach interrupted. "Just because you can *imagine* an extremely great being doesn't mean he exists."

"I agree," Suresh said. "I can imagine a rainbow unicorn with wings, but that doesn't mean it exists."

"Guys!" Hannah spoke sharply with just a hint of a smile. "Let him finish!"

"Hey, you interrupted first," protested Suresh.

"No problem." Angelo waved his hand and laughed. "The argument continues by saying that for anything to exist in reality is greater than for it to exist only in our minds, so the greatest possible being would necessarily have to actually exist to be the greatest. This doesn't mean we can imagine just anything, like a rainbow unicorn, but applies only to the greatest being overall."

"But how does any of this prove God?" Hannah couldn't help interrupting again.

"If you mean *prove* as in be irresistibly convincing for everyone, it doesn't." Angelo had asked his pastor the same question. "The point of this argument is simply that a truly greatest possible being would exist in reality and not just in our minds; therefore, it's entirely reasonable to believe in God. It is more of an argument or philosophical evidence than a proof."

"Okay, that is something to think about. Tell us another argument," Zach said.

"Another argument for the existence of God is related to the existence of the universe. If the universe had a beginning, which most scientists now believe, then something must have caused it. In fact, everything that had a beginning must be caused by something else, and the cause of the universe is God."

Angelo knew what was coming next.

"So what caused God?" Zach asked. This idea had crossed his mind before. He was sure it was the dagger in the heart of this argument.

"Good question. Christians believe that God is eternal, so he had no beginning and consequently no cause. He is self-existing. Everything else that exists has its genesis in him."

"That sounds like a cop-out if you don't mind me saying so," Zach said, his tone friendly.

"I don't mind at all. Those who ask that very question often think Christians are granting God an exception to the rule that everything that began to exist had a cause. But Christianity has always taught that God is the only one who is eternal. It's difficult to comprehend, but it's also difficult to escape the idea that *something* must be eternal. Otherwise, how would the something of existence ever get started since something cannot come from nothing?"

"But why can't something come from nothing?" Hannah asked.

"If you truly have nothing," Angelo said, "no elements, no chemicals, no physical material, not even time or space—how could something come from that?"

"Okay, I guess the nothing I'm thinking of isn't really nothing."

"Right. If something could suddenly come from truly nothing without a cause, how could we ever expect the universe to function in any predictable way?"

"You couldn't." Zach knew quite well that science depended on the uniform operation of the universe to act the same way every time.

"Exactly. Which brings us back to the argument that a self-existing, eternal God is the cause of everything that had a beginning. Otherwise, there is no good explanation for the origin of the universe."

Hannah looked at Zach. "Is that true? I always thought science had an answer for the origin of the universe."

Zach shifted in his chair. "I hate to admit it, but it's true. Although science can tell us much about the beginning of the universe and everything that exists now, the theories about the beginning of the universe all start with preexisting material of some kind. All the attempts to explain how something came from nothing actually begin with something, not nothing."

"That's one of the reasons why Eastern religion is so appealing to me," Suresh said. "Most forms believe in an eternal universe, which solves the problem of the question of beginnings."

"Except that science tells us the universe had a beginning," Zach countered.

"Yes, but what about other universes and realities beyond this one?"

"Guys, you're doing it again," Hannah said.

"This is fun," Angelo said, laughing. "I enjoy this banter and interaction."

"Me too," Suresh agreed.

"Please continue," Zach said.

"Not until I've refreshed my coffee," Angelo said, getting up to head to the counter.

* * *

After everyone had refilled their mugs and taken a restroom break, Angelo began.

"This argument about the origin of the universe easily transitions into the next one about the complexity and design of the universe. Not only is the universe incredibly intricate in its detail, but things seem to be designed for a purpose rather than being a result of a random process. That fits with the

Christian belief that God loves us and made the world for our good. Further, the complexity of the universe points to the fact that a creator would have to be intelligent beyond our comprehension. There are so many things in the natural world that we cannot duplicate, even with our best minds. This points to a creator."

"But why can't I simply believe that natural selection is the creator?" Zach asked. "Why should I believe that the creator is personal and is a god?"

"Well, many people do believe that," Angelo said. "But increasingly, some scientists—even those who don't believe in God—struggle to reconcile a random process with the seeming design found in nature. When we encounter something incredibly advanced like a space telescope or a nanobot, don't we automatically assume that a personal, rational being designed and built it? Why should we resort to an unintelligent explanation for even more complex things in nature?"

"I get it," Zach said. "Some scientists want to affirm some kind of intelligent source for the universe, so they resort to aliens as an explanation."

"No, they don't!" Hannah laughed out loud. "You're joking!"

"I'm dead serious," Zach said. "I don't go that far, but some do. I think they might be bothered by a lack of plausible explanation for the origin of the universe and want to credit someone or something with the beginning of it all."

"That's absurd. That simply pushes the question back a level—you have to ask where the aliens have their origin."

"I know," Zach said. "That's why I don't buy it as an explanation."

"I have a question," Suresh said, thinking about how the baby of some friends had died because of a birth defect. "While I can appreciate the intricate design in nature, aren't there also all kinds of things that point toward a breakdown as well, like mutations?"

"Well, that goes beyond the first plank of Christian teaching, the argument for design, but it fits with the second plank about the present world. After God created the world, the first man and woman sinned, and that brought a curse upon the world. Now everything in creation is affected. The Bible says that even nature groans to be restored to its original pristine condition."

"I see what you might call the effects of the curse constantly in my work," Hannah said. "Even though I don't believe the Bible, I can at least accept that part of the story."

"There are two more philosophical arguments," Angelo said. "The first is the fine-tuning argument, which says that life on Earth is so finely tuned that if any of almost two dozen factors were even slightly different, life here would be impossible. For example, if gravity, electromagnetic, and nuclear forces were any weaker or stronger, our present universe would have been impossible. Some of these constants could not differ from their present state in even the tiniest degree. If they did, the universe would either fly apart or collapse in on itself. Other factors include the thickness of the Earth's crust, the amount of water in the crust, the Earth's mass, the velocity of light, and more. The point of the argument is that the chances that life would be possible on Earth are so slim that they are very unlikely to exist without some intelligence directing them."

Everyone looked at Zach.

He nodded. "It's true. I'm not a cosmologist, but I remember discussions about fine-tuning while getting my master's. It's quite remarkable. Of course, my explanation for it is simply that given the age and vastness of the universe, chances are that life was bound to happen somewhere. But we can get into that in more detail when I present my case for atheism next week."

"The final philosophical argument," Angelo said, "is the moral argument that simply says that since a moral sense is universal, there must be a mind behind it. Morality isn't like a law of nature, such as gravity or the laws of thermodynamics. It is an internal sense that some things are good and some things are bad. Some thoughts, words, and actions are worthy of praise and contribute to the flourishing of life, and some thoughts, words, and actions are shameful and destructive to flourishing. It seems that a moral sense is universal, in that all recorded cultures have had a sense of morality. That makes sense if there is a holy God who has declared his will and made people in his image, possessing a sense of right and wrong."

The group fell silent for a moment.

"This last argument really challenges me," Hannah said. "I've seen so much that I would call evil that I cannot believe that morality is merely personal; otherwise my repulsion at evil would simply be my own taste or preference. It has to be more than just my dislike. I genuinely believe some things are wrong for everyone, even though that conflicts with my existentialism. This is the part of my former belief in God that I still hang on to."

Everyone stopped talking for a few moments as they contemplated the moral argument. It was clearly one of the most difficult questions in philosophy.

"You mentioned that there were other nonphilosophical arguments for God," Suresh said. "What are they? Believing in divine beings isn't a problem for me. But I gravitate toward the concept of multiple deities, which means Christianity's monotheism isn't an option."

"Well, there is the argument from miracles, which are a central belief in the Christian faith. But I have to acknowledge that other religions also believe in miracles, so that alone doesn't prove the existence of the Christian God. One miracle in particular serves as the ground for all Christian claims, and that is the resurrection of Jesus. Since his arrest, crucifixion, death, and empty tomb three days later have such significant historical evidence supporting them, they are often considered to be the prime historical case for Jesus being who he said he was—God in human form, Savior, and Messiah."

Angelo looked down at his notes. How could he articulate the connection between the historical events surrounding Jesus and the question at hand—the existence of God?

Zach picked up on it. "But the historicity and facts about Jesus have nothing to do with God's existence, so I don't see how that helps your case."

"I know what you're saying. The two may seem disconnected, yet because Christianity says that God's ultimate revelation of himself came in the incarnation—that is, the appearing of Jesus in history—the two are inextricably linked. We believe that the life, death, and resurrection of Jesus are the greatest proof not only of God's existence but also of his nature and his relationship with his creation, especially humans. So God's existence is more than the thirty-three years of Jesus' life, but it isn't less."

"This is such an impressive wealth of knowledge," Hannah said. "Any other evidence for God?"

"Yes," Angelo said after a pause, "and it's probably the most convincing to me. The first few arguments demonstrate that the existence of a God is a reasonable conclusion, I believe, and I find them convincing. But they don't require you to believe in an explicitly Christian God, simply a God who is beyond human understanding. As a result, you could use those arguments to support the existence of Allah or the god of the Deists, who wound up the clock of the world and walked away. He—or she, or it—might be super intelligent but maybe not infinite in his perfections."

"So what is this convincing argument?" Zach asked.

"It asks what kind of God would be necessary for the world in which we find ourselves. It moves beyond the general idea of a divine being to one that more specifically explains what kind of God is necessary for a world like ours. The Transcendental Argument for God—that's what it's called—says that apart from the Christian God, we cannot make sense of logic, knowledge, consciousness, and morals, among other things we presuppose in order to make sense of anything."

"Okay, you have my attention."

"Well, let's take logic, for example. Logic isn't dependent upon nature or anything physical, nor is it a physical reality. Logic is an abstract entity. It isn't the product of nature because if nature ceased to exist, then logic wouldn't be affected. It's not the product of human minds because most philosophers believe that logic existed before humans conceived of it. Yet clearly logic is something only comprehended by humans, who have the reasoning capacity that animals do not. Its genesis must be a mind—but not just any mind. It is a mind that created us to know truth and be able to hold it without contradiction.

"We are able to know anything because God made this world to be known. That is, the world is a revelation of what God wants us to know about himself, our world, and ourselves. He also made language so we can accurately communicate our knowledge of reality. Otherwise, how would we know if our language about external realities bore any resemblance to the reality?"

Zach had been writing down some notes while Angelo shared. "Thank you so much, Angelo. You offered ideas I've never heard or considered. And I'm glad to hear the arguments for God in a no-pressure environment from someone I know and trust. I hope I present my case for atheism with the same clarity and charity!"

"Yes, thank you, Angelo," Suresh said. "I also heard some arguments that were new to me and some questions that have me wondering how I would answer them. It was so intriguing for someone like me, who only marginally understood the Christian case for God."

Hannah also thanked Angelo. Then she turned to Zach. "So you're up for next time?"

"Yes, I am," Zach said with a smile. He knew he'd have to do his homework if he was going to be ready.

THEORY

In the dialogue, Angelo was rather informally attempting to do apologetics: He was attempting to make a case for theism. The English word "apologetics" comes from the Greek word *apologia* (ἀπολογία). It does not mean to apologize; it means to defend. An apologetic is a defense of a system of belief. There can be an apologetic for capitalism or socialism, for realism or idealism, for anarchy, monarchy, or democracy, etc. In this chapter we'll learn about theistic apologetics, which is the attempt to defend belief in the existence of God. In the next chapter we'll study atheistic apologetics, which is the attempt to defend the belief that God does not exist.

Arguments for God's existence are sometimes labeled "proofs," which relate to logic, wherein formal arguments are sometimes called proofs. Because the arguments for God's existence utilize logic, people have traditionally called them "proofs," too. However, this should not be mistaken as a claim that any of these arguments has proven God's existence with apodictic certainty.[1] It's doubtful that any human argument can provide that degree of certainty about anything. Considering the human propensity to err, an attitude of cognitive humility seems appropriate, and reasonable certainty seems like a more appropriate goal.

There are many arguments for the existence of God, and many kinds of evidence are used to support theistic beliefs. We'll discuss some classical arguments and some contemporary ones, but we cannot come even close to covering all of them.

---

1. Apodictic certainty is certainty that cannot possibly be mistaken. It contrasts with psychological certainty, which is a mere feeling of certainty that can be mistaken, and with reasonable certainty, which involves an evaluation that the probability of something being true is sufficient for it to be treated as certain.

The Ontological Argument

Ontology is the branch of metaphysics that studies the nature of being (existence). The ontological argument attempts to prove the existence of God by showing that his very nature somehow entails that he exists. The classical formulation of the argument comes from St. Anselm, whose definition of God we learned in the preceding chapter. When a theist like Anselm uses the word "God," he is talking about something that, if it were to exist, would be that being than which none greater can be thought. And such a being must exist, for if he doesn't exist, it's easy to think of something greater than him: Simply think of something that has all his attributes and actually does exist. But it's impossible to think of something greater than that being than which nothing greater can be thought. Hence, he must exist.

This argument can be diagrammed as *modus tollens*:

1. If God doesn't exist, then it's possible to think of a being greater than that being than which none greater can be thought.
2. It's not possible to think of a being greater than that being than which none greater can be thought.
3. Therefore, it's not possible that God doesn't exist.

Since *modus tollens* is a valid argument form, this argument is valid. Accordingly, if the premises are true, then the argument is sound and the conclusion is true. The minor premise certainly seems to be true: It's impossible to think of a being greater than that being than which none greater can be thought. The major premise also seems to be true: If God doesn't exist, then every human is more powerful, more knowledgeable, wiser, and more benevolent than God. Thus, this argument appears to be sound.

A number of objections to the ontological argument have been raised. In response, theists have developed newer versions of the argument and have attempted to refute the objections. You can read about these developments in the books recommended at the end of this chapter.

The Cosmological Argument

Cosmology is the study of the origin of and basic nature of the universe (the cosmos). Concordantly, the cosmological argument for God's existence argues that God is the best explanation for the existence of the universe. The first step is to show that there are two types of explanations of why the universe exists, those that say that the universe is eternal and those that say that it has a beginning. The former face the problem of needing to traverse an infinite number of past moments in order to get to the present. That would take an infinite amount of time. Therefore, it's argued, we would never get to the present. However, we are in the present, so it must be the case that the universe is not eternal. Therefore, the universe must have a beginning.

The second step is to show that the beginning of the universe must involve a supernatural cause. If the universe has a beginning, then something must have caused it to begin, since something that doesn't yet exist cannot cause itself. Hence, there must be something outside of the natural universe (i.e., something supernatural) that caused the natural universe. That sounds a lot like God. This step of the argument is a pure hypothetical syllogism:

1. If the universe isn't infinite, then it must have had a beginning.
2. If the universe had a beginning, then something outside the universe must have caused it to begin.
3. If something outside of the universe caused it to begin, then a supernatural cause like God exists.
4. Therefore, if the universe isn't infinite, then a supernatural cause like God exists.

Skeptics have objected that this argument repudiates the possibility of an eternal universe but then substitutes for it an equally problematic eternal cause. To this, some theists reply that God is **atemporal**, so his eternality does not face the same problem that an eternal temporal universe faces. It must be acknowledged, though, that an atemporal God faces other challenges.[2]

Another challenge is that the cosmological argument doesn't actually show that an infinite past is impossible; it only shows that we cannot

2. Atemporal means not existing in nor subject to time. Some theists believe that God exists outside of time.

comprehend how we would arrive at the present. That could simply be a problem resulting from the finite nature of the human mind rather than an actual impossibility. It's questionable whether humans can actually make sense of the infinite, as was pointed out nearly 2,500 years ago by Zeno of Elea.

Finally, critics of the cosmological argument point out that even if it is sound, it does not show that the supernatural cause of the universe is the maximal God of classical theism. Theistic apologists grant this point but reply that the argument does show that naturalism is false. Furthermore, they contend that the cosmological argument can be combined with other arguments into a cumulative case for classical theism. We'll say more about that later.

The medieval theologian Thomas Aquinas is perhaps the most famous advocate of the cosmological argument, which he develops in *Summa Theologica*.[3] The most influential contemporary proponent of the cosmological argument is William Lane Craig, who has published several books developing and defending it.[4]

The Teleological Argument

The term "teleological" comes from the Greek word τελος (**telos**), which means "design" or "purpose." The teleological argument is an inference from the elements of design that can be detected in the world to the conclusion that there must have been a designer. This argument was most famously articulated by William Paley, an eighteenth-century English philosopher.[5] He argued that if you were walking through a field and were to find a watch that was accurately keeping time, you would not think to yourself, "How strange—all these little pieces somehow came together and formed a

3. Thomas Aquinas, *Summa Theologica*, trans. Fathers of the English Dominican Province (Christian Classics, 1981), http://www.newadvent.org/summa.
4. E.g., Paul Copan and William Lane Craig, *Philosophical Arguments for the Finitude of the Past*, vol. 1, *The Kalam Cosmological Argument* (Bloomsbury Academic, 2018); Paul Copan and William Lane Craig, *Scientific Evidence for the Beginning of the Universe*, vol. 2, *The Kalam Cosmological Argument* (Bloomsbury Academic, 2019).
5. William Paley, *Natural Theology: Or, Evidences of the Existence and Attributes of the Deity* (Anodos Books, 2019).

functioning watch." You'd know that the watch is the result of a very precise design carefully executed. Similarly, when we look at the world and see its intricacy, detail, complexity, and functionality, we can infer that it is the result of an intelligent design carefully executed.

The logic at the heart of this argument is *modus ponens*:

1. If the universe exhibits design, then it had an intelligent, supernatural designer.
2. The universe exhibits design.
3. Therefore, it had an intelligent, supernatural designer.

This is a valid argument, and the major premise seems self-evident. The minor premise is the likely point of dispute. Not everyone agrees that the universe exhibits design. If it does, then the argument is probably sound. But naturalists and others who are skeptical of this argument often claim that evolutionary processes can explain the complexity and functionality of our world without recourse to a designer. If they're right, then even those things that look like they are designed may be the results of mindless processes, and the argument fails.

"Natural selection is the blind watchmaker, blind because it does not see ahead, does not plan consequences, has no purpose in view. Yet the living results of natural selection overwhelmingly impress us with the appearance of design as if by a master watchmaker, impress us with the illusion of design and planning." —Richard Dawkins

On the other hand, if the theist can come up with even one example of design that cannot be the result of natural evolutionary processes, then the argument succeeds. Many theists believe they can. One comes from Michael Behe, who at the time of writing teaches biochemistry at Lehigh University. He argues that there are some things that evolution cannot explain because they serve no evolutionary purpose until they reach the level of complexity at which they help the organism to survive. Behe terms these things "irreducibly complex." Before they reach this level of complexity, some other explanation of their existence is required. An intelligent designer would be such an explanation.[6]

Most scientists reject arguments like this as religious rather than scientific. Unfortunately, space does not permit us to explore that debate here. Others object that the teleological argument supports belief in an extremely intelligent designer but does not show the designer to be omniscient, omnisapient, omnibenevolent, etc. This is true: At best, the teleological argument gives us one piece of the puzzle. This is where the cumulative case comes into play. We'll get to that eventually.

The Fine-Tuning Argument

The fine-tuning argument is a modern version of the teleological argument. It utilizes scientific data and mathematics to calculate the probability of a life-sustaining universe coming into existence without the involvement of an intelligent force like God. The calculation is based on the laws of nature, the constants of nature, and the initial conditions that would need to be in place at the beginning of the universe in order to result in a life-sustaining universe.[7]

Here is a sample of the type of data that is utilized in this kind of calculation, taken from an article by Robin Collins:

1. If the initial explosion of the Big Bang had differed in strength by as little as one part in 10^{60}, the universe would have either quickly collapsed back on itself or expanded too rapidly for stars to form. In either case, life would be impossible.
2. Calculations indicate that if the strong nuclear force, the force that binds protons and neutrons together in an atom, was stronger or weaker by as little as five percent, life would be impossible.
3. Calculations by Brandon Carter show that if gravity had been

6. Michael Behe, *Darwin's Black Box*, 2nd ed. (Free Press, 2006).
7. Robin Collins, "The Teleological Argument: An Exploration of the Fine-Tuning of the Universe," in *The Blackwell Companion to Natural Theology*, ed. William Lane Craig and J. P. Moreland (Wiley-Blackwell, 2009), 211.

> stronger or weaker by one part in 10^{40}, then life-sustaining stars like the sun could not exist.[8]

The argument is abductive. There is a wide spectrum of possible ways that the universe could be, but only an extremely narrow range of these will support life. Hence, it is highly improbable that the universe would turn out to have one of the life-sustaining forms. But the universe does have one of those forms. How can that best be explained?

Collins summarizes the argument thusly:

1. Given the fine-tuning evidence, a life-sustaining universe is highly unlikely on naturalism.
2. Given the fine-tuning evidence, a life-sustaining universe is not unlikely on theism.
3. Therefore, by the restricted version of the Likelihood Principle, a life-sustaining universe strongly supports theism over naturalism.[9]

Skeptics have raised several objections to this argument. One is based on the "anthropic principle" and points out that if a non-life-sustaining universe were to exist, it would be natural that no one in that universe would wonder at the fact that the universe that exists is non-life-sustaining. Likewise, if a life-sustaining universe happens to exist and contains intelligent life forms, it's natural that they will wonder at the apparent unlikelihood that their universe is life-sustaining. However, if a universe exists, then it must be one or the other of these two types. Since it's the life-sustaining type that exists, it's no surprise that we marvel at our good fortune. This counter to the fine-tuning argument seems accurate as far as it goes. However, it does not repudiate the actual argument, which is that a life-sustaining universe is mathematically much more probable given theism than naturalism. The counter seems to miss the point.

---

8. Robin Collins, "A Scientific Argument for the Existence of God: The Fine-Tuning Design Argument," in *Reason for the Hope Within*, ed. Michael Murray (Eerdmans, 1999), 49.
9. This is a paraphrase of Collins' actual words. See Collins, "The Teleological Argument," 207.

Another objection to the fine-tuning argument is that if the current universe is merely the latest in an infinite series of universes, as the oscillating universe cosmology argues, then eventually every possible type of universe will come into existence. Hence "unlikely" types, such as life-sustaining ones, are inevitable. This seems like a strong counterargument, but only if there is an infinite series of universes.

The Moral Argument

There are multiple arguments from morality to the conclusion that God exists. Those of Immanuel Kant and C. S. Lewis have been widely studied, but contemporary philosophers such as David Baggett and Jerry Walls have also done considerable work on the moral argument.[10]

Lewis' version of the moral argument can be found in *Mere Christianity*:

1. If materialism is true, then there is no moral law.[11]
2. There is moral law.
3. Therefore, materialism is not true.
4. Either theism is true or materialism is true.
5. Materialism is not true (from #3).
6. Therefore, theism is true.[12]

Steps 1–3 present a *modus tollens* argument, which is a valid argument form. Steps 4–6 present a valid disjunctive syllogism. Hence, this two-step argument is logically valid. Therefore, if the premises are true, the conclusion must be as well.

The first premise seems accurate, because a moral law would be an abstract object, and if materialism (physicalism) is true, then abstract objects do not exist. The second premise is a little more controversial,

---

10. See David Baggett and Jerry Walls, *The Moral Argument: A History* (Oxford, 2019).
11. By "moral law," Lewis seems to mean a body of eternal moral truths that apply equally to all people at all times.
12. This exposition of Lewis' moral argument can be found in Christopher A. Shrock, "Mere Christianity and the Moral Argument for the Existence of God," *Sehnsucht: The C.S. Lewis Journal* 11 (2017): 103.

since it's common for ethical relativists to deny that there is a moral law. However, as we'll see in our unit on ethics, the arguments for the existence of moral law are much stronger than the arguments for relativism, so the second premise is probably also true. Number 3 is a conclusion rather than a premise. Since numbers 1 and 2 appear to be true and the logic leading from them to number 3 is valid, the argument appears to be sound and therefore, number 3 is true.

Number 4 could possibly be a false dilemma, since there are more options than Lewis presents. That he was well aware of other worldviews is clear from his writings. Interpreting him charitably, it seems likely that either he viewed theism and naturalism to be so much more likely than the other options that the others need not be mentioned, or he believed that, as far as the moral argument goes, the argument works even if deism, (theistic) polytheism, or panentheism is substituted for theism, and it works regardless of whether naturalism or pantheism is intended by "materialism" on the right side of the disjunct. In other words, we could rephrase number 4 as "Either some roughly theistic form of supernaturalism is true or some form of materialism is true." Those who prefer a nontheistic polytheism will still object, but the problems with that worldview are probably sufficient to justify Lewis' omission. Read this way, number 4 seems reasonable.

Number 5 was demonstrated to be true via numbers 1–3. Number 6 is the final conclusion of the argument. Since number 4 was shown to be reasonable and number 5 was found to be true, and the disjunctive argument from numbers 4 and 5 to 6 is valid, it appears that number 6 is also reasonable. Hence, the whole argument seems likely to be sound and the conclusion—that some sort of theistic supernaturalism is true—is probably correct.

The Argument from Miracles

Religious people generally believe in **miracles**, and this belief reinforces their conviction that their religion is true. In a way, they are viewing miracles as evidence supporting their religious beliefs. Skeptics, on the other hand, cast doubt on the truthfulness of miracle claims. Let's take a look at miracles and the evidence they may possibly provide for religious belief.

David Hume famously wrote that "A miracle is a violation of the laws of nature."[13] It's more than just an unusual occurrence, like an eclipse, or a snake with two heads, or the Buffalo Bills winning the Super Bowl. While those might be very unusual events, each of them has a natural cause. A miracle cannot be explained by natural processes and is therefore supernatural.

Many people have experienced things that they think are miracles. However, almost all these are the type of unusual event that could possibly be natural. Events that cannot be explained naturally seem to be rare. Hume, a skeptic, said that someone coming back from the dead would be a strong example of a miracle. Not coincidentally, some people believe that Jesus Christ miraculously came back to life. In fact, early Christianity appears to have taken this to be the definitive sign that Jesus is the Messiah. Of course, if Jesus did rise from the dead, it happened so long ago that it's difficult to verify today. However, apologists, including some trained historians, have argued that the historical evidence of Jesus' resurrection is strong.

A leading expert on the resurrection is the American scholar Gary Habermas. He has devoted much of his career to historical research on the life of Jesus of Nazareth. He says that the resurrection can be shown using nothing but facts that are accepted by secular researchers. Examine this modest list:

1. Jesus died by Roman crucifixion.
2. Jesus' disciples believed they saw the risen Jesus.
3. The disciples were transformed from despondent to zealous.
4. Proclamation of the resurrection began very early in the history of Christianity.
5. James, Jesus' brother, converted to Christianity subsequent to Jesus' death.
6. Paul, an oppressor of Christianity, attributed his conversion to seeing the resurrected Jesus.[14]

---

13. Hume, 55. We would prefer to say an *interruption* or *suspension* of the laws of nature, but "violation" will do.
14. Gary Habermas, *The Risen Jesus and Future Hope* (Rowman & Littlefield, 2003), 26–27.

Habermas' argument is abductive. There are a variety of theories about what happened to Jesus after his execution. Most of the theories are naturalistic—that is, they don't involve anything supernatural—but the traditional Christian theory is supernaturalistic: God miraculously raised Jesus back to life. Which theory best accounts for these six facts?

Naturalistic theories include the theory that the disciples experienced a mass hallucination in which they thought they saw the resurrected Jesus, the theory that Jesus swooned on the cross but didn't actually die, the theory that the disciples stole Jesus' body from the tomb and then lied about the resurrection, and the theory that the resurrection was not a feature of early Christianity but instead is a legend that developed later. None of these theories can account for the six widely accepted historical facts listed above, nor can a combination of those theories. However, the traditional Christian view that God supernaturally raised Jesus from the dead is able to account for all six facts, plus additional historical facts that weren't listed. Hence, Habermas concludes that the supernatural resurrection theory is the best explanation we currently have about what happened to Jesus and is therefore most likely true.

If the resurrection happened, then a miracle happened. If a miracle happened, then something supernatural happened. If something supernatural happened, then naturalism is false. If naturalism is false, then supernaturalism is true. It would be odd for a supernatural force to resurrect Jesus from the dead if it disagrees with Jesus' message. Therefore, it seems likely that the resurrecting force was the God that Jesus preached. Hence, it seems likely that God exists.

The Cumulative Case Argument

Each of the arguments that we've considered supports belief in only a small number of divine attributes. For example, the cosmological argument supports belief in divine omnipotence, the teleological argument divine intelligence, and the moral argument divine holiness. From the ontological argument we learn of God's maximal perfection, and from the argument from miracles we learn about God's providential presence. If we combine the results of multiple arguments, we end up with a list of attributes that is strongly suggestive of the God of classical theism. This is called the "cumulative case argument." If each of the aforementioned arguments succeeds, then we can add them together and get an outline of the nature of God.

Other Arguments

The existence of God may be the most foundational issue in the study of worldviews: Much hinges on the position one takes regarding the existence of God and/or the supernatural. There are many additional arguments for the existence of God. Unfortunately, space prevents us from discussing them, but the interested reader can find more arguments in the books listed below.

QUESTIONS TO PONDER

- Which of the arguments for the existence of God do you think is the strongest?

- Can you think of other reasonable arguments for the existence of God?

- How certain are you that God exists? Are you apodictically certain, reasonably certain, psychologically certain, skeptical, or convinced that he doesn't? Why?

TERMS TO KNOW

- ontology
- ontological argument
- cosmology
- cosmological argument
- atemporal
- telos
- teleology
- teleological argument
- fine-tuning argument
- moral argument
- abduction
- miracle
- cumulative case argument

FOR FURTHER READING

Cowan, Steven B. and Stanley N. Gundry, eds. *Five Views on Apologetics.* Zondervan Academic, 2000. This book studies the advantages and disadvantages of five different approaches to Christian apologetics. While the focus of the book is Christian, some of the arguments used could easily be adapted to other theistic religions.

Groothuis, Douglas. *Christian Apologetics: A Comprehensive Case for Biblical Faith.* 2nd ed. IVP Academic, 2022. This is perhaps the best single-volume book on apologetics currently available. It is broad but also detailed; scholarly but also comprehensible. Its 750 pages are written on the undergraduate level.

Sweis, Khaldoun A. and Chad V. Meister, eds. *Christian Apologetics: An Anthology of Primary Sources.* Zondervan Academic, 2024. This is a very helpful collection of primary sources ranging from the first to the twenty-first centuries.

15

ATHEISTIC APOLOGETICS

SYNOPSIS

Just as the previous chapter laid out a case for theism, this chapter will make the case for atheism. Commitment to faith in God or to unbelief is not merely an intellectual exercise in which one weighs arguments for or against. But faith includes reasons, and knowing why people believe what they do is important, especially if one wishes to engage in apologetics for one's position.

DIALOGUE

Angelo was looking forward to their next meeting. He was glad the burden was on Zach this week. He could sit back, listen, and ask questions. He was pretty sure what kind of case Zach would make for atheism, but he hoped there'd be some arguments for atheism he hadn't heard before, simply for the challenge it would present to his own beliefs. He had always wondered if his faith would stand up to scrutiny. Each week, as they talked, he found that his own beliefs were sharpened. Sometimes he encountered an idea for which he had no answers, and that always sent him on a search. He felt more confident in his faith than he ever had before.

Zach did not want to disappoint. Angelo's presentation had set a high bar, so Zach found himself driven back to some of his college textbooks on evolutionary biology and new books and websites that more directly made a case for atheism. The focus was energizing, and he went about the task with enthusiasm.

But unlike his early foray into atheism in his teens, Zach no longer felt the same zeal to convert others. Maybe it was maturity, or maybe he had been challenged with enough difficult questions from religious people that he no longer felt an evangelistic impulse. He knew there were questions he couldn't answer, but he remained confident that atheism was the most rational belief system.

After a quick catch-up on their week, Suresh turned to Zach. "Okay, buddy, what do you have for us?"

Zach nodded and looked down at his materials. "Thanks for giving me this opportunity, everyone. The teenage version of me probably would have seen this conversation as a chance to score some points and show you that to believe in any kind of deity is irrational and maybe even dangerous. But I've grown. You are my friends, and in the spirit of congeniality, I want to argue for atheism without being argumentative."

"I have no doubt you'll accomplish that goal." Angelo said, patting him on the back.

"Thanks for that vote of confidence!" Zach said. "Well . . . I guess I'll dive right in. I tried to narrow my reasons for being an atheist down to just three or four, so I'm going to focus on the arguments that seem most compelling to me.

"First, I think it's important to define atheism, or we may be talking past one another. I discovered, much to my surprise, that atheism is not monolithic. There are varieties of atheists who reject belief in God for very different reasons. The philosopher John Gray identifies seven types of atheism."[1]

"Seven?" Suresh said, his eyebrows raised. "I would have guessed two or three at most!"

"I was surprised too. But learning about the varieties of Buddhism, Hinduism, Judaism, and Islam, as well as the three major branches of Christianity—Catholic, Orthodox, and Protestant—made me realize it makes sense for there to be different types of atheists as well."

---

1. John Gray, *Seven Types of Atheism* (Picador, 2018).

Zach turned back to his notes. "Even though they are different, the common denominator is that atheists 'have no use for the idea of a divine mind that has fashioned the world.'[2] Essentially, atheism isn't a positive belief but rather a lack of belief. As a result, most atheists don't believe their viewpoint needs to be defended. Rather, religion needs to put forth a compelling case that deities exist. I don't have to prove a universal negative, such as that there are no naturally occurring hot pink swans in the world. Rather, someone who argues for their existence would have to present compelling evidence for such a claim to be plausible. In the same way, atheists don't believe in gods because they haven't found the arguments convincing."

"Or maybe also because the brokenness and absurdity of the world have eliminated the plausibility that deities, if they even exist, care about us. They don't help us, rendering them inconsequential to us," Hannah said. "That's the reason I abandoned belief in the Christian God."

"That is the seventh kind of atheism in Gray's book," said Zach. "It is an atheism of silence that summarizes life as pain, which would not be so if any kind of loving god existed. The divine may be identical with the world, and therefore not personal; in that case, it's easier to simply speak of the world and stop using the term *god*."

"I take it that's not your type of atheism?" Hannah knew she and Zach shared a disbelief in any kind of god but probably for very different reasons.

"That's right, although I'd add the heartlessness of the world to my list of reasons for disbelieving. It's not the main reason, but I agree with you."

"Red in tooth and claw?" Angelo asked.

He was met with blank stares.

Then he surprised everyone by quoting from Alfred Tennyson's poem "In Memoriam A.H.H.":

Who trusted God was love indeed
And love Creation's final law
Tho' Nature, red in tooth and claw
With ravine, shriek'd against his creed.[3]

---

2. Gray, *Seven Types of Atheism*, 2.
3. Alfred Tennyson, "In Memoriam A.H.H.," (1850) public domain.

"Wow, how did you do that?" Suresh said. He thought maybe he'd read that poem in high school but didn't remember it well enough to quote it.

"I have always loved poetry. I try to memorize poems that speak about belief or loss of belief in God. That stanza speaks about the challenge that the apparent cruelty of nature presents to belief in a caring God."

"I like poetry, but I don't think I have any memorized," Zach said. "Do you know any others?"

Angelo shook his head and looked down at his hands. "I don't want to distract from your presentation."

"It's not a distraction," Zach said.

"Okay, one more. This is from a poem called 'Dover Beach' from nineteenth-century English poet Matthew Arnold." Angelo looked into the eyes of his friends as he quoted the poem.

The Sea of Faith
Was once, too, at the full, and round earth's shore
Lay like the folds of a bright girdle furled.
But now I only hear
Its melancholy, long, withdrawing roar,
Retreating, to the breath
Of the night-wind, down the vast edges drear
And naked shingles of the world.[4]

"Ooh, that one gives me shivers," Hannah said. "It reminds me of my own journey out of faith."

"Okay, I humored you," Angelo said with a smile. "Now let's get back to your presentation, Zach."

"I'd place myself in the category of scientific atheism. I believe it's rational to embrace only ideas that can be scientifically proven. The scientific method has brought us advances in the last few hundred years that were inconceivable for all of human history prior. It wasn't religion that brought us these advances but science."

Angelo inhaled slightly, as if he was preparing to interject.

---

4. Matthew Arnold, "Dover Beach," (1867) public domain.

"I know what you're going to say, Angelo. You were about to say that science has also brought the world suffering and death, and I agree with you."

"I'm glad you're willing to admit that. Not every atheist is."

"There was a time when I would have argued with you on that, but I've come to see that sometimes the most advanced societies commit the greatest atrocities, like Nazi Germany. Rather than using their advanced scientific brilliance for good, they channeled it into becoming more efficient at killing. That shows me, without doubt, that science needs something directing its efforts toward good. You've actually helped me see that religion can, in some cases, influence science to strive toward human flourishing and not world domination." Zach patted Angelo on the back.

"Thanks, man."

"One idea I find helpful is that extraordinary claims require extraordinary evidence. If, for example, someone claimed to have formulated a new drug that could cure all forms of cancer in twenty-four hours with one dose with no side effects, the medical testing for that drug would take many years and millions of dollars. That's because there are between one hundred and two hundred kinds of cancer, depending on how they're classified.[5] The miracle medicine would have to be tested on every type of cancer over a long period of time, first with lab rats, and then with many human subjects willing to undergo the treatment. The test subjects would then have to be followed for decades to see if, in fact, there were no deadly side effects. Because the claim is extraordinary, it couldn't be considered accepted science until extraordinary evidence supported it."

"I've never thought about that," Suresh said.

"The claim that there are invisible deities is extraordinary, according to most atheists," Zach said, "requiring extraordinary evidence. I'm not sure if other atheists think this next thought—I've never read it anywhere—but I find Suresh's belief in multiple deities or one deity that permeates the universe and is identical with it more plausible than the Christian God."

---

5. The Cleveland Clinic claims one hundred types of cancer (https://my.clevelandclinic.org/health/diseases/12194-cancer), while Cancer Research UK claims there are more than two hundred types (https://www.cancerresearchuk.org/about-cancer/what-is-cancer/how-cancer-starts/types-of-cancer).

Angelo and Suresh looked at each other in surprise.

"Why is that, Zach?" Hannah asked.

"I think my struggle with the Christian God is the fact that he's personal. He reveals, speaks, loves, and relates to creation in a personal way. That entails obligation to him and implies that he can be known—truly known—as one person knows another. Atheists typically find that too far-fetched. If God exists and is like that, why isn't he more obvious and known by every person? Why does he seem to be hiding so well that the majority of people in the world don't believe in him and science can't prove his existence?"

"That's tricky," Angelo said. "Christians believe he *is* known by every person because he has revealed himself to us in the way that the world and we have been created, but people suppress that truth because they don't want to be accountable to God.[6] The problem isn't that God can't be found but that people don't want to know God apart from his work of drawing them to him. They don't want to acknowledge God's lordship, his right as Creator to deserve their worship and hold them accountable."

"Yes, I'm remembering this line of thinking from your argument for Christianity," Zach said. "So you're saying that God can be known and is known but is rejected because people want to do what they want?"

"Essentially, yes," Angelo said.

"Do you have a poem for *that*?" Zach asked, half joking.

Angelo laughed. "I actually do . . ."

Hannah leaned forward. "Wait. Are you kidding, Angelo?"

"You must be," Suresh said.

Zach waved his hand, inviting Angelo to share.

"This one is called 'The Garden of Love' by William Blake." Angelo looked at the ceiling for a moment to gather his thoughts. Then he closed his eyes and began to speak.

I went to the Garden of Love,
And saw what I never had seen:
A Chapel was built in the midst,
Where I used to play on the green.

6. Rom 1:18–32.

And the gates of this Chapel were shut,
And 'Thou shalt not' writ over the door;
So I turn'd to the Garden of Love,
That so many sweet flowers bore.

And I saw it was filled with graves,
And tomb-stones where flowers should be:
And Priests in black gowns, were walking their rounds,
And binding with briars, my joys & desires.[7]

Angelo opened his eyes and looked around at his friends.

"Forgive me," Suresh said. "I'm not sure what the poet is trying to say."

"He's talking about how religion, portrayed as a church building, commandments, tombs, and priests, has ruined the pursuit of his desires, which he calls the Garden of Love."

"I think it has an even deeper meaning," Hannah said. "Isn't the writer sort of implying something about the Christian story of the fall into sin? Rather than the garden being where God originally was found and worshiped by the people made in his image, the garden in the poem is a paradise of following your own desires that is ruined by the presence of God."

"Whaa . . . ?" Angelo's mouth fell open. "I've never thought about it that way."

"That was a good one," Zach said. "I may need to revisit it later."

He looked around the table.

"In some of my reading in philosophical atheism to supplement my scientific arguments against the existence of God, I came across an author, J. N. Findlay, who proposed an idea that resonated with me. He said that if there is a God—and I believe he's referring to the Christian God—and if he were able to satisfy the claims made about him, he'd have to be 'in every way inescapable, One Whose existence and Whose possession of certain excellencies we cannot possibly conceive away.'"[8] Zach looked up from his notes.

---

7. William Blake, "The Garden of Love," (1794) public domain.
8. J. N. Findlay, "Can God's Existence Be Proved?" in *The Impossibility of God*, ed. Michael Martin and Ricki Monnier (Prometheus, 2003), 24. Findlay capitalizes

"That sums up well my view of the nonexistence of God. I don't believe in any God, let alone the Christian God, because I can do without him. I don't need to believe in God to do science or to be a good person. Does that make sense?"

Zach repeated his question before realizing that Angelo wasn't listening. Angelo's eyes were fixed on something beyond Zach's left shoulder.

"Angelo, did you hear Zach?" Hannah asked.

Suresh had already traced Angelo's gaze to its target. A man was standing near the entrance of the coffee shop, close to the back of the small line at the register. His appearance was unremarkable—average height, dark brown hair, neatly dressed. Nothing unusual. Nothing that is, except his eyes. The man's eyes swept slowly left to right and then back again. As his gaze turned toward their table, Suresh felt a shiver run down his spine. The man's eyes were cold and lifeless and somehow menacing. Suresh was startled by his eyes and the brain's ability to perceive this unusual characteristic in a total stranger standing twenty-five feet away. But it was unmistakable.

Panic rose in Hannah's throat. Angelo had clearly tuned them and everything else in the coffee shop out. She thought about what had happened at Suresh's restaurant a few weeks before. She suddenly felt unsafe. She had experienced this feeling before, usually when making a home visit without anyone accompanying her.

Angelo didn't move his head. His reflexes kicked in, and he reflexively slid his right hand down to his side. Nothing. He remembered that he was off duty and wasn't carrying his sidearm. As the man near the door began to look his way, Angelo dropped his eyes to his coffee cup to avoid alerting the man that he was watching him. When Angelo sensed the man's gaze moving away from him, he looked up again. It was unmistakable—the man was surveilling the room. Angelo quickly glanced around the cafe. No one else—besides his friends—seemed to be paying attention to the man.

Angelo quickly made mental notes about the man's appearance, especially his facial features. Mid-thirties. He noted the man's hairline, build, and clothing. He seemed to be fit, with no sign of a belly, but not overly muscular

---

the pronouns in this sentence, presumably to indicate the kind of respect such a being would merit.

either. No visible scars or tattoos. His earlobes were attached—significant as only 2–3 percent of the US population has that feature. The figure could be as high as 50 percent in other countries, but Angelo couldn't determine this man's ethnicity. He really did blend right in. Angelo's assessment of the man took mere seconds.

Am I being paranoid? The man wasn't doing anything suspicious beyond his methodical visual sweep of the room, which he had now done three times. But with everything that was going on in Greenfield, Angelo wasn't taking chances. The recent training they'd received from the FBI said not to ignore their instincts. Sometimes the intangibles tipped off law enforcement to criminals or terrorists.

"Angelo, what is it?" Hannah's voice was low and edged with fear. Zach never turned around, as he sensed Angelo was locked onto something of concern. He had noticed when Angelo's hand drifted down to his side. He too felt the chill of fear without ever seeing what was causing it.

A noisy group of six teenagers burst into the coffee shop, and like magic, the man disappeared out the door. Angelo caught a quick glimpse of him walking away down the sidewalk before he vanished entirely. Angelo leaped to his feet. "I'm sorry, everyone. I need to go to the police department."

Hannah grabbed his arm. "What did you see, Angelo?"

"I saw it too, Angelo." Suresh knew what he saw, even if he couldn't explain exactly what "it" was.

Angelo shook his head. "Something was off about that man by the counter. I don't like the way he was methodically looking at the customers here."

He looked at Hannah. "Please don't worry. I just need to file a report while his face is fresh in my mind. With everything going on around Greenfield, it's better to be safe."

"Go," Zach said. "Do what you need to do. And thank you for everything you do to keep the community safe."

THEORY

In the dialogue, our friends discussed some of the reasons that atheists reject belief in God. The conversation was more than polite: It was friendly, even though the stakes are high. As we said in the previous chapter, the existence of God may be the most foundational issue in the study of worldviews. Let's take a more systematic look at some of these arguments.

Perhaps this is a bit counterintuitive, but it's often harder to prove that something doesn't exist than it is to prove that something does. Take, for example, black swans: If I believe that black swans exist but you believe that all swans are white, all I have to do to prove that black swans exist is to show one to you. On the other hand, to prove that they don't exist, you can't simply show me a white swan; you have to somehow prove that there are no black swans anywhere on this entire planet—nor on any other. That's a pretty tall task!

Atheism is claiming that there is no God, not here, not out there, not anywhere. Thus, from the very start atheistic apologetics faces a challenge. This is further complicated by the fact that God, if he exists, is incorporeal. That you can't see, touch, or detect God with any of your senses doesn't constitute evidence against him. How should atheists proceed?

Epistemologically speaking, this must be done rationally rather than empirically: Rather than appealing to sensory data to disprove God's existence, atheists will need to use abstract arguments. Many such arguments have been formulated; as with the arguments for theism, there are more than we can cover. Therefore, we're limiting ourselves to the ones that seem to be most influential. The "For Further Reading" section at the end of the chapter covers many more.

The Moral Argument for Atheism

Many people reject belief in God because they find the gods of specific religions objectionable. The gods of polytheism are generally on par with humans as far as morality goes: They squabble, lie, and betray both humans and each other. The God of Judaism is portrayed in some parts of the Hebrew Bible in very human ways, as if he loses his temper, becomes vengeful, and punishes innocents along with the guilty. In Islam, Allah is sometimes pictured similarly, and it is common among Muslims to affirm that God can do anything he chooses to with complete moral impunity. Related to this is the common objection that many religious people are hypocrites and therefore their religions are false and their gods don't exist.

Let's see if we can formalize this argument. Some people express the argument as a logical contradiction, something like this: "If God exists, he's the greatest possible being, but the God of the religions is morally flawed and therefore not the greatest possible being, so God does not exist." Or it could be like this: "All the world's religions claim to be following God, but the world's religions are responsible for wars, oppression, pedophilia, and other terrible things, so either God condones such things and therefore, isn't worthy of worship, or God doesn't exist."

The underlying argument seems to be something like this:

1. If God exists, he would be morally perfect.
2. But God, as the religions describe him (or as they reflect his nature), isn't morally perfect.
3. Therefore, God doesn't exist.

This is *modus tollens*, which is a valid argument form, so let's examine the premises to see if the argument is sound. Theists, deists, pantheists, and panentheists would probably agree with the statement "If God exists, then he would be morally perfect," so that premise stands.

There's some truth to the minor premise too: Some religions seem to understand God in a way that views him as less than morally perfect. But it seems likely that describing God as morally flawed is a mistake, so rather than concluding that God doesn't exist, we should conclude that some interpretations of God's nature are flawed. Furthermore, the argument seems to be saying that when religious people don't accurately reflect God's moral perfection, that proves God doesn't exist. But when we state it that way, it's a rather obvious *non sequitur* unless we assume determinism. That's because, if religious people have free will, then even if a maximally perfect God exists, it's possible for them to freely make poor choices without impugning God's holiness, with the result that even though God exists, religious people sometimes do not live in a way that reflects their belief in him.

Finally, it must be pointed out that the minor premise doesn't sufficiently reflect the major premise. The major premise speaks of God *simpliciter*, while the minor premise speaks of God "as the religions describe him (or as they reflect his nature)." If we change the major premise so that it matches the minor premise, the argument becomes this:

1. If God, as the religions describe him (or as they reflect his nature), exists, then he would be morally perfect.
2. But God, as the religions describe him (or as they reflect his nature), isn't morally perfect.
3. Therefore, God, as the religions describe him (or as they reflect his nature), doesn't exist.

Here the conclusion of this argument isn't that God doesn't exist, but rather that God as the religions describe him or reflect his nature doesn't exist. In other words, the argument is reduced to saying that the religions are doing a poor job of describing God or reflecting his nature. Hence, even if this argument is sound, it does not prove that God does not exist.

Belief in God Is Not Scientific[9]

Another common objection to belief in God is that it's not scientific. A simple version of this argument can be seen as another *modus tollens*:

1. If God exists, then we should be able to prove it scientifically.
2. We cannot prove God's existence scientifically.
3. Therefore, God does not exist.

Modus tollens is logically valid, but right away the major premise seems suspect. If God is incorporeal, then he is not part of the natural world: He's supernatural. Science, on the other hand, has to do with the natural world. There seems to be a mismatch here. Perhaps a methodology other than science would be more appropriate for learning about God. On the other hand, though, some scientists think that science does hint at the existence of God. This could be because the creation reflects certain truths about its creator, similarly to how pottery formed on a potter's wheel reflects the potter's hands. So to demand scientific proof for the existence of God might

9. Stephen Hawking, quoted in Jamie Ducharme, "Stephen Hawking Was an Atheist. Here's What He Said About God, Heaven and His Own Death," *Time*, March 14, 2018, https://time.com/5199149/stephen-hawking-death-god-atheist/.

be a mistake, but to allow for it might not be.[10] And that calls into question the minor premise. With both premises in doubt, it doesn't seem likely that this is a sound argument.

"God is the name people give to the reason we are here. But I think that reason is the laws of physics rather than someone with whom one can have a personal relationship." —Stephen Hawking

Theoretical Simplicity

There's a more sophisticated version of the argument from science that is not so easily dispatched. In short, the argument is that since science can explain everything, God isn't needed. You remember Ockham's razor: "Entities should not be multiplied beyond necessity." Ockham's point was that if we must choose between a theory or explanation that relies on unproven assumptions or postulated entities and a theory or explanation that doesn't require such things, the latter theory is generally preferable as long as it can explain the phenomena in question. In other words, the simpler theory is better, if it can do the job.

When we apply this to **the God hypothesis** (as it's sometimes called), the argument is that a theory that doesn't require a God-like being to explain the origin of the universe and other things is simpler than a theory that does, and hence theories that don't involve the God hypothesis are preferable to theories that do.[11] This argument can be expressed as *modus ponens*:

1. If there's a simpler explanation for the universe, design, morality, etc., then the God hypothesis isn't justified.
2. There is a simpler explanation for the universe, design, morality, etc.
3. Therefore, the God hypothesis isn't justified.

---

10. See Henry M. Morris, *Men of Science Men of God: Great Scientists of the Past Who Believed the Bible* (Master Books, 1982).
11. The God hypothesis is the theory that God exists and that his existence provides an explanation for the existence of various other things, such as the universe, the appearance of design in the universe, timeless moral truths, etc.

What would this simpler explanation be? That depends. If we're trying to explain the existence of the universe, then the simpler explanation would be a naturalistic explanation like the Big Bang theory. This is a simpler explanation because it requires belief only in the existence of physical matter, while the theistic explanation requires belief in the existence of physical matter and also an eternal God. Similarly, regarding the existence of advanced forms of life, evolution is offered as a simpler explanation than intelligent design; regarding morality, social contract theory is a simpler alternative to divine command theory; and so on.

Theists raise several objections to this argument. First, it's difficult to explain where the matter that caused the Big Bang came from. To this, some naturalists respond that the universe is a closed system, and that according to the principle of the conservation of mass, the amount of matter within a closed system neither increases nor decreases, and therefore, the matter within the universe doesn't "come from" anywhere: It's eternal. Contemporary quantum physics calls this into question, but quantum physics is a rapidly developing field, and the quantum view of the source and nature of matter is still evolving.

Second, supernaturalists can object that even if it's true that matter is eternal, naturalism does not have a cogent explanation for many other aspects of reality, such as the appearance of design and the probable existence of immaterial things like abstract objects. Most naturalists reject the claim that the physical world evidences design, and many of them are nominalists regarding abstract objects, so while these are important objections, they are also controversial. The argument from theoretical simplicity is a sophisticated and important argument, but it's not easy to determine which side it supports the most, naturalism or supernaturalism.

The Ateleological Argument

In the chapter on theistic apologetics we discussed the teleological argument for the existence of God. There is an argument for atheism that is nearly its opposite. It is the argument that the lack of design in the world is evidence that there isn't a designer. This is the ateleological argument, "a" meaning "no" (as in atheism), and "telos" meaning "purpose" or "design."

David Hume made a seminal presentation of this argument in *Dialogues*

Concerning Natural Religion.[12] He explains that if an inference is made from the nature of the world to the nature of its designer, then the nature of the designer will turn out to be as imperfect as the world is. Since the world is full of natural disasters and moral failures on the part of its inhabitants, if it has a designer, that designer must be either incapable of designing or unwilling to design a perfect world. In the former case, the designer isn't omnipotent; in the latter, it's not morally perfect. Either way, the designer is significantly flawed and therefore cannot be the maximally great God of classical theism.

"I cannot, for my part, think that so wild and unsettled a system of theology is, in any respect, preferable to none at all." –David Hume

Hume's argument is interesting in that it attempts to force the theist to choose between the teleological argument and a perfect God. If the theist insists that the teleological argument works, then he'll have to grant that God's not perfect. On the other hand, if he insists that God is perfect, he'll have to abandon the teleological argument.[13] Theists would generally prefer to abandon the teleological argument rather than the perfection of God, but many attempt to refute Hume's argument by attempting to show that it's possible for the designer of the universe to be perfect but somehow not responsible for the imperfections and calamities in the world. Can that be done? Perhaps. This brings us to the final argument for atheism: the problem of evil (the **POE**).

The Problem of Evil

It's possible that the most widely used argument for atheism comes from the problem of evil. It was famously posed 2,300 years ago by Epicurus, an

12. David Hume, *Dialogues Concerning Natural Religion and the Posthumous Essays* (Hackett, 1980), 35–40. More recent versions of the ateleological argument can be found in Wesley Salmon, "Religion and Science: A New Look at Hume's Dialogues," *Philosophical Studies* 33 (1978): 143–76; and Michael Martin, *Atheism: A Philosophical Justification* (Temple University Press, 1990), 317–33.
13. This is called a constructive dilemma. It's an argument form not covered in our logic chapters.

ancient Greek philosopher, who wondered, "Is God willing to prevent evil, but not able? Then he is not omnipotent. Is he able, but not willing? Then he is malevolent. Is he both able and willing? Then whence cometh evil? Is he neither able nor willing? Then why call him God?"[14] Epicurus is suggesting that an omnipotent and omnibenevolent God should be able to prevent evil and should want to prevent evil, so since evil exists, God must lack one of these attributes that make him worthy of being called God. Hence, Epicurus implies, no one worthy of the title God exists.

Epicurus seems to assume divine omniscience, and as such he overlooks the possibility that God doesn't prevent evil simply because he doesn't know about it. Classical theism sees God as omnipotent, omnibenevolent, and omniscient. If God is all of those things, then he knows about all the evil in the world, desires to prevent all that evil, and has the ability to prevent all that evil. Therefore, no evil should exist. But clearly it exists, so such a God must not. This argument is a *modus tollens*:

1. If there is an omnipotent, omniscient, omnibenevolent God, then he would prevent all evil.
2. He hasn't prevented all evil.
3. Therefore, there isn't an omnipotent, omniscient, omnibenevolent God.

Modus tollens is always logically valid, but it's only sound if the premises are true. Theists grant the minor premise, but they have various reasons for objecting to the major premise. Some object that God may allow specific instances of evil because he knows that they will result in greater goods. For instance, God may allow a student to fail an exam despite the student's prayers to pass so that the student learns a lesson about the importance of studying adequately. This is called the **greater good argument**.

J. L. Mackie, a twentieth-century Australian philosopher, thought that the existence of God and the existence of evil are logically incompatible.[15]

14. This is attributed to Epicurus by ancient sources, but Epicurus' own text has been lost.
15. J. L. Mackie, "Evil and Omnipotence," *Mind* 64 (1955): 200–12.

This view of the POE has become known as the logical problem of evil. The late American philosopher William Rowe thought that some evil is compatible with the existence of God, but that any evil that is truly **gratuitous**—in other words, any evil that is not justified by resulting in some equal or greater good—is incompatible with the existence of God and thus stands as evidence for atheism.[16] This has become known as the evidential problem of evil. The American philosopher James Sterba has argued that there are truly horrendous evils that are so great that it's not even possible for them to be justified, and that these are incompatible with the existence of God.[17] The Holocaust is a vivid example of such an evil.

These are serious challenges to belief in God. Theists have responded to them in a variety of ways. For example, Irenaeus, a second-century leader of Christianity, argued that God allows evil to happen to people because it strengthens, deepens, or purifies people's character.[18] A twentieth-century philosopher named John Hick argued for this, too.[19] This is sometimes called the **Irenaean theodicy** (named after Irenaeus).

"The sun shines and warms and lights us and we have no curiosity to know why this is so; but, we ask the reason of all evil, of pain, and hunger, and mosquitoes, and silly people."
—Ralph Waldo Emerson

Christian intellectuals like St. Augustine of Hippo and the contemporary American philosopher Alvin Plantinga have argued that a world wherein humans are free necessarily involves the possibility that they will make choices that result in evil but that there are certain

16. Rowe's seminal essay is "The Problem of Evil and Some Varieties of Atheism," *American Philosophical Quarterly* 16 (1979): 335–41.
17. James Sterba, *Is a Good God Logically Possible?* (Palgrave MacMillan, 2019).
18. Irenaeus, *Adversus Haereses (Against Heresies)* (T & T Clark, 2023). Available online at https://en.wikisource.org/wiki/Ante-Nicene_Fathers/Volume_I/IRENAEUS/Against_Heresies:_Book_I.
19. Hick calls this the "soul making theodicy." See John Hick, *Evil and the God of Love*, rev. ed. (Harper, 1978).

goods that result from human freedom that justify God in giving humans freedom anyway. For example, C. S. Lewis argues that genuine love would not be possible if humans weren't free.[20] This is called the **free will defense**.

Gottfried Wilhelm Leibniz, a seventeenth-century German philosopher, argued that the world in which we live, even with all its problems, is the best possible world. A world devoid of problems would also be devoid of the learning that comes from solving problems; a world without pain would be a world wherein pleasure is less appreciated; a world without evil would be a world that never experiences the triumph of good over evil. When we compare the present world, with all its defects and all the victories that they make possible, to a world without evil, the latter, it can be argued, turns out to be shallow and bland. Furthermore, if we have good reason to believe that God designed this world, that is a good reason to believe that this is the best possible world, for God could do no less.[21] This is called the **best possible world** theodicy.

CONCLUSION

At the end of the chapter on theistic apologetics we stated that there are many more arguments for the existence of God and we referred the reader to the suggested readings at the end of the chapter in order to explore those. We must say the same thing here: There are many more arguments for atheism, and we encourage you to consult the suggested readings below.

The existence of God is a perennial discussion in philosophy. There are very intelligent people on both sides. There are famous atheists who have converted to theism and famous theists who have converted to atheism. This is not an issue that can be decided easily. Nonetheless, each of us should wrestle with it and attempt to decide. Again, that's because it is one of the most foundational issues to your worldview. Much hinges on whether you believe or disbelieve in God. Therefore, we strongly recommend that you continue to study the issue on your own.

20. C. S. Lewis, *Mere Christianity* (Simon & Schuster, 1996), 52–53.
21. G. W. Leibniz, *Theodicy: Essays on the Goodness of God, the Freedom of Man, and the Origin of Evil*, trans. E. M. Huggard (Open Court, 1985).

QUESTIONS TO PONDER

- Is it possible to prove that something doesn't exist? How would you go about doing that?
- Which of these arguments for atheism do you think is the strongest? Does it succeed?
- Do you think that simpler explanations are generally superior to complex ones? Why?
- Do you believe in evil? What makes something evil? Is the existence of a perfect God compatible with the existence of evil?

TERMS TO KNOW

- the God hypothesis
- ateleology
- POE
- greater good argument
- gratuitous evil
- Irenaean theodicy
- free will defense
- best possible world theodicy

FOR FURTHER READING

Bullivant, Stephen and Michael Ruse, eds. *The Oxford Handbook of Atheism*. Oxford University Press, 2013. This is a broad introduction to atheistic thought.

Campbell, Ronnie P., Jr. *Worldviews and the Problem of Evil: A Comparative Approach*. Lexham, 2019. This book examines how the POE is handled by the adherents of various worldviews.

Martin, Michael and Ricki Monnier, eds. *The Impossibility of God*. Prometheus, 2003. This is a multi-author collection of deductive arguments.

Martin, Michael and Ricki Monnier, eds. *The Improbability of God*. Prometheus, 2006. This companion to the previous book is a multiauthor collection of inductive arguments.

Sterba, James, ed. *Do We Have a Logical Argument from Evil?* MDPI, 2024. This is a multiauthor collection of articles written by theistic and atheistic philosophers arguing the POE.

ETHICS

16

RELATIVISM/ SUBJECTIVISM VS. ABSOLUTISM/ OBJECTIVISM

SYNOPSIS

This chapter launches a three-chapter section on ethics, the philosophy of morality. The first question to be settled, perhaps, is whether morality is fixed and eternal, the same in all places and times, or relative to individuals and/or cultures.

DIALOGUE

Angelo rose quickly from his seat and sidestepped Hannah, who was sitting between him and his target, the man with the dead eyes who had been surveilling the crowd at the coffee shop. Angelo drew his sidearm and barked in a commanding voice, "Freeze! Put up your hands!" Angelo's field of vision was narrowing into a tunnel, a dangerous reaction to his brain's hyperfocus. He fought to maintain his peripheral vision. The man locked eyes with Angelo, and as he did so, he raised his arm.

He was holding a large pistol.

Instinctively, Angelo squeezed the trigger of his gun—but nothing happened. He squeezed harder, desperately, as he saw the man's weapon now pointed directly at him. Life and death were a matter of a fraction of a second. The two men stood only twenty feet apart, so missing was unlikely. Angelo frantically squeezed the trigger with all his might, but it wouldn't fire.

The man now opened his mouth, unnaturally wide, and a deafening sound erupted from it. The man's gun wasn't firing. But the bone-chilling noise from his mouth kept getting louder, and Angelo felt his entire body tense.

Angelo bolted upright in bed, drenched in sweat, his heart racing. The noise coming from the man's mouth was the ringtone on his phone, a combination of clanging bells and a blaring emergency warning sound. The sound filled the room.

Adrenaline coursed through his veins as he leaped out of bed, knocking over his nightstand lamp, breaking the bulb. His hands trembled as he searched for his phone in the dark. He always laid it facedown on the dresser five feet from his bed, but with the lamp broken, he fumbled to find his phone's exact location. Angelo often emptied his pockets onto his dresser every night, so it was crowded with junk. He finally located the phone and answered it, relieved that the intense noise was silenced.

"Hello?" he said in a shaky voice. The voice on the line was familiar, brief, and authoritative. It was his captain.

"Get dressed and come straight to the police station."

Before Angelo could say a word or ask any questions, the call went silent. The time on his phone said 2:08 a.m.

Ten minutes later, he was racing through empty streets to the police station. He guzzled a protein shake as he drove and hoped someone had made coffee—although he wasn't even a little tired at this point.

When he turned onto Chestnut, his jaw dropped. Flashing lights set the night sky ablaze. There must have been two dozen police cars, lights flashing red and blue, spread out over multiple streets. The effect was blinding. Something big was up. He rolled up to a barricade. Two heavily armed SWAT officers approached his car, one directly and one off to the side, with their M4 combat rifles half raised. Angelo lowered his window and squinted as the closer officer shined his flashlight in his eyes.

"Are you Cassarino, the courthouse guard?"

Angelo nodded. "Yessir!"

"That's him," said the second officer, who quickly lowered his weapon. "I recognize him."

Angelo squinted. The flashing lights made it difficult to see. *Oh! It's Mack Ryan!* Mack had led some specialized training with Angelo's unit the previous year.

The first officer waved Angelo through the barricade and spoke into his radio as Angelo drove through. A uniformed officer wearing a high-visibility safety vest that practically glowed in the dark directed him to a parking space in front of the police station. Angelo quickly donned his service cap and stepped out of his car. Another police officer on the sidewalk motioned to him.

"You can leave your car there, Cassarino. The captain is waiting to see you."

Angelo nodded and thanked the officer, still bewildered about the whole scene. He hurried up the stairs and through the front door, which was also manned by a uniformed officer.

Inside the station, he saw dozens of people scurrying around, their clothing bearing the insignias of multiple agencies, including the FBI, ATF, and DEA.

It's a real alphabet soup in here, he thought to himself.

He saw Captain Lennox through the crowd and made his way toward him.

"Cassarino! You made it!" The captain motioned to Angelo and turned to a grave-looking man in a dark suit, who appeared to be an official of some government agency. "This is the officer I told you about."

Angelo's heart pounded. What was all this?

The man thrust out a hand, his steely eyes fixed on Angelo's. "Good work, son," the man said, a hint of southern drawl in his voice.

Angelo reached for the man's hand and made contact with what felt like granite. That hand couldn't possibly be flesh.

"Tom Blane, Special Agent in Charge. You're responsible for all this," he said, waving his arm to indicate the frenzy of activity in the station.

Angelo winced. *Oh no. What does* that *mean?*

"Your tip about the man at the coffee shop was a breakthrough. The way you described him, as bland and unremarkable as he is, triggered something for an analyst in DC, which set off a chain of connections that have led us to this point. A perceptive guard at the courthouse tonight noticed what appeared to be a person experiencing homelessness in the doorway of a closed restaurant across the street. But the guard thought something might be going on."

"Wow," Angelo said.

"He called it in, and SWAT was able to secure the man. Among his belongings, disguised as bags of clothing was surveillance equipment and a ghost gun made up of untraceable parts. More important, we identified the man as Sam McBride. He's been seen, but never identified, at multiple locations where the cartels operate. We also found a trigger device—to what, we don't yet know. This man is a high-value target, and every agency is going to want a crack at him."

Angelo tried to take it all in. Then he remembered that he had been called down to the station in the midst of what looked like a national emergency.

"Why was I called down here in the middle of the night?" Angelo looked back and forth between Captain Lennox and Agent Blane.

Blane fixed his eyes on Angelo. "Because he asked for you."

"Who asked for me, sir?"

"McBride."

"What?"

Angelo instinctively took a step back, his mind reeling.

"How is that possible, sir?" He looked back and forth at Agent Blane and then at Captain Lennox. "How does he know who I am? We locked eyes for only a moment, and then he disappeared from the coffee shop."

None of this made sense. Panic crept into his heart like icy fingers grasping for his very life. Angelo's legs suddenly weakened, and he swayed a bit.

"Cassarino, snap out of it." Captain Lennox's voice brought him back to reality. Angelo tried to gather himself.

"I'm sorry sir," Angelo blurted, straightening himself as if at full attention. "What do you need me to do?"

"We just want you to talk to him," Blane said. "I don't know what he wants with you, but he won't talk until he speaks with you."

"Just go in there and see what he wants," Captain Lennox said, placing his hand on Angelo's shoulder. "You aren't trained as a detective or interrogator, so there's no pressure here. We want to watch while he talks to you to see if we can gain insight about whether something is at the other end of that trigger."

Angelo nodded. "I'm ready, sir."

The captain and special agent led Angelo down the hall. Several SWAT officers stood guard as they turned the corner to an interrogation room. Representatives of the various agencies were standing in front of a two-way mirror.

"That him?" a DEA agent murmured to another agent, nodding in Angelo's direction. The second man shrugged.

As Angelo passed the window, he looked into the room and saw Sam McBride sitting at a heavy metal table, his hands cuffed to a thick steel ring embedded in the table. He was looking straight into the mirror. Even though Angelo knew McBride couldn't see them, it felt like he was looking straight through Angelo.

A shiver ran down Angelo's spine.

McBride's dead, cold eyes suddenly began to twinkle.

He was smiling.

* * *

Angelo entered the interrogation room and walked to the chair across the table from Sam McBride. Angelo had been instructed to let McBride lead the conversation. He wasn't to try questioning him about the trigger device they had found or about McBride's presence in Greenfield. Angelo was nervous, but his nerves gave way to a surprising calm as he sat down. McBride smiled at him but didn't say anything right away. Angelo studied his eyes, surprised that the man seated across from him now seemed like a normal guy.

Finally, McBride spoke. "How did you know?"

He seemed amused with Angelo.

Angelo decided to mirror him as much as possible. "Know what?"

"How did you know I was surveilling the coffee shop?"

Angelo *wanted* to interrogate him. But he knew he'd get in over his head quickly. Agent Blane had warned that McBride was dangerous and very intelligent. Angelo knew his limits. And he didn't want to accidentally tell McBride something that would put him or others in danger.

"That's a good question. I'm not sure. It was intuitive, I guess. I sensed it before I knew it."

"So you're more than just a rent-a-cop then. But you clearly aren't a shooter."

McBride meant he wasn't an experienced and highly trained soldier such as a member of the special forces.

"I'm not."

"Yet you recognized what I was doing that day. It's impressive. Maybe you have more potential than you realize. I've done this for years, and I don't know if I have ever been caught red-handed like that." McBride laughed. "You could have fit a pineapple in the mouth of the guy sitting next to you. He was so shocked by your reaction to me that his mouth almost hit the floor."

Angelo didn't say anything.

"Why were you there that day? I stood outside for a while. Your group was talking quite intently. What was it . . . three guys and a girl?"

Angelo nodded. He didn't like that McBride had noticed the others at the table.

McBride must have glimpsed Angelo's concern. "Don't worry. They aren't in danger," he said. "I don't believe in unnecessary collateral damage or retribution. It's part of my code."

The look in his eyes troubled Angelo.

"We were having a philosophical discussion," Angelo said, instantly regretting that he had given McBride any information.

McBride raised his eyebrows. "Philosophy? So you're no empty uniform. I minored in philosophy in college, you know."

Angelo stared back at him.

"Surprised?"

Shoot. Angelo's face had betrayed his thoughts again.

"You know I'm a bad dude, don't you? Did they tell you that?"

Angelo nodded.

"If you studied philosophy," Angelo blurted out, "then why are you . . . ?" He stopped himself. He didn't know what McBride's profession was. He only knew he shouldn't be doing all the talking.

McBride smiled. Not even the authorities were aware yet of what he did. But they'd figure it out sooner or later.

McBride's smile curved with a touch of something sinister. It unsettled Angelo.

"Why didn't your study of philosophy lead you to embrace virtue instead of whatever it is you do?"

McBride's smile dropped, and he leaned forward. "I did embrace what I learned but probably not the way you'd like."

Angelo stopped himself from shuddering at the sinister tone in McBride's voice. McBride leaned back in his chair.

"I favored the more radical philosophers, like Friedrich Nietzsche. He argued that the prevailing culture of his day was too beholden to Christianity and its ethic of compassion and pity for the poor, the weak, and the sick. He called it a slave religion and said that continuing in that direction would only weaken humanity and poison it. He called for a revaluation of morals consistent with Darwin's work on evolution. Strength, aggressiveness, selfishness, and assertion were what would push man's development to the next level. I was attracted to these ideas because I came to believe that following the path of evolution, not the Enlightenment, was our best hope for the future. I devoured the pessimistic philosophy of Schopenhauer, who said that raw will was what drove the universe. I embraced Thomas Hobbes's idea that an all-powerful ruler, the Leviathan, was needed to subjugate humanity to end war and conflict as we know it. I became a relativist who believes that we each make our own morality and have no right to tell others how they should live. We each get to exercise our will to power for our own good, so 'bad' is simply anything that hinders or weakens my own power, and good is anything that advances it. When I made these ideas my guiding principles, I began to grow in power and to advance as I never had before."

Behind the two-way mirror Captain Lennox and Agent Blane looked at each other, both raising an eyebrow. The courthouse guard was not getting any specifics out of McBride, but the conversation was certainly giving some insight into their captive.

After an awkward silence McBride asked a question.

"Are you one of those people who believes in absolutes?"

"I am," he replied. "I believe that morals are woven into the fabric of the universe because God has written moral law on our hearts. In addition,

God has revealed our moral obligations in the Bible and will someday judge the world, declaring all who have failed to keep his law to be condemned. Only those who have put their trust in God's Son, Jesus Christ, the innocent one who suffered for the guilty, will be welcomed into eternal life. I believe everyone knows the absolute right and wrong and that no excuses will be accepted on the day of judgment." Angelo realized he was talking too much.

McBride's previously blank face was now the one that betrayed what he was thinking. His expression was a combination of genuine interest and skeptical wonder.

"You really believe that, don't you?" McBride asked.

"I do," said Angelo, surprised at his own boldness. "Further, I find your relativistic morality to be unrealistic. You may believe that raw power and self-assertion are acceptable because no real morality forbids it, but I'd guess you're counting on your employers to hold some kind of absolute morality."

McBride's lips tightened in a thin line. "What do you mean by that?"

"I'm sure you've heard the saying that 'There is no honor among thieves.' What happens if those who are paying you decide you're no longer worth the risk now that you've been arrested? What if they decide to cut you loose, or even worse, make sure you don't live long enough to tell the authorities who they are and what they're doing in Greenfield?"

McBride slammed his fist on the table, the cuffs clanging against the metal top. He raised up partway from his chair and bared his teeth like a wolf. "They wouldn't dare," he growled. "I'm too valuable. I know too much. There's a code, and those who violate it don't last for long."

Angelo jumped a little when McBride slammed the table. But then a sense of calm washed over him. Was it because he'd gotten McBride to break character, or because he'd suddenly spotted a chink in McBride's fortress of self-assurance?

"I have no doubt there's a moral code," Angelo said calmly, "even among criminals. Otherwise they wouldn't be able to work together. But what if your employers didn't have opposition from law enforcement and could act with impunity? What kind of world would they bring about?"

McBride didn't say anything. How had some low-level security guard gotten him riled up? He was used to dealing with dangerous people and practiced self-control in every aspect of his life. He could even control his heart rate in stressful situations.

But this guy had raised a question he'd never allowed himself to contemplate during his years working with criminal elements. He had self-consciously developed a philosophy of life and morals characterized by Nietzsche's "will to power," which encouraged self-assertion and self-interest above all, but he counted on those he dealt with to be less reflective.

Something Angelo said was bothering him, in part because it might be true. Now that he was in custody, would his employers consider him a liability? The world he had so carefully crafted might be vanishing.

He realized that Angelo was speaking.

"What did you say?"

As Angelo repeated the question, McBride replied, "I imagine the vision of that kind of future would be strong men carrying out their will and accruing power to themselves. I plan to be on top when that happens."

"As long as you're on top, that's all that matters?"

"That's right," he said. "Only the strong survive. And that's what moves humanity to the next stage of evolution."

At that moment, the door swung open, and Agent Blane strode in.

He nodded at Angelo and said, "That'll be all."

That was Angelo's cue to leave. He looked over his shoulder as he left the room. McBride's eyes were dead once again.

* * *

Angelo got home as the sun was rising and crawled into bed, exhausted. In seconds, he was fast asleep. He slept fitfully for the next few hours. When he awoke, he texted the group to see if anyone could get together. He needed to talk to someone. Captain Lennox hadn't put any restrictions on talking about the encounter since no real interrogation had occurred.

Surprisingly, everyone was free.

Angelo told the group about the arrest of the man they'd seen in the coffee shop that night and Angelo's interaction with him.

Zach, Hannah, and Suresh couldn't believe their ears.

"I don't think he'd ever considered that others might treat him with the same relativistic morals by which he lives. He seemed to assume that the criminals he is involved with will abide by some code of honor and deal honestly with him."

"I suppose even criminals expect a person to keep their word and be honest, even if the focus is on criminal behavior," Suresh said.

"I was surprised he hadn't seriously considered that his employers might double-cross him now that he's been caught. As long as he was succeeding in his role, he didn't have to worry about it. But that has all changed . . ." Angelo's voice trailed off.

"Part of me pities him, which I'm sure he would hate," Angelo said. "His philosophy of life is worthless to him now. His only hope at this point is that the justice system will show some leniency if he cooperates, but I don't see that happening. When you commit to a way of life, I guess it's not easily abandoned."

Angelo looked around the table. He was so thankful for these friends and that they could talk about serious matters. Little did he know how important this group would become to him in the weeks to come.

THEORY

Angelo's conversation with McBride showed that different people approach the subject of ethics differently. But does that mean that ethics is relative to individual people? The following discussion will attempt to answer that question.[1]

Everyone experiences moral dilemmas. Sometimes they are big and obvious, like the temptation to plagiarize a term paper or steal something while shopping. Sometimes they are much smaller, like when you are tempted to roll through a stop sign while hurrying to an appointment,[2] or much more

1. Portions of this section of the chapter were previously published in Michael S. Jones, *Moral Reasoning: An Intentional Approach to Distinguishing Right from Wrong* (Kendall Hunt, 2017).
2. Some would argue that this is a legal issue rather than a moral one. The distinction between what is moral and what is legal is important but beyond the scope of this book.

difficult, like when you must choose between paying your bills on time or buying groceries for your family. Morality affects each one of us.

Everyone has opinions on moral issues. Some people think that drinking alcoholic beverages is simply a lifestyle choice, while others are convinced that it's highly immoral. What interests philosophers is how such opinions are justified. That is where ethics comes in. **Ethics** is the study of morality and theories about what is morally right and wrong. **Morals** are a person's beliefs about what is ethically right and wrong.

Two additional terms must be introduced: metaethics and applied ethics. **Metaethics** is the study of the theoretical foundations of one's moral beliefs. The prefix meta- indicates something lying beyond or behind something else, such as in the term "metalanguage" (which is a language created to talk about language) and "metaphysics" (which is the attempt to get beyond our assumptions about reality in order to investigate reality's true nature). In metaethics we are attempting to get beyond our assumptions about morality to investigate whether and how our assumptions are justified. **Applied ethics** is what most people think of when they hear the term "ethics." It is the attempt to evaluate the morality of specific actions or activities such as abortion, capital punishment, defensive warfare, in vitro fertilization, and many others. It is called applied ethics because it involves applying an ethical theory to some practical moral issue.

All of this assumes that there is right and wrong, that morality isn't completely subjective or some kind of **category mistake**.[3] This brings us to the issue of ethical relativism, which is one of many important metaethical issues that we need to discuss. Let's turn our attention to that.

Ethical Relativism

Ethical relativism is the view that morality varies from one person or group of people to another. In other words, morality is relative to one's culture.

3. A category mistake is a fallacy that is committed when one assigns something to a category in which it doesn't belong. For instance, if someone would say, "The Green Bay Packers are the best team in the AFC," that would be a category mistake, since the Packers are actually in the NFC. An example from ethics is when abortion is called "contraception," since by definition a contraceptive prevents conception, but abortions happen only after conception.

While this has never been the dominant view in the West, it gained ground throughout the twentieth century and continues to be a major current today. If ethical relativism is true, then the approach we must take to determining what is morally right will be very different from the approach that we would take if relativism is false, which is why we treat this issue at the beginning of our study of ethics.

There are several different types of ethical relativism. One is essentially epistemological in nature. It argues that moral judgments are completely subjective; that is, it holds that there is no possible way to be objective about morality. This view is called **moral subjectivism**. The opposite of moral subjectivism is **ethical objectivism**, which holds that ethical principles are not completely subjective but rather can be known objectively. Moral subjectivism may seem strange to the reader who has never encountered it before, but it's not so odd: After all, we have no problem saying that what kind of food tastes best, what kind of music sounds best, and what kind of painting looks best are completely subjective issues. "Beauty is in the eye of the beholder," as they say. The moral subjectivist is saying that morality is also a matter of personal taste or preference. One person prefers a society in which taxes are high in order to provide social benefits for even the neediest people in that society, while another person prefers a society in which both taxes and social benefits are minimal in the belief that this will result in a thrifty and industrious working class. Obviously there are advantages and disadvantages to both of these approaches; the subjectivist argues that which one is best is simply a matter of taste.

Another type of relativism is **cultural relativism**. This is the view that what is right or wrong is determined by the culture in which you live. Many examples of cultural relativism can be given. In some indigenous cultures women wear no shirts and this causes no scandal. It doesn't cause men to lust after them; in fact, men don't even notice. However, if a woman walks across the campus of a university in North America with her upper body unclothed, that would probably be more than merely a *faux pas*. It would be immoral, for it would both contradict the **mores**[4] of American culture

4. In ethics the word *mores* is pronounced "morays." Mores are moral values shared by a group of people.

and be very disruptive to the functioning of the campus. But in the USA it is common for women to wear short skirts, halter tops, and to swim in public wearing swimsuits that cover very little of their bodies. This is accepted in the American culture, but can you imagine what would happen if a woman were to dress that way in public in Saudi Arabia? What Americans take to be moral is not the same as what people in other parts of the world take to be moral. And here's the kicker: Each moral system—be it in an indigenous culture, in North America, in China, or in Saudi Arabia—works for the people living therein. According to cultural relativism, each society or culture has its own system of moral values that determines what is morally right and wrong in that society.

Arguments for Relativism

We've already seen some examples of the sort of evidence that leads people to conclude that morality is relative. Some take the wide diversity of ethical systems and moral convictions found throughout the world as evidence that there are no universal moral truths. This has been called the argument from the diversity thesis. The **diversity thesis** affirms that there are no moral principles that are held by all people (no **universals**). Based on this, relativists draw two conclusions: (1) Moral values are cultural constructs, and (2) there are no moral absolutes. (A **moral absolute** is an ethical principle that is binding on all people.)

Whether relativists are correct that there are no universal moral truths is open to debate,[5] but they are right that there is a great deal of diversity on moral issues. However, even if the denial of moral universals can be sustained, many ethicists are concerned that the argument from the diversity thesis to relativism is a ***non sequitur***.[6] It seems that the problem here is an

---

5. Several moral values and principles have been defended as being universal. One example is the Golden Rule ("Do unto others as you would have them do to you"), which appears in religions and philosophies from every part of the world in very diverse epochs. See Leonard Swidler, "Toward a Universal Declaration of a Global Ethic," *Journal for the Study of Religions and Ideologies* 3 (2004): 33–36, https://jsri.ro/ojs/index.php/jsri/article/view/157.
6. A *non sequitur* is a fallacy committed when the conclusion doesn't follow from the premises that are used to support it.

unfortunate **conflation**[7] of the concepts of "universal" and "absolute." The former is a moral value that is acknowledged by all people—a value that occurs universally throughout the human race. Even if there aren't any universals, that doesn't entail that there are no absolutes, no moral values that *should* occur universally. For example, most societies hold that it is wrong to torture innocent people. This may not be universal, for there may be some societies that hold that it is acceptable to torture innocent people. But perhaps those societies are simply mistaken. If so, then even though "thou shalt not torture innocent people" is not a universal (for it is not universally accepted), it is still an absolute. Universals and absolutes are not the same, and proving that the former don't exist doesn't prove the nonexistence of the latter. Hence, this argument for relativism seems unsuccessful.

That, of course, does not prove that there actually are absolutes. It simply shows that disproving the existence of universals would not disprove the existence of absolutes. Those who maintain that relativism is mistaken should go on to give reasons for believing that there really are ethical absolutes. Can that be done? Well, at the very least it can be stated that there are some actions that are very difficult to conceive as not being absolutes. For example, could it ever be immoral to "do unto others as you'd have them do to you" (the Golden Rule)? If not, then this principle would be an ethical absolute. Can you imagine a time when it would ever be right to torture a child simply for the fun of it? If not, then prohibiting it seems like a strong candidate for another ethical absolute.

Now let us return to the first conclusion that the relativist draws from the diversity thesis: Moral values are cultural constructs. A "cultural construct" is a belief, value, or tradition that is created by and becomes part of a particular culture. When relativists assert that morals are cultural constructs, they are saying that morals don't exist independently of culture but instead are created by a culture, perhaps unconsciously over a long period of time in response to events that happened in that culture or needs of the people in that culture. For example, a cultural relativist might point out that, for most of human history, slavery was not considered immoral, but today it

7. Conflation is the combination or equating of two distinct ideas as if there are no relevant differences between them.

is. She would then argue that contemporary culture has developed a moral value that was absent in earlier cultures: freedom.

Once again, the relativist has hit on some truth. There certainly are things that we consider moral and immoral today that were not considered moral or immoral at other times, and some of them are very significant—equal rights for women and minorities, for example. But the underlying argument, that the diversity thesis shows that moral values are cultural constructs, seems to commit the very same fallacy that was committed earlier: conflation. In this case what is conflated are the concepts of moral values and ethical absolutes. The term "moral values" connotes what people believe is right or wrong: their opinions. The term "ethical absolutes," on the other hand, refers to what actually is right or wrong independent of what people think. If **ethical absolutism** is correct, then binding moral principles do exist (in some fashion—we'll discuss this in a later chapter), regardless of what people believe.

You see, the fact that there are a great many opinions about what is right and wrong does not necessarily mean that all the opinions are equally true. It would be strange if every time there was widespread disagreement on a subject, the disagreement would be seen as evidence that all the disputants are equally correct. For the diversity thesis to work as evidence for relativism, either the absence of absolutes must be presupposed (which would **beg the question**[8]) or some additional evidence must be added.

One piece of additional evidence often thought to be relevant is the observation that those who hold to absolutism seem to have a tendency to be intolerant of those who disagree with them on moral issues. The basic line of reasoning is simple: People have a right to their own opinions, and therefore, people ought to tolerate those who hold opinions other than their own; absolutism seems to cause people to be intolerant of those with different opinions; hence, absolutism is incompatible with the principle that people ought to tolerate others' opinions. Therefore, absolutism should be rejected.

This can be viewed as a disjunctive syllogism:

8. Begging the question is a fallacy that was introduced in chapter 3.

1. Either tolerance (and therefore relativism) or intolerance (and therefore absolutism) is preferable.
2. Intolerance (and therefore absolutism) is not preferable.
3. Therefore, tolerance (and therefore relativism) is preferable.

This syllogism is logically valid, but for it to be sound, the premises must be true, so let's examine the premises. We all want our opinions to be tolerated by others, and it would be hypocritical to expect others to tolerate our opinions but to think that we don't need to tolerate the opinions of others. Hence, at least ***prima facie***,[9] tolerance seems to be worth preserving, and if absolutism undermines tolerance, it should be viewed with suspicion.

However, with a little reflection a person quickly realizes that there is a wide range of possible beliefs that just about everyone would agree should *not* be tolerated. For example, very few would argue that we should tolerate the opinions of Nazis wanting to resume the Holocaust or the terrorist belief that attacks on innocent bystanders are a viable way to advance a cause. In fact, the entire legal system seems to be predicated on the assumption that society has the right to limit or even prohibit the practice of many beliefs (the belief that I can drive on public roads at any speed that I want to, that I can take what I want from others without paying, etc.). We object to some of these beliefs because of moral values other than tolerance. We object to tolerating antisemitism because antisemitism is a grievous injustice; hence, in this context we are valuing justice above tolerance. We object to tolerating terrorism because terrorism is a violation of other people's right to life; hence, we value life over tolerance. This suggests that even though we should value tolerance, it is not the only moral value that we prize. We have a range of moral values of which tolerance is but one. This calls into question the major premise, which appears to assert that either tolerance or intolerance is *always* preferable. Because the situation appears to be more nuanced than that, it appears that this argument isn't sound.

---

9. *Prima facie* means "at first appearance." A *prima facie* conclusion is a conclusion that one arrives at when one first looks at the evidence on some topic, but such a conclusion may turn out to be wrong, and hence one should not put too much stock in *prima facie* conclusions. A conclusion arrived at after a thorough scrutiny of all the considerations pertinent to the subject is called ***ultima facie***.

Arguments Against Relativism

Several arguments attempt to show that ethical relativism is false. One is called **the problem of specificity**. Cultural relativism states that moral beliefs are constructed by social groups and hence each set of moral beliefs is binding only within the particular social group that constructed it. But large social groups are composed of smaller social sub-groups, which are themselves composed of even smaller sub-groups, etc. On the broadest level, perhaps all of humanity forms one large social group; on the narrowest level, perhaps each individual is his or her own very small social group, having his or her own cultural peculiarities and moral views. The question, then, is of which level the relativists are thinking when they affirm that moral beliefs are constructed by and only binding on a social group. Clearly they're not thinking of the whole human race but rather some subset. Is it the nation? Or the region? Or the race? Or the race within that region? Or the class? Or the class within that nation? Or perhaps it's individuals? It's not clear that there is any good answer to this question. But without a good answer, the view becomes problematically vague.

If the relativist takes the broadest view possible, that the social group that determines morality is the whole human race, then even if moral values are social constructs, they are binding on everyone and hence universal. That is as much a version of absolutism as it is relativism, and it's not what relativists are arguing for. If the relativist takes the narrowest view possible (the social group is the individual), then what the cultural relativist is talking about is no different from moral subjectivism, to which we'll return shortly. If the relativist takes any position between these two extremes, then she needs to provide a good reason for taking that position or else her choice is arbitrary. An arbitrary position is not based on a good reason, and therefore, there isn't a good reason to think that it is correct.

Regarding moral subjectivism, if it is true, then each person gets to choose not only what to *believe* is right and wrong but also what to *act upon* as right and wrong. And no one can judge an individual's choice as wrong. So if someone chooses terrorism as his or her morality, then terrorism is right for that person. Whatever a person chooses is right, be it antisemitism, racism, slavery, cannibalism, or whatever else you can imagine. But that seems absurd.

This argument is a ***reductio ad absurdum***. We've seen *reductio* arguments before. They work by showing that some principle or idea, if followed to its logical end, will lead to a conclusion that is so unlikely that it seems absurd. Here it is being used to show that adopting moral subjectivism would lead to the conclusion that anything at all can be moral if an individual decides that it is moral, which seems absurd.

Here's another *reductio*. If cultural relativism is true, then whatever a society believes is moral actually is moral for the members of that society. Therefore, it would be a mistake for people from other societies to judge the practices of that society. Based on this, it would be wrong for us to judge the antisemitism of Nazi Germany as morally reprehensible, or the racism of the antebellum South, or the cannibalism of various tribes in Papua New Guinea. But surely it's appropriate to judge antisemitism, racism, and cannibalism as morally reprehensible. Therefore, it's likely that cultural relativism is wrong.

A similar *reductio* can be constructed about moral progress. If relativism is true, then whatever a society currently accepts as moral actually is moral for that society. If that's the case, then doing anything other than what is currently accepted as moral is doing something that is not moral. Hence, no moral changes should be viewed as moral progress, for they will always involve moving away from what is currently accepted, which is moving away from what is moral. In short, if relativism is true, then there's no such thing as moral progress.

Here's one last *reductio*. If cultural relativism is true, then all moral reformers are actually corruptors of the morality of a culture. That's because if cultural relativism is true, then whatever a culture says is moral actually is moral. So any reformer—like William Wilberforce, who ended the British slave trade, or Martin Luther King Jr., who championed civil rights in the US—who is trying to improve a culture is actually corrupting the culture, since he's trying to move it away from the traditional practice. But that hardly seems right: People like Wilberforce and King are rightly viewed as heroes, not villains. Therefore, cultural relativism must be mistaken.

CONCLUSION

Relativism begins with some legitimate insights. For one thing, that moral *judgments* are culturally conditioned seems obvious. This explains the diversity of moral views in the world. Furthermore, we can agree that one ought to be tolerant of the views of others as long as those views do not lead to unacceptable consequences. However, neither of these points actually supports the conclusion that there are no moral absolutes once we recognize the important distinction between moral judgments and moral absolutes. That the former are relative does not at all entail that the latter are relative (or that the latter do not exist).

We have seen that the arguments for relativism are not very strong. On the other hand, the arguments against relativism seem convincing. Therefore, the most reasonable conclusion is that relativism is mistaken. If relativism is not true, then morality is not relative. If morality is not relative, then morality must be absolute. If morality is absolute, then absolutism is true; ethical absolutes exist.

If we are right in concluding that absolutism is true, then our meta-ethical question becomes, "What are the moral absolutes?" But in order to answer that question, we must first answer the question, "How can we find the moral absolutes?" We will turn to that question next.

QUESTIONS TO PONDER

- Where did you get your own ideas about what is ethical and what isn't?
- How would you define moral relativism? Is there any sense in which moral relativism is true? In what sense or senses is moral relativism false?
- How would you define moral absolutism, and what would you consider to be examples of moral absolutes?

TERMS TO KNOW

- ethics
- morality
- metaethics
- applied ethics
- ethical relativism
- moral subjectivism
- cultural relativism
- ethical absolutism
- ethical objectivism
- mores
- diversity thesis
- moral universals
- moral absolutes
- category mistake
- *non sequitur*
- conflation
- beg the question
- *prima facie*
- *ultima facie*
- the problem of specificity
- *reductio ad absurdum*

FOR FURTHER READING

General resources on philosophical ethics:

Becker, Lawrence C. and Charlotte B. Becker, eds. *Encyclopedia of Ethics*. 2nd ed. Routledge, 2003.

Bourke, Vernon. *History of Ethics*. 2 vols. Axios, 2007.

Feinberg, John S. and Paul D. Feinberg. *Ethics for a Brave New World*. 2nd ed. Crossway, 2010. This is an introductory ethics textbook.

On relativism and absolutism:

Mackie, J. L. *Ethics: Inventing Right and Wrong*. Penguin, 1990. This is a philosophically rigorous argument for relativism.

Pojman, Louis P. "A Defense of Ethical Objectivism." Pages 38–59 in *Moral Philosophy: A Reader*, edited by Louis P. Pojman and Peter Tramel. 4th ed. Hackett, 2009. This is a short but cogent rebuttal to relativism.

Pojman, Louis P. and James Fieser. *Ethics: Discovering Right and Wrong*. Wads worth, 2011. This is a book-length discussion and critique of relativism.

17

ETHICAL THEORIES

SYNOPSIS

Having dealt with the broad categories of ethical relativism and absolutism in the last chapter, this chapter will explore various ethical theories. A great many systems have developed over time to explain the existence of morality and to help people make moral decisions. This chapter will look at several of the major attempts.

DIALOGUE

A few days after their impromptu get-together, the friends still met for their normal Thursday evening gathering.

"I've been bothered by something," Hannah said, "but I don't want to be paranoid."

She paused for a moment.

"We got so focused on our chat about ethical relativism that we didn't ask: Was McBride doing surveillance on *us*? I know that sounds crazy, but Angelo and Suresh were at the shooting, and Zach has been involved in something related to it. McBride even said he saw us that night. Besides, who else in the coffee shop would have drawn the cartel's attention?"

Suresh agreed. "It's definitely confusing—and a little alarming."

"McBride said none of us are in danger, but he didn't tell me the purpose for the surveillance," Angelo said.

"I'm just a chef," Suresh said. "The chase through Studio 31 seems to have been random. I don't see how the cartel would have any concerns about me."

"They might want revenge against me since I was part of the effort to stop the men, but I'm just a security guard. I can't imagine a gun-running cartel considering me a threat."

"My only involvement has been providing social services to the witnesses of the shooting. It all just feels weird," Hannah said.

Zach sat quietly. He was struggling with what he could tell his friends.

"I can't say much, guys, but you're right that I've been involved. I was working at an FBI forensics lab. I can't share details. But no one except the FBI knows what I've been doing."

"You haven't talked to *anyone* but FBI agents?" Suresh asked.

Zach's stomach dropped.

"I did have a strange conversation with Tristan Lancaster last week."

"The former mayor's son?"

"Yes . . ."

"What's strange about that?" Angelo asked. "You and Tristan go back, don't you?"

"Yes, but I haven't spoken to him in a few years. He called out of the blue and asked me about my work with the FBI."

"How did he know about it?" Suresh asked.

"He claimed someone he knows at the courthouse mentioned that a chemist from my company was working on the case, and he guessed it was me. And then he said someone he knows at the FBI had confirmed it. It was a strange conversation, and his explanation didn't make sense."

Hannah furrowed her brows. "Do you think Tristan is somehow involved in the cartel and McBride was sent to watch you?"

"I don't want to jump to conclusions," Zach said. "There may be a perfectly reasonable explanation. All we know right now is that the son of the mayor, who is facing severe criminal charges, knew things about me he shouldn't have, and a gunman working for the cartel was watching the cafe where we meet."

Angelo thought for a moment. "I think we should return the favor."

"What do you mean?" Suresh asked.

"Let's find out where Tristan Lancaster lives. I'll do some surveillance on him to see if he's involved in anything suspicious."

"If Tristan is involved with a criminal organization, that could be very dangerous," Hannah said. "Maybe we just should tell the police."

Zach shook his head. "I'm not sure we have enough to take to the police. But I won't let you do this alone, Angelo."

"Me too," Suresh and Hannah said almost simultaneously.

"I can talk you guys through a few pointers on staking out a residence. I'll work out a schedule, and we can start right away. With our work schedules, we won't be able to maintain constant surveillance, but who knows. Maybe we'll figure out if he's up to something. Can't hurt to try."

"It might hurt if we get caught," Suresh said.

* * *

"Anything else you guys want to talk about?" Zach asked. "I'm in no hurry to call it a night."

"What Angelo shared about his conversation with McBride got me thinking about how I would establish my ethics," Suresh said. "I think I'm basically a good person, but all this conversation has me wondering about my ethical assumptions."

"Maybe it'll take our minds off current events to talk about it." Zach said.

"I, for one, don't know much about ethical theory," Angelo said. "Maybe we could brainstorm ways people might justify their ethical decisions? Then we could do some research and see how close we came."

"My training included some study of ethics," Hannah said. "Maybe I'll have some insights once we start. You might even stumble onto some of the major theories."

"Nice," Suresh said. "Hannah can give points to whoever gets closest to a known theory. Winner gets coffee on us for the next two weeks."

"I didn't say anything about it being a competition! But if that's what motivates you *boys* . . ."

Zach was laughing by now. "I'll go first!"

"Okay," Hannah said. "Here's a scenario: Suppose a woman finds out that the person in the cubicle next to her is stealing small items from the office. How does she decide whether to report the coworker?"

"That seems straightforward," Zach said. "If people are allowed to steal without consequence, it may be just a stapler today, but it could be thousands of dollars tomorrow. The lady must report the theft. That's the only reasonable and consistent option."

"Is that one of the ethical theories?" Angelo asked. "Zach's reasoning makes sense, but is it the only possible answer?"

"Indeed it is," Hannah said.

She explained what she could remember of Kant and what is known as duty ethics, based on what he called the Categorical Imperative, which is a moral law that must always be followed, regardless of circumstances or personal desires.

"People should always choose what they think everyone should do in that situation," Hannah said.

"Zach, you seem to think this principle is obvious," Angelo said. "But do you think ethical situations can always be reduced to rules with no exceptions? Didn't the Underground Railroad, for instance, work precisely because some people thought it was moral to break bad laws and hide runaway slaves? It seems like duty ethics doesn't allow for exceptions to the rules."

"I see your point. I guess I'd formulate a law that says a person should always value life over telling the exact truth. That would make it a duty for people to hide Jews from Nazi soldiers, wouldn't it?"

"It might," Suresh said, "but if you formulate a new rule for each exception, it doesn't seem to be much of a *general* rule."

"I think Suresh is on to something," Hannah said. "My recollection is that Kant didn't think categorical imperatives could be formulated for particular situations. The whole genius of this system is that it determines ahead of time what the right action will be in all similar situations."

"Interesting," Zach said. "I see the problems. Maybe doing one's duty isn't the entire explanation for how to make ethical decisions. I did come up with a valid ethical system. So how many points do I get?"

"Fifty points," Hannah said. "Your turn, Suresh."

"I think the lady should think through the consequences of the other person's theft and of her reporting it. After all, if the thefts aren't doing any harm and if her reporting it would cause the coworker to get fired over something trivial, she shouldn't report. But if the thefts are genuinely hurting the company and a confrontation would benefit the thief, then it would be right to turn her in."

"I guess we all make calculations like that about decisions," Angelo said. "And considering what we were just talking about, it seems similar to the thinking of people who hid runaway slaves and Jews destined for prison camps. I'm not sure I completely agree with it as an ethical system though."

"Suresh has come up with a legitimate ethical system," Hannah said.

Zach looked surprised. "People actually think the morality of an action can be determined by its outcomes? We may use calculations like that sometimes, sure. But I don't see how the outcome renders the decision moral or not. That seems very problematic. What is this ethical system called, Hannah?"

"Broadly, I think it is a type of consequentialism—the name sort of explains itself. An action's being moral or not is determined by its consequences. The most famous example of a consequentialist system is probably utilitarianism."

"Utility . . . that means usefulness, doesn't it?" Angelo asked.

"That's right. Utilitarians deem an action useful if it does the most good to the most people. Utilitarianism argues that being useful equates to being right. The most useful action is the one that helps the most people, and that makes it ethical."

The guys were beginning to wonder if Hannah had read an ethics book recently; they were impressed by her knowledge of the subject. They didn't know that Hannah herself was surprised by how much of her ethics class was coming back to her.

"I still don't see why you're troubled by consequentialism, Zach. And, Angelo, you seem to have some reservations as well. It seems like a very reasonable way to arrive at ethical conclusions," Suresh said.

"I can't speak for Zach," Angelo said, "but my initial concern is that it's often very hard to tell what the consequences of an action will be. Does an action have no moral character until the consequences are assessed? And when is the assessment made? An action might look like it benefits a lot of people in the short term, but in the long run it might cause a lot of harm. Was it moral for a while and then it turned immoral?"

"Furthermore," Zach interrupted, "some actions I think most people would find objectionable might have positive consequences."

"How many points did I get?" Suresh asked.

"We've got a tie!" Hannah sad. "Fifty for Zach and fifty for Suresh. The pressure's on, Angelo!"

"Based on what I know, it seems that both duty ethics and consequentialism focus on what a person does, but isn't morality deeper than that? Doesn't it matter more what a person *is* than what a person *does*? If the lady at the office is a virtuous person, she'll know the right thing to do. Do any ethicists argue along these lines, Hannah?"

"This way of addressing the question goes back to Plato and Aristotle. It's called virtue ethics, and it's still a very popular ethical system," Hannah responded. "The Greek thinkers argued that one could, through analysis, arrive at the most virtuous behavior."

"As a Christian," Angelo said, "I'm aware of virtue lists in the Bible that help us know what kind of character God desires. But how did the Greeks determine what behaviors are virtuous?"

"Aristotle wrote a book on ethics and explained the concept of the golden mean," Hannah said. "The virtuous action will find the balance between extreme behaviors."

"Such as?" Suresh asked.

"We've all known corrupt people," Hannah continued, "but the opposite extreme, legalism, is hardly better. The mean between these, according to Aristotle, is integrity. Or, for another example, we might say that diligence is the mean between laziness and workaholism. See how it works?"

"That makes sense," Suresh said.

"Fifty points for Angelo!" Hannah said, before anyone could jump in and ask for points. "It looks like we have a three-way tie . . . You guys up for a second round?"

"In fairness to Angelo, we should go in reverse order. Going first is a big advantage," Zach said.

"Thanks, Zach! Of course, that means I have to come up with something right away while you get to think about it."

"You're on to me!"

Angelo stood up. "But first I'm heading to the bathroom and then, ironically, I'm going to refill my coffee."

Angelo's three friends all followed his example. When they reassembled, Angelo began. "I think the Bible teaches me ethics. I look for the commands of God in the Bible that apply to me, and I try to obey them. Of course, I think this defines true virtue; I follow the Golden Rule, which I think is somewhat like Kant's categorical imperative; and I believe that doing the right thing will usually lead to positive consequences. Regardless, God's commands define morality for me."

"My ethics teacher probably wouldn't have thought much of that answer," Hannah said, "but he did acknowledge that billions of people around the world base their ethics on their religion's sacred text." Hannah checked her phone and discovered that this ethical system is called divine command theory. "That's good for fifty points, Angelo!"

"Wait a minute," Suresh said. "Are you saying that an action is moral because God commands it, or are you saying that God commands things because they are moral?"

Angelo had no idea how to respond to that. The friends waited patiently while he searched on his phone. After a few moments, he said, "You've raised an issue called the Euthyphro Dilemma, Suresh. Apparently, many Christians respond by teaching divine nature theory, the idea that morality is neither above God, holding him accountable, nor a result of his sheer will. It teaches that morality expresses God's moral nature and is part of who he is."

"Do I lose points because I had to look that up?" Angelo asked.

"No, you're still sitting at one hundred points. You're up, Suresh."

"You guys are probably going to think I'm nuts, but a couple of years ago I read *Atlas Shrugged* by Ayn Rand," Suresh said. "She argues that there is only one criterion for right and wrong: Does it benefit me? Rand regarded altruism as counterproductive and therefore immoral. We're all trying to survive, so the best thing a person can do is whatever it takes to survive."

"How exactly is that an *ethical* system?" Zach asked.

"Rand claims that pursuing one's own goals aligns best with human evolution and, therefore, will ultimately benefit everyone else. Sacrificing for others runs counter to survival of the fittest and is unethical in that it hurts humankind."

"Let me get this straight," Angelo said. "Every person should seek his or her own benefit in all decisions—and doing so is good, ethical conduct—but the person is simultaneously caring that these decisions benefit others? Doesn't caring about the results for others contradict the basic premise? And what if a particular decision doesn't benefit others?"

"I'm not advocating for Rand's view," Suresh said. "I just found it interesting. Is it a real viewpoint, Hannah, or just Rand's private idea?"

"Rand isn't the only person to advance that ethics structure. It's called ethical egoism," Hannah answered. "It's a particular form of consequentialism. Instead of asking how to do the greatest good for the greatest number, like utilitarianism, it asks a much simpler question: How will my action benefit myself? You explained it well, Suresh, especially considering your knowledge came from a novel.

"Angelo's critique is representative of what many critics say. Someone, for instance, who assassinated a king and took his place, would presumably benefit considerably from the action if he got away with it. But if he was a poor ruler, it's hard to see how the action would bring general benefit to others. Considering it an ethical act is certainly counterintuitive."

By this time, Hannah was using her phone quite a bit. Her memory of ethics class only went so far.

"I guess it's my turn," Zach said.

"It is, but let's give Suresh his fifty points first! I'm having a hard time distinguishing between you guys."

Zach laughed. "Okay. How about this? As a scientist, I think nature itself shows us how to live. Evolution has hardwired the world so that doing the right thing matches the way things are, if you will, and doing the wrong thing doesn't."

"Aspects of that resonate with me," Angelo said. "Of course, I'd argue that *God* embedded morality in nature. I doubt that morals would evolve naturally, but I agree with your basic premise."

"Your position is known as natural law ethics, Zach. There are naturalistic and Christian versions of it—as you and Angelo have illustrated—and the primary concern is that nature doesn't always send sufficiently clear signals for people to know what their ethical responsibilities are," Hannah said.

"You guys are amazing," Hannah said, clapping her hands together. "When we started this 'game,' I had no idea you'd come up with six ethical theories. How am I supposed to pick a winner?"

"Have I mentioned how beautiful your eyes are, Hannah?" Suresh gave his most disarming smile as he said it.

"Is that really how you are going to try to win an *ethics* contest?" Hannah asked, rolling her eyes. "Okay, Angelo you buy coffee for Zach; Zach, you buy it for Suresh; and Suresh, you buy it for Angelo. You're all winners."

* * *

Two days later, Zach and Angelo were in Angelo's car about half a block from a very nice home. Angelo had gotten Tristan Lancaster's address, and he and Zach were doing the first stakeout on the team's schedule.

At 11:00 p.m., a white van drove up to Lancaster's gate, and the driver spoke into a speaker mounted there. A few moments later, the gate opened, and the van entered the property. They'd never be able to tell much from ground level, half a block away. Angelo began scanning for a higher spot from which to observe what was happening on Tristan's property. A brick wall circled the property—several of the homes in this rather exclusive neighborhood had perimeter structures. Angelo wondered if they could scale the wall to see what was happening inside.

When he told Zach his idea, Zach looked at him like he was crazy. "You want us to walk right up to Tristan's property, *climb* the surrounding wall, and try to watch the property from on top? What ethical theory justifies that, dude? Certainly not ethical egoism. Are you trying to get us arrested or killed?"

"Okay, but aren't you curious about that white van?"

"Be patient, man. On every cop show, surveillance always looks like a long, tedious process. This is our first shift. Let's write down what we saw and see where it leads."

Angelo took a breath. His heart was beating out of his chest. *Who am I?*

I was suggesting scaling the wall around the property of someone who might be involved in criminal activity!

Zach was right. They'd keep watching the property. Perhaps they'd follow Tristan if he left the house at an odd hour. But they would avoid doing anything irresponsible or illegal. Hopefully they'd get to the bottom of this.

THEORY

In the previous chapter we learned that metaethics is the study of the theoretical foundations of one's moral beliefs. This chapter will lay out various metaethical options and explain the reasons why some people prefer one while others prefer another.[1] When studying metaethics, there are two different types of questions that need to be answered. One type is metaphysical in nature and includes questions like the following: "What is the nature of morality?" "Why does morality have the nature that it does?" "What is the source of morality?" and "What makes some actions moral and others immoral?" Anytime we're trying to figure out the nature of something, we're investigating its ontology, and ontology is a subset of metaphysics.

The other type of question is epistemological. Examples include "How can we discover the nature of morality?" "How can we find out what its source is?" and "How can we determine whether an action is moral or immoral?" Anytime we're asking how something can be known, we're doing epistemology. Since the nature of a thing sometimes has a direct bearing on how that thing can be known, we'll begin with the metaphysical questions.

Metaphysical Options

What is it that makes one action moral and another immoral? One answer to this question dates back to ancient Greece: **Platonic moral realism**. Plato believed that moral principles are an immaterial part of reality that exist even though they cannot be seen or felt, similar to the laws of logic and the principles of mathematics. It's called "realism" because it says that ethical absolutes really exist. Furthermore, they exist independently of any

---

1. Portions of this section of the chapter are adapted from Jones, *Moral Reasoning*, and Michael S. Jones, Mark J. Farnham, and David L. Saxon, *Talking About Ethics: A Conversational Approach to Moral Dilemmas* (Kregel Academic, 2021).

being, human or divine. Many moral realists, both naturalists and theists, believe that moral principles are necessary truths that would pertain in any possible world.[2] Platonic moral realism fits well with ethical absolutism. Most Americans who are not relativists are probably Platonic moral realists.

Despite its popularity, Platonic moral realism faces objections. For the theist, an important objection is that this view implies that there's a set of moral standards or laws to which even God is subject, which seems to impugn his sovereignty. Naturalistic moral realists face the problem that moral absolutes aren't physical and thus shouldn't exist on naturalism. If it's argued that moral truths are necessary truths that are neither corporeal nor incorporeal, that preserves the absolutist aspect of Platonic moral realism but at the risk of replacing realism with nominalism.[3]

Another venerable theory that supports moral absolutes is **divine command theory** (DCT). Many ethicists have held that what is good is good because God commands it, and what is evil is evil because God prohibits it. They reason that if God is the source of all things, he must be the source of morals. Furthermore, they reason that if God is sovereign and omnipotent, then he has both the authority and the power to decide what will be moral and immoral.

Obviously, naturalists will reject DCT because they don't believe in God. However, even for theists there are serious challenges to divine command theory. The heart of the problem was hinted at long ago in a story told by Plato. He has Socrates ask a young acquaintance named Euthyphro a series of questions leading to the following exchange:

> **Euthyphro:** Piety, then, is that which is dear to the gods, and impiety is that which is not dear to them.
> **Socrates:** There was a notion that came into my mind while you were speaking; I said to myself: "Well, and what if Euthyphro

---

2. A necessary truth is a statement that cannot possibly be false, like one plus one equals two. Necessary truths are true in any possible world.
3. The book *God & Morality: Four Views* contains chapters defending atheistic moral realism and theistic moral realism as well as atheistic moral constructivism and modified divine command theory. See R. Keith Loftin, ed., *God & Morality: Four Views* (IVP Academic, 2012).

> does prove to me that all the gods regarded the death of the serf as unjust, how do I know anything more of the nature of piety and impiety? For granting that this action may be hateful to the gods, still piety and impiety are not adequately defined by these distinctions, for that which is hateful to the gods has been shown to be also pleasing and dear to them." And therefore, Euthyphro, I do not ask you to prove this; I will suppose, if you like, that all the gods condemn and abominate such an action. But I will amend the definition so far as to say that what all the gods hate is impious, and what they love pious or holy; and what some of them love and others hate is both or neither. Shall this be our definition of piety and impiety?
>
> **Euthyphro:** Yes, I should say that what all the gods love is pious and holy, and the opposite which they all hate, impious.
>
> **Socrates:** The point which I should first wish to understand is whether the pious or holy is beloved by the gods because it is holy, or holy because it is beloved of the gods.[4]

The last line poses what has famously become known as the **Euthyphro dilemma**. It is called a dilemma because regardless of which of the possibilities Euthyphro opts for, he's in trouble. If he chooses the first option—that something is beloved by the gods because it is holy—then he has the problem that holiness is something that exists independently of the will of the gods. This is a problem because, if being holy is what causes the gods to love something, then the fact that the gods love it does not explain why it is holy. On the other hand, if he opts for the second possibility—that whatever is holy is holy because it is loved by the gods—then he implies that anything that the gods love would be holy. This is a problem because it makes holiness arbitrary, so that anything could be holy, depending on the whims of the gods.

Don't be distracted by the obvious polytheism here. The issues that Plato (via Socrates) points out are challenges to a monotheistic divine

4. The complete text of Plato's *Euthyphro* can be read online at http://classics.mit.edu/Plato/euthyfro.html.

command theory, too. Skeptics of divine command theory ask, "Is what is moral determined by the will of God, or is God's will determined by what is moral?" If the theist replies that God's will determines what is moral, that implies that nothing is inherently immoral, with the result that God could choose to make anything at all moral. This is a problem for several reasons, including that it makes morality arbitrary, that it deprives us of any sort of explanation for why God chooses one thing to be moral instead of another, and that if true, then things like torturing innocent little children for fun could be moral if God so chooses (which seems highly improbable to many people).

On the other hand, if the theist says that God's will is determined by what is moral, that implies that there is a standard of morality that is independent of God and to which God's will must conform in order for God to be moral. But that implies that there is a moral authority higher than God, which impugns God's sovereignty. It also fails to answer the question of the source of morality, for saying "God's will is determined by what is moral" does not explain how "what is moral" became moral. So divine command theory faces serious challenges.

A third theory on the nature and source of moral goodness is **social contract theory**. Its roots go back to early modern philosophers like Thomas Hobbes (1588–1679), John Locke (1632–1704), and Jean-Jacques Rousseau (1712–1778). It postulates that our ideas about what is moral are the result of an implicit agreement between the members of a society that facilitates the functioning of that society. It is like an unwritten contract between you and those living around you that guides your behavior so that you can get along with each other.

Prima facie, this seems like a very reasonable suggestion. There certainly do seem to be a lot of unspoken rules that help us get along with one another. For example, some people like loud motorcycles, other people like loud music, and some people like it quiet all the time. If a given neighborhood contains a mix of people who have each of these preferences, that could result in considerable conflict. But most people refrain from making loud noises at nighttime in order to preserve the peace. Loud motorcycles and loud music during the day don't usually cause problems; quiet at night seems to be a nearly universal compromise.

It makes sense to say that our ideas about what is right and wrong reflect, at least to some extent, the implicit beliefs of our culture. However, inasmuch as this is basically a form of cultural relativism, it is subject to the same objections as cultural relativism. And there is another significant objection to social contract theory. It says that each society has its own social contract, and that the contract of one society may differ significantly from that of another. Critics point out that it seems to be at least theoretically possible to compare the social contracts of various societies and evaluate which contracts are the most restrictive, the most permissive, the fairest, the most just, the most effective at promoting the flourishing of the society, etc. But some of these categories are clearly moral categories, and the conclusions drawn in such an evaluation will be, at least in part, moral conclusions. That means that we will be determining which social contract is the most moral. If that's the case, though, then there must be a standard or a conception of morality that is over and above the social contracts being compared, some moral standard up to which each contract can be held. But social contract theory cannot explain where this transcendent standard of goodness comes from. Thus, while social contract theory seems partially correct, it cannot be the final explanation of the nature and source of morality.

Recently some ethicists have argued for a **modified divine command theory** that some are calling **divine nature theory**.[5] They believe that an improved version of divine command theory can better account for the origin and nature of morality than the other theories we've looked at. They argue that we can solve the problems with traditional divine command theory by viewing morality as inherent in the nature of God himself rather than as something that God creates through issuing commands. God's commands do not determine what is good; they only communicate it. If this is the case, then moral principles are not arbitrary, as one horn of the Euthyphro dilemma implies, nor are they cultural constructs, as social contract theory implies. Instead, what is good is a reflection of a changeless, omnipresent

---

5. One influential figure in this movement was the ethicist Robert Adams, who taught philosophy at leading schools in the USA and Great Britain. See the further readings section of this chapter for information on one of his books.

God. And that's why moral truths are absolutes: Since they are part of God, they, too, are changeless and omnipresent.

This theory combines elements of divine command theory and moral realism. It does so in a way that shows the Euthyphro dilemma to be a false dilemma, for there is a workable third option. Divine nature theory denies that morality is arbitrarily determined by God's choices, for if morality reflects the unchanging nature of God, then no choice is necessary. Thus, it overcomes the arbitrariness objection. And it overcomes the objection from a standard of morality existing outside of God to which God's commands conform by making the standard internal to God—in effect, God is the standard.

The main objection to divine nature theory is that it requires the existence of God. Consequently, it's not an option for atheists. However, it may be a very good option for theists.

Epistemic Options

"Epistemic options" in the study of ethics refers to theories about how we can know whether an action is moral. There are many theories of this sort. Let's begin by examining theories that could work for naturalists. As explained above, naturalism is not compatible with any kind of divine command theory, nor does it fit well with moral realism. It makes the most sense for naturalists to embrace social contract theory. Therefore, naturalism is going to need an epistemology that focuses on socially generated moral truths, does not rely on any sort of divine revelation, and does not presuppose the existence of abstract objects. That rules out several theories, but it allows other options that do not involve anything transcendent.

One option is **ethical egoism**, the view that it is every individual's duty to look out for himself or herself and therefore the most moral option will always be the one that is most advantageous to the individual making the choice. It may not be immediately apparent how this is a moral theory; at first glance, it seems too self-serving. But the ancient Greek philosopher Epicurus argued that what's in one's best interest is often a path of moderation, helping others, and being an all-around good person. That's because how you treat others often determines how they treat you, and much of our happiness comes from our relationships with those around us. So for Epicurus, his concern for his own well-being leads him to be good to others.

Another ethical egoist is the Russian-American author Ayn Rand. She was born in Russia and lived through the Bolshevik Revolution, experiencing firsthand the poverty and oppression of the Soviet Union. She fled to the US and became an outspoken advocate of capitalism, freedom of speech, individual rights, and ethical egoism, which she saw as interrelated issues.

Rand argues that a system that places responsibility for having a good life on individuals and frees individuals to succeed will naturally tend to thrive, for it builds on the intrinsic motivation to be industrious in order to survive and flourish. Furthermore, she argues that capitalizing on this motivation will lead to economic prosperity that benefits all of society. In short, she argues that prioritizing the rights of the individual is what is best for everyone.

These examples of egoism are attractive because they manage to balance concern for individuals with concern for societies. They are attractive to naturalists because they don't require belief in God or abstract objects. However, there are some concerns with ethical egoism. Perhaps the most obvious is that egoists' concern that their theory benefits all of society in addition to individuals seems to be in strong tension with their foundational principle: that the most moral choice will always be the one that's most advantageous to the individual. It's easy to think up scenarios in which some choice would benefit an individual at the cost of the rest of society. Thus, there may be self-referential incoherence here.

There are other possible problems with egoism, too. For example, it seems to imply that an act that would ordinarily be considered evil should be viewed as good if it is beneficial to the individual performing the act. It also seems to rule out all altruism. The Randian version could lead to a sort of dog-eat-dog mentality of ruthless competition. But ethical egoism isn't the only option that is compatible with a naturalistic worldview.

Utilitarianism, the view that the most moral choice will always be the one that provides the most benefit to the greatest number of people, is another possibility for naturalists. Consider this: While the death penalty clearly involves a very significant loss for one person, if it has an even greater benefit to the rest of society, perhaps as a deterrent or through some other means, then isn't the death penalty moral? A utilitarian ethicist would answer "yes."

Utilitarianism has been a major approach to ethics in the twentieth and early twenty-first centuries. The founders of utilitarianism were the nineteenth-century philosophers Jeremy Bentham and John Stuart Mill. More recent utilitarian thinkers include R. M. Hare and Peter Singer.

Utilitarianism seems like a good fit for those who hold to social contract theory, which says that mores are a result of an unspoken agreement between the members of a society to live according to certain rules that will help that society flourish; utilitarianism says that we can figure out what is moral by figuring out what is best for society. Basically, social contract theory and utilitarianism are two sides of the same coin, one side answering the metaphysical question and the other answering the epistemic one.

Although utilitarianism seems like a straightforward approach to ethics, there are concerns. For example, the emphasis on doing what's good for society implies that we should not take into consideration the impact of actions on ourselves. Hence, the individual is sacrificed on the altar of the group. Egoists aren't the only ones who would be concerned by this. Other concerns flow from the fact that utilitarianism, like egoism, is a consequentialist approach to ethics. **Consequentialism** is the view that the morality of an action is entirely dependent on its consequences: An action with favorable consequences is moral, while one with detrimental consequences is immoral. One problem with consequentialism is that it can be difficult to predict the consequences of our actions. Because of this, consequentialist theories like utilitarianism and egoism provide little guidance about the morality of actions the consequences of which are in the future. Additionally, consequentialism seems to imply that immoral means can be used to achieve moral ends, since on consequentialism nothing is inherently moral or immoral, but rather actions become moral or immoral by producing desirable or undesirable consequences.[6]

A nonconsequentialist theory that might be compatible with naturalism is **virtue ethics**. This theory dates back to Aristotle (fourth century BC). It

---

6. Consequentialists would say that this objection begs the question by assuming that there are immoral means that produce moral ends.

views ethics as primarily concerned with a person's character, believing that what you do follows naturally from the sort of person you are. The virtuous person will naturally do the right thing. Therefore, virtue ethics recommends that those who want to be moral focus on cultivating a virtuous character. To do that, you need to know which traits are virtuous and which traits are not. Aristotle proposed that we can identify virtuous character traits by looking for traits that evidence balance by falling midway between two extremes. For example, courage strikes a balance between rashness and cowardice. He called this balance the **golden mean**.

There is much to like about this approach to ethics. For one thing, it prepares us to face ethical dilemmas by requiring us to cultivate a moral character well in advance of any future moral quandary. This is very useful, for once you are caught up in a moral crisis you may have neither the time nor the patience to contemplate what character traits should be guiding you. Furthermore, it builds on the insight that what we do flows from who we are. As Jesus put it, "The good person out of the good treasury of his heart produces good, and the evil person out of his evil treasury produces evil, for his mouth speaks from what fills his heart" (Luke 6:45).

Virtue ethics would be incomplete if it were to tell us how to identify virtuous character traits but not how to identify what course of action a virtuous person should take. To identify the moral course of action, virtue ethics advises us to ask ourselves what a virtuous person would do if he or she was faced with the same dilemma. This advice may sound circular, but vicious circularity can be avoided by thinking of a concrete person, such as Confucius, Jesus, St. Teresa, or closer to home, a virtuous parent, teacher, or minister. Ask yourself what he or she would do—or give him a call!

Since virtue ethics doesn't explicitly require the existence of a divine lawgiver or abstract objects, it is compatible with social contract theory and the naturalistic worldview. On the other hand, it doesn't explicitly rule out the existence of God or abstract objects, either, so it's also compatible with theism and divine nature theory.

Another approach that has roots in Aristotle—and was further developed by Thomas Aquinas—is **natural law ethics**. This is predicated on the belief that God created the universe with scientific laws that govern the natural world and moral laws that govern human interactions.[7] Moral laws are woven into the fabric of reality and can be discovered through careful study of the natural world, human nature, and human social interactions.

Examples of such careful analysis abound. For example, comparison of truth telling and lying shows the inherent superiority of truth telling: Lying frustrates communication, undermines trust, and can destroy relationships. This example illustrates how the very nature of reality encourages certain paths in life that are conducive to flourishing rather than being destructive. These are the choices that the natural law theorist views as moral. It's not that they are moral because they produce flourishing—that would be consequentialism. Rather, they produce flourishing because they are moral. Good actions naturally tend to result in a good life.

There's a fly in the ointment, though: There's disagreement about what moral conclusions the examination of reality actually supports. Take polygamy, for example: Although most people in Europe and the Americas view polygamy as clearly immoral, polygamous groups have long argued that polygamy is healthy for both men and women. A marriage involving multiple wives enables them to share childcare and household responsibilities, which not only makes life easier for them, but it can also free them up to pursue education and career opportunities that are often difficult to combine with motherhood. They can also provide companionship to each other and more easily satisfy the romantic desires of their husband. To be sure, monogamists can point out problems with polygamy, so this is a difficult issue for natural law ethics to decide.

Another theory comes from the German philosopher Immanuel Kant, whose approach to ethics focuses on fulfilling a person's moral obligations and is called **duty ethics**.[8] The central principle of duty ethics is the

---

7. Natural law has traditionally been a Christian—especially Roman Catholic—approach to ethics, but some secular ethicists advocate similar approaches. These ethicists reject relativism in favor of moral realism, and they argue that moral truths can be discoverable facts about the world. Neo-Aristotelian naturalism and Cornell realism are schools of thought within this movement.
8. Duty ethics is also called deontological ethics. **Deontology** is the study of moral duty.

categorical imperative: Act only according to that principle that you could consistently will to become a universal law. This means you should only do what you wouldn't mind others doing. That is similar to the Golden Rule.

Kant didn't conceive of the categorical imperative as an emotional test, as if what matters is what you would *prefer* to have done to you. Rather, he conceived of it as a logical test: Do only that which will not involve you in a logical contradiction. You contradict yourself if you say that what is acceptable for you to do would not also be acceptable for others to do. You are making yourself an exception to the rule.

Lying is a good example of this. If I were to adopt as my guiding principle "I should lie when it's convenient for me," I would have to be willing for everyone else to also live by that principle. Otherwise, I would be involving myself in a contradiction by saying, on the one hand, that it is moral to lie (for me), and on the other hand that it's not moral to lie (for others). In contrast, if I were to adopt as my guiding principle "always tell the truth," I would have to be willing for everyone else to always tell the truth. That's an outcome that I would consider to be desirable, and since I would be adopting the same principle for myself as I would want others to live by, I wouldn't be contradicting myself. Hence, "always tell the truth" is the moral choice.

Kant strongly believed in moral absolutes. He also clearly rejected consequentialism. It's not easy to determine whether Kant was a Platonic moral realist, held to some form of divine command theory, or held to something else entirely. However, it is clear that Kant believed in God, so some theistic approach to ethics would be a good fit for him.[9]

Duty ethics sounds promising. However, there are difficulties. For example, like cultural relativism (discussed in the preceding chapter), duty ethics faces a "problem of specificity": How specific should our moral principles be? We may not want to universalize the principle that lying is good. However, perhaps we should universalize the principle "lying is good when it saves a life." Here we can think of the familiar scenario of a family harboring Jews in Nazi Germany. If the Secret Service would knock on the

9. Kant saw God's existence as a necessary condition of morality. See Peter Sjöstedt-Hughes, "Kant's Moral Argument for God," https://www.philosopher.eu/texts/kants-moral-argument-for-god/.

door and ask whether the family was harboring Jews, the family would be faced with a difficult choice: Should they lie to protect the Jews, or should they tell the truth, with the very likely result being that the Jews would be sent to a concentration camp? Surely in such a situation it is more moral to lie than to tell the truth. But if we say that, then we seem to have abandoned our principled approach to ethics in favor of an approach that says that we should base our moral decisions on the consequences that we anticipate our actions will have. In short, we've traded duty ethics for consequentialism. Kant would urge us to stand firm and tell the truth, even if that doesn't feel right.

Religious traditions bring another option to the table: **revelational ethics**. All the world's major religious traditions have scriptures that contain moral teachings. In fact, the *Analects* of Confucius are primarily concerned with moral and political thought. The Hebrew Bible and the Christian Bible contain a considerable amount of moral instruction, as do the Qur'an (Islam), the Gathas (Zoroastrianism), and the scriptures of other religions. These are a potentially rich resource for ethical decision making.

The view that revealed scripture can be a source of moral truth fits well with divine command theory, both traditional and modified. If God exists, is the foundation of morality, and has revealed truth to us in scripture, then looking to scripture for guidance is an obvious move. Naturalists reject these premises, of course, but theists accept them. This gives rise to several questions, including whether God exists, whether he has inspired scripture, and which scripture he has inspired. Unfortunately, we do not have space to address these questions here.

The Metaphysical Options, the Epistemological Options, and the Worldviews

We have studied four theories on the metaphysics of ethics: Platonic moral realism, divine command theory, social contract theory, and divine nature theory. We've seen that social contract theory fits well with a naturalistic worldview and that divine nature theory is a good choice for those holding to theism (and deism). Regarding an epistemology of ethics, since naturalism rejects belief in anything supernatural, it is incompatible with any option that involves God or abstract objects. That leaves ethical egoism, utilitarianism, and perhaps virtue ethics as live options for naturalists. One might think that duty ethics would also be a possibility, but duty ethics implies the existence of moral absolutes and therefore is not compatible with social contract theory, which implies cultural relativism.

Because theism and divine nature theory are complementary, theists can avail themselves of any epistemic theory that is compatible with divine nature theory. That would include revelational ethics, natural law ethics, and duty ethics. It would also include ethical egoism, utilitarianism, and virtue ethics, since these don't rule out belief in God.

It's quite possible to combine several of these theories. This must be done with care, though, in order to avoid combining incompatible systems. Naturalists may want to combine utilitarianism and virtue ethics, which seem complementary. Christian theists may benefit from combining revelational ethics with natural law ethics, duty ethics, and virtue ethics, each of which reflects a principle contained within the Christian Bible.[10]

10. For natural law ethics, see Rom 2:14–15; for duty ethics, see Matt 7:12 (the Golden Rule); for virtue ethics, see Matt 15:17–20. Some form of utilitarianism may also be biblical; an omnibenevolent and omnipotent God would arguably want the best outcome for the most people, and a number of passages urge us to care for others, such as Rom 12:10; 15:1–3; Phil 2:3–4; and Heb 13:16.

QUESTIONS TO PONDER

- Is morality relative? What does it mean to be "relative"?
- What is a "moral absolute"? Are there moral absolutes?
- How can we decide whether any given act is moral or immoral?
- If there is no God, what makes one action moral and another immoral?

TERMS TO KNOW

- social contract theory
- divine command theory
- the Euthyphro dilemma
- Platonic moral realism
- divine nature theory
- modified divine command theory
- ethical egoism
- utilitarianism
- consequentialism
- virtue ethics
- golden mean
- natural law theory
- duty ethics
- deontology
- categorical imperative
- revelational ethics

FOR FURTHER READING

Two very readable introductions to ethical theories are:

Jones, Michael S. *Moral Reasoning: An Intentional Approach to Distinguishing Right from Wrong*. Kendall Hunt, 2017. This small book was written by one of the authors of *Talking About Worldviews.*

Wilkens, Steve. *Beyond Bumper Sticker Ethics.* InterVarsity Press, 1995. This includes chapters on ethical theories and applied ethics.

For those desiring more advanced reading:

Becker, Lawrence C. and Charlotte B. Becker, eds. *Encyclopedia of Ethics.* 2nd ed. Routledge, 2003. As the title suggests, this is a broad resource covering many ethical issues from a variety of perspectives.

Bourke, Vernon. *History of Ethics.* 2 vols. Axios Press, 2007.

Feinberg, John S. and Paul D. Feinberg. *Ethics for a Brave New World.* 2nd ed. Crossway, 2010. This book treats ethical theories and applied ethics. It's a fairly advanced reading that approaches ethics from a theistic perspective.

18

APPLIED ETHICS: RACISM

SYNOPSIS

Ethical theory is valuable because it shows *how* ethical thinking should be done. It's important, though, for the theory to be utilized for actual ethical problems, such as capital punishment, abortion, and preserving the environment. This chapter will address a perennial ethical problem in human history: racism.

DIALOGUE

Even though Angelo's schedule called for two people to stake out together, it was long and boring. They had a new appreciation for those who did this all the time.

Unfortunately, they hadn't seen much. Most of their stakeouts were in the evenings because of work, so they knew very little about Tristan Lancaster's daytime routines.

The one thing that occurred regularly was the arrival of a white van around 11:00 p.m. four or five times a week. While it seemed odd for a van to arrive at that time of night, they had no idea what it contained, who was driving it, or what its purpose was.

By the third week, they were tired and frustrated.

Angelo decided to use his vacation days to do some daytime surveillance. Surprisingly, Hannah joined him so that he'd have company and backup. Zach had missed so much work while he was with the FBI that he didn't have that option, and Suresh was still working overtime.

The following Monday, Angelo and Hannah were in his car outside Tristan's house at 6:00 a.m. They had started early in hopes of catching Tristan's daytime activity, possibly even following him to work.

At 7:30, the gates opened, and a silver Lexus pulled out of the driveway. It turned toward Angelo and Hannah and drove slowly in their direction. Angelo was suddenly glad Zach wasn't with him because Tristan had no reason to recognize him or Hannah. As Tristan drove past them, he glanced at the two people in the parked car on the side of the road. Angelo thought he saw confusion (or was it worry?) on Tristan's face.

After the car was out of sight, Angelo made a U-turn and headed after Tristan's car, hoping to spot it before it turned. Nothing ventured, nothing gained.

Hannah glanced at him and nodded her approval. They were tired of sitting for hours on end. They were ready to get some info.

Following Tristan didn't end up being very difficult. He drove straight to the courthouse, where Angelo spent most of his working hours. Hannah checked the news on her phone. Mayor Lancaster was there for a pre-trial hearing. Tristan was there to support his dad. Angelo and Hannah watched him park and then circled the building and left, somewhat disappointed by how little they had learned. Suresh and Zach were scheduled to watch the house that evening.

No new information the next day, as Tristan never left his house. Was this just a wild goose chase? Zach and Suresh hadn't seen anything suspicious the night prior. The white van hadn't even come. Angelo didn't have much vacation time and was close to calling the whole thing off when there was a new development.

On the third day of their daytime surveillance, the white van came up the street behind them. It usually came at night, from the opposite direction. Fortunately, Angelo caught them in his rearview mirror before they drove by. He saw that the driver and passenger were both Hispanic. The van slowly drove past, unaware of them, and turned into Tristan's driveway.

"Did you see them?" Angelo asked Hannah. "They were Latino; they must be affiliated with the cartel."

"Because they're Latino?" Hannah said.

"What do you mean?" Angelo said. "Many cartels originate in Mexico and other Hispanic countries. This operation probably has ties to one of the Latino cartels."

"I'm not so sure. Granted, we've been doing all this under the assumption that Tristan is involved in the cartel and that whoever was driving the white van might be implicated. But to assume we know more because they're Latino seems like a reach. I'm sorry, Angelo, but that feels like racial stereotyping."

"I'm not a racist," Angelo said, gripping the steering wheel. "I guess we'll wait and see. But I think I'm right."

"Whether you end up being right isn't the issue," Hannah said. "Applying the characteristics of a group to an individual isn't justified, whether we end up being right or not."

"Whatever," he mumbled.

Hannah let it go, but for the first time, she was very frustrated with Angelo.

Nothing happened for the remainder of their shift, and Angelo drove Hannah home. A few minutes into the drive, Angelo glanced at Hannah. "I think someone is following us."

"That would be ironic," Hannah said.

But Angelo kept glancing in the rearview mirror and seemed genuinely concerned.

"Don't turn around, but do you see that light blue car a few cars back? I've made four turns since Turret Street, and it has matched every turn, keeping its distance but maintaining contact. I'm going to make another turn and see if it follows us."

The blue car turned and continued to follow them.

In fact, it began to close the distance between the two vehicles. Angelo sped up a bit. He turned several more times, almost at random, and then got on the interstate past the west side of Greenfield. The blue car stayed on his tail.

He decided to drive to the police station. If the car had criminals inside, they'd be less likely do something with police around. After another fifteen pulse-pounding minutes, Angelo and Hannah pulled into the police station parking lot. Angelo made sure he had easy access to his pistol.

The blue car pulled up directly behind them, and a large, imposing Hispanic man got out of the car. The man approached their car, right there in the police department parking lot, walking to the passenger side at the curb. Angelo's hand tightened on his gun.

"Don't worry, Hannah."

The stranger tapped Hannah's window and motioned for her to roll it down. He produced an FBI badge. "You guys led me on quite the chase. I'm Agent Esposito. We need to talk."

Hannah glanced over at Angelo.

"We've contacted Zach Williams and Suresh Bakshi. They'll be here soon," said Agent Esposito.

Angelo and Hannah were relieved that the driver wasn't criminal, but why did he want to talk to them? They walked into the police station with him and were ushered to a private room. Zach and Suresh were already there. The four friends greeted one another a bit uneasily and sat down at a long rectangular table. Esposito and another man took seats on the opposite side.

Esposito spoke first, "Thank you for coming. Collecting Mr. Cassarino and Miss Maplewood was a bit more challenging," he glanced over at Angelo, "but how that happened will make sense."

Esposito motioned to the man next to him. "This is ATF Agent Johnson. He's investigating primarily the gun-running operation. Chemical weapons are my specialty, so I was brought in because of the sarin gas. We think the same group is involved in both."

Hannah couldn't believe what she was hearing. "Why are you telling us these things?"

"You have put yourselves in a very dangerous situation," Esposito said. "I don't know why you're watching Tristan Lancaster, but you were naïve to think bad people wouldn't notice."

Angelo turned pale. He had put his friends in danger.

"Some things happened that made us suspicious," Hannah said.

"But we didn't think we had enough to bring the police into it," Zach said. "Watching his house seemed like the most reasonable option."

"Mr. Cassarino, you did a good job spotting my tail."

Angelo looked at him and then down at the table.

"But if you were able to spot me, don't you think Mr. Lancaster might have noticed you following him?"

Johnson spoke. "We've been watching Lancaster's residence since before you guys showed up. Once we realized what you were doing, we kept an eye on you."

"And you're just now calling us off?" Angelo asked.

"Frankly, we weren't sure of your involvement with Lancaster. Once Mr. Lancaster's people realized you were watching them, we couldn't interfere without tipping them off to our presence. The drive across town tonight gave us this opportunity."

"How do you know they figured out we were watching?" Angelo asked.

"An embedded agent picked up bits of conversation inside the house."

"So you have people on the inside?" Zach asked.

"Yes," Esposito said. "They were talking about how to eliminate the four of you."

Hannah gasped and put her hand to her mouth. Angelo turned pale while Suresh and Zach exchanged dour looks.

"They originally sent Sam McBride, primarily because of their interest in Mr. Williams."

The friends looked at Zach. What could they want with Zach?

"McBride's arrest infuriated the cartel," Johnson said. "They were going to come after you anyway, but the stakeout made it much easier."

"We're in the middle of a mess," Suresh said.

"I know," Esposito said. "That's why we're talking to you today. We are close to breaking open a national operation. You guys, to be frank, are a distraction and are risking the operation."

"It's national?" Zach asked.

"Would you believe that the bombing of Chesterton Bridge was a diversion and part of the cartel's overall plan? Big things are happening, and Tristan Lancaster and the sleepy town of Greenfield seem to be in the middle of it."

"What do you want from us?" Suresh asked.

Esposito's voice was firm. "Get out of our way. Stop this silly 'surveillance.' Keep your heads down."

“I thought you said we’re in danger,” Hannah said. “Will keeping our heads down keep us safe?”

“The Greenfield PD is cooperating on this operation, and they are loaning us some officers to keep an eye on you. We’re watching Lancaster. We will do our best to keep you safe. We think Lancaster and the cartel have bigger fish to fry. If you stay out of the way, we doubt you’re worth the trouble to them at this stage in the game.”

“You doubt?” Angelo asked. “That’s not very comforting.” He was wondering how he was going to obey all the verses in the Bible about not worrying.

“No more vigilante antics!” Esposito said. “Go about your normal lives, and hopefully you’ll see breaking news headlines in a few weeks.”

“If you say so,” Zach said.

* * *

The four friends tried their best to return to normal routines. But life felt anything but normal after hearing that a dangerous cartel wanted them dead.

The group decided to get together at a different location this week since the cartel knew about their regular meeting spot. Instead, they met at Zach’s place, the first time they’d been there. It was small, but he had good coffee, and his dog was cute.

They settled into conversation about McBride, Tristan, the FBI, their car chase, and the mysterious white vans. When the vans came up, Hannah decided to bring up Angelo’s assumption about the Hispanic drivers.

Angelo immediately apologized. “I’ve thought about what I said, and I see now that I was jumping to conclusions. I was a poor representative of Christian ethics. Racism should have no part in a Christian’s life.”

“Would any ethical system condone racism?” Hannah asked.

“Perhaps,” Suresh said. “We should explore the various systems and see. At least it will get our minds off Tristan Lancaster.”

Zach said. “What exactly do we mean by *racism*? For that matter, what is a race?”

“Good point,” Hannah said. She grabbed her phone and did a quick search. “Here’s a definition from *Merriam-Webster*: ‘any one of the groups that humans are often divided into based on physical traits regarded as common among people of shared ancestry.'"[1]

"Makes sense," Angelo acknowledged. "And *racism*?"

"'A belief that race is a fundamental determinant of human traits and capacities and that racial differences produce an inherent superiority of a particular race.'"[2]

"So racism has two distinct components," Suresh said. "Not only is it racist to think a particular race is inherently superior to others, but it's racist to assume that 'human traits and capacities' should be attributed primarily to race."

"So it would be racist for me to think, for instance, that Asians, especially those from the Far East, are good at math because they're Asian," Zach said. "Even though I'm not saying something critical of them . . ."

"Yes, because you're still diminishing the individual achievement of a particular Asian person by attributing their skill at math to their race," Hannah said.

"Given that definition, many of us probably stumble into racism quite often."

"I certainly did," Angelo said. "I associated the men in the van with criminal activity based on their racial features—they appeared Latino—much more quickly than I might have had they been of some other race. Maybe the word *cartel* had my mind oriented that way, but I have no excuse."

Angelo leaned back in his seat.

"I don't believe God favors one person over another based on 'human traits or capacities.' After all, God creates those characteristics and seems to love variety. If his nature determines morality, racism wouldn't be an acceptable option for Christians."

"I've never thought about it through this framework," Hannah said.

"And there's another thing," Angelo continued. "If a person takes the origin stories in the Bible literally, Scripture teaches that all people are

1. *Merriam-Webster,* under "race," https://www.merriam-webster.com/dictionary/race.
2. *Merriam-Webster,* under "racism," https://www.merriam-webster.com/dictionary/racism.

descended from the same original ancestors, Adam and Eve, meaning the differences that now exist between groups of people are less significant than the similarities they inherit from their common ancestry. In fact, many Christians are uncomfortable with the word *race* because they are convinced that all people belong to the same race. We tend to use *ethnicity* or some other synonym, although there doesn't seem to be a perfect term."

"So how did slavery flourish for so long among Christian people?" Suresh asked. "Many 'Christians' seemed to regard other races—particularly the Black race—as inherently inferior. Was that some alternate way of understanding Scripture?"

"I'd say any such interpretations are *mis*interpretations, and I believe strongly that racism contradicts the heart of the Christian faith. The Bible makes no distinctions based on race between those who are sinners, those God loves, and those Jesus Christ died for," Angelo said, looking around the room.

"I hope it doesn't sound defensive to also point out that slavery has been a worldwide problem, involving people from almost every world faith. In England and America, primarily Christians fought against the slave trade—because of proper interpretation of Scripture."

"That's a good reminder," Suresh said.

"It seems to me that an evolutionary hypothesis in which different people groups are viewed as arising from different ancestors would have a more difficult time establishing racial equality. What do you think, Zach?"

"There is the question of objective differences between people of different races," Zach said. "It's undeniable that groups of people have shared characteristics that distinguish them from others. Otherwise we wouldn't be having this discussion. Distinct evolutionary development may contribute to these differences, but Angelo is right that the differences are statistically minimal compared to the massive similarities between all races. Evolutionists would simply say that all people belong to the same species, *Homo sapiens*. When you apply ethical theory to how we should treat one another, an atheist finds no basis for racism."

"Can you elaborate?" Hannah asked.

"I haven't completely settled on which ethical theory I prefer, but utilitarianism makes a lot of sense. If we make decisions based on what will bring the greatest benefit to the greatest number of people, then making decisions for only a segment of any population, even if it is the majority, won't be as ethical as making decisions to benefit the entire population."

"But couldn't this reasoning sometimes undermine the rights of minorities?" Hannah asked. "Let's say a city official has to make a decision that will either benefit the majority race, say 75 percent of the population, or the minorities who make up the other 25 percent. If she used utilitarian thinking, wouldn't she be obligated to choose what benefits the majority? How would this kind of ethic guard the rights of minorities?"

"That's a good question, but I think it proceeds based on a false disjunction: that the official must choose for the majority or for the minorities. In most cases, there is a third way, namely making a choice that benefits a significant percentage of both the majority and minority populations. I read an article recently by John Stuart Mill in which he responded to a challenge that his philosophy threatened the rights of minorities. He essentially said that a democracy of ideas benefits *everyone* in the population. Therefore, protecting minority rights ends up bringing the most benefit to the most people.[3] Like Angelo's Christian ethics, utilitarianism could be *misinterpreted* to always favor the majority, but that's not a sophisticated reading of it."

"Suresh and I had a conversation about ethical theory after our group meeting on the topic," Hannah said, "and we found ourselves leaning toward virtue ethics. It doesn't seem like virtue ethics would ever support racism. Looking down on others, feeling superior, and mistreating people because of racial characteristics could hardly ever qualify as virtuous."

"I fully agree," Suresh said. "The key in virtue ethics seems to be identifying the virtues against which a person measures his character. Angelo says he gets his list from the Bible; I see the virtues embodied in the great works of Eastern literature; Hannah extracts them from her work in the social sciences. In all cases, the character traits that emerge directly contradict the attitudes that generate racial animosity."

Zach looked at the time.

---

3. Mises Wire and Michael Rectenwald, "John Stuart Mill, 'The Marketplace of Ideas,' and Minority Opinion," *Mises Wire*, June 22, 2021, https://mises.org/mises-wire/john-stuart-mill-marketplace-ideas-and-minority-opinion.

"It's getting late. Thanks for coming over, everyone," Zach said. "We should probably all catch up on our rest after everything that has happened."

"Whatever lies ahead, I hope we hear about some resolution on the news."

"Amen," Angelo said.

THEORY

In the dialogue, Angelo showed how easy it is for people to slip into discriminatory thinking if they're not careful. To avoid this hazard, it's important to have a clear system for determining right from wrong and then to apply it consistently. The following discussion will illustrate this by exploring how each major ethical theory addresses the issue of racism if it's applied consistently.

The first step is to define the term "racism" so that we know exactly what we're talking about. To define racism, we must first define "race," which is a bit trickier than one might expect. Many people think of race in terms of skin color, but a careful examination of the data shows that there's more involved. Consider these facts:

- In Brazil, siblings can be categorized as different races based on appearance even if they share the same parents.
- In Great Britain the term "Black" refers to all non-Whites (medium- and dark-skinned Africans, American Indians, Asians, etc.).
- In the US, anyone who has any African ancestry and has skin that's slightly darker than northern Europeans is usually considered "Black," even if their African ancestry is considerably less than 50 percent. On the other hand, it is not at all the case that anyone who has any northern European ancestry and has skin that's slightly lighter than Black Africans is considered "White."

During the nineteenth century, when several million Irish and Italian immigrants came to the United States, they were not considered "White." They were Caucasian, but their skin tones and hair color were different from most Americans, their English had pronounced accents, their religion was different (most were Roman Catholic rather than Protestant), and their diets, customs, and cultures differed from other Americans. It's interesting that they weren't simply viewed as Whites who were different in various ways; they were considered non-Whites.

Data like this suggests that race involves both objective and subjective elements. The objective elements include things like ethnicity, skin color, speech patterns, and so on. The subjective elements are generally regarded as social constructs, each society evolving its own categorization of various groups of people in a subconscious process that sociologists call "racial formation."[4] So **race** can be defined as a set of objective and subjective characteristics that differentiate one group of people from others within a given society.

Building on this, **racial prejudice** is somebody's preconception that certain people are inherently more worthy than others simply because of their race (as defined above); it is the view that some race or races are inherently superior to others.[5] The term racism is often used as a synonym for racial prejudice. Therefore, we now have one definition of racism: **Racism** is (sometimes) the view that some race or races are inherently more worthy than others. Corresponding to that, a **racist** is a person who harbors such racial prejudice.

This sort of racism is an attitude or belief held by one individual toward others and can be called **individual racism**, for it occurs in the minds and hearts of individual people. However, that's not the only kind of racism. Another kind is impersonal: **Systemic racism** refers to policies and/or practices that exist in a society or organization that result in an unfair advantage to some people and unfair harm to others based on race. Systemic racism

---

4. Michael Omi and Howard Winant, "Racial Formations," in Charles Gallagher, *Rethinking the Color Line: Readings in Race and Ethnicity*, 7th ed. (Sage, 2022), 35.
5. It may be that some races have certain advantages (or greater strengths) over others. Physical prowess, mathematical abilities, or financial savvy may be exhibited more in one race than another. At the same time, another race could surpass the first one in other ways. Attempting to make an evaluation of which race is superior based on an analysis of the comparable strengths and weaknesses of these races would be a project fraught with problems. That's why it is preferable to say "worthy" rather than "superior," for all people of all races are of equal intrinsic worth, even if some individuals are more gifted than others and as a result may have greater instrumental value.

can be invisible and unintentional. Societal structures that evolved or were put in place generations ago can affect people long after and are sometimes accepted as natural and even inevitable. Systemic racism can even exist in societies that no longer exhibit individual racism.

An example of systemic racism comes from how public schools are funded in the United States. Most public school funding comes from property taxes. Thus, the more valuable the property in a given school district, the better funded the schools are. Better funding often results in better education. Therefore, the public schools in areas with higher property values often provide better education than do schools that are in areas with lower property values.

Minorities, especially Black and Hispanic minorities, tend to live in school districts with lower property values, while Whites tend to live in districts with higher property values. No one forces minorities to live in low-income neighborhoods, but they live there because often that's what they can afford. One of the reasons that they cannot afford to live in more affluent neighborhoods is that in order to get a job with better pay, you need a good education, but if you can't afford to live in a more affluent neighborhood, you probably can't afford private school, either, so you go to the public school in that neighborhood, which will be underfunded due to the low property values in that neighborhood. Minorities are often caught in a vicious cycle of poverty that, even if unintentional, is built into the system for funding public schools.[6]

Some object that this is a poverty issue rather than a racial one. Clearly it is a poverty issue, but we need to ask why minorities tend to live in lower-income school districts. Very few people prefer to live in low-income districts. Most who live there can't afford to live in more affluent areas. Why can't they "pick themselves up by their bootstraps"? If it was because they are less intelligent or somehow less capable, then the fact that Blacks and Hispanics tend to live in low-income districts more than Whites do would

---

6. On the very large financial gap between Blacks and Whites in the USA, see Thomas Shapiro, Tatjana Meschede, and Sam Osoro, "The Roots of the Widening Racial Wealth Gap: Explaining the Black-White Economic Divide," in Gallagher, *Rethinking the Color Line*, 66–74.

imply that Blacks and Hispanics tend to be less intelligent or less capable than Whites are. But no research supports that conclusion.

Thinking abductively, a more plausible explanation seems to be historical in nature. Freed slaves were very poor, and many immigrants aren't much better off. They had (and often have) little choice but to settle in places where the costs of living (including rent) were low. If the schools in those places were funded by real estate taxes, they were schools with marginal finances. Consequently, the children of the freed slaves and/or immigrants who attended those schools received lower-quality educations. As a result, it was difficult for those children to compete in the job market with people from more affluent areas, and accordingly they wouldn't be able to get jobs with salaries that were sufficient to enable them to move to more affluent neighborhoods. This results in their children facing the same challenge. This is one way the cycle of poverty begins. Generation after generation is raised in poverty and has little hope of escape.

This description makes it seem like the situations resulting in systemic disadvantages to minorities arise naturally and unintentionally. Sometimes that's the case, but sometimes the process is more nefarious. A well-documented example of this is "redlining," which is the practice of divvying up towns and cities into majority neighborhoods and minority neighborhoods and restricting minorities, through various means, from moving into majority neighborhoods.[7] Intentional systemic racism has also reared its head in immigration policy, public health, criminal justice, and various other areas of public life.

While individual racism occurs in the minds and hearts of people, systemic racism occurs in societies and in social structures. Both can be either overt or covert. Both deserve to be addressed. Because systemic racism cannot be addressed until racial prejudice is addressed, we will address the latter and leave systemic racism for another day. Our methodology for addressing individual racism will be to apply each of the ethical theories that we studied in the previous chapter to racism to see what attitude

---

7. On redlining, see Thomas Sugrue, "'Detroit's Time Bomb': Race and Housing in the 1940s," in *The Origins of the Urban Crisis: Race and Inequality in Postwar Detroit* (Princeton University Press, 2014), 33–56.

should characterize someone who adheres to that ethical theory. We utilize this approach because we believe that allowing an ethical theory to guide your thinking is the approach that is most likely to lead you to the correct conclusion.

Racial Prejudice and Naturalism

As we saw in the preceding chapter, social contract theory is the theory about the nature and source of moral truth that is most consistent with naturalism, and ethical egoism and utilitarianism best complement social contract theory. Let's attempt to apply ethical egoism and utilitarianism to the problem of racism.

Ethical egoism says that one should always do what is in one's best interest. *Prima facie*, it seems like this would lead to racism on the part of at least some people. One might think that, on egoism, all those who can find a way to employ racial prejudice in their favor should do so. However, we learned from Epicurus that our concern should be for what is in our long-term best interest, so we must ask ourselves whether racism is in our long-term best interest. One consequence of racism would be that I will view others as inferior, which means that my character might take a turn toward undesirable traits like arrogance, disdainfulness, and intolerance. Furthermore, I would be likely to treat others as inferior, which would probably provoke those people to be resentful and hostile to me. Consequently, they might take various harmful actions against me and those connected to me. Furthermore, it could contribute to developing a culture of racial tension, or of judgmentalism, or, at the very least, of disunity. Embracing racism could lead to a whole range of negative consequences.

Rejecting racism would deprive me of the ability to tell myself that my race is more worthy than some other race or races, so I'd lose one possible source of self-worth and pride. But on the other hand, it could improve my relationships with people from other races, which could lead to having more friends and also a more diverse set of friends, and the latter can be very enriching. It could also help contribute to developing a tolerant and inclusive community wherein people are able to look past their differences and see each other as intrinsically worthy. That will benefit me, since I want people to see me as worthy. In short, rejecting racism could help foster a culture in which respect and friendship are predominant rather than division and hate.

This evaluation of the consequences of racism is necessarily incomplete. Nevertheless, it does seem to indicate that a solid case can be constructed showing that ethical egoists should view racism as immoral. Given more time and space to continue this investigation, it seems probable that this conclusion would become even clearer.

Utilitarianism says that I should do whatever produces the most benefit for the greatest number of people. *Prima facie*, this also seems like it could lead directly to viewing racism as moral in at least some circumstances. In a society with a clear majority/minority bifurcation, viewing the minority as inferior and legitimately subject to discrimination and subjugation could benefit the majority. This could take the form of social disapproval, restricting the minority to menial occupations, outright slavery, or, in the worst case, genocide.

However, this may be an erroneous assessment of how utilitarianism applies to the issue. John Stuart Mill, the most famous utilitarian ethicist, was a committed abolitionist who stood up for minorities. Since the central principle of utilitarianism is something like "whatever produces the most good for the greatest number of people is moral," it's easy to see why Mill would choose egalitarianism over racism. At best, racism privileges the majority over minorities; sometimes it privileges a minority over other minorities or even over majorities. Egalitarianism, on the other hand, sees all races as of equal worth. Accordingly, egalitarianism benefits all people by making everyone equal. So, egalitarianism benefits more people than racism does, which is why utilitarianism supports an egalitarian view of the races.

It's interesting that ethical egoism and utilitarianism take different paths but arrive at the same conclusion: Racism is immoral. Now let's examine the ethical theories that complement a theistic worldview to see what conclusions they lead to.

Racial Prejudice and Theism

We have seen that the theory about the nature and source of moral truth that is most consistent with the theistic worldview is divine nature theory and that revelational ethics, duty ethics, virtue ethics, and natural law ethics are ethical theories that are compatible with divine nature theory and offer epistemic methods for discovering moral truths.[8] Now we'll apply each of these to the issue of racial prejudice to see what position a theist should take on the issue.

To apply **revelational ethics** to any moral issue, we must determine what qualifies as revelation. Each religion has its own writings that it considers to be revelation, and in addition to written revelation, there could also be spoken revelations, visions, and general revelation. An adequate treatment of all these factors would require a second book. Since the authors of the current volume are most familiar with the Christian tradition and the Christian Bible, we will use the Bible to give an example of how revelational ethics would handle racism.

The Bible pictures humanity as one race descended from two original ancestors: Adam and Eve. This is the unified picture from Genesis through the book of Revelation. That's why the apostle Paul said, "From one man he made every nation of the human race to inhabit the entire earth" (Acts 17:26). *Prima facie*, there doesn't seem to be any basis for racism here.

The Christian belief that all humans are of equal worth ties into the biblical doctrine that we are created in the image of God. Genesis says, "Then God said, 'Let us make humankind in our image, after our likeness, so they may rule over the fish of the sea and the birds of the air, over the cattle, and over all the earth, and over all the creatures that move on the earth.' God created humankind in his own image, in the image of God he created them, male and female he created them" (Gen 1:26–27). This doctrine carries over into the New Testament, where James observes, "With it we bless the Lord and Father, and with it we curse people made in God's image" (Jas 3:9). Each person is made in God's image and thus is of tremendous worth.

The universality of God's redeeming love is stated in John 3:16, one of the most well-known verses in all the Bible: "For God so loved the world, that he gave his only begotten Son, that whosoever believeth in him should not perish, but have everlasting life" (KJV). If God is the standard of moral

8. Aspects of ethical egoism and utilitarianism may also be compatible with divine nature theory, but since the egoist and utilitarian views of racism have already been investigated, there's no need to cover that ground a second time.

goodness and if God loves all people, then we are morally obligated to love all people. That our love and compassion ought to extend beyond those who are like us to include even those who are the least like us in racial, social, and religious ways is the very point of Jesus' parable of the good Samaritan in Luke 10:25–37. This parable was told to a Jewish audience that despised Samaritans. Someone in the audience had asked Jesus whom he was morally obligated to love. Jesus answered with a parable that featured a Samaritan as the unexpected hero who helped a Jew who had been mugged. This was Jesus' way of saying that we should love all people, even those whom we are inclined to despise. It leaves little room for racism.

This teaching is consistent with Jesus' Golden Rule, "Treat others in the same way that you would want them to treat you" (Luke 6:31). The apostle Paul emphasizes ethnic equality among Christians, mentioning it in both Galatians and Colossians. Colossians 3:11 says, "Here there is neither Greek nor Jew, circumcised or uncircumcised, barbarian, Scythian, slave or free, but Christ is all and in all" (see also Gal 3:28).

More could be said about race and racism in the Bible, but what has been mentioned here is a good starting place. A revelational ethic utilizing the Christian Scriptures supports a very egalitarian, non-racist view of humanity. It also leads to the conclusion that racism is not moral.

Next, let's attempt an application of **duty ethics** to racism. Kant's **categorical imperative** states: "Act only according to that principle that you could consistently will to become a universal law." If I seek to justify racism, I will have to embrace the principle that it is moral to treat the members of other races as if they are inherently less worthy than the members of my own race. However, if it is moral for me to treat the members of other races as if they are inherently less worthy than the members of my own race, it must be moral for all people to treat the members of other races as if they are inherently less worthy than the members of their own race. But that would entail either that my race is both superior to other races and inferior to other races at the same time, or that I should believe that my race is superior to other races while at the same time other people should believe that their races are superior to my race. Both of these options involve a logical contradiction. Therefore, embracing racism leads to a logical contradiction and so fails the test of the categorical imperative.

Kant has a second formulation of the categorical imperative called **the principle of ends**.[9] It states that we should treat all people never merely as a means to an end but always also as ends in themselves. In contemporary parlance, we could say that you should never treat anyone as a tool, but instead you should respect them as real persons. Slavery treats enslaved people as tools. Racists treat the members of other races as tools even if they don't enslave them, because devaluing people of other races is a strategy to get ahead at someone else's expense.[10] They are using people of other races as a means to an end rather than as ends in themselves.

John Rawls was an influential twentieth-century proponent of duty ethics who devised a thought experiment that can be used to evaluate the morality of racism: the **veil of ignorance**. Imagine that before you are born, you somehow have the ability to determine what the world you are going to be born into will be like, including how the races treat each other. Here's the catch: You do not know what race you will be born into. In light of this fact, how would you want the races to treat each other? You probably wouldn't want to be born into a situation wherein you are viewed as inferior to others simply because of your race. Hence, you would probably want all races to be viewed as equal, since that's the only way to ensure that you won't be born into an oppressed group. This thought experiment helps us see that racism is immoral, for no one wants to experience racism.

Now let us apply **virtue ethics** to racism. Virtue ethics emphasizes the importance of developing your inner character so that when you are faced with a moral dilemma, you respond in a moral way, using the **golden mean** to determine which character traits are virtuous. Aristotle proposed this list of virtuous character traits: courage, temperance, liberality, munificence, magnanimity, patience, truthfulness, wittiness, friendliness, shame, justice, and modesty.[11] This isn't necessarily exhaustive, but it's a good starting point. Would someone with this kind of character be a racist?

---

9. Kant scholars have identified four distinct formulations of the categorical imperative, each of which emphasizes a different nuance of morality.
10. Sometimes racial prejudice is a way of getting ahead emotionally rather than financially: Disvaluing others can be a strategy to bolster someone's weak self-image.
11. See Aristotle, *Nicomachean Ethics*, trans. Joe Sachs (Focus, 2002), Book Two.

Traits such as courage, patience, and wittiness may not be decisively incompatible with racism, but quite a few of the others seem to be. **Liberality** has to do with having a generous spirit, and someone with a generous spirit probably wouldn't unfairly judge others as inferior. Someone who is **truthful** will admit that people of all races have strengths and weaknesses. Someone who is genuinely friendly is friendly to people regardless of their race. Someone who is **just** will treat others how they deserve to be treated without regard to race. Someone who is **temperate** will exercise self-control; consequently, such a person will consciously limit the influence that cultural prejudices have on his or her thinking. People who are **modest** have a realistic self-image and don't view themselves as inherently more valuable than others. In the end, it seems that those who hold to virtue ethics will probably conclude that personal racism is immoral.

The last ethical theory to attempt to apply is **natural law ethics**, which holds that the universe is governed by laws woven into the fabric of reality. An implication of this is that moral acts will be conducive to flourishing. We have seen that racism is not conducive to flourishing. One might think that racism would sometimes benefit those individuals and/or races who are in power, but on a more careful analysis, it seems likely that racism would be more detrimental than helpful, both on an individual level and corporately. Hence, it seems that natural law ethics would probably lead to the conclusion that racism is immoral.

Additionally, since the physiological differences between the various races are superficial in comparison to the tremendous similarities, and since there don't appear to be any inherent psychological differences, there is very little reason not to view and treat their members as equals. From a theistic perspective, it seems likely that any feature of any race reflects a genetic potential that was built into the human genome by its designer. Therefore, racial diversity should be viewed positively, since it was most likely part of God's plan from the very beginning.

CONCLUSION

After examining racism through the lens of these ethical theories, we have found that they lead to the conclusion that racism is immoral. The reader may be surprised that the naturalistic and theistic theories lead to the same conclusion. Perhaps that won't always be the case, but it's interesting that, if natural law theory is correct, then this is exactly the result that we would expect. That's because if natural law theory is correct, then studying the universe and humanity (which is part of the universe) and the moral problems that humans face should uncover truths about nature, humanity, and morality. Regardless of whether we're asking what's best for individuals, or for society, or what actions can be universalized, or what the moral laws are, or even what God has revealed about morality, we should arrive at the same conclusion vis-à-vis any particular moral issue. That's encouraging, isn't it?

QUESTIONS TO PONDER

- What is the difference between "race" and "ethnicity"?
- Have you ever asked yourself if you harbor any racial prejudices?
- How would you define racism? What is a racist?
- Do you think racial prejudice is immoral? Why or why not? Is it ever moral?

TERMS TO KNOW

- race
- racial prejudice
- racism
- racist
- individual racism
- systemic racism
- redlining
- ethical egoism
- utilitarianism
- revelational ethics
- duty ethics
- categorical imperative
- principle of ends
- veil of ignorance
- virtue ethics
- golden mean
- natural law theory
- natural law ethics

FOR FURTHER READING

Gallagher, Charles A., ed. *Rethinking the Color Line: Readings in Race and Ethnicity*. 7th ed. Sage, 2022. This anthology has become a standard university textbook on race and racism.

Hawkins, J. Russell and Phillip Luke Sinitiere, eds. *Christians and the Color Line: Race and Religion After Divided by Faith*. Oxford University Press, 2014. This anthology features Christians wrestling with the issues of race and racism.

Taylor, Paul C. *Race: A Philosophical Introduction*. 3rd ed. Polity Press, 2022. This book attempts to construct an actual philosophy of race and racial relations.

JURISPRUDENCE

HUMAN RIGHTS

SYNOPSIS

Chapters 19 and 20 form a unit on jurisprudence, which deals with philosophical issues related to laws and legality. The first such issue to be discussed is of great importance: human rights. Much is said about this topic in the modern world, but this chapter addresses the topic philosophically.

DIALOGUE

After weeks of tumult, the four friends found themselves in a lull of activity. They began to breathe a sigh of relief. No one was calling or meeting with them to address crises. No surprises at work. No requests from law enforcement. It was almost eerie after all they had experienced.

The group met at Suresh's apartment this time.

"Did you have a quiet week like I did?" Suresh asked. "I was on edge for several days before I could finally relax."

"Same," said Hannah. "When I got up this morning, I was thinking about how on edge I've been the last few weeks. It's so nice to hang out and feel a sense of normalcy again."

After a long pause, Zach said, "Well, should we dive in? The subject this week is human rights. It seems to be something we can all agree on, at least to a certain extent."

"Don't be so sure!" Angelo said. "We can disagree about almost anything."

"True," Zach said, laughing.

"On this topic, I have a funny feeling we'll all agree at least to the reality and goodness of human rights. We may diverge on the origin and number of human rights, but I bet we can arrive at similar conclusions."

"I'm just giving you a hard time," Angelo said.

"Let's start by defining *human rights*. The *Stanford Encyclopedia* defines them as 'norms that aspire to protect all people everywhere from severe political, legal and social abuses.'"[1]

"So human rights are protections," Angelo said.

"I guess so," Zach said. "But maybe they're not limited to protections. Maybe they also constitute guarantees from some kind of authority, the guarantee of life, liberty, and the pursuit of happiness, for example."

"So human rights are protections that would guarantee certain ideals," Hannah said.

"I have so many questions," Suresh said. "How many rights do we have? And what are they?"

"Let's make a list of what we believe are or should be human rights." Zach retrieved a notebook and pen from his bag.

"I'll start," Angelo said. "I'd think an obvious one would be protection from violence and mistreatment. Along with that would be just laws and the enforcement of those laws. Without those, it seems like every other human right would be in danger of being violated."

"I agree," Hannah said. "Freedom from slavery and discrimination seem like basic rights as well. The right to feel safe and secure is necessary if a person is to live freely."

"What about the right to speak freely and express opinions, even if they're not popular?" Suresh asked.

"Definitely," Zach said, jotting down the ideas as they shared them. "If

---

1. James Nickel and Adam Etinson, "Human Rights," in *The Stanford Encyclopedia of Philosophy*, ed. Edward N. Zalta and Uri Nodelman (Fall 2024 ed.), https://plato.stanford.edu/archives/fall2024/entries/rights-human/.

you can't express your opinions and can only parrot what you are forced to believe, freedom would be severely limited."

"Here's one," Hannah said. "I was watching a documentary about the death of Princess Diana. The paparazzi that followed her everywhere was so intrusive. Their invasion of her privacy ultimately led to the car crash that killed her. Technology feels like a different version of this intrusion—the way our phones passively listen to us, surveillance cameras everywhere, our online footprints, and even drones. How much privacy do we even have? Did you guys ever read *1984* by George Orwell?"[2]

Orwell's book had been pivotal in Angelo's high school curriculum and for Zach in college.

"I remember it being very troubling," Zach said.

"I haven't read it, but I'm familiar with the story," Suresh said.

"The dystopian picture of the future and the totalitarian government it portrays is pretty terrifying," Angelo said.

"To some degree, a right to privacy must be considered a human right," Hannah said. "Governments that intrude on the privacy of individuals' homes are not good for their people."

"And not just governments," Suresh said. "The right to privacy from other people's intrusion in your private affairs is critical. I guess that goes alongside free speech and protection from violence. A person should be able to trust that his home can't be entered and violated by another person."

"What about education and healthcare?" Hannah asked. "Those seem like rights every person should have."

"Hmm, I don't know," Zach said, scratching his chin. "Those are good and important things, but are they rights?"

Hannah looked surprised and slightly irritated. "How can you say that? Do you deny that people need education and healthcare?"

"Of course, I want everyone to have access to healthcare and opportunities to get an education," Zach said. "Surely universal education would benefit societies, and the more healthcare is made available, the better off a culture would be. My question is whether they're human rights. If they are, the lack of these things would be criminal or deserving of international

2. George Orwell, *1984*, 75th Anniversary Edition (Berkley, 2003).

action. Yet many people in the world lack these things. Either human rights are lacking in many places, or these things aren't really human rights and are rather goals of a flourishing society."

"That's an interesting thought," Angelo said. "Are human rights different from the good things a just and flourishing society might strive for? What was the definition of *human rights* again, Zach?"

Zach looked down at his phone. "'Norms that aspire to protect all people everywhere from severe political, legal, and social abuses.'" He looked up at the group. "This definition is aspirational—societies should strive for these things to protect and benefit their citizens."

"If that's the case, education and healthcare would fit into that category, don't you think?" Hannah said. "After all, an educated person is protected against abuses by others if they know the law."

Angelo tapped his notebook in thought. "I agree, and I certainly want education and healthcare for everyone in the world, but it still seems to me that there is a dividing line between the idea of rights like fair trial and freedom from slavery and the elements of life that would encourage flourishing. Otherwise, we'd need to add to that list things like housing, transportation, clothing, and more. We want all people to have those things, but do they rise to the level of 'rights?'"

"Ah, I see," Suresh said. "Some people might say employment is a human right. I've even heard people online advocating for a universal basic income—every person would receive an income to cover basic necessities."[3]

"Some of that seems to be tied to an economic system, doesn't it?" Zach asked. "In a more socialist economy, a regular payment from the government seems more likely than in a free-market economy. I suppose there are benefits of a universal basic income, but I can't imagine the tax burden it would place on working individuals."

"Okay, I'm seeing how this fits together," Hannah said. "If we extend human rights to every aspect of an ideal life, we have a serious problem

3. Universal Basic Income is also sometimes called *social minimum*. See Stuart White, "Social Minimum," in *The Stanford Encyclopedia of Philosophy*, ed. Edward N. Zalta and Uri Nodelman (Fall 2024 ed.), https://plato.stanford.edu/archives/fall2024/entries/social-minimum/.

of—how would it be paid for and managed? I wonder what the United Nations includes in its statements on human rights. Surely they address these issues."

"Why don't we look?" asked Angelo. He began searching on his phone and texted a link to everyone. "It looks like there are thirty articles in the United Nations Universal Declaration of Human Rights."[4]

Everyone read quietly for a few minutes.

"The first fifteen articles are primarily about human dignity, free speech, legal protections, privacy, freedom of movement, and the right to have a nationality," Hannah said. "Those seem like the most basic needs of life for someone to live with any degree of security. Can you imagine living in a society where these things weren't guaranteed?"

Suresh shook his head. "A lot of refugees work in the restaurant business. I've talked to many about their experiences—being arrested or beaten by police or thrown in jail without a trial. Some had no protection against corrupt government officials stealing all they had worked for. And in some places, the media is run by a dictatorial government. The people don't even know what is actually happening in the country."

"That's wild," Zach said. "I rarely even think about things like this."

"One woman I worked with told me that her cousin was walking down the street when a van pulled up next to him and uniformed soldiers got out and grabbed him. She never heard from him again."

"I can't even imagine that," Angelo said. "We have our fair share of corrupt public officials and abusive law enforcement officers in America, but at least there is recourse in a court of law, even if imperfect. Can you fathom living in a country where there was no way to appeal for justice? Or the perpetrators are the very officials who are supposed to enforce the law?"

Zach was still looking over the list. "Beginning with Article 16, it seems like people might start to resist some of these articles based on culture. Article 16 says that no one should have to enter a marriage against their consent. Wouldn't this violate cultures that still have arranged marriages?"

"Some of my relatives still live in countries with arranged marriages,"

4. Universal Declaration of Human Rights, https://www.un.org/en/about-us/universal-declaration-of-human-rights.

Suresh said. "For them, arranged marriage is viewed positively and is considered not only normal but also a protection of the interests of the families involved."

"Article 17 ensures the right to private property. Does this mean that a communist economic system is a violation of human rights since the government owns the means of production?"

"I see your point," Hannah said. "Some of these don't seem to fit in certain cultures or economic models—whether we agree with those models or not. The UN might not consider communism to be a violation of human rights, but most expressions of communism and dictatorships have historically denied some or all of these rights. Maybe it's a matter of degree?"

"What do you mean?" Zach asked.

"It seems that many of these rights don't necessarily have to be absolute, as if a society with any limitations is violating human rights. For example, the right to free speech probably has some limitations no matter how free a society is. The right to religious expression probably has limits as well, even in countries that protect religious freedom. Would our government allow a public animal sacrifice or nudity—even if a religion claims that such expressions are essential to its practice?"

"I guess since no society is perfect," Angelo said, "as long as a country mostly adheres to these points, it wouldn't be considered to be violating human rights. Correct? Otherwise, every country in the world would be open to the charge of violating human rights."

"Why don't we look through the rest of these and each pick one that raises a question." Zach said. "I know we're running out of time, and I have a few other questions about human rights not related to the specifics on this list that I'd love to have time to talk about."

The group took a moment to look through the list again.

"I'll go first," Angelo said. "Article 23 seems problematic to me: 'Everyone has the right to work, to free choice of employment, to just and favourable conditions of work and to protection against unemployment . . . Everyone who works has the right to just and favourable remuneration ensuring for himself and his family an existence worthy of human dignity, and supplemented, if necessary, by other means of social protection.'"

He looked up from his phone. "Of course, this is ideal, but how do we judge what level of pay ensures a family a dignified existence? In the US, if someone makes less than fifty dollars a day, they are considered below the poverty level. But in many parts of the world, people exist on less than five dollars per day. How is that evaluation made and by whom?"

"Exactly," Zach said. "And now I have questions about the very nature of human rights. What are they, where do they come from, and who enforces them?"

"Ugh," Hannah said. "Why do we have to discuss the meta questions? Can't we just take them for granted?"

"Ha! No way!"

"Fine, Zach. You go first."

"Well, to be consistent with my atheism," Zach said, "I would argue that human rights aren't really things in themselves. There is no realm of 'rights' floating around out there. Like all ideas, they are thoughts in our brains that we have decided are important for human flourishing. Don't get me wrong; I support them all, at least the ones that don't require us to do away with human responsibility. But I think they're essentially behaviors that humans have identified as conducive to a long and happy life."

Zach paused for a moment. "Where do they come from? To me, it seems that individuals, organizations, and cultures that have fine-tuned flourishing tend to recognize these behaviors and articulate them. So they come from the human mind. As far as who enforces them, that seems to be the role of government. Organizations like the United Nations exist in part to ensure that human rights are protected across governments and cultures. One distinction is that I didn't note the UN appealing to any transcendent source such as a god as part of this list of rights. That would lead me to conclude that religion isn't necessary to establish human rights."

"I agree with you about that last part, Zach," Angelo said, "but I think your statement is incomplete."

"How so?"

"The expression of various human rights can be found in most religions and philosophical positions, but the bigger question is whether a secular and humanist basis can consistently ground them in anything firm. You may ground them in universal agreement, but with an evolutionary history, you have to admit that change is inevitable and might not follow the present trajectory. The next stage of evolution may require the denial of at least some of what are presently considered human rights. To me, that's the drawback of not grounding rights in anything transcendent."

"This reminds me of our discussion of morals and ethics," Zach said. "I guess to be consistent, I have to admit that you might be right. But I reserve the right to optimistically believe that we will only progress forward in human rights."

Zach and Angelo could go round and round on this issue all day.

"Fair enough," Angelo said, smiling.

"From an Eastern perspective," Suresh said, "human rights are of utmost importance. There have been many widespread violations in Cambodia, Tibet, and Myanmar since the 1960s, including summary executions, forced labor, condoned rape of women and children, suppression of free speech, and children forced into the military. With Buddhism's focus on right living and respect for all things, virtuous behavior is foundational. Traditional Buddhism has no concept of a 'right' like we think of it in the West, but it does acknowledge the inherent equality of all humans and the value of all things. Since humans can attain enlightenment, they have inherent dignity and value. This moves Buddhists toward a central ethic of nonviolence. This would serve as the transcendent basis for human rights.[5]

"As far as what a human right is? I don't know." Suresh scratched his head. "I don't think that question would ever occur to me. I'd simply say that a human right is something real that people are obligated to acknowledge. Maybe I'd describe it as a duty. I think everyone has a responsibility to work toward the realization of the ideals of the UN Declaration, but ultimately enforcement falls upon the government."

"That's a helpful perspective," Hannah said. "I think I'd ground human rights in the necessity of every person to will his essence into existence. For an existentialist, it's necessary to have self-determination because no identity

---

5. Sallie B. King, "Buddhism and Human Rights," in *Religion and Human Rights: An Introduction*, ed. John Witte Jr. and M. Christian Green (Oxford University Press, 2011), 106–107.

is given by God or the universe. Since that's the case, freedom of thought, expression, and movement, as well as protection from slavery and coercion, are critical to anyone choosing their own concept of being.

"One philosopher summarizes the foundation of human rights as the capacity to say yes or no to oneself, to communicate and argue, to live with others around a common plan of life, and to be a participant in that life.[6] Human rights must come from human will in society. What they are metaphysically, I'm not sure. I suppose a government that reflects the will of rational people would be the ones to enforce them."

Angelo looked around the room. "You probably know by now what I'm going to say about anything metaphysical."

Everyone laughed. Angelo had been consistent.

"I believe human rights reflect the inherent value of human life as made in God's image. The ideals of freedom and protection have their genesis in the way God originally made the world—without sin, evil, or a curse. We have had to articulate human rights and pass laws because of the corrupt and fallen nature of the human heart since Adam and Eve's fall into sin.

"Human rights are directly tied to justice, which we can discern from natural law because God has revealed his nature to us. And while Zach is correct that the UN Declaration doesn't ground its rights in religion, many of the historical documents that enshrined human rights did. Think of the Magna Carta, for example, signed in 1215. Or the Declaration of Independence. Both of these documents recognize the need for a transcendent source of the rights granted by God so they wouldn't be perceived as a gift from kings and later taken away."

"We may not agree on where rights come from and what they are, but I do see what you're saying," Zach said. "I'm comforted that we all seem to broadly agree on what rights a flourishing society should protect."

"The similarities and differences are pretty amazing," Hannah said. "I think we might agree more on this topic than on anything else we have discussed."

---

6. Massimo La Torre, "Human Rights: Existential, Not Metaphysical," *Ratio Juris* 31, no. 2 (June 2018): 193.

THEORY

Hopefully, you are picking up on a theme of this book: What one thinks in *any area of life* results from prior worldview commitments. The following discussion will address how various worldviews conceive of human rights.

The Universal Declaration of Human Rights

Article 1
All human beings are born free and equal in dignity and rights. They are endowed with reason and conscience and should act towards one another in a spirit of brotherhood.

Article 3
Everyone has the right to life, liberty and security of person.

Introduction

The Declaration of Independence of the United States affirms, "We hold these truths to be self-evident, that all men are created equal, that they are endowed by their Creator with certain unalienable Rights, that among these are Life, Liberty and the pursuit of Happiness."[7] Many Americans accept these as common-sense truths, as do many people from other parts of the world. Some people do not, though, and historically speaking, these ideas were considered radical at the time of the American Revolution.[8] Such disbelief notwithstanding, in 1948 the United Nations officially adopted the *Universal Declaration of Human Rights*, which shows that the concept has widespread international support.[9]

---

7. Here we are referring to *The Unanimous Declaration of the Thirteen United States of America*, which can be read on the webpage of the National Archives of the United States, accessed November 23, 2004, https://www.archives.gov/founding-docs/declaration-transcript.
8. On the history of the concept of human rights, see Micheline R. Ishay, *The History of Human Rights: From Ancient Times to the Globalization Era* (University of California Press, 2008).
9. The Universal Declaration of Human Rights can be read on the webpage of the UN, accessed November 23, 2004, https://www.un.org/en/about-us/universal-declaration-of-human-rights.

Many people believe in something called "human rights." But what exactly are they? We can find various lists of things people believe are human rights, but what kind of thing is a human right? It's not a physical object, is it? If it's not, then is it even real? Now we're doing metaphysics again!

Physicalism

If you think back to the chapters on metaphysics, you'll probably remember a chapter on monism and dualism (chapter 8). Monism is the view that reality is, in some sense, one. One form of monism is physicalism, the view that all of reality shares one nature: It's all physical. Physicalism leads to the conclusion that if human rights aren't physical, then they don't exist. This leaves physicalists with two options: Either there are no human rights, or they are physical.

Some physicalists bite the bullet and affirm that there are no human rights. They argue that such rights are simply a human invention meant to curb the abuses of those in power. This is much like the social contract theory discussed earlier. It can be traced back at least as far as the seventeenth-century philosopher Thomas Hobbes.

There are other physicalists, though, who consider human rights to be very important and who strive to make room for them in their metaphysical views. Some take the social contract theory approach, but rather than concluding that human conventions are less than fully real (and therefore human rights are less than fully real), they argue that human conventions are real and therefore human rights are real. This raises the question of what "real" means in this context, since such conventions don't seem to be physical, but perhaps it could be argued that they actually are physical. If human rights are beliefs accepted by the members of a given society, or perhaps agreements between the members of that society, then they are thoughts in human minds. If the physical brain is the only mind that humans have, then beliefs and thoughts are physical activities of the brain. Therefore, if human rights are beliefs or agreements accepted by the members of society, then they are physical activities of the brain. Of course, the activities of the brain are real, so human rights are real.

This attempt to reconcile physicalism and human rights makes sense if we grant physicalism. It succeeds in making human rights real. However, they are not real in the Platonic sense: They're not real because they are eternal and unchanging principles or anything like that. In fact, despite the reality of human rights (on this view), if each society creates its own social contract, then it seems likely that human rights could vary considerably from society to society. If we want a set of rights that's universal, as both the Declaration of Independence and the *Universal Declaration of Human Rights* indicate, then we need a different ontology of human rights.[10]

Dualism

The chapter on monism and dualism also talked about the dualistic view of reality. This is the view that reality contains both physical things and immaterial things. As was explained in the chapter on abstract objects (chapter 9), if dualism is true, that opens up the possibility of the existence of a whole range of immaterial things, including real numbers, the laws of nature, the laws of logic, timeless moral truths, and universal human rights. These things are categorized as abstract objects. Abstract objects are non-physical and non-mental, but according to some people, they are real.

You may recall that chapter 9 discussed two different ways that abstract objects could be real: Platonic realism and conceptualism. Platonic realism affirms that abstract objects exist independently of anyone or anything else. They are eternal, omnipresent (in an incorporeal sense), self-existent truths. Naturally, this view is not compatible with physicalism. Concordantly, it's neither compatible with naturalism nor a good fit with theism, since it makes abstract objects eternal and unchanging like God and sets them up as an authority higher than God in the areas of mathematics, logic, and morality.

Conceptualism, on the other hand, holds that abstract objects exist as thoughts. Thoughts are real, even though they aren't physical, so on this view, abstract objects are real immaterial entities. However, if abstract objects are real because they exist in human minds, then they can vary from one mind to another. In fact, they may be completely lacking in some minds. This suggests that they are not universal; it may also suggest forms of relativism.

In order for conceptualism to avoid relativism and to yield abstract

10. Ontology is the study of the nature of something.

objects that are universal, abstract objects must exist in a mind that is eternal and unchanging, such as the mind of God. If abstract objects exist in the mind of God, then since God is eternal, omnipresent (in an incorporeal sense), and self-existent, so are abstract objects. They are an aspect of God and share in his attributes. We'll call this version of conceptualism "theistic conceptualism." It is, of course, incompatible with physicalism (and therefore with naturalism).

The three options just presented parallel the options that we saw in the chapter on ethical theories (chapter 17). There we encountered social contract theory, Platonic moral realism, and divine nature theory. Social contract theory holds that morality is a social construct, while Platonic moral realism holds that there are eternal, unchanging moral truths that exist apart from society (and God), and divine nature theory holds that moral truths are eternal and unchanging because they are part of the nature of God, who is also eternal and unchanging.

The same three options appear to pertain to human rights. We've already seen the equivalent of social contract theory in the naturalistic approach to human rights. We've also seen Platonic realism applied to human rights. Theistic conceptualism is the human rights equivalent of divine nature theory. Human rights could be a reflection of God's just, fair, loving, and generous nature.

Ontological Distinctions

Ontology is the study of the nature of something. There are several aspects of the nature of human rights upon which we should comment. The first is the distinction between negative rights and positive rights. **Negative rights** involve freedom from interference, like the right to life, the right to free speech, and the right to worship in the manner that you choose. Under normal circumstances, no one has the right to take your life or to prevent you from expressing your opinion or worshiping as you see fit. There are conditions under which a person could sacrifice these rights, but these rights are the norm. **Positive rights** involve an entitlement to something, such as a right to food and shelter or to education or healthcare.

Another distinction is between legal rights and moral rights. **Legal**

rights are rights that are conferred on people by the laws of the society in which they live. The right to vote and the right to bear arms are rights that are conferred by the local, state, or federal government. The right to work out in the gym or the right to borrow books from the library are conferred, respectively, by the gym to which you belong and the library from which you have a library card.

Moral rights, on the other hand, are more universal. Although they may be recognized, confirmed, and protected by governments, they don't seem to be created by governments. Human rights, such as the right to life, liberty, and personal safety, fall into this category. These rights seem innate rather than bequeathed.

One last thing: Rights implicate duties. If you have a right to life, then everyone else has a duty not to take your life. Put differently, if you have a right to life, then everyone else has a duty to respect that right. It would be contradictory to say that you have a right to life but at the same time no one has a duty to respect that right, for that would be the same as not having the right in the first place.

That rights implicate duties seems logical and unproblematic when we're talking about negative rights. Some people, however, think that the situation is different regarding positive rights. If positive rights implicate corresponding duties on the part of others, then your right to healthcare, for example, makes it someone else's duty to provide that healthcare. Likewise, your right to food and shelter implies that someone else has a duty to provide food if you lack it. If that's the case, though, your right to food could infringe upon my right to sell food (if I'm a gardener or a grocer) for the best price I can get (or something similar to that). Hence some people have reservations about the existence of positive rights.

Epistemology

If human rights are real, how can we find out what they are? As in the chapter on ethical theories, the answer to this epistemological question depends on one's metaphysical perspective. If the perspective is that human rights are human constructs bequeathed upon individuals by the society in which they live via custom or legislation, then the way to discover what human rights there are will be to examine the customs and/or legislation of a given society. As this implies, different societies may have different customs and different laws. Thus, people living in one society may have different human rights from people living in other societies. In some societies people may not have the right to life, liberty, or the pursuit of happiness, while in other societies people may have all these rights and more.

If, on the other hand, human rights are universal, eternal, unchanging truths that are not created by societies, then a very different epistemology will be needed. To determine the nature of that epistemology, we would first need to discern whether human rights are truths that exist apart from God, as is maintained by Platonic realism, or whether they are thoughts in the mind of God or perhaps aspects of God's own nature, as maintained by theistic conceptualism.

If the former is true, then human rights should be discoverable, just as the laws of nature and of morality are discoverable. The difficult question is how to discover them. Here we can learn a lesson from our discussion of consequentialism and of natural law ethics: If human rights are real, then respecting them should be conducive to both individual and societal flourishing. Additionally, respecting them universally, as the UN statement urges us to do, will prevent us from logically contradicting ourselves by saying that it's good to treat some people (namely ourselves) as having such rights while denying that others have such rights. This mirrors what we saw when we studied duty ethics.

There are challenges for Platonic realism, though. While it avoids the cultural relativism that seems to follow from the view that human rights are a social construct, it doesn't explain why human rights exist. Platonic realism specifically eschews the suggestion that God created them; to take that option would be to affirm that they aren't eternal. Are they necessary truths, something that just couldn't be any other way, like a triangle necessarily having three sides or a bachelor necessarily being an unmarried male? Saying that a bachelor is a married male reveals a misunderstanding of the meaning of the term. But at least *prima facie*, saying that people don't have the right to life and liberty doesn't seem to reveal any misunderstanding of the terms. The basic laws of thought—the law of identity, the law of noncontradiction—seem to be necessary truths, because denying them leads to logical absurdities. But again, saying that people don't have the right to life and liberty doesn't lead to any obvious contradiction.[11] So Platonic realism has this key problem: It fails to explain why human rights exist.

That brings us to theistic conceptualism. If theistic conceptualism is true, then human rights should be discoverable in the natural world because the natural world reflects the mind and nature of God, its creator. This is similar to natural law ethics, only it's applied to human rights. They could be discovered via strategies like those proposed by consequentialism and natural law ethics: We would look for rights that will lead to individual and societal flourishing. This is because the sort of rights that would issue from a wise and omnibenevolent God would be rights that contribute to the flourishing of the beings that he has created.

Furthermore, if theistic conceptualism is true, then perhaps God has communicated something about human rights via revelation. Here the details are similar to those discussed in chapters 17 and 18 in relation to divine command ethics. There are at least two possible types of revelation: general and special. Both could be used to communicate truths about human rights. The strategies employing general revelation will be those found in natural law ethics. To utilize special revelation, we must determine which claimants to the status of "revelation" are actually from God, and then we must study those to learn what they say about human rights.

Theistic conceptualism avoids relativism by anchoring human rights to the unchanging nature of God. It answers the question of why human rights exist: They exist because God exists. As to why God exists, Anselm (and others) argued that God exists necessarily. Non-theists will reject that claim, of course, which reveals the major problem facing theistic conceptualism: It requires belief in God. Since we've devoted two full chapters to the question of the existence (or nonexistence) of God, we won't revisit that issue here.

---

11. This point could be argued. Some, like Kant, would argue that those who deny that human rights are universal fail to see the logical implications of the concept. If some humans have innate human rights, and if they have those rights because they are human, then all humans have those rights, for all humans are human.

Worldviews and Human Rights

The Declaration of Independence clearly attributes the existence of universal human rights to God. This is no surprise, since the Founding Fathers of the United States were theists and deists. The metaphysical position on human rights that best complements theism (and deism) is theistic conceptualism, and the epistemic theories that best complement theism, deism, and theistic conceptualism are the consequentialist, natural law, revelational, and perhaps Kantian approaches mentioned above.

Not surprisingly, the UN's *Universal Declaration of Human Rights* avoids addressing the source of human rights. No doubt this was intentional, so that the declaration will be acceptable to people from all worldviews. Those who hold to Platonic realism can accept the UN's declaration as compatible with their view. Platonic realism is the best option for worldviews like polytheism, panentheism, and paganism, which believe in the supernatural but do not believe in an all-powerful God as is found in theism and deism.

Those who hold to naturalism and pantheism can accept the UN's declaration as compatible with the view that human rights are bestowed on people by the society in which they live. There could be some tension between this view, the fact that some societies do not grant universal human rights, and the UN declaration that human rights are in fact universal. Naturalists who favor human rights can hope that those who don't believe in them can be persuaded that recognizing human rights is in everyone's best interest.

Each of these theories has strengths and possible criticisms. Theistic conceptualism avoids relativism, sees human rights as universal, and provides a straightforward explanation of why human rights exist, but it requires belief in God, which many find difficult. Platonic realism avoids relativism, sees human rights as universal, and doesn't require belief in God, but it fails to explain why human rights exist. Social contract theory provides a straightforward explanation of why human rights exist and does not require belief in God, but it leads to relativism and is not conducive to viewing human rights as universal.

QUESTIONS TO PONDER

- How many human rights are there? How many can you list?
- Do you think human rights are an invention? If not, then where do they come from?
- Which of the theories—Platonic realism, theistic conceptualism, and social contract theory—do you think makes the most sense?
- Which theory fits best with your worldview?

TERMS TO KNOW

- human rights
- Declaration of Independence
- *The Universal Declaration of Human Rights*
- physicalism
- dualism
- ontology
- negative rights
- positive rights
- legal rights
- moral rights
- epistemology
- metaphysics
- abstract objects
- social contract theory
- Platonic realism
- theistic conceptualism

FOR FURTHER READING

The first ten amendments to the Constitution of the United States of America, referred to as The Bill of Rights, can be read on the website of the National Archives: https://www.archives.gov/founding-docs/bill-of-rights/what-does-it-say.

The Universal Declaration of Human Rights can be read on the webpage of the UN: https://www.un.org/en/about-us/universal-declaration-of-human-rights.

Hayden, Patrick, ed. *Philosophy of Human Rights: Readings in Context*. Paragon, 2001. This is an anthology of classical and contemporary essays on human rights.

Ishay, Micheline R. *The History of Human Rights: From Ancient Times to the Globalization Era*. University of California Press, 2008. As the title suggests, this is a broad history of the gradual development of the concept of human rights.

20

PHILOSOPHY OF LAW

SYNOPSIS

While chapter 19 addressed the somewhat narrow topic of human rights, this chapter broadens to consider philosophy of law in general. The friends stumble into this topic, unaware of its importance. The topic, however, intersects several earlier topics and is again helpful in identifying the link between worldview and specific applications.

DIALOGUE

"Good morning, Zach." Mr. Hargrove, vice president of Bradley Pharmaceuticals extended his hand. "I need to talk with you about something."

Zach had never been in such a large or plush office. He knew about Jerry Hargrove, of course. If one went far enough up the org chart, he was Zach's boss. But Zach never expected to have a direct conversation with him.

Mr. Hargrove motioned for Zach to take a seat across from his desk.

"We approved your time with the FBI and have heard great things about the assistance you rendered."

Zach had requested the time away, but he had no idea the FBI had shared any of what he was doing with the company. Did everyone in Greenfield know about his "secret" work for the FBI?

"This work has brought you, and therefore this company, to the attention of a dangerous organization."

Zach's stomach dropped.

"Sir—" Zach interrupted. "I know this is unusual. And I don't know what information you have or how, but the FBI hasn't cleared me to discuss any of it with you or anyone in this company."

"I understand. Very few people at Bradley know about your involvement, but the FBI contacted us directly when they needed your services for so long."

Zach nodded.

"By the way, we've decided to compensate you for your time away."

"What? Wow. Thank you, sir."

"That's not the reason I called you in." He paused and looked directly at Zach. "We've received a tip that directly relates to you and your friends. Yes, we know about your three philosophy friends," Hargrove added, seeing Zach flinch at the mention of his friends.

"The cartel hasn't forgotten about you and is laying plans to exact vengeance because of the assistance you've given law enforcement agencies. I don't have details, but you and your friends should take precautions. You are in considerable danger."

Zach sat for a moment, trying to absorb what he'd just been told.

How could an executive at a pharmaceutical company get access to such information? If he learned it from the FBI or ATF or even the police, why wouldn't they have told Zach and his friends directly?

Something about this felt strange. Zach decided not to ask any further questions. He looked Mr. Hargrove in the eye. "Thank you, sir," he said, closing the office door behind him.

* * *

"It's done," Hargrove said into the phone. "They've been warned, just as you requested. What if they go straight to the FBI? I don't want to be implicated in this . . ."

"Don't lose your nerve, Jerry," Tristan Lancaster responded. "The whole point is to create a diversion. If the FBI is concerned about four philosophy weirdos or even the VP of Bradley Pharmaceuticals, they aren't looking at the cartel."

"I know. But I don't want my name involved."

"This whole deal is going down very shortly. If they come after you, we can get you out of the country, and I assure you the compensation will be well worth it."

Hargrove shook his head as he spoke quietly. "When I agreed to supply chemicals to you, I didn't know I was sacrificing my life in America, Tristan."

"The kind of money we're about to make will support you more than comfortably anywhere you want to go. And if you even think about turning on us now," Tristan's voice took on a sharper tone, "you will indeed sacrifice your life in America."

Hargrove struggled to respond before the line went dead.

* * *

Zach texted his friends that he needed to talk to them about something important. He didn't tell them the details, just that he'd had an alarming conversation with the VP at his company.

"We need to meet as soon as possible," he texted.

"Where?" Hannah texted. "I'm nervous to meet in any of our homes."

Angelo suggested the courthouse. A friend could get them into the building. Angelo could get permission for them to hang out there for the evening.

They assembled at the courthouse right after Hannah got off work. Angelo had arrived early and talked to his friend, public defender Sharise Cunningham, about allowing the group to use a conference room adjoining her office. Sharise and her husband attended church with Angelo. Although he couldn't explain everything to her, Angelo made it clear that real danger was involved.

Zach, Suresh, and Hannah arrived and were taken to Mrs. Cunningham's second-floor office suite. She escorted them to the conference room where she normally met with clients. Angelo promised they'd turn off the lights and lock up on their way out.

The friends felt safe for the first time in several hours.

Now that they were safe in a private room, Zach recounted the details of the conversation with his boss.

"Do you think he's involved with the cartel?" Angelo asked abruptly. "I don't think he should have this kind of information."

"He said he learned about it from the FBI. I immediately called Agent

Esposito and left a message. I still haven't heard back though. And I'm not comfortable talking to anyone else."

"I don't blame you," Hannah shuddered as she spoke. "I can't believe any of this is happening. And I don't know who we can trust. But I do know we need to stick together."

"We also need to avoid any independent actions," Angelo said. "Agent Esposito made it clear that we aren't qualified to take on the cartel. I almost got us killed."

"None of us blames you about the stakeout. We all agreed to do it and thought it was a good idea," Suresh said. "And you *are* a professional when it comes to physical threats, certainly more than the three of us are."

Zach's phone rang. It was Agent Esposito.

Zach briefly explained his conversation with Hargrove and that he and his friends were in a private conference room at the courthouse.

Esposito listened quietly and didn't say much. He told Zach not to worry. They were closing in on Lancaster. It would all be over soon. The officers assigned to watch them knew they were gathered at the courthouse and would keep Esposito apprised.

But this wasn't any kind of reassurance for the friends.

There was a soft knock at the door. Mrs. Cunningham had returned. She had forgotten some files she needed before taking her work home. She pointed out the coffee maker and invited them to make themselves at home.

"Are you the philosophy group Angelo has mentioned?"

The friends nodded.

"What are you discussing right now?" she asked.

There was an awkward silence as the friends looked back and forth at each other.

"We don't have an agenda at the moment," Angelo said. "We might not even talk about philosophy tonight."

"Have you considered the philosophy of law?" she asked. "It overlaps with several other fields of philosophy, such as metaphysics and religion, that might be interesting to you. I'd love to hear your thoughts if you have time."

Zach stepped forward and extended his hand. "Hi, I'm Zach. I initially organized the group, and I've mostly been the person recommending topics for discussion. The philosophy of law hadn't crossed my mind," he said. "I guess it doesn't look like a philosophical topic to me. Societies need structure and boundaries to thrive, and they mutually agree to place limitations on themselves for that purpose. How could that be metaphysical or religious? It doesn't even seem philosophical."

"You don't want to restrict philosophical inquiry in that way, do you, Zach?" Hannah said. "Over the last year, you've helped us see that careful, analytical thought about anything is philosophical. Even if you're right about the pragmatic nature of law, it would still be an appropriate subject for us, wouldn't it?"

Hannah turned to the lawyer and waved. "I'm Hannah. It's nice to meet you."

"And I'm Suresh." He smiled broadly.

"So good to meet you all. Please call me Shari."

She pulled out a chair and sat down. "Hannah makes a good point. Your understanding, Zach, if correct, is still philosophical in nature. In fact, you are arguing for what is known as legal positivism. You view laws as simply social constructs, created by societies for practical purposes with no eternal grounding in reality."

Zach furrowed his brow, "Are you suggesting that some see laws as having some kind of eternal existence apart from specific legislation?"

"I am," Sharise said. "There are two ways to argue for that idea. One group of thinkers, who wants to avoid religious overtones, says that laws are eternal abstract objects, realities that underlie specific legal codes. Others embrace a theistic explanation and say that laws are reflections of God's morality and are communicated via divine revelation. Both reject legal positivism."

"I think I'm with Zach on this," Suresh said. "I saw on social media the other day that Bulgarians are required by law to carry a fire extinguisher in their cars.[1] How does that express some kind of eternal abstract object? Sure, 'Don't kill' may have some basis in reality, I suppose, but the majority of laws are very context specific. They don't look like the abstract objects we often discuss."

Angelo looked at Shari. "Correct me if I'm wrong, but I don't think these

1. This is not fictitious. See "Driving in Bulgaria," https://www.avis.co.uk/drive-avis/driving-guides/road-rules/bulgaria#.

more realist positions are arguing that every single legal stipulation has an eternal formulation. That would be nonsense. I think they're arguing for something more foundational."

"You're right, Angelo. Built into the nature of reality or revealed by God is the idea that people should show concern for others by making preparations on behalf of their welfare. This eternal principle might look like putting a fence around a flat roof, a law in Old Testament legal code; salting icy driveways in the Midwestern or Northern United States, a requirement in some localities; or carrying a fire extinguisher in one's car if you live in Bulgaria. The applications may be context specific, but each is rooted in something more fundamental, something eternal."

"Interesting . . ." Hannah said. "These realist positions, as you call them, seem to be adding complications to a simple situation. Like Zach and Suresh, I've always viewed laws as determined by their societal setting. After all, laws change with cultures as human needs develop. Why try to penetrate to some abstract level when legal positivism, as you call it, provides a solution unencumbered by metaphysics?"

Angelo looked around the room. "It appears I'm the only person who finds legal positivism unattractive. You could probably say that my religious orientation pushes me in that direction, and I suppose you'd be right in a way. Zach's naturalism, Hannah's existentialism, and Suresh's pantheism all work well with positivism, it seems, but theism points in a different direction. Just as I've argued in the past that morality is an expression of God's eternal nature, I would source law in God as well.

"What about an argument for realism that might or might not be religious? Hannah, you mentioned that laws change as human needs change. Would you say laws get better or worse?"

"Probably both," she replied. "Coercive, tyrannical states create and enforce evil laws sometimes; when the dictators fall, it's often necessary to replace the bad laws with good laws."

"But how do you know if a particular law is good or bad? What makes a law tyrannical or evil, as you put it?"

"A good law," Zach said, "brings benefits to the society, and a bad law brings detriment. Does that cover it?"

"Is it that simple?" Angelo asked. "A law in Mississippi in the late 1800s that 'colored people' couldn't drink from the water fountains of white people benefited the majority of the citizens—at least in their view. Would you say that was a good law?"

"Obviously not."

"What are you measuring the law against?" Angelo asked. "Is there some 'right' way to treat minorities? Do the laws create the right way, or do good laws reflect the right way and bad laws undermine it? Do you see what I'm getting at?"

Sharise smiled broadly and nodded.

"You all have laid an excellent philosophical foundation for Angelo to make those connections to philosophy of law so quickly. I think Angelo's point is important. Can I make two related points?"

"Of course," Zach said.

"Suresh, you alluded to the fact that murder might 'have some basis in reality,' if I remember your wording. If you grant that some laws—indeed, the most important and universal ones—have eternal grounding in abstract principles, then you are no longer a consistent legal positivist. Realists are willing to concede that there are occasional particular laws—like 'eat all your peas before you get dessert'—that may have little or no connection to eternal abstract principles, but the existence of *any* eternal abstract principles underlying law defeats legal positivism.

"Which brings us to an important point: What if a society decided that murder was okay in certain instances? Let's say we can kill everyone over sixty or who has a terminal disease or who is the result of an inconvenient pregnancy. Would legal positivism have any basis for denying the legitimacy of such a law? Good and bad laws can be characterized only by comparison to a fixed standard; similarly, obviously unjust and evil laws have no restraint without a fixed standard.

"This leads, then, to a final observation: The diversity in legal codes is more apparent and surface-level than real and deep. There is surprising uniformity of legal principles underlying legislation from around the world and across time. It's difficult to explain along positivist lines but makes good sense if either form of realism is true."

"You've given us a lot to think about," Hannah said. "I still prefer the simpler solution, and I think maybe human and societal evolution might explain the commonality of laws that support flourishing cultures. But at the moment, I don't see how my positivism can guarantee that every culture would have a law against murder or even that it should."

* * *

Just then, a rush of footsteps could be heard in the hall. Agent Esposito and three other uniformed men burst into the room.

Everyone jumped up from their seats.

"An agent embedded in Lancaster's home overheard that a major operation is underway to take out the four of you," Esposito said.

Hannah sank back into her chair, and Suresh rushed to make sure she was okay.

"Our intelligence says that approximately ten heavily armed men are preparing to descend on the building."

"How did they find out we're here?" Zach asked.

"They've had a man shadowing you. He followed you here when you got off work."

Zach groaned.

"They wouldn't seriously consider attacking a government building, would they?" Angelo asked. "Why do something so visible to get at us? We're nobodies."

"We don't know. Our first priority is to get you to safety. We have a safe house a few blocks from here where we can guard you with a lot less personnel than it would take to defend this facility. These men are members of the Greenfield PD and will get you to safety."

Angelo recognized two of them but knew only one of them, a SWAT team member, Mack Ryan.

"I'll be praying for you," Sharice said as they left the room. After they left, they heard Esposito promise Shari an escort to her home.

* * *

"Are you sure that FBI plant overheard our plans at the courthouse?" Lancaster asked one of his assistants.

The man assured him that he had.

"Good. Notify Hargrove and the buyers that the deal is going down in the next twenty-four hours. And I want that FBI snitch dealt with."

"Yes, sir."

THEORY

The dialogue portion of this chapter illustrates that philosophy of law flows out of our other philosophical commitments. What follows will lay out the topic in a more systematic manner.

Introduction

Philosophy of law is the utilization of the techniques of philosophical investigation to examine various issues that relate to governmental rules that citizens and corporations are required to obey. Perhaps the most central issues in philosophy of law are those about the nature and source of governmental authority and laws.

In the chapters on ethics and human rights we've seen that although they are distinct subjects, they have significant similarities. This is true for philosophy of law too: It overlaps with ethics and human rights, but it's not reducible to either of them. Somehow these three topics are interrelated even though they are distinct from each other.

Here's an example. Route 80 is an interstate highway that crosses the USA from New Jersey in the east to California in the west. In many places along Route 80 the speed limit is 65 mph. There are some places where the speed limit is only 55, though, and there are places where it's 70. There's nothing inherently immoral about driving 55 mph, 65 mph, or even 70 mph. However, it is illegal to drive 70 in a 65 zone, or 65 in a 55 zone. So, it can be illegal to do something even when the act isn't inherently immoral. However, some argue that it is the moral duty of citizens to abide by the laws established by their governments. If that's correct, then it's immoral to break the speed limit. In that case it would be immoral to drive 70 in a 65 zone or 65 in a 55 zone, even though there's nothing inherently immoral about driving at these speeds.

This illustration shows at least two things: first, that "moral" and "legal" are not exact synonyms, and second, that there is some overlap between them. But what exactly is the difference between them? And how much do they overlap? These are metaphysical questions, and answering them requires careful thought.

Metaphysics (Again)

In the chapter on ethical theories we saw three basic approaches to the question of the source and nature of morality: social contract theory, Platonic moral realism, and divine nature theory. Social contract theory views morality as a human creation, Platonic moral realism views morality as eternal and impersonal, and divine nature theory views morality as a reflection of the nature of an eternal, personal God. We saw something similar in the chapter on human rights, only there the options were social contract theory, Platonic realism, and theistic conceptualism. Social contract theory views human rights as human creations, Platonic realism views them as eternal and impersonal, and theistic conceptualism views them as eternal ideas in the mind of God. There are similar options when it comes to the nature of laws.

When we're talking about laws, social contract theory becomes **legal positivism**, the view that laws are social constructs created by a society that determine what is permissible and not permissible for the members of that society. Metaphysically speaking, this is a nominalist view of laws, since it denies that laws have any real existence independent of human and divine involvement. Platonic realism becomes **legal realism**, the view that laws are based on or instantiations of eternal truths that exist apart from gods and humans.

The theistic approach to laws is metaphysically conceptualist. That means that it attempts to take a middle position between realism and nominalism, arguing that, contrary to what realism affirms, laws don't exist apart from minds, but they are nonetheless real, contrary to what nominalism affirms.[2] They are real in the same sense that thoughts are real, since laws are viewed as thoughts in the mind of God. This is akin to the theistic conceptualism that we discussed in the chapter on human rights, but in the context of philosophy of law, this view is called **natural law theory**.

---

2. Nominalism, realism, and conceptualism were first introduced and explained in chapter 9 (abstract objects).

Prima facie, legal positivism seems to have an advantage in this debate. Many laws appear to be nothing more than practical agreements among the members of a society or arbitrary requirements that governments enact rather than instantiations of eternal truths or reflections of God's nature. Take, for example, speed limits. Thinking abductively, does it seem likely that the law establishing a 40-mph speed limit on unmarked country roads in Alabama and the law imposing a 55-mph speed limit on such roads in Virginia are both instantiations of an eternal, transcendent truth about speed limits? Does it seem likely that they are a reflection of the nature of God? Or is it more likely that speed limits are agreements between the Alabama Department of Transportation and the Alabama State Police about what would work best in Alabama, and the Virginia Department of Transportation and the Virginia State Police about what would work best in Virginia?

Here's another example. Many countries do not practice capital punishment. Others do practice it, but with varying regulations. Does it make the most sense to view this diversity of approaches to capital punishment as a result of a transcendent, eternal principle? Or does it make better sense to say that it's a reflection of the nature of God? Or is it more likely that capital punishment laws are the result of various societies coming to different conclusions about what will work best for each society? Thinking abductively, which of these theories best accounts for the diversity of laws?

The Arguments

Many people who have thought about the explanatory power of legal positivism have concluded that it presents the best account for the diversity of laws that we see around the world. And that's not the only argument favoring legal positivism. Another argument comes from how easily it accounts for changes in laws within a society. Each society's legal system evolves—or at least changes—over time. Things that used to be legal are sometimes outlawed, such as selling cigarettes to minors and using lead as an additive in house paint. Other things that used to be illegal become legal, such as shopping on Sundays and driving faster than 55 mph on some highways.

Another argument for legal positivism is its ontological parsimony. This was mentioned as an argument for nominalism in the chapter on abstract objects. Ontological parsimony is stinginess about what things exist: The fewer unnecessary things there are, the better. A parsimonious theory is one that doesn't make up unnecessary things. As Ockham's razor puts it, "Entities should not be multiplied beyond necessity." When it comes to legal positivism, legal realism, and natural law theory, legal positivism is the most parsimonious. All three theories believe in laws; legal realism adds to that eternal truths, and natural law theory adds God. Legal positivism, on the other hand, doesn't add anything.

Another way of viewing this argument is via the contrast between physicalism and dualism. Physicalism is ontologically more parsimonious than is dualism, since physicalism believes only in the physical world, while dualism believes in the physical world plus something (or things) that is (are) immaterial. Legal positivism is compatible with a physicalist view of reality, but legal realism and natural law theory aren't. If physicalism turns out to be true, then legal realism and natural law theory cannot be true. Hence, if physicalism is true, then legal positivism must be true, too.

However, rejoinders to these arguments must be considered before one can draw a conclusion. For example, when we discussed Ockham's razor in the chapter on abstract objects, we pointed out that it's not teaching that we should automatically accept whatever theory is simplest even if that theory doesn't do a very good job explaining the phenomena in question. If a theory is too simplistic, it's much better to opt for a more complicated theory that does a better job explaining things. Many critics of legal positivism grant that laws are made by humans and vary significantly from society to society. However, they argue that the underlying goals of each society's laws are universally the same: protecting the weak and defenseless, ensuring justice, facilitating a flourishing society, and so forth. In a way reminiscent of how advocates of Platonic moral realism and divine nature theory respond to the use that advocates of social contract theory make of Ockham's razor, critics of legal positivism argue that it does not adequately account for these universal underlying values.

This brings up a common misconception about legal realism and natural law theory. It is sometimes assumed that legal realism holds that each earthly law is a reflection of a specific transcendent law. In other words, if there's a speed limit for Interstate 95 in the United States, it's because there's a specific I-95 speed limit in the world of the forms. Similarly, it's sometimes thought that natural law theory teaches that all earthly laws are directly created by God, or at least directly reflect some idea in God's mind, or something along those lines. But while some who hold to these views may espouse such positions, there are other ways to interpret legal realism and natural law theory.

Perhaps most salient to our discussion is the theory that earthly laws that work well do so because they harmonize with the nature of reality. Both legal realists and natural law theorists have made this argument. They grant that earthly laws—speed limits, tax laws, laws against assault and robbery, and so on—are human creations. However, they argue that humans create these laws because humans have figured out, to one degree or another, what laws contribute to a safe, just, and flourishing society. And these laws contribute to such a society because they reward behavior that is in keeping with truths about how people need to behave for safety, justice, and prosperity to prevail. Legal realists will view these truths as existing as eternal abstract objects, while divine nature theorists will hold that they reflect, in some way, the nature of God, but both groups will agree that without such transcendent truths, there's no accounting for why good laws are successful at bringing about a better society.

By this point, the reader can probably anticipate how critics of legal positivism would respond to the first two arguments given in support of it. Legal positivists think that positivism has an easier time explaining the diversity of laws in the world. Legal realism and natural law theory can respond to this by pointing out that although they believe that laws should perfectly align with the transcendent ideal, they recognize the obvious: This often doesn't happen. This failure is because earthly laws are made by humans. Factors like human creativity, varying circumstances, and uncertainty about which laws will work best combine to result in societies enacting laws that vary considerably from one society to another, but this does not entail the conclusion that there is no transcendent ideal.

Legal realism and natural law theory can also explain the fact that laws change over time. Ideally, perhaps, human laws would exactly mirror their transcendent counterparts. However, due to the facts referenced above, this is often not the case. Consequently, human laws don't function perfectly.

Societies modify and replace them, endlessly attempting to come up with laws that work perfectly but always falling short.

What arguments are there in favor of legal realism and natural law theory? Let's start with the abductive arguments. The variety of laws around the world notwithstanding, there are also significant commonalities. Nearly all—perhaps literally all, though that can be debated—societies develop some sort of legal system to guide or regulate the behavior of their members. Some have argued that this is best explained by the natural tendency of people to care for those closest to them (called "kin altruism" or "group altruism") because doing so leads to an ethos that benefits everyone, both individually and as a group. That seems like a reasonable view, but it's not clear why it would necessitate a body of laws.

Alternatively, it could be that laws are just the best way to structure a society so that it results in what's best for everyone, or the majority, who lives in that society. It could be that, given enough time, each society discovers this truth and structures itself accordingly. But look at what is being said: There's a universal truth about the best way to structure a society. That sounds a lot like legal realism, doesn't it? It could also fit with natural law theory.

How can we best explain the fact that all (or most) societies develop laws protecting life, liberty, property rights, and so on? Once again, the legal positivist may argue that it's natural for societies to develop laws that strengthen the society by protecting its members and their individual and corporate interests, and that all laws that do that well will look at least somewhat similar. Fine, but what is it about a particular set of laws that makes it effective at promoting well-being? Legal positivism doesn't seem to have an answer to this question.

On the other hand, legal realism argues that laws promote well-being when they are in conformity with eternal truths about the nature of reality. Whether we like that answer or not, at least it's an answer. Natural law theory asserts that laws promote well-being when they cohere with God's design for the world, because a God who is omniscient, omnisapient, and omnibenevolent will design the world in a way that is conducive to the flourishing of those who inhabit it. Once again, some people won't find this answer satisfying, but at least it's an answer.

Epistemology

The three theories that we've been discussing are, essentially, ontological: They are theories about the nature of laws. However, these ontological views may have epistemic implications. As was the case in our study of ethics, one's view of the nature of laws may have implications for how one thinks that laws can be known. Let's take a look at that.

Since legal positivism says that laws are social constructs, with each society creating its own set of rules for its members and with nothing transcendent (like Platonic forms or divine commands) involved, the way to know what laws there are is to read the legislation in whatever society interests you. That seems very straightforward, and that could be a real advantage to legal positivism vis-à-vis the other views. However, this approach assumes that we do not want to venture beyond a descriptive attitude toward laws: The only knowledge that interests us is the facts about what laws have been legislated in a given society.

Some would find this limitation unacceptable. They would want to go beyond the merely descriptive and ask questions of a more prescriptive nature, such as "What laws should there be in this society?" There have been many societies in which the laws that were enacted did not result in the kind of society that the legal positivist would want, a society with laws that protect the individual and corporate interests of its members (or something along those lines). It could be very useful to know what laws *should* be enacted. For this, we will need an epistemology that helps us discover not only what laws are the case, but also what laws *should be* the case, so that we can move from an ineffective set of laws to an effective one. But that suggests that there's a transcendent standard that laws can be judged against. Such a standard is not a good fit for legal positivism: It's too much a Platonic or theistic ideal, and as such it seems more fitting for legal realism or natural law theory.

Since legal realism says that human laws are ideally based on or are instantiations of eternal truths that exist apart from gods and humans, its epistemology needs to provide a way of determining what these eternal truths are so that the laws that humans enact will accurately reflect these truths. That's a challenge, but not one that we haven't encountered before, for the same challenge arose in our discussions of ethics and human rights.

In those discussions we saw that if morals and human rights are real, then living morally and respecting human rights should be conducive to individual and societal flourishing. The same thing should be true regarding laws. If human laws accurately correlate to truths about the nature of reality, then they should result in stable societies that facilitate human flourishing. A sort of pragmatic epistemology is in play here: The best system of laws is that which works best because the best system of laws is the one that corresponds to truths about the way human societies function.

Because natural law theory views laws as human creations that, at their best, reflect the divine mind, the epistemology of natural law theory will be much like the epistemology of divine nature theory. Hence, it will require that God reveal to humanity those aspects of his nature that are relevant to good governance. God can do this through nature (general revelation) and through special revelation. Special revelation can take many forms: It can come through angels, human messengers such as prophets, dreams and visions, thunderous voices or a still, small voice (1 Kgs 19:12), and through inspired Scripture. God can also take on human form and speak directly to humans.

Since natural law theory believes that an omniscient, omnisapient, and omnibenevolent God would design the world in a way that is conducive to the flourishing of those who inhabit it, it follows that laws that cohere with God's design for the world will promote the well-being of the people living therein. Hence, there can be a pragmatic test of the correspondence between any human law and the divine plan: Laws that do not contribute to flourishing are probably not in correlation with God's plan and thus are not good laws.

Worldviews and Philosophy of Law

By this time it's probably fairly obvious which views on the nature and source of laws (and the principles that lie behind laws, if such principles exist) best complement which worldviews. Nonetheless it's good to make it clear. Since naturalism denies the existence of anything immaterial, it is incompatible with legal realism and natural law theory. It requires a theory about the nature and source of laws that does not involve anything immaterial. Legal positivism is the only such option. Conversely, since legal positivism denies that there are eternal truths that, in some way, lie behind human laws, it is a nominalist view regarding the nature of laws, and nominalism fits well with naturalism. The considerations that render legal positivism a good choice for naturalists also render it a good choice for pantheists; pantheism and naturalism have a lot in common.

Since legal realism affirms the existence of eternal truths that exist independently of humanity, it's not compatible with naturalism. On the other hand, since these truths form a standard that exists independently from God, impugns God's sovereignty, and affirms eternal existents in addition to God, it's not compatible with classical theism or deism. However, it could be reconciled to polytheism, which allows for the existence of multiple eternal entities, and many forms of polytheism do not have a supreme deity like theism and deism have. It is compatible with panentheism and paganism for similar reasons.

Since natural law theory is based on the belief that God's omnibenevolent design is woven into the fabric of reality, this view is explicitly theistic. It's also compatible with deism, which can be viewed as "absentee theism." Classical natural law theory is not compatible with worldviews that lack a creator God, so it's not compatible with naturalism, pantheism, panentheism, paganism, and most polytheisms.

QUESTIONS TO PONDER

- Do we really need laws? Why or why not?
- Are all laws created by humans?
- Are there things that should be outlawed in every society?
- What makes a law a good law?
- Where do governments get their authority from?

TERMS TO KNOW

- philosophy of law
- legal positivism
- legal realism
- natural law theory
- nominalism
- realism
- conceptualism
- abduction
- ontological parsimony
- Ockham's razor
- physicalism
- dualism
- ontology
- descriptive
- prescriptive

FOR FURTHER READING

Feinberg, Joel, Jules Coleman, and Christopher Kutz, eds. *Philosophy of Law*. 9th ed. Cengage, 2013. This is a solid anthology representing all three traditions and covering a nice range of issues.

Finnis, John. *Natural Law and Natural Rights*. 2nd ed. Oxford University Press, 2011. This is a detailed exposition of the natural law approach to philosophy of law.

Kramer, Matthew H. *In Defense of Legal Positivism: Law Without Trimmings*. Oxford University Press, 1999. This is an exposition and defense of legal positivism.

Wacks, Raymond. *Philosophy of Law: A Very Short Introduction*. 2nd ed. Oxford University Press, 2006. This is a brief, readable introduction to philosophy of law.

PHILOSOPHICAL ANTHROPOLOGY

PERSONAL IDENTITY

SYNOPSIS

The last four chapters in this book address important questions in philosophical anthropology, the study of humanity. This chapter addresses the significant but easily overlooked issue of personal identity. The role of worldview in answering the questions this issue raises will again be prominent and important.

DIALOGUE

It was 11:30 p.m. Angelo wanted to peek out of the window of the safe house to see if anything was happening. He rose to his feet and took a step toward the window.

Across the dimly lit room, he saw Mack Ryan staring him down. Mack had volunteered to "babysit" inside the safe house while the Greenfield PD covered the outside of the building. A presence inside the dwelling in case the cartel broke through the outer defenses seemed wise.

It felt like the threat to their lives was increasing by the hour. *Why would the cartel even consider them a threat?* Mack had broken his steely silence only once when they entered the house to say that he believed that Tristan Lancaster was a homicidal maniac who had become fixated on the four of them and was angling for revenge for their roles in interfering with his plans.

Angelo stopped when he caught Mack's eye and saw him shake his head slowly. Mack was one step ahead of him. At 6'5" and 260 pounds of lean muscle, Mack seemed to be cut from stone. He wore a Level IV armored vest, and his index finger rested lightly on the frame of his M4 rifle. Mack was no one to trifle with. Angelo felt safe but still wished he knew what was happening.

After an hour of struggling to find a comfortable position on the couch, Hannah sat up. The rest of the group took that as a signal that they wouldn't be disturbing the others if they gave up their battle to sleep. They looked at each other through the gloom. Only one light shone in the house, from the kitchen down the hall. Mack stood illuminated in the hallway, a menacing silhouette driving home the point that this was no normal night.

Suresh spoke first, "What's everyone thinking?"

Hannah rubbed her eyes. "How surreal all this is . . . I'm not even sure I'm thinking anymore. I feel numb and like my mind is on automatic, just working to survive."

"I don't know how to make sense of everything that has happened," Zach said. "Just a few months ago, we were getting together to talk about philosophy, and now we're embroiled in a deadly conspiracy involving international cartels?"

"I certainly didn't think being a courthouse guard would lead me here." Angelo rubbed his hands together as if trying to get warm even though the room wasn't cold. "I took this job because one of my friends said it was easy and nothing ever happened on the job."

"And I never imagined," Suresh added, "that cooking in a high-end restaurant would result in a shoot-out and surveillance."

Everyone was quiet for a moment.

"How does someone end up in a criminal syndicate?" Hannah asked. "What kind of person do you have to be to take up a life of law-breaking and harming others? I don't mean the morality of it, but rather, who takes on the *identity* of a criminal?"

It was a puzzling question.

"I'm not sure you can separate the morality of criminal acts from the question of identity, but I see the dilemma," Angelo said. "I'm curious whether these cartel members think of themselves as good people, or have they embraced their identity of criminals? Surely they don't think they're humanitarians, do they?"

Zach shook his head. "I can't imagine anyone could be that self-deceived, but who knows?"

"Surely some of them have families, right?" Suresh asked. "How does someone who kills during the day sit down with his kids at night to play and read? The cognitive dissonance of being daddy to his kids and the worst nightmare to his enemies . . . Dr. Jekyll and Mr. Hyde. Could you prosecute and imprison the evil killer without also condemning the loving father? Obviously I'd like to see these cartel members caught and punished, but think about what that would be like for the person's children, who only know him as their dad."

"But the law can't go easy on dangerous people just because they have families . . ."

"Of course not," Suresh said. "I'm just thinking about the complexity of a person's identity. It is easy to see an evil person from only one angle and forget that they are more than their evil deeds."

"Okay, I see what you're saying. The guy might be two different people to the public and to his family, but that doesn't mean he can escape responsibility for his actions."

"And what about the mothers of these criminals?" Hannah had visited many homes where she saw conditions and parenting styles that seemed to be a breeding ground for criminal behavior. "Just think, at one point, these criminals were little children being raised in a home with a mom, maybe a dad, and siblings. They played with toys and used their imagination. What happened to turn them from innocent, wide-eyed children into people who spend their life in criminal activity, even to the point of harming or killing others? Are they even the same person as when they were little?"

"Wow, Hannah," Angelo said. "It's so much more emotionally complex than I've considered. I never would have imagined these dangerous people as children, even though at some point, all of us were children"—he looked over at the imposing figure in the hallway—"even Mack."

Angelo thought he caught a faint smile on Mack's face.

"And you raise a good point, Hannah. Are they even the same people?"

"I can think of one way in which they aren't the same," Zach said. "Have you ever heard of the Greek myth of the ship of Theseus? The warrior Theseus sailed to Crete and defeated the minotaur, a creature with the body of a bull and the head of a man. When he returned to Athens, his ship was kept in the harbor as a memorial to his great victory. Over time, parts of the ship decayed and were replaced with new lumber. Eventually, the entire ship was made of new wood, and philosophers began to debate whether the ship was even the same as the one on which Theseus sailed. Some argued that since none of the original parts were the same, the ship in the harbor was no longer the ship of Theseus. Others argued that it was the same ship since it looked identical to the one on which Theseus returned after his famous battle."

"Where did this story originate?"

"A historian, Plutarch, recorded it in the second century. But it gets better," he said with a smile. "In the seventeenth century, English philosopher Thomas Hobbes added a new wrinkle. He imagined that the person who repaired the ship as it decayed kept the original planks and over time reconstructed the original ship of Theseus. So now there were two identical ships (minus the decay). So which ship was really the ship of Theseus?"[1]

"Wait," Suresh said. "I don't even understand this."

"Mind bending, isn't it? It raises the question of whether a person remains the same over time. I read one time that the average age of all cells in the body is seven to ten years.[2] Some cells, like muscle and fat cells, can last seventy years, while others are replaced every week, like the cells in your colon. If the very cells that make up who you are change, how can you be the same person? Maybe prison sentences should last no longer than seven to ten years so we don't punish those who were entirely different people when they were sentenced."

"You're not serious, are you?" Angelo asked.

"No, of course not." Zach laughed. "It was just a thought experiment."

---

1. Thomas Hobbes, *Elements of Philosophy: The First Section* (R&W Leybourn, 1656), 100.
2. Chris Opfer and Allison Troutner, "Does Your Body Really Replace Itself Every Seven Years?," in *How Stuff Works*, September 22, 2022, https://science.howstuffworks.com/life/cellular-microscopic/does-body-really-replace-seven-years.htm.

"A similar thought experiment is Ludwig Wittgenstein's idea of language games."

Everyone turned their heads toward the shadowy figure standing in the hallway. Mack had been listening to the conversation while monitoring through his earpiece the chatter of the officers outside.

"What do you mean, Mack?"

Angelo was the only one on a first-name basis with the officer.

"How do you know about Wittgenstein?"

Mack laughed, a deep rumble emerging from his chest. "Do you think you're the only ones who read? When I was stationed overseas with the 75th Ranger Regiment, we had a lot of downtime between missions. Rather than playing video games or cards, I worked my way through the base library. Someone had stocked it with a well-rounded section on philosophy. I read Wittgenstein and was intrigued by his language game theory. He argued that the meaning of words is found in the context in which they are written or spoken. If you start to change the context, the meaning of the words changes with it. He gave the example of a ball game in which you slowly start to change the rules. At some point, the modified game ceases to be the original game. For example, let's say you replaced a soccer ball with a volleyball, but you kept all the rest of the rules of soccer. Would it still be a soccer game?"

"Sure it would," Suresh said. "A slightly different ball wouldn't change it all that much."

Mack stepped a little further into the room as he talked. "Yes, but if you kept changing the rules, at some point it wouldn't be soccer anymore. What if you used a football and raised the goals so they were six feet off the ground? Eventually it wouldn't resemble soccer at all."

"What does that have to do with our discussion about the cartel?" Hannah asked.

"Just as the ship of Theseus would eventually become another ship given enough replacement parts and one game would change into a new game with enough changes to the rules, so people in some ways become different when they change or when life changes them. That doesn't mean they aren't responsible for their choices or actions, but it does help us understand to some degree why people can change so dramatically over time."

Hannah thought about that for a moment. "That makes sense. I've seen all kinds of change in people because of circumstances, often in destructive ways. As a social worker, I unfortunately sometimes have a front-row seat to people's negative transformation."

Mack turned his head to reply to a radio check. He waved his hand to indicate his departure from the conversation and stepped back into the hallway.

"So are we agreed that even though these cartel members were once innocent children, they are still the same people and are responsible for their actions?"

Everyone nodded. Even though the discussion had raised interesting questions about identity, they all still held strong views about the need for people to be accountable for their choices. After all, if people could escape culpability because of something that happened to them, how could anyone be convicted of a crime? A person's identity must have some stability despite the changes that time and circumstances might bring.

"You know," Suresh said, "we've been talking so much about the cartel members and their identities that perhaps we haven't considered our own. The shooting at the restaurant has forever changed me, but I don't know if it's an essential change in who I am or simply a change in my emotions and thoughts. If I'm honest, it feels like an alteration to my very being, but I haven't thought about it enough to know for sure."

"I guess that would depend on our understanding of who we are," Hannah said. "I'd have to say that our essence as individuals changes as we choose new conceptions of ourselves. I think about my previous life as a Pentecostal Christian and how radically my sense of self changed when I abandoned that identity."

"But you're still the same person, aren't you?" Angelo said. "I struggle to separate identity from beliefs. For example, your beliefs changed, but you as a person remained the same, right?"

"I don't know that I did . . ." Hannah began. "Since I don't believe that our fundamental identity is as a person made in God's image, my concept of the self is determined by my will or creative activity to declare myself. As such, my identity will always be in flux, always making myself new as circumstances change.[3] So it's not just my beliefs that change but rather who I am—since my beliefs and my choices *are* who I am."

"I guess that makes sense—if you're right that we don't have a given nature from God. If you don't believe you're a special creation by virtue of being made in the image of God, then I guess all you have left is your will to create and recreate yourself," Angelo said, scratching his head. "I have to ask, though, isn't that terrifying at times?"

Hannah sighed. "Yes, sometimes it is. Not having a god to turn to and find my identity in can be a burden at times. At other times, it is exhilarating and gives me a sense of genuine freedom. One of Sartre's famous sayings is, 'Man is condemned to be free.' Which reminds me of a book a friend was reading recently. The first sentence struck a nerve: 'I don't believe in God, but I miss him.'[4] The author, Julian Barnes, is a self-declared agnostic."

Even Zach seemed moved by this statement.

"It really resonated with me," Hannah said. "I envy you, Angelo. To know who you are because God has told you, and to know that it is a lofty identity, must provide a real sense of security and stability."

A great sadness washed over Angelo as Hannah spoke. He didn't always think about all the implications of his Christian worldview, but Hannah's words reminded him what a precious gift his sense of identity was.

"I don't always appreciate what I have in my faith," he said. "When I do think about it, I am very grateful. I think every person has inherent worth and dignity because of the image of God in them. But since the fall, that image has been marred, or disfigured. Every person still bears that image, but the corruption of sin has distorted their likeness to God. When I came

---

3. The *Stanford Encyclopedia of Philosophy* states, "Existentialists forward a novel conception of the self not as a substance or thing with some pre-given nature (or 'essence') but as a situated activity or way of being whereby we are always in the process of making or creating who we are as our life unfolds. This means our essence is not given in advance; we are contingently thrown into existence and are burdened with the task of creating ourselves through our choices and actions." Kevin Aho, "Existentialism," in *The Stanford Encyclopedia of Philosophy*, ed. Edward N. Zalta and Uri Nodelman (Summer 2023 ed.), https://plato.stanford.edu/archives/sum2023/entries/existentialism/.
4. Julian Barnes, *Nothing to Be Frightened Of* (Knopf, 2008), 1.

to believe that Jesus Christ was the Savior I needed, I experienced the regenerating power of the Holy Spirit and the transformation that comes with it.

"I'm not perfect by any means. I still struggle with sin and foolish choices, but I have embraced what the Bible says about those who believe in Christ: I have become a child of God.[5] Even though I fail to live up to this ideal, my confidence is in God, who has promised to complete the work of transformation he began in me. You're right . . . it does allow me to live with a secure identity. And I'm grateful for that."

Suresh leaned forward. "I take a very different view of human identity. Buddhism teaches that personal identity is a delusion and that each of us as a differentiated self doesn't actually exist. Our desire to have an identity is a significant source of suffering. Our goal should be nirvana, which is a state of nonself, or liberation. At death, the self disappears.[6] In this life, the self or person, conceived as an enduring entity, simply does not exist. Everything is a succession of moments and is in flux."[7]

"Those are complex ideas," Angelo said. "In some ways, it sounds similar to Hannah's view, and in other ways it seems to mirror Zach's view. Isn't it interesting how our views seem to overlap at times, at least a little?"

"It *is* interesting," Suresh said.

He started to comment further on that overlap when Mack suddenly stepped into the room. He held a finger up to indicate that he needed silence while he listened intently to the voice in his earpiece.

"What is it?" Hannah mouthed.

Mack paused and finally spoke. "Sorry," he said quickly. "I didn't mean to startle you. The agent in charge started to ask a question about you, and then someone else interrupted. He wanted to know if any of you have slept yet in case your testimony or ability to identify people is needed."

"We haven't slept at all," Zach said.

"Could everyone try to get some sleep so he doesn't chew me out?"

---

5. John 1:12 states, "But to all who did receive him, who believed in his name, he gave the right to become children of God" (ESV).
6. Yung-Jong Shiah, "From Self to Nonself: The Nonself Theory," *Front Psychol* 7, no. 124 (2016).
7. K. T. S. Sarao, "Anātman," in *Oxford Bibliographies*, https://www.oxfordbibliographies.com/display/document/obo-9780195393521/obo-9780195393521-0193.xml.

The friends laughed. Even this huge, formidable soldier didn't want to get in trouble.

"Sure," Angelo said. "We'll try."

And with that, everyone got comfortable again and did their best to chase some rest.

THEORY

Philosophical Anthropology

Our four friends expressed different approaches to personal identity depending on their worldviews. While helpful, we will see that the issues involved are even more complex than the dialogue suggests, and it's just one of the issues that arise in the study of philosophical anthropology. Anthropology is the study of humanity. Anthropologists, sociologists, psychologists, theologians, and philosophers study humanity. Each discipline has its own unique tools and approaches anthropology in a unique way. Philosophers study humanity using the tools of any philosophical investigation: an open mind, curiosity, and critical thinking. So philosophical anthropology is the philosophical study of human nature.

Our unit on philosophical anthropology contains four chapters dealing with four subjects: personal identity, human uniqueness, the meaning of life, and the nature of death. There are quite a few other topics that we could investigate if we had the space, but unfortunately, we don't. However, some of the topics that we've already studied could fit into this unit, such as the mind-body problem, free will vs. determinism, and ethics. Each of those deals, in one way or another, with the nature of humanity. In truth, every chapter in this book deals with the nature of humanity either directly or indirectly.

Personal Identity

Superhero movies and TV shows are very popular. There's an interesting pattern in most of them: The superhero is an alter ego of someone who, when not "wearing the cape," appears to be an ordinary person. Superman is Clark Kent, Batman is Bruce Wayne, Wonder Woman is Diana Prince, the Black Panther is T'Challa, and so on. We would probably agree that Superman and Clark Kent are identical—the only difference is their clothing. Clark Kent *is* Superman.

On the other hand, some superheroes don't seem to be identical to their alter egos. For example, Peter Parker didn't become Spiderman until he had been bitten by the radiated spider and had undergone significant physiological changes. So the normal Peter Parker and the one that is Spiderman aren't identical. In one sense Peter Parker is Spiderman, but in another sense Spiderman is different from Peter Parker—from the original, unbitten Peter Parker. We can't really say that the original Peter Parker is Spiderman, can we? We can say that the later Peter Parker is Spiderman, though. And this raises an interesting question: Can we say that the original Peter Parker is the same person as the later Peter Parker?

The case of Bruce Banner and the Hulk is even more radical. When Bruce Banner turns into the Hulk, everything changes. His body changes tremendously—and so do his mind and his personality. He goes from being a calm, intellectual scientist to being a raging, inarticulate monster. Is Bruce Banner the Hulk? What is it that makes a person that person? Is it having the same body? Is it having the same personality? What do we mean by "the same"?

In attempting to answer these questions, it is useful to make a distinction between qualitative identity and numerical identity. Two things are **qualitatively identical** when they share all the same qualities but are located in different places. For example, if you drive an old, beige Ford F150 pickup, and you meet someone else who drives a truck of the same make, model, year, and color, you might exclaim, "You drive the same truck I do!" You don't mean that the two of you share one truck but rather that his truck is qualitatively identical to yours.

Numerical identity, on the other hand, is when two qualitatively identical objects are located in the exact same place at the same time. In that case, they're really only one object. This is the case when Alfred and Commissioner Gordon are in the same room and Batman walks in. Commissioner Gordon sees Batman, the tall, muscular, caped defender of Gotham City. But he doesn't know that he's also seeing Bruce Wayne, the wealthy, spectacled philanthropist: He has no idea that Bruce Wayne is Batman and doesn't associate the two with each other at all. In his mind, they probably aren't even similar. But Alfred has known Wayne since he was a child and has helped in all of Wayne's crime-fighting capers. When

Batman walks in, Alfred sees Bruce Wayne in a cape. Bruce Wayne and Batman are numerically identical.

It's clear that Bruce Wayne is Batman and the spider-bitten Peter Parker is Spiderman. But it's not clear that Bruce Banner is the Hulk. They're neither qualitatively identical nor numerically identical. Is there some other sense in which the two could actually be one person?

The question of **personal identity** doesn't just apply to fictional superheroes: It applies to all of us. What makes you, you? Does putting on a costume make you a different person? Or putting on a uniform? Is the version of you that your mom calls "honey" the same person as the version that your buddies call "pal" and that the police sternly call "young man" when they pull you over for a traffic violation? You probably answered "yes" to some of those, but how about this: Is the you that's reading this book the same person as the five-year-old you that barely knew the alphabet? That little kid was you, right? But it's not the you of today. The two actually share rather little in common. So what makes you, you?

Theories of Personal Identity

There are nearly a dozen different theories on the nature of personal identity, on what makes you "you." Some of them focus on qualitative identity, some on numerical identity, and some center on something else. Let's take a look at them.

1. **Qualitative bodily identity** says two beings are the same person if they have qualitatively identical bodies. If they are exactly the same height, weight, skin tone, hair color, eye color, and everything else, but they're not in the same place, they are the same person. If this is true, then a man and his clone would be one person. But that seems problematic, because if one of them died, they wouldn't both die. Furthermore, if you were to tell that man that you were going to kill him but that he shouldn't be upset because he'll live on in the clone, I don't think he would feel reassured. Even if their bodies were exactly the same, they would have their own minds, beliefs, desires, and will to live. So this theory seems unsuccessful.
2. **Qualitative mental identity** says that two beings are the same

person if they have identical thoughts, feelings, beliefs, and memories. This view focuses on a person's mental life as the locus of personal identity. *Prima facie*, that seems like a good move. However, we can imagine scenarios wherein two qualitatively different bodies have minds with identical thoughts, feelings, beliefs, and memories. For example, newborn fraternal twins will have different bodies but may have had the same experiences—they were conceived at the same time, they gestated in the same womb, and they will have been born at almost the same moment—and therefore, they may have identical thoughts, feelings, beliefs, and memories (to the extent newborns have these things). Surely we wouldn't say that they are one person.

3. **Numerical bodily identity** says two beings are the same person if they have numerically identical bodies. Since numerical identity involves having qualitatively identical bodies that are in the same location, this adds up to just one body. This is what's happening when Alfred sees Bruce Wayne while Commissioner Gordon sees Batman, but they're really seeing the same person. Wayne and Batman are numerically identical and are the same person. This view comes closer to explaining personal identity than the previous two, but it cannot account for identity over time. It does not explain how the five-year-old you and the current you are the same person, even though most people would say that they are. Furthermore, mind-body dualists would have another objection to this view: If dualism is true, then it's possible to exist without a body, so locating personal identity in one's body is a mistake.
4. **Numerical mental identity** says that two beings are the same person if they have numerically identical thoughts, feelings, beliefs, and memories. Remember: Numerical identity involves having the same qualities in the same location. This theory seems to be very close to correct. However, it still faces the problem of identity over time. How could you say that the five-year-old you and the present you are the same person, since the thoughts, feelings, beliefs, and memories that you currently have were not had by the five-year-old you? And you probably don't have all the same thoughts,

feelings, beliefs, and memories that the five-year-old you had. Your thoughts, etc., are simply not numerically identical.

5. **Bodily continuity** says that two beings are the same person if they share the same body but at different times. This view is specifically crafted to handle the problem of identity over time, and it almost pulls it off. However, the sense of "same" is unclear here: It's certainly not numerical identity. Furthermore, the cells that make up your body are constantly dying and being replaced by new ones. In just seven years almost all the cells in your body have been replaced. It doesn't really seem like the present you and the five-year-old you share the same body. Dualists would also object to focusing exclusively on the body.
6. **Mental continuity** says that two beings are the same person if they share the same thoughts, feelings, beliefs, and memories but at different times. This is another attempt to overcome the problem of identity over time. It succeeds in avoiding the problems of the bodily continuity view, but it has other problems. For starters, on this view, a person with acute amnesia, Alzheimer's disease, or a similar condition would literally not be the same person she was before contracting the condition. This is good fodder for a *reductio ad absurdum* argument. There are other possible problems, too, having to do with multiple personality disorder and duplicate persons. Finally, if physicalism is true, then mental continuity is the same as bodily continuity and therefore has all the problems that bodily continuity has.
7. **Spiritual continuity** says that we are spirits, souls, or minds that inhabit bodies but are not identical to them. Therefore, two beings are the same person only if they have numerically identical spirits but at different times. That's like saying that Bruce Wayne is Batman (and vice versa) not because they have the same body, or the same thoughts, feelings, beliefs, and memories, but because they both have the same soul. While it's true that they both have the same body, that's not what makes both of them him, so to speak. What makes Wayne and Batman the same guy is that they have the same spirit. This view seems to overcome all the problems of

the preceding views, including the problem of identity over time. However, it does assume mind-body dualism and is not compatible with physicalism.

8. The **personal narrative** view says that two beings are the same person if their personal histories are numerically identical. This is different from the spiritual continuity view: Two beings (like Bruce Wayne and Batman, for example) can have the same narrative even if physicalism is true, so this view is compatible with physicalism as well as dualism. However, it falls to the problem of identity over time, for the five-year-old you and the present you don't have the same histories: You have all the history that the five-year-old had and lots more, but the five-year-old has only a fraction of your history.
9. The **bundle theory** says that there is no "self" *per se*, but instead, your idea of self is a mental construct that you form to help you process the stream of experiences, thoughts, and memories that you have throughout your life. There's no objective self, only a bundle of mental experiences and activities to which you assign the label "self." The mental experiences are real, but the self is not. On this view, personal identity is rather like a useful fiction.[8] The bundled theory is a challenge to personal identity—it seems to undermine the very concept. However, when advocates of this view say that the self is a construct, it raises the question of who or what is doing the constructing. What bundles the mental experiences and activities together and assigns the label "self" to them? It seems like there needs to be something like a self that does these things. Furthermore, in order to have thought, there must be a thinker, which seems to imply that the self is real.
10. The **anatman** (no self) doctrine also says that there is no self, but for different reasons than the bundle theory. Anatman is the Buddhist teaching that there is no persisting, enduring self. Instead,

8. This view is advocated by David Hume in *A Treatise of Human Nature*, 2nd ed. (Hackett, 1993). Hume has some interesting arguments in support of this view, but we cannot discuss them here.

there is a long series of causal relationships (karma). That which exists at any moment ceases to exist in the next moment and transfers all its causal force into its replacement. In other words, the present you causes the next you, which causes the next you, and this goes on over and over again. The present you is an effect of the previous you and the cause of the next you. No particular you is the enduring you that Westerners think of when they talk about the self. The goal of Buddhism isn't to have an enduring self but rather to escape this endless, karma-caused cycle of cause and effect. (It's called "dependent origination."[9]) In a sense, the goal is to extinguish the self. While this is primarily a Buddhist approach, it could be attractive to people who are not Buddhists but do subscribe to process metaphysics. **Process metaphysics** is the view that reality is not constituted of enduring substances but rather of the processes that all substances undergo.[10]

This is quite a range of approaches to the issue. It's interesting that they all seem to have some sort of weakness, small or large. Some of them have very serious problems; others seem to be satisfactory if one accepts certain presuppositions.

Practical Implications

The question of the nature of personal identity is not simply theoretical. It has many practical implications. For example, if we adopt qualitative bodily identity as our theory of identity, then two different people who are physically identical would be treated as if they are the same person. So if one of them performs a moral act—perhaps tells a lie—they would both be culpable. If we adopt numerical mental identity as our theory, then two beings are the same person if they have identical thoughts, feelings, beliefs, and memories. But imagine a scenario in which someone is robbing a convenience store

9. See "Anatman," in *Buddhist Encyclopedia of Philosophy*, accessed December 13, 2024, https://encyclopediaofbuddhism.org/wiki/An%C4%81tman.
10. For an explanation of process metaphysics, see J. R. Hustwit, "Process Philosophy," in *Internet Encyclopedia of Philosophy*, ed. James Fieser and Bradley Dowden, https://iep.utm.edu/processp/.

and shoots and kills somebody. He gets away but has to flee the state. He moves far away and changes his name, appearance, and occupation. Feeling guilty, he embraces a new religion, and this results in a reformation of his values and personality. Now he has different thoughts, feelings, and beliefs, and many new memories, too. But if the police catch him, they're going to believe that he's still responsible for the crimes that he committed, even though on the numerical mental identity theory, he's not the same person who committed those crimes. But is he?

If we adopt spiritual continuity as our theory, then two beings living at different times are the same person if they have the same soul. But how can we tell if they do? If a child is smart, talented, and precocious at five years of age, and is still that way at ten, and also at fifteen, we would expect that the child has the same soul throughout that period because we assume that souls normally remain in the same body, and this belief would be reinforced by the observed continuity of personality throughout that time period. But how about a man and a woman who are married for fifty years? At the age of seventy, the husband succumbs to Alzheimer's disease. Initially he loses his memory, and then he loses his intellect. Eventually he loses his mobility and is confined to bed. Is he the same person that his wife was married to for fifty years? Should she view him as her husband, or is he only the shell of her husband? Is it rational for her to continue feeling love and affection for him? We might assume that his soul has remained in his body, but we lack the sort of confirming evidence that we had in the preceding scenario.

If we accept the bundle theory or the anatman doctrine, then there is no enduring self. If that's the case, then can there be any hope for life after death? The bundle theory provides little hope for an afterlife since there's no self that could potentially survive the death of the body. Perhaps some advocates of the bundle theory would argue that mental activities like thoughts and memories can survive the death of the body, but how that would work is unclear. The anatman doctrine is clear on this issue: The causal momentum of this life automatically results in a new life once this one ends. That seems like a plausible theory, but an alternative possibility is that the causal force of this life is used up during this life. On this view, death is a result of the exhaustion of that causal force. This, too, seems like a plausible theory. Lacking a self as the vessel to carry the causal force into the next life, the latter view may be the more cogent option.[11]

Worldviews and Personal Identity

The connection between one's worldview and one's view on personal identity is fairly straightforward. The spiritual continuity view does a pretty good job of avoiding the problems faced by many of the other views. Its main problem is that it's not compatible with mind-body physicalism: It's an inherently dualistic view. Therefore it's not an option for those worldviews that are incompatible with dualism, such as naturalism and pantheism. On the other hand, it seems like a strong choice for any worldview that is compatible with dualism, so it's a good option for theists, deists, panentheists, and polytheists.

Naturalism and pantheism are compatible with nearly all the other options. However, some of these have problems that are so significant that they really aren't worth considering. Perhaps the bodily continuity view would be the best choice for naturalists and pantheists. On the other hand, some naturalistic philosophers who are inclined toward a strongly empiricist epistemology seem to find the bundle theory appealing.

Buddhism is an interesting worldview. Although it is not a physicalist worldview (it does not reduce everything to physical components), it denies the existence of human souls. When it comes to personal identity, it embraces the anatman approach.

CONCLUSION

We began this exposition of personal identity by discussing superheroes and their alter egos, which illustrates some of the issues involved in personal identity. The spiritual continuity view seems best able to handle the difficult cases. Peter Parker is likely to have had the same soul after he received his superpowers as he had before receiving them. This seems to be the norm:

11. This is a severely truncated discussion of the Buddhist view of reincarnation (a term that many Buddhists find inadequate). Buddhist philosophy is a venerable tradition that deserves more interaction, but that is simply beyond the scope of this book.

People seem to have the same soul from birth until death. This presumption is reinforced by the fact that each of these people retains the same basic personality, beliefs, memories, values, etc., following reception of their superpowers. So the spiritual continuity view succeeds in explaining why Peter Parker is Spiderman.

Bruce Banner and the Hulk are more difficult, because although we may assume that Bruce Banner retained the same soul even after he became the Hulk, this assumption is not backed up by consistent retention of basic personality traits, beliefs, memories, values, etc. after receiving his superpower. On the contrary, the Hulk barely resembles Banner, if he resembles him at all. However, we should avoid overstating this, for whenever the Hulk reverts to being Banner, he immediately resumes all his old personality traits, beliefs, memories, values, etc. This suggests that the Hulk does indeed have the same soul as Banner. In the end, if we can accept mind-body dualism, then the spiritual continuity view seems to be the theory that is most able to explain the personal identity of Bruce Banner and the Hulk.

QUESTIONS TO PONDER

- Do you think Bruce Banner and the Hulk are the same person? Why and how?
- Which of the ten theories of personal identity seems strongest to you? Why?
- Can you think of any alternatives to the ten theories that were listed?
- Are you the same person you were fifteen years ago?

TERMS TO KNOW

- philosophical anthropology
- personal identity
- qualitative identity
- numerical identity
- qualitative bodily identity
- qualitative mental identity
- numerical bodily identity
- numerical mental identity
- bodily continuity
- mental continuity
- spiritual continuity
- personal narrative
- bundle theory
- anatman doctrine
- process metaphysics

FOR FURTHER READING

Gallagher, Shaun, ed. *The Oxford Handbook of the Self.* Oxford University Press, 2011. This is a large collection of articles on many topics related to personal identity.

Noonan, Harold. *Personal Identity*. 3rd ed. Routledge, 2019. This is a standard introduction to the issue of identity that, while challenging, is very informative.

Kitcher, Patricia. *The Self: A History*. Oxford University Press, 2021. This is a history of the development of the concept of the self in the Western philosophical tradition.

22

HUMAN UNIQUENESS

SYNOPSIS

What distinguishes humans from other living creatures? Our second philosophical anthropology topic is human uniqueness, what sets us apart. It is a difficult question, again tied to one's worldview.

DIALOGUE

Tristan Lancaster checked his watch. The time for the deal was drawing near.

Over the previous two years, through enormous and careful efforts, Tristan had accumulated a significant cache of weapons. His ultimate goal was to become a major player in an international criminal cartel that dealt in drugs, sex trafficking, weapons, and a host of other lucrative illegal activities. Today's deal would prove him to the highest echelons of that organization and, if all went according to plan, usher him into the halls of power, prestige, and magnificent wealth.

Not bad for a kid from Greenfield.

The buyers were from a European terrorist organization with deep pockets. How they had managed to accumulate the nearly fifty-five *million* dollars involved in this purchase, Tristan neither knew nor cared. His bosses in the cartel trusted that the buyers would come through, and at least one of those bosses, Michael Fridley, had arrived the night before. The cartel would take most of the money, of course, but Lancaster planned to pocket nearly twelve million himself.

Lancaster had arranged to use a large warehouse on the west side of Greenfield. Very few people outside his small circle knew about the location. He was confident that the FBI and other law enforcement officers crawling all over town had no idea either. He smiled with smug satisfaction that the bumbling involvement of the four thirtysomethings had produced a useful sideshow to occupy officers that might otherwise pose a problem.

He'd have to send them a thank-you note when this was over.

Tristan's men spent the morning moving his various weapons collections—firearms, bombs, and the prize of the collection, chemical weapons—from their hiding places around the county to the warehouse. This was done very carefully, in small quantities, in common vehicles (they avoided white vans). By noon, the entire collection was at the warehouse, and Lancaster was reviewing them with Fridley and two of his associates. The buyers were set to arrive at three.

* * *

It was a slow morning at the safe house. Everyone had finally crashed on the living room furniture and slept. But after just a few hours, they awakened, hungry and immediately aware that the strange dream that they were being guarded by armed men so that other armed men wouldn't kill them was actually real. Mack Ryan stood as alert and motionless in the hallway as he had been when they had fallen asleep.

"What time is it?" Suresh asked, eyes squinting.

Zach looked at his phone. "Nine forty-five. I think we slept for about four hours. I'm thankful we got that much."

"I'll see if there's any food in the kitchen," Suresh said.

It didn't hurt to have a chef in the house.

The smell of cooking bacon began wafting out a few minutes later. Soon Suresh had whipped up omelets with some deli meat and veggies that had been in the fridge. The anxiety was palpable, but a hearty breakfast helped everyone get their bearings.

As they ate and sipped coffee, their conversation naturally drifted to the ideas they were always talking about. Hannah kicked things off with a question that left everyone laughing.

"Why do people act like animals?"

Angelo about spit out his coffee. "Okay . . . I guess we're diving in."

"Hahaaa. Sorry!" Hannah said. "What I mean is that people are threatening our lives for little or no reason. Humans are supposed to be better than that!"

"I know what you mean," Zach said, "and I'm certainly disappointed when humans act in ways that harm other people. But I'm not sure I'd say it that way. After all, humans *are* animals, right?"

"I suppose, biologically speaking, that humans are animals," she said. "But surely we're different. I've always thought of humans as fundamentally different from animals."

"In what ways?" Suresh said.

"Aren't we distinguished by being more advanced in how we think and communicate?"

"Well, many animals think and communicate, especially some of the higher animals, such as apes, dolphins, and elephants," Zach said. "The key to your statement seems to be that humans are 'more advanced' in how we do these things. If so, are you saying that we're different from animals in degree but not relative to what kind of being we are?"

"Yes, I think that's right."

"It would be hard to disagree with that. But just because humans are currently farther along on the evolutionary scale doesn't mean we always will be. And perhaps we'll meet life forms out there who will be more different from us than we are from gorillas and chimpanzees."

Suresh set down his fork. "Animals don't seem to be spiritual beings though. Sure, they can think, but are they self-aware? Do they have a conscience? Moral awareness? Do they form communities with loyalty and self-sacrifice?" he asked. "Humans seem quite different."

"Depends on who you listen to," Zach said. "Scientists are finding indications of community among some animals that involve both loyalty and self-sacrifice. Some researchers attribute these behaviors to instinct, but one could just as easily claim that humans act instinctively."

"It's hard to respond without access to the studies," Suresh said, "but I remain a bit skeptical. You believe everything consists of matter, but I believe in both matter and spirit. The religious tradition I've been reconnecting with holds to transmigration of souls, that people reawaken after death in a new form of life. This obviously depends on man being more than just a body. Transmigration, which is also called reincarnation, also teaches that people can regress into animal forms through bad karma. This has usually been portrayed as a significant step down on the path to enlightenment. Animal-human continuity seems to challenge that worldview."

"I don't think it would necessarily be a challenge," Zach countered. "I'm not arguing that animals are as advanced as humans. I'm simply denying any essential difference between them. If I wanted to look for superiority, I'd investigate physical things, like erect posture, opposable thumbs, a more advanced brain, and the like."

Angelo had been quietly listening but now joined the conversation. "I understand what you're saying, Zach, and I've come to admire the consistency of your positions. But I think Scripture teaches a clear distinction between humans and animals. I'm not sure what to make of the current scientific thinking I've read on levels of rationality, communication, tool-use, emotion, etc., in animals. Like Suresh, I'm inclined to be a bit skeptical of some of it, but my position isn't affected one way or the other.

"When the Bible records the creation of man, it carefully distinguishes man from animals by saying that we are created in God's image or likeness. Because humans are in God's image, they can fulfill their purpose on earth: to rule it and fill it. God is the ultimate ruler, but he has put humans in charge of creation, and humans' similarity to God—in whatever respects—enables that mission. Animals, and even angels for that matter, don't have that job."

"So you define the uniqueness of humans along strictly theological lines?" Hannah said. "Presumably you'd apply this distinction to all humans, not just Christians, but your explanation of it is specifically Christian."

"Yes, that's right," Angelo acknowledged. "I think my view has many benefits, but I won't belabor them since they're ultimately persuasive only for Christians or, at least, theists. I'll just say that the doctrine of the image of God gives humans a unique dignity: Humankind alone can portray the character of God to other creatures. A proper understanding and application of this doctrine will prevent discrimination and other mistreatment of people—after all, every human is in God's image—and will lead to self-respect and environmental responsibility."

"You are a very compelling advocate of your view," Suresh said warmly.

They continued to chat pleasantly for a while and then wandered back to the living room. It looked like it was going to be a long afternoon. Fortunately, the police had helpfully brought necessities and even a few novels and games to help them while away the time. Meanwhile, they were safe and they were together.

* * *

By 3:15, Lancaster was seething. Where were the buyers? He didn't like being jerked around, and this was the biggest day of his life.

Fridley, noticing his agitation, said, "Relax. I've done several transactions with this organization, and they almost always show up late. It's a cultural thing. They'll also almost certainly object to something and make us scramble to complete the deal. But they pay as well as anyone. Chill out. We'll be considerably richer in a few hours."

"If you say so," Lancaster mumbled.

Sure enough, a silver Mercedes followed by a second vehicle arrived ten minutes later. Two heavily armed bodyguards emerged from the front doors, and moments later, two men in expensive suits exited from the backseat. Four dangerous-looking men came out of the second car and positioned themselves strategically. Lancaster tried to be patient as the two leaders went through elaborate greetings and had their men do a brief scan of the area to confirm that they considered it safe. Lancaster himself had eight armed men stationed around the property; there was nothing to worry about.

The buyers began inspecting the weapons. They were meticulous, so it took longer than Lancaster had expected. When they came to the prize weapon, an explosive designed to release a lethal chemical toxin, the Europeans talked for several minutes in a language Lancaster couldn't understand. He had hired chemical engineers to create this weapon, using Bradley Pharmaceuticals to procure the toxins. He knew how effective and deadly the weapon could be.

Abruptly, one of the men spoke in clear English. "How do we know these chemicals will do what you claim? We want you to demonstrate that we're getting exactly what you told us."

Lancaster was about to explode in anger, but before he could say what he was thinking, Fridley spoke.

"Of course. That's perfectly reasonable."

Tristan thought it the most unreasonable thing he'd ever heard.

Fridley turned to Tristan. "I believe you've been working with a nearby lab. Could you get a chemist here to prove to these gentlemen that we're acting in good faith?"

Despite his annoyance, Lancaster decided to humor them. He would do a lot for twelve million dollars. He stepped away and called Jerry Hargrove. *This fool better not have fled the country.* Hargrove picked up, and Lancaster told him he needed a chemist to verify the makeup of the weapon.

Hargrove's answer infuriated him.

"Sir, only one person at Bradley has the knowledge and experience to do what you're asking: Zach Williams."

The other end of the line was silent.

"That's why the FBI recruited him."

Tristan nearly threw his phone. "Are you serious? No one else?"

"Not with millions of dollars on the line, no."

"Then this is what you're going to do, Jerry," Tristan said, spitting every word like a dagger. "Call Williams. Tell him you got caught up in a terrible criminal plot but you've had a change of heart. Then tell him you know where the big deal is going down and give him the following address."

"What good will that do?"

"Do what you're told and leave the thinking to me!"

* * *

At the safe house, Mack had collected the friends' phones and was ignoring the various calls and texts from friends and family. When Zach's phone rang at 4:40 and displayed Jerry Hargrove's name, Mack thought Zach should take the call.

Zach told everyone to be completely silent and answered on speakerphone.

Hargrove told Zach exactly what Lancaster had told him to say, and given how much actual remorse Hargrove was feeling, his stricken conscience came off as authentic.

Mack immediately called Agent Esposito, told him about the conversation, and gave him the address north of town. Esposito had Mack ask Zach if he believed Hargrove.

"He sounded genuine. But I have no way of knowing," Zach said.

Soon they heard vehicles pulling away from the safe house. Esposito and the Greenfield PD were marshaling as many forces as possible. Mack and two other officers were left to guard the foursome, who they now realized must have only been a decoy. Two other officers were sent to Bradley Pharmaceuticals to arrest Hargrove.

* * *

Tristan's plan had worked perfectly. Three cars full of armed men were on their way to grab Zach (one of Lancaster's men had watched as the friends were transported from the courthouse to the safe house). Twenty minutes after Zach's conversation with Hargrove, they arrived.

Gunfire erupted outside, and Mack hustled the four friends into an inner bedroom with no exterior windows.

"Let me help," Angelo told Mack. "You don't have many men, and you know I'm capable with a sidearm."

Mack looked reluctant, but he handed Angelo his Glock 22. Mack had an M4 and looked ready. As the shooting continued outside, it became evident that they were outnumbered.

Soon the two officers outside were down, and assailants were smashing through doors and windows. Mack and Angelo positioned themselves behind furniture with visibility of the entrances and opened fire as soon as they saw motion.

They immediately took down four men.

And then Mack took a bullet.

Built like a Tiger Tank, Mack kept firing through the obvious pain. Within moments, men were in the room and flanking their positions. Angelo emptied the Glock, realizing that in their hurry, Mack still had the rest of the ammunition, and Angelo could no longer reach him. Mack had stopped firing and was slumped over. As Angelo lunged toward Mack to try to get cover and reload his gun, a slug pierced through his chest and he fell back against the wall.

Ignoring Mack and Angelo, the gunmen strode through the living room to the locked door where Suresh, Zach, and Hannah were hiding.

In just a few hard slams, they battered down the door and found three frightened people huddled inside. Following Lancaster's instructions, they seized all three. Hannah and Suresh were taken to guarantee that Zach would follow instructions. As they were dragged through the living room, they saw Angelo leaning against the wall, his chest covered in blood, his face drained of color.

"Nooooooo!" Hannah screamed, bursting into tears and fighting against her captors.

Zach felt like he might vomit.

Neighbors had called the police when they heard the gunfire, but it happened so fast that the first police car didn't arrive until after the perpetrators had left.

Police found a terrible scene. One of the outside officers was dead, shot multiple times. The other was in serious condition. Entering the house, they found Mack and Angelo; both had severe injuries but were still breathing. Multiple ambulances raced to get them to the nearest hospital.

* * *

By 6:00, the cars with the three captives had arrived at the warehouse. Suresh and Hannah were taken to the far side of the facility and put in a small room with one guard, a fresh-faced young man who seemed a little ill at ease with his rifle.

Zach was taken to Tristan.

"Nice to see you again," Tristan said, a smirk on his face.

"Can't say the same."

"Enough chitchat. I need you to verify the chemical composition of the fluid in the weapon."

"I can't do that without lab equipment," Zach said. "At the very least, I need access to some basic instruments to do the testing."

"I'll kill your friends if you don't cooperate."

"I don't know what to tell you, Tristan. I can't verify it without equipment. Any chemist would tell you the same thing."

Fridley laid a firm hand on Lancaster's arm.

"Send a couple men with Zach to get what he needs at Bradley. It's our best option. He'll be at gunpoint if he tries anything," Fridley said, looking over at Zach. "If you try anything, you'll never see your friends again."

* * *

Jess Casey and Pedro Gomez were a little disappointed that Agent Esposito had given them the low-stakes assignment of arresting a pharmaceutical exec when the real action was going down north of town.

They flashed their badges at the front gate, and the guards admitted them, but it took a few minutes to locate the correct building. The receptionists on the main floor asked if they had an appointment. But after seeing the agents' badges, they pointed them toward Hargrove's office. He often left around this time, 5:30, so the front desk staff also indicated the entrance to the executives' private parking garage.

Gomez made his way to the parking garage while Casey went to the fifth floor to find Hargrove's office. After the two agents left, one receptionist called Mr. Hargrove to warn him.

"Stall them!" he hissed into the phone.

Before the receptionist could reply, he had dropped the phone and was headed for the back exit from his office.

Agent Casey reached the fifth floor and stepped out of the elevator. As he approached Hargrove's office, Hargrove's assistant asked how he could help.

Casey flashed his badge.

"I need to speak with Jerry Hargrove."

Suddenly Casey heard Gomez's voice in his earpiece.

"I spotted him, Jess. When he saw me in the garage, he headed back to the office. I don't know his plan, but I think he's trying to escape," Gomez said. "I'm right behind him. Be careful . . ."

Casey motioned for the assistant to get down as he drew his weapon. He walked past the assistant's desk to the door to Hargrove's office, but just then, a gunshot rang out from inside the office.

He rushed in and found Hargrove slumped over his desk, a small 22-caliber pistol in his hand, a pool of blood forming around his head.

Gomez arrived moments later, and the two men ordered the assistant to get everyone off the floor, which was beginning to fill with other employees curious about the gunshot.

They cordoned off the area and waited outside Hargrove's office.

First responders began to arrive by 6:15, and Gomez and Casey prepared to turn over the crime scene when they saw something suspicious through Hargrove's fifth-floor window. A car had parked outside an adjoining building, which had been identified as the main laboratory.

As they watched, two men got out, and they seemed to be guiding a third. They were too far away to see who the men were until, that is, the third man glanced up toward Hargrove's office.

Zach Williams.

Gomez had helped ferry the four young people to the safe house, and he was almost sure that was one of them.

The two officers quickly made their way outside and headed to the main lab. It was after five, so the place was almost deserted. But as they entered, they saw the three men, who appeared to be gathering some equipment.

"Hey guys," Casey said. "What's going on?"

Two of the men pulled guns, and Casey dove for cover. Gomez had positioned himself out of sight and shot one of the men, who dropped to the ground.

"Stand down!"

The other turned to fire, and Gomez took him down as well. His hands were sweating, and his mouth was suddenly dry. Eight years in the FBI, and he'd never had to shoot someone.

Zach raised his hands and shouted, "I'm Zach Williams. They held me hostage! Tristan Lancaster has my friends and is trying to sell a huge load of weapons just west of here. I can take you to them!"

Casey contacted Esposito, and soon a cavalcade of law enforcement officers headed to the warehouse in west Greenfield.

* * *

By 6:45, Lancaster knew something had gone wrong. Efforts to contact the two men who had taken Zach were proving unsuccessful. The buyers were beginning to panic that their presence would be detected, and Fridley, while outwardly trying to keep everyone else calm, was getting dangerously angry. With two of Fridley's men gone with Zach, Lancaster had more men in the warehouse than the terrorists and Fridley combined. If they turned on him, he thought he could win a shootout. He'd kill the chef and the social worker, gather his weapons, and flee to a new location. He still had millions of dollars in merchandise. Lancaster was sure he could handle this situation.

When the law enforcement vehicles began arriving, the men inside the warehouse suddenly realized how outnumbered they were. Their only hope was Suresh and Hannah, who they planned to use as hostages.

But the young man watching Hannah and Suresh was having terrible misgivings about being a party to all this. When he realized that law enforcement vehicles were arriving, he decided to cut and run. He snuck out a back door and tried to escape on foot. He was caught within sight of the warehouse and arrested.

Once their guard was gone, Suresh and Hannah decided to run for it also. They were just reaching the door when more of Tristan's guards appeared and moved forward to grab them. Hannah and Suresh froze at the barked command from the guards.

As they were slowly turning, they heard, "Drop!"

They hit the ground as gunfire exploded through the windows just ahead of them. Their guards took gunfire and went down quickly, and FBI agents and police officers burst through the door. A couple of officers hustled Hannah and Suresh out of the building.

Hannah and Suresh would never forget what they experienced in those next few minutes.

Gunfire, screaming, and the smell of gunpowder and blood filled their senses. A number of people, including Tristan Lancaster, died in the firefight. Fridley and the two Europeans were injured but captured.

The entire weapons cache was recovered.

It was a notable day for Esposito and all law enforcement involved. Despite the challenges, the cartel had taken a major hit, and there were no civilian casualties. That is, unless, they counted the young security guard at the safe house.

* * *

Wrapped in blankets, Hannah, Suresh, and Zach sat in a room at the Greenfield Police Department, sipping hot coffee and trying to process the last twenty-four hours.

Angelo was in surgery.

"I guess you're right, Zach," Suresh said sadly. "People really are animals."

"I don't know, Suresh," Zach said. "I think Angelo looked a lot like God today."

THEORY

The exciting climax to the narrative contained a brief exploration of human uniqueness. The following discussion will try to break down the topic by looking at various alternatives, defining key ideas, and once again showing the correlation of various answers with one's worldview.

Is Humanity Unique?

In the previous chapter we introduced the concept of "philosophical anthropology" and evaluated various views on personal identity, trying to figure out what makes you "you." Now we will investigate another issue that arises in anthropology: what makes humans unique. In the chapter on logical fallacies, we introduced the "complex question" (or "loaded question"), which is a question that assumes a specific answer to a logically prior but unstated question. The question "What makes humans unique?" is a complex question. It assumes that we've already asked whether humans are unique and that we've answered that question in the affirmative. However, we haven't asked (nor have we answered) that question. It would be good to begin by asking if humans actually are unique.

Asking if humans are unique is not the same as asking if you are special. Each one of us is special: No one has your precise mix of gifts, experiences, and character traits, and hence no one is quite like you. You are indeed special! But that's a different question from ours. Our question is about the human race in general. Is humanity special?

As a species, humanity is unique. But then again, all species are, aren't they? That being the case, the question "Is humanity special?" must be asking more than merely whether as a species humanity differs from every other species in some way. What is this question asking?

Many—perhaps most—people desire to be special in some way. When we consider this desire, perhaps what people want is to be, in some way, better, more valuable, or at least uniquely valuable in comparison to all the other kinds of things that exist in this world. Maybe what we are asking in this chapter is whether humanity is unique in some way that makes us more valuable than other things. It's interesting that both theists and naturalists tend to affirm that humanity is special in this sense—theists because we are supposedly the pinnacle of God's creation, and naturalists because we are supposedly the most evolved species. Are they right?

Theories of Human Uniqueness

One way to find out if we're special is to ask whether we can pinpoint anything that makes us so. If we can, then we'll know that we are in fact special. If we can't, then we're not justified in claiming that we are. Over the years quite a few things have been suggested as to what makes us special. Here are some of the candidates:

1. **Erect Posture**: Some have argued that standing erect sets humanity apart from the rest of the animal kingdom. Erect posture has several benefits: It enables us to see greater distances, which helps us see approaching predators, locate food from a distance, and perhaps most significantly, it frees up our hands to grasp weapons and tools. The ability to grasp weapons and tools has been hugely beneficial to humanity. On the other hand, though, there are quite

a few species of animals that can stand and walk erect, and there are some for which erect, bipedal locomotion is the norm, such as kangaroos and wallabies. Hence, erect posture does not make us unique.

2. **Opposable Thumbs:** It has been suggested that having opposable thumbs on our hands sets humanity apart from other species. It's our thumbs that enable us to grasp things. Hands wouldn't be nearly as handy if we didn't have opposable thumbs! However, humanity isn't the only species possessing opposable thumbs. The fairly long list of animals with opposable thumbs includes baboons, monkeys, chimpanzees, and gorillas, to name just a few. Furthermore, some animals have opposable thumbs on their feet as well as their hands, which can be very useful. Koalas have two opposable digits on each hand and one opposable toe on each foot. Clearly our modest number of opposable digits is not that special.
3. **Use of Tools:** We already alluded to the importance of being able to use tools. Some have suggested that creating and using tools makes humanity special. Other animals are stronger than us and faster than us; many swim better and some can even fly. But through the use of tools we surpass them all: Forklifts enable us to lift more weight than an elephant can, motorcycles enable us to travel faster than a cheetah, jets help us fly farther than any bird, and with ships we can swim around the globe. Tools multiply our abilities in almost every area. Robots help us build, computers help us think, musical instruments help us sing. With tools we far overcome our weaknesses. However, we are not the only species that uses tools. Chimpanzees, for example, use stone hammers and wooden spears. Orangutans fashion leaves into whistles that they use to communicate. Elephants form branches into fly swatters. These are much simpler tools than those humans have created, but they are tools nonetheless, so fashioning and using tools does not make us unique.
4. **Use of Language:** Some have argued that our highly developed linguistic ability makes us unique. Humans benefit greatly from the ability to preserve information linguistically and to pass it from

one generation to another. This enables a gradual accumulation of knowledge, so that each generation can build on the information received from the previous one. The value of this can hardly be overstated.[1] However, humans are not alone in using language. The most famous example of a non-human using language is Koko, a gorilla from the San Francisco Zoo who learned to communicate using over one thousand signs (sign language). Parrots, crows, and bottle-necked dolphins have been found to communicate linguistically, too. At this point, it appears that animals that communicate linguistically do so at a much more basic level than humans do, but it does not appear that language is exclusively a human thing.

5. **Intelligence:** Many have thought that our high degree of intelligence makes humanity unique. This seems to be a very common view among humans in general. The term "brute beast" used to be a common way to distinguish intelligent humans from unthinking animals. Corresponding to that, humans who were physically powerful though not very sharp mentally were sometimes characterized as "brutes." We don't really know just how much intelligence dolphins and whales have, but *prima facie*, it does seem likely that humans are by far the most intelligent members of the animal kingdom. Nonetheless, that does not necessarily entail that we are the *only* intelligent animals. Scientists have found that chimpanzees, bonobos, orangutans, dolphins, elephants, and other kinds of animals have some mental capacity that is analogous to human intelligence but at a more basic level.[2] So humans may be the smartest, but we're not the only ones with intelligence.
6. **Emotion:** Some have asserted that only humans have feelings and that this makes humanity unique. Humans certainly do have a rich

---

1. Kevin Laland argues that it is this cumulative aspect of human culture that makes humanity special. Kevin N. Laland, "These Amazing Creative Animals Show Why Humans are the Most Innovative Species of All," *The Conversation*, April 20, 2017, https://theconversation.com/these-amazing-creative-animals-show-why-humans-are-the-most-innovative-species-of-all-75515.
2. Dan Sharp, "The Smartest Animals on Earth," Factanimal.com, accessed December 19, 2023, https://factanimal.com/animal-facts/smartest-animals-on-earth/.

variety of emotions that add beauty and significance to our lives. However, some humans, due to damage to certain parts of their brains, do not experience emotions.[3] If feelings are what make us special, then such people aren't special, which is a troubling conclusion. Furthermore, that some animals also experience emotions is well documented.[4] Hence, emotions are probably not what make us very special.

7. **Free Will:** Another suggestion is that humans alone have free will. As we saw in a previous chapter, not everyone is convinced that humans have free will, but those who do believe in free will might find this argument attractive. However, there's ample evidence that some animals also exercise free will: They can choose when to get up and when to lie down, to eat or not to eat, etc. They may not be aware that they are making choices, but that does not entail that they aren't making them. Furthermore, some may be aware that they are making choices, and humans are often unaware that they are making choices when they make them. Hence, in the final analysis this doesn't seem to make humanity special.
8. **Morality:** It has been argued that only humans have morality. Only humans have the emotion needed to feel empathy for others, the intelligence needed to contemplate the morality of an action, and the volition needed to choose between options that are moral and immoral. But there are several problems with this argument. First, some humans don't seem to have any sense of morality, either because they lack the ability to feel empathy or because they lack the needed intelligence due to some cognitive impairment. If morality is what makes us special, then they're not special, which seems like a problem for this theory. Second, we've already seen that some animals have emotions, intellect, and will, so it seems possible that some animals do have morality. Finally, some researchers confirm

3. "What Is a Flat Affect?," Moody Neurorehabilitation Institute, accessed December 19, 2024, https://www.moodyneuro.org/what-is-a-flat-affect/.
4. Klaus Wilhelm, "Do Animals Have Feelings?" *Scientific American Mind* 17 (2006): 24–29, https://www.jstor.org/stable/24939403.

that some kinds of animals do have a basic sense of morality.[5] So morality does not seem to make humanity unique.

9. **Creativity:** Humans are wonderfully creative. We create music, visual art of many kinds, literature, drama (movies, plays, musicals, etc.), architecture, cuisine, crafts, technology, and on and on. No other creatures rival humans in breadth of creativity. Perhaps that makes us special. But there are many examples of creativity in the animal kingdom. Think of the beauty of birdsongs on a summer morning and of spider webs sparkling with morning dew. Of course, the birds and spiders may not be aware that what they are making is beautiful, but whether such awareness is required for an act to be creative is debatable. Various captive animals—chimpanzees, orangutans, elephants, even birds—have been trained to draw and/or paint, and some have even done it without being trained. It has been argued that some of these acts involve self-awareness and intentionality and are therefore sufficiently like intentional human creativity to count as animal creativity.[6]
10. **The Soul:** Some argue that only humans have souls and that makes us unique. This assumes mind-body dualism, of course, and it assumes that animals don't have souls. Not all dualists agree with that. Dualists typically recognize many components, aspects, or functions of the immaterial side of a person, such as the soul, spirit, mind, heart, conscience, and will. Typically, it's thought that the mind does the thinking, the heart does the feeling, the conscience provides moral guidance, and the will executes decisions. There's less agreement about the roles of the soul and spirit, though. Some say that the spirit is what relates to God and the soul is what relates to other humans. Some reverse this. Some say the spirit facilitates interpersonal relationships while the term "soul" is a general term

5. See Simon Fitzpatrick's review of the arguments in "Animal Morality: What Is the Debate About?" *Biology & Philosophy* 32 (2017): 1151–83, https://doi.org/10.1007/s10539-017-9599-6.
6. An interesting anthology devoted to the question of animal creativity is Allison B. Kaufman and James C. Kaufman, eds., *Animal Creativity and Innovation: Explorations in Creativity Research* (Academic Press, 2015).

that includes all the other components.[7] The exact meanings of these terms aside, since some of the arguments that dualists use to show that humans have an immaterial side would work equally well for animals, there is some reason to reject the idea that only humans possess an immaterial side that makes us unique. An additional reason for reticence about denying animal souls comes from dualistic religions such as Judaism and Christianity, the scriptures of which support the idea that both humans and animals have an immaterial aspect but with different destinies.[8]

11. **The Image of God:** Some religions hold that humanity is unique because only humanity is created in the image of God (Latin, ***imago Dei***). Exactly what constitutes the *imago Dei* is debated. If it were a physical feature, one would expect God to be a physical being, but most religions reject that.[9] If it's some attribute like intelligence, morality, relationality, or creativity, then since it seems likely that some animals also have these attributes (albeit in reduced capacity), we would have to grant that some animals also bear the *imago Dei* (though to a reduced degree), and therefore, it would not make humanity unique. However, there's more to say about this, so we'll return to the *imago Dei* before the end of the chapter.

Degree vs. Kind

While many of the attributes examined above come close to providing a basis for believing that humanity is special, none of them really seems

7. Jesus, who was a very influential dualist, seems to use "soul" and "spirit" interchangeably (as he does "body" and "flesh"). Compare Matt 10:28 and 26:41.
8. See, for example, Eccl 3:19–21: "For what happens to the sons of men also happens to animals; one thing befalls them: as one dies, so dies the other. Surely, they all have one breath; man has no advantage over animals, for all is vanity. All go to one place: all are from the dust, and all return to dust. Who knows the spirit of the sons of men, which goes upward, and the spirit of the animal, which goes down to the earth?" (NKJV).
9. Some theologians, though acknowledging that God is spirit rather than body, nevertheless believe that the *imago Dei* includes the physical body because that is the vehicle by which man uniquely expresses God-like characteristics in the created order.

to succeed. Perhaps this is because we haven't been sufficiently precise in defining what we mean by "special." A philosophical distinction may help us in our quest: uniqueness of degree vs. uniqueness of kind. Uniqueness is basically the quality of being one of a kind. **Uniqueness of degree** is possessed by something when it is one of a kind because it has more of some attribute than any other thing has, even though there are other things that have that attribute in a lesser quantity or to a lesser degree. For example, cheetahs have a degree of uniqueness because they are the fastest land animals, even though there are other animals that are almost as fast; elephants have a degree of uniqueness because they are the strongest land animals, even though there are other animals that are almost as strong.

Many of the characteristics discussed above may provide this sort of **relative uniqueness** to humanity, including use of tools and language, intelligence, emotion, free will, morality, and creativity. We can say that humanity has a degree of uniqueness because it has the most intelligence, or the most freedom, or something along those lines. Furthermore, it's possible that humanity is unique not because of any one of these things but instead because humans are the apex species for multiple attributes. If cheetahs are fastest and elephants are strongest but humans are smartest, most creative, with the most acute sense of right and wrong, the best at making and using tools, the most linguistic, with the broadest range of emotions, and with the most free will, then that abundance of things that humans are best at makes humanity really special! Of course, gods, angels, and other supernatural beings, if they exist, could surpass humanity in many or even all these areas, but if we're limiting our comparison to natural beings, this sort of analysis does seem to support the conclusion that humanity is unique. One more caveat must be stated, though: If evolution is ongoing, then in theory other species could eventually surpass humanity in one or more of these categories, thus diminishing humanity's relative uniqueness.

In contrast to uniqueness of degree, **uniqueness of kind** is possessed by something when it is the only kind of thing that has that attribute. This is **absolute uniqueness**. A good example would be God: God, if he exists, is the only being that is omniscient, omnipotent, omnisapient, omnibenevolent, etc. That makes him completely unique: He's the only being who has those attributes. Many have argued that humanity has uniqueness of kind.

Typically this takes the form of an assertion that animals don't have one of the attributes discussed above; only humans do. This strategy doesn't seem very successful in light of our analyses above, though it's difficult to be sure, since it could turn out to be true that only humans have one or another of those properties.

The Judeo-Christian tradition offers an interesting argument for viewing humanity as having uniqueness of kind. It's connected to the aforementioned doctrine of the *imago Dei*, but with a significant addition. The *imago Dei* is first mentioned in the Bible near the very beginning, in the first chapter of the first book (Genesis). It reads:

> Then God said, "Let us make humankind in our image, after our likeness, so they may rule over the fish of the sea and the birds of the air, over the cattle, and over all the earth, and over all the creatures that move on the earth." God created humankind in his own image, in the image of God he created them, male and female he created them. God blessed them and said to them, "Be fruitful and multiply! Fill the earth and subdue it! Rule over the fish of the sea and the birds of the air and every creature that moves on the ground." . . . The LORD God planted an orchard in the east, in Eden; and there he placed the man he had formed . . . to care for it and to maintain it. (Gen 1:26–28; 2:8, 15; cf. Ps 8:3–8)

In this passage the *imago Dei* is connected to a special responsibility that God assigns to humanity: God gives to humanity the unique role of stewards of his creation. This gives us, then, another candidate for the basis of human uniqueness:

12. **Stewardship:** Humans are stewards of God's creation. Genesis does not explain why humanity was selected for this enormous responsibility, but it seems likely that among all the earthly creatures that God created, humanity most reflects God's own intelligence, creativity, moral sensitivity, and other qualities that make humanity better qualified for the role than any other member of the animal kingdom. Hence, humanity's various uniquenesses of degree qual-

ify it for a uniqueness of kind. Only humanity is appointed steward of God's creation.

Worldviews and Human Uniqueness

This chapter began with the statement, "both theists and naturalists tend to affirm that humanity is special." That does not imply that a person's worldview plays no role in how he or she views human uniqueness; however, one's worldview significantly influences what one thinks about this issue. For example, naturalism and pantheism imply physicalism regarding both the nature of reality and the nature of humanity. Therefore, many factors that could potentially make humans unique are not options for those who hold to these worldviews. They see humanity as the result of natural evolutionary processes. Accordingly, they see humanity as positioned at the upper end of a continuum with all other living organisms. Humanity is winning the evolutionary race: We've evolved further than any other species. This is a uniqueness of degree rather than a uniqueness of kind, but we are currently the most adaptive species on the planet.

Supernaturalistic worldviews tend to be dualistic and therefore have more options for human uniqueness available to them. In addition to those available to naturalists and pantheists, they can consider options involving an immaterial soul or a supernatural creator. Our analysis of these options, though, found that most of them also only claim a degree of uniqueness. On this score, supernaturalistic worldviews and naturalistic worldviews are about equal.

The clear exception to this is the Judeo-Christian view of the *imago Dei* as a position of stewardship of God's creation (option #12). This interesting option actually provides both uniqueness of degree and uniqueness of kind. It is explicitly related to belief in a single, maximal God, and therefore it is only compatible with supernaturalistic worldviews like theism and deism. As was seen, it's explicitly advocated by Judaism and Christianity.

QUESTIONS TO PONDER

- Are humans animals?
- Is there anything wrong with wanting to be special?
- If humanity is special, what makes us special?
- What conclusion does your worldview lead to regarding the uniqueness of humanity?

TERMS TO KNOW

- *imago Dei*
- uniqueness of degree
- uniqueness of kind
- relative uniqueness
- absolute uniqueness
- stewardship

FOR FURTHER READING

Hoekema, Anthony. *Created in God's Image*. Eerdmans, 1994. This volume is a biblical, theological, and philosophical study of the *imago Dei* and related anthropological issues written by a Christian theologian.

Tattersall, Ian. *Becoming Human: Evolution and Human Uniqueness*. Harcourt, 1998. This highly regarded volume explores human uniqueness from a naturalistic and evolutionary perspective.

Vanden Berg, Mary L. *Aquinas, Science, and Human Uniqueness: An Integrated Approach to the Question of What Makes Us Human*. Cascade, 2022. This is a scholarly Christian exploration of human uniqueness with an Aristotelean flavor.

THE MEANING OF LIFE

SYNOPSIS

Some of the most basic and fundamental questions in philosophical anthropology relate to the meaning of life. After listening to the friends wrestle with this question in light of the tragedy they experienced, this chapter will develop the topic relative to the major worldviews.

DIALOGUE

Later that evening, Zach, Hannah, and Suresh were taken to their homes and told to try to sleep, which was no easy task. The next day, police officers picked them up for a day of questioning. It was a long day, and they were heartsick while trying to get through the next steps.

Police insisted that they remain at the station for a series of debriefings and meetings with counselors. Through it all, their thoughts (and prayers, if they were honest—although it was a fuzzy category for all three of them) swirled around Angelo. Since they weren't family, they had received very little information.

Late in the afternoon, Sergeant Johnson of the Greenfield PD gave them the encouraging news that Officer Mack Ryan had come through his surgery and appeared to be out of danger. They didn't know Mack well, but he had nobly done his duty to protect them.

They learned that many of the people they had seen shot had survived.

The death toll was considerably less than they had expected. News outlets later reported only eight fatalities among the dozens of people involved in the shooting.

This included Tristan Lancaster, the mastermind of the operation.

The entire experience had caused life and death to take on a new vividness, if that was the right word. Johnson stepped in and said they were free to go home. The investigation would continue for some time, but for now, they were no longer required at the station.

Suresh asked Hannah and Zach if they wanted to get a light dinner at his restaurant. None of them felt much like eating, but they knew it would be good to get something in their stomachs—and also just to be together outside the police department.

As they ate, Suresh sighed deeply. "This whole thing has caused me to question so much about my life. It almost ended at just thirty years old." He paused, his fork midair. "Angelo . . ."

But Hannah and Zach would never know where that sentence was going because Suresh was suddenly weeping. Hannah and Zach both reached out to comfort Suresh. But soon both of them were also crying as the reality of the experience fully hit.

Hannah blew her nose. "This whole thing, and confronting death, has me asking questions. Why are we here? Why are we alive? Why do we exist? Do we have a purpose in life? And if we do, how do we find out what it is?"

Neither man seemed to have an answer.

"Assuming, of course, that there is a purpose for humanity or, more specifically, for individual people," Zach said. "I don't want to be dismissive, Hannah, but if our worldviews are right and humans are currently the most advanced mammals on Earth, who's to say we even have a purpose? I mean, do cows have a purpose?"

"I see what you're saying," Hannah said, "and I'm committed to an evolutionary framework. Comparing humans to lesser animals doesn't feel quite right, but I'm not sure how to answer."

"It's really hard to talk about this while Angelo is hanging between life and death, but perhaps this discussion can be a distraction. I'm inclined to say that cows do have a purpose," Suresh said. "That purpose is foisted upon them, I suppose, but they do provide excellent steaks, not to mention milk, butter, and other byproducts."

Zach nodded.

"At least one of their purposes," Suresh said, "seems to be providing benefit to humans or other animals that eat them. Obviously, I differ from my Hindu friends on this issue, who see cows in a different light. But it seems like purpose can arise from function. Somewhat similarly, humans produce and accomplish, benefiting each other and other species and, ultimately, improving Earth. Am I way off?"

"I don't think you're way off," Zach said. "You're answering the question in a particular way though. Do you guys know the word *teleological*?"

Both Suresh and Hannah shook their heads.

"Something is teleological if it was designed for a purpose. You're talking about results, Suresh—people do this or that—and using those results to explain purpose. But isn't there a precursor? Cows are used by others for various purposes, but are cows here because they had those purposes for existing?"

Zach paused to let the question sink in.

"I'm not sure we can ever discover a teleological purpose for anything that currently exists because we would have to know *why* the universe brought it into being. Cows evolved. The Big Bang released energy that eventually organized itself as organic matter; millions of years later, that organic matter has evolved into cattle. The cattle have their place in the circle of life, including providing an occupation for someone like you, Suresh, and nourishment for those of us who eat meat. But I don't think the universe did any of this *on purpose*. It just happened."

"That seems reasonable," Hannah said, "given your naturalistic and my existential commitments. When I apply this logic to human beings though, it feels dissatisfying. I've given my life to helping people through challenges and crises in their lives—in fact, I'll probably get a call from one of my colleagues in a day or two.

"The police often provide my agency with a list of people potentially needing counsel after events of this nature . . ." She paused. "For the first time, I'll be on the list."

Hannah looked down at the tissue in her hands.

"I can assure you, my counselor won't say, 'You survived, but you don't have any purpose for being alive, so if you hadn't survived, no big deal.' She also isn't likely to say, 'You bring benefits to other people. Your colleagues would miss you; your cat would miss you. So it's good that you survived.' What I expect her to say—because I've said it to many people—is, 'It's wonderful that you made it through. You're important. You have value.' But is that counselor telling the truth?"

"You're asking about *intrinsic* worth," Suresh said. "Am I understanding correctly? Whether people have value in themselves, simply because they exist? One of the reasons I first spoke in terms of work and contribution is because that's a typically Buddhist way of addressing meaning. Buddhists find meaning in their teleological purpose—I like your word, Zach. They are seeking enlightenment. It won't likely be achieved in this lifetime, but it remains the distant goal of life, the end of all striving and suffering. Humans are here for that pursuit. The question of why we were put here in the first place simply isn't important to most Buddhists. It's all about where we're going."

Hannah nodded, remembering something. "I read an article about Ikigai. Are you familiar with that? I may have mispronounced it. I-k-i-g-a-i."

"I have a Japanese friend who talks about Ikigai occasionally, but I haven't paid close attention," Suresh said. "Can you tell us more?"

"A little . . ." she said.

Hannah drew a picture on a napkin to illustrate the concept. "Many Japanese Buddhists believe that Ikigai is achieved by balancing passions, abilities, vocation, and mission. They think this will result in a balanced life, especially between caring for oneself and meeting others' needs. It's intriguing."[1]

"This is fascinating," Zach said, "and it looks useful. But I think we're fleshing out a distinction. Each of us can think of ways to *make* life

---

1. For details, see Francesc Miralles and Hector Garcia, *Ikigai: The Japanese Secret to a Long and Happy Life* (Efinito, 2022). For the Ikigai graphic and a brief discussion of meaning in Buddhism, see Emily Shipp, "The Downside of Happiness: What I Learned About Purpose from a Buddhist Monk," accessed August 25, 2025, https://questionsonpurpose.org/blog/the-downside-of-happiness.

meaningful. The question remains: Is life itself *intrinsically* meaningful? It seems like we would prefer that to be true. Hannah expressed her desire for such meaning, but I admit that I would be comforted to think that my life has meaning whether I contribute to society or do anything of value," Zach said.

"I simply don't see a rational basis in my worldview for affirming intrinsic value. Maybe Angelo has thoughts on this . . ." Zach's voice trailed off.

* * *

Zach's phone rang. Suresh and Hannah watched his face as Zach got an update on Angelo.

"The surgeons are optimistic. The bullet missed his heart. He had a collapsed lung, internal bleeding, and a few other issues, but the blood never stopped flowing to his brain or other crucial organs. It was a high-caliber bullet and passed entirely through him, which the doctors say was a good thing. They are confident he will survive."

Hannah and Suresh practically cheered when they heard the news. And then they all teared up again.

Angelo was going to be okay.

They might not be able to explain why, but his life had a great deal of value to them.

* * *

They weren't allowed to see Angelo for several days. In the meantime, they met his parents—a sweet Italian couple—and a young lady, Allison, who was a friend of Angelo's from church. She seemed nice.

Over the next week, they returned to their jobs. Suresh found the restaurant a welcome haven from the turmoil. As news outlets gradually released information about the cartel, the federal investigation, and, to some extent, their involvement, Hannah, Suresh, and Zach became minor celebrities. Suresh downplayed his involvement and tried to go about his business.

Zach received a hero's welcome at Bradley Pharmaceuticals. Zach's work was as meaningful as ever. It was all he needed.

Hannah had the hardest time reintegrating into her old job. Her instinct that people have intrinsic worth and the conflict of that instinct with what she believed about the evolutionary origins of humanity bothered her and became a distraction. *What's the use of helping this or that person through a particular problem if the person's whole life doesn't matter? Were her existentialist teachers right that a person has to make her own meaning?* Sartre spoke about angst and despair over realizing that people have no fixed nature or purpose, and Hannah was feeling that right now.

The day finally came when Angelo was moved from the ICU to a normal hospital room and his friends could visit.

"You look good, man," Zach said.

After gentle hugs, which resulted in a few winces, the friends lightheartedly caught Angelo up on their lives for the last couple of weeks. He drank up their words, so happy to be with them.

"So what philosophy have you been discussing lately? I'm sure something must have come up in the wake of, shall I say, our *adventure*."

"How did you know?" Zach said, laughing. "We've been talking about the meaning of life."

Zach paused for a moment, seeming to need to compose himself.

"We didn't know if we'd ever see you again. Our own lives were threatened too."

"It really got us thinking about life itself," Hannah said. "Why we're here . . . whether we have a purpose, and, more fundamentally, whether we're here on purpose?"

"This has been a wakeup call like no other," Suresh said. "I've made some major changes."

"Such as?" Angelo asked.

"We can talk about it more later, but Hannah introduced me to a Japanese Buddhist philosophy of life called Ikigai. It doesn't answer all the questions we worked through, but I really like it. It speaks about meaning as path and destination. It doesn't worry about purpose in the sense of why we're here in the first place."

"We haven't found much of an answer as to why the universe put us here," Hannah said, smiling at Angelo. "But I bet you have a Christian answer, don't you?"

"I do . . . It's a very important doctrine in Christianity, although not all Christians frame it the same way."

"Does the Bible directly address this question?" Suresh asked.

"The apostle Paul makes several sweeping statements that relate to human purpose. He says, for instance, 'Therefore, whether you eat or drink, or whatever you do, do all to the glory of God.'[2] He says something similar in his letter to the Ephesians: 'In Him (that is, Jesus Christ) also we have obtained an inheritance (that's our goal), being predestined (that's God establishing the goal for us in advance) according to the purpose of Him who works all things according to the counsel of His will, that (this word expresses purpose) we who first trusted in Christ should be to the praise of His glory.'"[3]

---

2. 1 Cor 10:31 (NKJV).
3. Eph 1:11–12 (NKJV).

"What does it mean to 'be to the praise of his glory'?" Zach asked.

"It means to live in such a way that we cause other people to recognize that God is glorious and praise him as well," Angelo said. "My life is for the purpose of glorifying God."

"So the Bible teaches that God created people so they will make him look good?" Zach was dubious. "Doesn't that make God selfish and arrogant? No offense, my friend."

"It would certainly be selfish and arrogant for me to want other people to glorify me," said Angelo. "I suppose we all do some things that are praiseworthy. Heaven knows, I've had a steady stream of relatives visiting and telling me how brave and wonderful I am."

"And they're right!" Hannah said.

"Yeah, whatever," he said, laughing a little. The laughter made him wince. "In the last analysis though, I'm pretty mediocre. I have limited power, limited knowledge, limited everything. God is quite different. As we saw in our discussion a few months ago, God, if he exists, is omnipotent, omniscient, omnibenevolent, eternal, and unchanging. He *deserves* everyone to make much of him. In fact, it's wrong—the Bible calls it idolatry—when anything or anyone else is given the glory that only God deserves.[4] So God is right to demand worship and would be acting immorally if he allowed or encouraged the worship of anything else. So it's not selfish or arrogant at all. I would add, by the way, that God has arranged the universe in such a way that when the beings he has created glorify him, they find themselves the happiest and most fulfilled."

"Does this tie in with the discussion of the image of God we had during the crisis of two weeks ago?" Zach asked. He was listening closely and trying to connect the dots.

"It does! Good observation, my friend," Angelo said. "If the Bible is truthful when it says that God created humanity in his own image, then

---

4. See, for instance, Isa 42:8: "I am the LORD, that is My name; And My glory I will not give to another, Nor My praise to carved images" (NKJV). Carved images were a particular form of idolatry in the ancient world, but the principle applies to any alternative object of worship.

the implication is that humans express God's nature—his moral nature—when they carry out their God-ordained task of ruling this world correctly. When I look like God in my love and justice and truthfulness, then people form a right opinion about God, and he is glorified. It all works together in Christian theology."

"That seems like a tall order," Hannah said. "You've already said God is infinite in all these things. How could someone like you or me ever give people the right impression of him through our actions?"

"We can't do it in our own power," Angelo said, a gleam in his eye. "In fact, because of our sinfulness, we mostly fail to bring God glory in our lives. As Paul puts it in Romans, 'We fall short of the glory of God.' But God's Son, Jesus Christ, who, according to Scripture, is God in the flesh, bore our sins on the cross so that we can be forgiven. The third person of the Trinity, then, the Holy Spirit, comes into our lives and gives us strength to do things that bring God glory, and we become more and more like Jesus. Until we die—and are *glorified*—we won't follow the Spirit perfectly and look like Christ completely, but in the meantime, we do our best to please God. One could almost say that our purpose could be boiled down to pleasing God."

"Are you saying humankind's purpose is to glorify God or to please him?" Suresh asked.

"Yes," Angelo said, gently changing his position in the hospital bed. "Humans are created in God's image and have intrinsic value in God's sight. But I'm not actively pleasing God unless I'm living in such a way that makes others find him glorious, and I'm not glorifying God unless I try to live in such a way that pleases him. This is my game plan for life."

"Angelo," Zach said, tears welling up in his eyes, "you know I haven't come to faith in your God. But this I will say: I've never met anyone who caused me to think better of God, if he exists, than you have."

"Absolutely," Suresh said.

"I'll go a step further," Hannah said. "When you put yourself in harm's way, willing to sacrifice yourself to save our lives, I was reminded of the Sunday school stories I heard as a child of Jesus laying down his life for others."

"Thank you, Hannah," Angelo said softly. "There's a big difference, though: Jesus laid down his life for us while we were his *enemies*.[5] That's how much intrinsic value he places on humanity."

THEORY

The final two chapters, which cover life and death, are outstanding examples of the divide between naturalistic philosophies and supernaturalistic philosophies. One's worldview substantially shapes how a person views her reason for existing. The following discussion will lay out how philosophers have addressed this important issue.

The Question

The third chapter in our unit on philosophical anthropology is about the meaning of life. For philosophers, a seminal text on this topic is Plato's *Phaedo*, which in ancient times was titled *On the Soul*.[6] If it is an actual historical account, then it records a conversation between Socrates and some of his friends that took place while Socrates was in jail awaiting execution. They discuss justice, the meaning of life, the nature of death, why it's wrong to kill someone, whether suicide is immoral, and other related issues. It ends with Socrates' execution.

Phaedo was written almost 2,400 years ago. It's remarkable that people are still wrestling with these same issues. Doubtless that's because these are some of the most important issues that humans face. At some point, almost everyone wonders what he or she is supposed to do with his or her life. Questions like "Why am I here? What's the meaning of all this? How can I feel more fulfilled? How can I have a more meaningful life?" seem to arise naturally in everyone's mind. However, these are notoriously difficult questions to answer.

The question, "What is the meaning of life?" is one of the most famous questions in philosophy, and it's as difficult to answer as any. No doubt part

---

5. Rom 5:8, 10: "But God demonstrates His own love toward us, in that while we were still sinners, Christ died for us. . . . For if when we were enemies we were reconciled to God through the death of His Son, much more, having been reconciled, we shall be saved by His life" (NKJV).
6. Plato, *Phaedo*, trans. Benjamin Jowett (Internet Classics Archive), accessed December 26, 2024, https://classics.mit.edu/Plato/phaedo.html.

of the reason for this is that it's not very clear what the question is even asking. Perhaps part of the reason for that is that it's a complex question. You remember what a **complex question** is: It's a question that assumes a specific answer to a logically antecedent question that was never actually asked. The question "What is the meaning of life?" assumes that we've already asked the question "Does life have meaning?" and that we've answered that question in the affirmative. But what if life doesn't have meaning? Clearly, we need to back up a step and ask, "Does life have meaning?"

"The hour of departure has arrived, and we go our separate ways, I to die, and you to live. Which of these two is better only God knows." –Socrates

An Antecedent Question

The question "Does life have meaning?" is also pretty tricky. What exactly is it asking? Some have objected that this question commits the **category mistake** fallacy. This fallacy is committed when you assign something to a category in which it doesn't belong. For example, if someone were to say, "Pluto is the smallest planet in the solar system," that would be a category mistake, because Pluto doesn't fit into the "planet" category (as it is currently defined). The statement "whales are the biggest fish" is also a category mistake, since whales are mammals rather than fish.

The reason some people think that the question about life having meaning commits the category mistake fallacy is that they think that only communicative acts have meaning. Speech has meaning: It says something. Writing has meaning. Gestures, like a thumbs-up or nodding your head or pointing, have meaning, since they communicate something. Signs have meaning: A street sign with a jumping deer on it tells you to drive carefully because deer frequently cross the road in that vicinity. But life isn't a communicative act. It's not trying to say something. And for this reason, they argue, life doesn't have meaning.

There's a problem with this argument, though, because it seems to misunderstand how the word "meaning" is being used in the questions about the meaning of life. Most words have what is called a **semantic range**, which is the range of meanings that a given word has. For example, the word "light" can mean a form of radiant energy that makes things visible, but it can also refer to radiant energy that does not make things visible (such as ultraviolet light), and to the object that produces the illuminating energy (like a lamp or a flashlight), and to something that is used to ignite a cigarette ("can you give me a light?"), and it can be an adjective that describes something that is a brighter shade than something else ("it's light green"). It has other meanings, too. All these meanings make up the semantic range of the word "light."

The word *meaning* has a semantic range that includes a concept being communicated ("what he meant to say"), the concept behind something ("the meaning of the word is . . ."), an intention ("she was meaning to go"), a degree of significance ("his glance was full of meaning"), and a particular purpose ("What was the meaning of coming here, anyway?"). The way to tell which of these connotations is the one that's intended is to examine the context of the statement in which "meaning" is being used. If we try to think of contexts in which people talk about the meaning of life, we will come up with things like someone going through a very hard time and asking, "What is the meaning of life?" or asserting, "My life is meaningless!" In other words, "What is the point of me being here? There is no point!" This suggests that they're using the term with reference to purpose—the last option mentioned above.

Historical Explanations vs. Teleological Explanations

So now our question has become "Does life have purpose?" By "purpose" we mean the reason for which something exists. Why are we here? Do we exist for a specific reason? How you answer this question will depend on your worldview.

Naturalism and pantheism offer a **historical explanation** for our existence. Current scientific **cosmology** (the branch of science that deals with the origin and development of the universe) holds that the universe began with the Big Bang, which sent matter flying in every direction, causing the formation of meteors, comets, planets, stars, and other heavenly bodies. Galaxies and solar systems were formed. On a planet in one of those solar systems, organic matter developed and began to evolve, eventually resulting in vertebrates, mammals, and then humans. In brief, the naturalistic (and pantheistic) answer to the question of the reason for our existence is historical in nature: We are the product of natural processes that eventually resulted in the human race.

Bringing this to a more personal level, a question that relates to "Why are we here?" is "Why are you here?" The naturalistic/pantheistic answer to this personal question is also historical: You are here because evolution resulted in the lives of your distant ancestors, who gave birth to succeeding generations of nearer ancestors until eventually your parents were born, met, and gave birth to you.

These answers are historical in nature. They explain why humanity is here and why you are here in the sense of explaining the historical factors that led to the existence of the human race in general and each one of us in particular. But the questions "Why are we here?" and "Why are you here?" can have another sense, a teleological one. **Teleology**, as we learned in the chapter on theistic apologetics, has to do with purpose or design. A **teleological explanation** of human existence will talk about more than just the historical events that brought about our existence. It will talk about *why* those factors led up to our existence: Did something or someone intend for us to exist? Are we part of a great, cosmic plan? Do we exist to serve some special purpose?

These are difficult to answer on naturalism and pantheism. In fact, naturalists and pantheists would probably consider the whole teleological perspective on human existence to be another category mistake: Things that have teleological explanations come about as the result of some plan created by an intelligent being. Since (according to naturalism and pantheism) humans came about by natural processes that don't involve any such being and plan, it's fallacious to expect them to have a teleological explanation.

On the other hand, supernaturalistic worldviews like theism and deism attempt to provide both historical and teleological explanations for humanity and humans. Theism and deism see the universe as created by God (historical explanation), and they believe that God has good reasons for everything he does. Concordantly, they believe that everything that God created has a purpose (teleological explanation). Things that God created directly and things that he created indirectly have a purpose. While the very first humans fall into the former category, most humans fall into the latter category: God created them through creating their distant ancestors and endowing them with the ability to reproduce. But even though God didn't create you directly, theism teaches that you are part of God's plan, and he created you for a purpose.

Extrinsic vs. Intrinsic Purpose

This brings us to the question, "What is our purpose?" And that's the question with which this chapter began: What is the meaning of life? The French call this our *raison d'être*, our "reason for existing." What is our reason for existing?

Naturalism is likely to respond that there is no teleological reason for our existence. That seems like a logical implication of naturalism, which sees humanity as a result of non-sentient natural processes. However, many naturalists have found this answer unsatisfying. That is understandable, since the thought that life is purposeless—meaningless—is rather depressing. Therefore, some naturalists have argued that, even without a divine design, life can have purpose. In particular, existentialist thinkers like Friedrich Nietzsche and Jean-Paul Sartre have argued that we can make our lives meaningful by devoting ourselves to a worthy cause, such as eradicating poverty, finding a cure for cancer, or promoting world peace.[7]

"Life has no meaning, the moment you lose the illusion of being eternal. Life has no meaning *a priori*... It is up to you to give it a meaning, and value is nothing but the meaning that you choose."
–Jean-Paul Sartre

This brings us to another distinction: extrinsic purpose vs. intrinsic purpose. **Extrinsic purpose** is conferred on your life by something else, something other than life itself. The sort of purpose that naturalistic

7. Labelling Nietzsche an existentialist is somewhat anachronistic, since by most accounts existentialism as a movement didn't begin until well after he died, but he's generally seen as a forerunner to the movement.

existentialists advocate is extrinsic. You can make your life meaningful by devoting it to a worthy cause, or to your family, your job, or whatever you are passionate about. And most of us do: Most people enrich their lives in this way. It's a good thing to do!

However, there is a problem—an inherent danger, even—in extrinsic purpose: It can be lost. If your sense of meaningfulness and significance comes from your job and you lose your job, or from your family and through some tragedy you lose your family, or from serving the poor at a soup kitchen and the kitchen closes down, you could find yourself feeling empty, your life could seem pointless, and you could spiral into depression. This is a serious problem that many people face. It can even lead to suicidal ideation.[8] Hence, although external sources of purpose and meaning are good, they also involve a degree of risk.

If life were intrinsically meaningful rather than merely extrinsically so, then we wouldn't run this risk. **Intrinsic purpose** is purpose that is inherent in life itself. Is life intrinsically meaningful? Does it have intrinsic purpose?

Theism (and deism) holds that God created humanity for a purpose. Therefore, according to theism, life is inherently meaningful. Accordingly, if theism is true, then life is intrinsically meaningful. This is not the place to debate the truth of theism, though: that's already been done in chapters 14 and 15 (and in numerous books that you can find in libraries and bookstores).

The Meaning of Life

Now it's time to attempt to answer the question: "What is the meaning of life?" Here we'll assume that life has meaning and attempt to identify what that meaning is.

Naturalistic existentialists view life's meaning from an extrinsic perspective. For them, life has whatever meaning you instill in it. You may choose to view life as meaningless, or as yours to enjoy to the fullest extent

8. According to the CDC, suicide is one of the leading causes of death in the US (https://www.cdc.gov/suicide/facts/index.html). If you know anyone who is struggling with suicidal thoughts, please inform them that they can contact a trained counsellor by calling or texting the Suicide and Crisis Hotline at 988 or direct them to the Suicide and Crisis Hotline webpage: https://988lifeline.org/.

possible, or as an opportunity to serve humanity. So from a naturalistic perspective, there are at least three possible purposes for your life:

1. **Nihilism**: There is no meaning to life.
2. **Hedonism**: Maximal pleasure or happiness is the meaning of life.
3. **Altruism**: Selflessly serving others is the meaning of life.

Existentialists emphasize that it is your choice which of these is going to be the meaning of your life. Since it's your life, you get to decide. There is no intrinsic meaning that you need to discover and then fulfill.

Aristotle, in *Nicomachean Ethics*, seems to suggest that happiness should be the supreme goal of life:

> And of this nature happiness is mostly thought to be, for this we choose always for its own sake, and never with a view to anything further: whereas honour, pleasure, intellect, in fact every excellence we choose for their own sakes, it is true, but we choose them also with a view to happiness, conceiving that through their instrumentality we shall be happy: but no man chooses happiness with a view to them, nor in fact with a view to any other thing whatsoever.[9]

At first that might sound rather hedonistic, but that conclusion would be hasty. According to Aristotle, lasting happiness is acquired by achieving contentment. So how is contentment achieved? By understanding and fulfilling your *telos* (a very Aristotelian word). That leads us back to our original question: What is my *telos*? According to Aristotle, our ability to be virtuous sets humanity apart from the rest of the animal kingdom. Whether he is right about that can be debated, but if he is, then it could be that this singular ability is what God has put us here for. If that's correct, then we should intentionally cultivate our own inner virtue. By doing that, we fulfill

9. Aristotle, *The Nicomachean Ethics*, ed. David Ross and Lesley Brown (Oxford University Press, 2010), Book I, ch. 7, p. 10.

our *telos*, and by fulfilling our *telos*, we achieve a fulfilling life, which will produce contentment resulting in lasting happiness.[10]

Aristotle's answer to our question combines intrinsic and extrinsic aspects in a way that makes them complementary to each other. This seems like a good move, for the intrinsic aspects are invulnerable to the vicissitudes of life, but the extrinsic aspects add human involvement and action that lead to visible expression of our intrinsic *telos.*

A more overtly theistic answer that also combines intrinsic and extrinsic elements comes from the New Testament. Have you ever wondered why God would create the human race, with all its flaws, fighting, and other failures? If he's omniscient then before he created humanity he knew how cruel we would be to each other, how some of us would deny his existence, and that some of us would do terrible things in his very name. Of course, he would know about all the good things and all the beautiful things that we do, too. In the final analysis, perhaps the good outweighs the bad, and God, knowing this, was motivated by that knowledge. Perhaps. But perhaps not. Perhaps he created us out of pure love, not because we do more good things than bad but because he knew that we'd enjoy living, and he, being omnibenevolent, takes pleasure in seeing us enjoying life. That's speculation, of course. In the final analysis, all we can say for sure is that if God created us, he did so because he wanted to. For if he hadn't wanted to, he wouldn't have done it.

That's basically the answer that the New Testament gives to the question of the meaning of life. Revelation 4:11 says that it was God's will to create the universe and all that lies therein, "You are worthy, O Lord, to receive glory and honor and power; for You created all things, and by Your will they exist and were created" (NKJV). Colossians 1:16 indicates not only that God created all things but that they were created *for him*: "For by Him all things were created that are in heaven and that are on earth, visible and invisible, whether thrones or dominions or principalities or powers. All things were created through Him and for Him" (NKJV). According to theism, this is the intrinsic meaning of life: We exist because God wants us to. It pleases the almighty God that you exist. On theism, you are inherently

10. C. D. C. Reeve, *Action, Contemplation, and Happiness: An Essay on Aristotle* (Harvard University Press, 2012).

and eternally important to the almighty creator of heaven and earth. That's something, isn't it?

The extrinsic aspect is found in the teachings of Jesus. When asked by some of his interlocutors which is the greatest commandment in the Jewish law, he replied, "'You shall love the Lord your God with all your heart, with all your soul, and with all your mind.' This is the first and great commandment. And the second is like it: 'You shall love your neighbor as yourself.' On these two commandments hang all the Law and the Prophets" (Matt 22:37–40 NKJV). According to theism, God wants us to reflect his benevolent nature by being benevolent ourselves. This pleases and glorifies God. As Angelo put it, "Man is created in God's image and has intrinsic value in God's sight. But I'm not actively pleasing God unless I'm living in such a way that makes others find him glorious, and I'm not glorifying God unless I try to live in such a way that pleases him."[11]

Returning to the questions at the beginning of the chapter, here is how theism answers them:

- Why am I here? Because God wants you here.
- What is the purpose of life? To please and glorify God.
- How can I feel more fulfilled? By realizing that you please God.
- How can I have a more meaningful life? By reflecting God's benevolence to others.

11. There was quite a bit of discussion among the authors of this book about what the ultimate purpose of human existence is. All three see pleasing God and glorifying God as important. One thought that pleasing God is the broader category that includes glorifying God as one component, while the other two thought that glorifying God is the broader category that includes pleasing God as a component. In the end, we decided to mention both. Both play a role, and the question of which one is more foundational to the other is difficult to answer.

QUESTIONS TO PONDER

- Do you think it makes sense to seek a teleological explanation for our existence? Why or why not?
- Do you think your life has a purpose? If you do, what do you think it is?
- If you think your life has a purpose, where do you think that purpose comes from?
- If you don't think life has a purpose, do you think that's a problem? Does that make life seem less meaningful?
- Do you find the existentialist attempt to instill meaning into life effective?

TERMS TO KNOW

- *Phaedo*
- complex question
- category mistake
- semantic range
- purpose
- cosmology
- teleology
- historical explanation
- teleological explanation
- *telos*
- extrinsic purpose
- intrinsic purpose
- nihilism
- hedonism
- altruism

FOR FURTHER READING

"The Gospel According to Matthew." In *The New King James Bible, New Testament*. Thomas Nelson, 1979. This is one of the earliest and most detailed accounts of the teachings of Jesus, who had a lot to say about the meaning of life. His perspective is theistic.

Plato. *Socratic Dialogues: Meno, Euthyphro, Apology, Crito, Phaedo*. Translated by Cathal Woods and Ryan Pack. Broadview, 2024. Plato's dialogues are among the most seminal texts for discussions on the meaning of life in the Western intellectual tradition. The perspective is broadly polytheistic.

Sarte, Jean-Paul. *Existentialism is a Humanism*. Translated by Carol Macomber. Yale University Press, 2007. This is one of the most foundational texts on the meaning of life from the perspective of a naturalistic existentialist.

Seachris, Joshua W., ed. *Exploring the Meaning of Life: An Anthology and Guide*. Wiley-Blackwell, 2013. This is a wonderful collection of classic and contemporary texts on a range of issues related to the meaning of life.

24

THE NATURE OF DEATH

SYNOPSIS

This chapter concludes our investigation of philosophical anthropology by considering a sobering but important topic: the nature of death. Death is an inescapable reality for all people, and people address it in a variety of ways. As with the other topics in this book, it is important to think critically—that is, to think philosophically—about this important issue.

DIALOGUE

Three weeks went by after that visit to the hospital. Life settled back into a routine, and the friends found themselves busy yet again—so busy that their attempts to get together fell through again and again. And they didn't want to meet until *everyone* was available, including Angelo.

Suresh, Hannah, and Zach arrived around the same time. They got their drinks and went to their usual spot. When Angelo finally arrived, he walked through the door slowly and made his way to the counter. They finally got a good look at him when he got to the table.

Hannah gasped.

Suresh leaped from his chair to offer Angelo assistance.

"Are you okay?" Zach asked.

Angelo's face was pale and drawn. He'd lost so much weight that his belt was cinched tight around his pants, which were clearly too big for him now.

"Hey, friends," he said weakly. "Thanks for waiting for me. It took me longer than I expected to get ready today. I'm fighting some serious fatigue."

Hannah placed a hand over Angelo's. "Should you be here today? Don't get me wrong. We're so glad to see you, but you don't look so well."

"I had to get out of the house," Angelo said. "But I have to admit that this is pushing it. The doctors keep saying I should be feeling stronger every day, but I don't feel stronger. Maybe I just need a few more weeks . . ."

Zach made eye contact with Hannah, a look of concern in his eyes.

"Now that I'm here," Angelo said, "I'm sure I'll be fine." He sat back in his seat and drew his coffee cup to his lips.

Suresh and Zach sat back down, and there was an awkward pause as everyone stared at Angelo, uncertain what to do next.

"Do you feel up to discussing philosophy today?" Hannah asked. "If not, that's fine. Or we can talk about what happened if anyone wants to."

No one knew what to call what had happened the month before and the months leading up to it. They alternately referred to it as "the ordeal" or "the attack" or "the incident," but none of those terms seemed adequate. It *had* been an ordeal, a long, drawn-out succession of events that culminated in the most traumatic day of their lives. It had spawned nightmares, panic attacks, and general anxiety for each of them. Hannah was the most informed on the process people experience in the aftermath of intense trauma, so she wasn't surprised at the feelings that arose over the intervening weeks. But all her education hadn't prepared her for her own involvement in the Tristan Lancaster ordeal—or the subsequent emotional difficulty.

"I'd rather not talk about it again for a while if I can help it," Angelo said. "Between recounting the incidents to my parents again and again and answering questions from every relative and friend, I feel like I've said all that can be said. I would love to move on, heal, and get back to life as I used to know it, if that's possible."

He looked around the table, his eyes warmer and filled with more love than they'd seen before. "I appreciate so much the kindness all of you have shown me. I mean it."

He set his cup back down. "So what is the last topic we have to discuss from the book?"

Zach cleared his throat.

Hannah put her hand on Angelo's again. "That's why we weren't sure if we should dive into this last chapter. It's a touchy subject considering all we have been through. The topic is death."

Angelo blinked, seeming to fall deep into thoughts none of them had access to.

"Maybe we should skip it for now," Zach said.

"Oh wow," Angelo said, "that's a tough one! I think we were all closer to our own deaths and the death of others than at any other point in our lives, wouldn't you say?"

"Without a doubt," agreed Zach.

"Are you okay with talking about it?" Suresh asked.

"Yes, let's do it. The reality is that we will all die someday, and there's no point in talking about it in a detached and clinical manner when we all know how real and emotional the moment of death really is."

Angelo had expected to die when he was shot in the chest, and ever since then he had been trying to evaluate that experience and remember what went through his mind.

"It was real, so real, and yet the whole thing seems like a bad dream at times," Zach said. "I was so sure I was going to die, regardless of what I did or didn't do for Tristan. I have never felt such fear in my life and such a sense of powerlessness. It felt like he could have made me do almost anything he wanted because he had all the power."

Zach shuddered. "I don't think Tristan would have thought twice about killing me if he thought it would help him succeed. Over the last few weeks, I have tried to analyze why I was so afraid . . ."

"How could you *not* be afraid?" Suresh said. "How could any of us be anything but absolutely terrified?"

"I know you're right," said Zach, "but if I am being consistent with my atheistic beliefs, death would simply be the cessation of my life, my consciousness, and myself. I wouldn't feel anything after death because there would be no me to feel or think."

Zach turned toward Hannah. She was watching Angelo closely and didn't meet Zach's gaze. Zach looked at Angelo too. He wasn't moving. His face was white, and he was swaying slightly in his seat. Suddenly he began to list to one side. Zach jumped up and caught him before he hit the floor.

"Help me lower him to the floor," Zach said as Hannah rushed over and grabbed Angelo.

Suresh stood abruptly, his chair clattering to the floor.

"Someone call 911!" he yelled.

A young woman made a beeline toward them from across the room. She knelt next to Zach and quickly began checking Angelo's pulse.

"My name is Kelcey. I'm an emergency department nurse. Can you tell me anything about this man? Is he your friend?"

"Uh, yes, he—he's my friend. He's recovering from a gunshot wound to the chest. It happened about, uh . . ." Zach looked at Hannah.

"It happened four weeks ago," she said.

Kelcey checked his pulse, then opened Angelo's shirt. The surgical scar was bigger than anyone expected and still quite angry looking. His abdomen was swollen. "We need to get him to the hospital now. What's his name?"

"Angelo," Suresh said, a little pale, his hands visibly shaking.

"Angelo, I'm Kelcey." She tapped his chest, trying to get a response. "Can you hear me? How are you doing?"

Angelo's breathing was shallow and labored, and faint groans escaped his throat.

The ambulance arrived within minutes. Two paramedics burst through the door with a gurney and quickly conferred with Kelcey as they loaded Angelo onto it. The vehicle roared off with a scream of sirens and flashing lights.

The three friends watched helplessly. Once again, they were swallowed up in grief. How could this be happening? They thought they lost Angelo the day he was shot. Now his survival was in question once more.

Death was once again looming over them like a dark cloud.

Over the next few days Angelo hovered between life and death. Everyone tried to maintain their normal routines but had little interest in work—or anything for that matter. They waited eagerly each day for an update from Angelo's parents. Death was on their minds constantly.

* * *

Zach shuffled through each day, overwhelmed with his new duties as lab director at Bradley Pharmaceuticals. Many of his coworkers knew he had been embroiled in the events surrounding the death of Tristan Lancaster and the exposure of a cartel operating in the area. Those who knew tried to help Zach any way they could. One person in particular kept his eye on Zach: Dr. O.

As a child, Dr. O had lived through the Nigerian Civil War and lived with the aftermath that struck his family, who had lost friends, relatives, and neighbors. He knew firsthand about the long-term effects of trauma. Dr. O was alarmed to discover that Zach returned to work just a week after being taken hostage. Now the security guard who had been shot, Zach's friend, was in the hospital and might not survive.

Dr. O walked past the lab at lunchtime three days after Angelo was readmitted to the hospital. Zach hadn't gone to lunch the past few days. He had stayed in his office, busying himself with paperwork. As the rest of the scientists trickled out for lunch, Dr. O slipped past and made his way to Zach's office. He peered around the doorway. Zach was sitting at his desk staring absentmindedly at some papers. After a few moments, Dr. O cleared his throat.

"Dr. O!" Zach stood up quickly and tried to appear composed. "What can I do for you?"

Dr. O shook Zach's hand warmly. "Sit down, Zachary. This is a personal visit. Are you headed to lunch?"

"Um, no, I wasn't planning to eat today. To tell you the truth, I haven't had much of an appetite lately."

"That is perfectly understandable, considering what you've been through." Dr. O was always able to put Zach at ease. He spoke as a man who genuinely cared for others, and everyone who worked with him felt it.

"I wanted to see how you're doing, Zachary. I heard that your friend is back in the hospital. What is his condition?"

Tears sprang to Zach's eyes. He was so choked up he couldn't speak for several minutes.

"Take your time, friend," Dr. O said, deep compassion in his voice.

With that, Zach burst into tears. He put his head on his desk and sobbed. Dr. O pulled his chair around the side of Zach's desk and sat next to him with an arm on Zach's shoulder. Such a gesture from any other coworker would have been awkward, but not from Dr. O.

Dr. O held out both arms with his palms up in an open gesture. "Zachary, you know you can talk about anything with me."

"I know," said Zach. "This whole ordeal has rattled my confidence in atheism as the answer for life. I believe that death is the end and that's it. But another part of me hopes that Angelo is right, that if he dies, he will go into the presence of God and live forever where there is no pain or death or evil, only joy and light. Can I hope that is true for him even if I don't believe it will be true for me? I have never wanted different belief systems to be true simultaneously more than I do now."

Dr. O smiled and nodded. "Nothing is true simply because it is comforting, so I am not suggesting that you abandon your atheism simply because the Christian teaching on death and the afterlife consoles you. But have you considered the possibility that it is comforting because it's true? Maybe the Christian faith isn't wishful thinking by those who are afraid and want there to be something beyond the grave. Maybe the reason all religions teach life after death is because it's true and we are hardwired to long for it."

Zach groaned as he considered Dr. O's words.

"If that's too much for you right now, then perhaps you should consider other options for what you believe. I must say, the idea of cessation of consciousness and life at the moment of death is bleak and depressing to me." Dr. O could say things that Zach would never accept from someone else.

"Not that that makes it untrue," Zach said half-heartedly.

"True, Zachary." Dr. O rose from his seat and clapped a hand on Zach's back. "I don't know what this means to you, Zachary, but I want you to know that I am praying for you, and I am always here if you want to talk." With that Dr. O bid Zach goodbye.

Zach felt strangely better. He didn't know why.

He couldn't pray for Angelo, but he would hope for his recovery.

* * *

Across town, Hannah was experiencing her own crisis of faith over Angelo's condition. She found it difficult to concentrate when meeting with clients and couldn't seem to muster her usual compassion.

She felt like she was at a breaking point.

Her parents tried to comfort her, but they resorted to talking about God's power to heal and about heaven. She didn't want to hear it. If God was real, this wouldn't have happened to one of his most faithful followers. Angelo had restored Hannah's faith in religious people after many years of disillusionment. But now this. What was it all for? She saw no sense in it.

After an unusually difficult home visit, Hannah called it a day. Her house was quiet and cozy, but it seemed empty and silent, cold and foreboding. She didn't want to think about Angelo. It was too painful. And yet thinking about death is one of the best things a person can do because it puts everything in perspective.

It was easier to think about her own death than about Angelo's. As a temporary being, she had long ago accepted her mortality. In fact, all of life was an alignment of oneself toward the inevitable day of death. This mindset had enabled Hannah to create for herself a life of meaning, albeit an often grim life.

As she sat in her quiet house alone, Hannah spent time in deep reflection. Her declared freedom came with a cost. If she had died in the warehouse, she would have continued to exist only in the memories of her family, friends, colleagues, and the clients she had helped through the years. After she died, it would be as if a tree was cut down in a dense forest. Within a few years, the forest would reclaim the space where she had been, and eventually there would be no evidence that she ever existed.[1]

Death is truly the great enemy, and no one is coming to rescue us, she thought.

Hannah closed her eyes. The sadness and despair engulfed her. She could embrace her mortality and the mortality of everyone she knew. But she could only do it intellectually. She could not wrap her heart around the idea that Angelo might die. Maybe she simply hadn't delved deeply enough into existentialism. Maybe further reading would unlock new ideas about death that would ease the pain in her heart.

Somehow, she doubted that any philosophy could override how she felt about her friend.

---

1. See Sarah Bakewell, *At the Existentialist Café: Freedom, Being, and Apricot Cocktails* (Other Press, 2016), especially ch. 13.

* * *

Suresh was in the zone. Sometimes when he cooked, he entered a trancelike state where his hands moved quickly and effortlessly. He and his colleagues called it "the dance." He and others moved throughout the kitchen as if interlocked in a choreographed performance. For hours, they moved from station to station, dish to dish, and stove to stove, creating culinary delights that earned Studio 31 rave reviews online and in the upscale city magazine *Verde*.

As food service began to wind down and orders slowed to a stop, Suresh chanced a glance at his phone.

Nothing.

He was hoping for an update on Angelo. He wasn't worried, but he didn't want to see Angelo suffer. In the last few months, Suresh had become more confident in his Eastern beliefs. Disha had played a significant part in that process. As Suresh contemplated the possibility that Angelo might die, his sadness was mixed with hope. Even though he might never see Angelo again in his present form, Angelo would never cease to exist. He would simply be reborn in a new form on his way to escape from the endless wheel of life and death until finally he achieved enlightenment.

Suresh was learning to detach himself from desire and from others so as to embrace the impermanence of life. This didn't mean he wouldn't form close relationships with others, but it did mean he would hold all things loosely. All was impermanent, including his love for his friends. Everything was destined to become one, so there was ultimately nothing to grieve.

And yet. And yet.[2]

---

2. The poet Kobayashi Issa (1763–1827) wrote this famous haiku:
   So this world of dew
   Is a world of dew,
   And yet, and yet.

   Pico Iyer explains that Issa wrote this verse after suffering the death of both his parents and several of his children. Pico Iyer, "About a Poem: Pico Iyer on a Haiku by Kobayashi Issa," in *Lion's Roar: Buddhist Wisdom for Our Time*, September 1, 2009, https://www.lionsroar.com/about-a-poem/.

* * *

Angelo's girlfriend, Allison, texted the three friends. Angelo's condition hadn't improved. He was in a coma, and his organs appeared to be failing. The medical team had advised that Angelo's family and friends should plan to say goodbye.

Hannah, Zach, and Suresh texted each other after receiving Allison's text. They decided to meet at the hospital at seven that night.

They found each other in the lobby and embraced for a long time. Hannah buried her face between Zach and Suresh and sobbed. The dam of emotions burst as soon as she saw them. Zach and Suresh fought back tears. When Hannah caught her breath, she wiped her eyes and said, "Okay, let's be strong for Angelo."

They proceeded to the front desk and got Angelo's room number. They rode the elevator to the fifth floor and found Room 516. Zach knocked lightly and heard a voice tell them to come in.

The sight of Angelo, intubated and connected to so many machines and IVs and wires, intensified the soberness of the moment. Allison was sitting next to the bed holding Angelo's hand.

"I am so glad you came," she said, her smile bright alongside her tears. "Angelo has told me many times how precious your friendship is to him."

They introduced themselves and stood awkwardly looking at Angelo.

"We'd hoped Angelo would have shown some improvement by now," Allison said. "The doctors are concerned that the longer he remains in a coma, the less likely it is that he'll come out of it. Our whole church is praying hard."

"When Angelo slumped in his chair that night," Zach said, "he was in the middle of telling us what Christianity teaches about death. He said something about experiencing bliss forever and ever. Even though we aren't Christians, I think it would be comforting for us to hear something about that."

"I'd be happy to read some passages from the Bible about a Christian's death," Allison said.

She opened the Bible and flipped a few pages.

"'Even though I walk through the valley of the shadow of death, I will fear no evil, for you are with me; your rod and your staff, they comfort me.'"[3]

"That's from Psalm 23, isn't it?" Hannah asked. "I memorized it as a kid."

"It is," Allison said. "Here's another one from Romans 8: 'For I consider that the sufferings of this present time are not worth comparing with the glory that is to be revealed to us. For the creation waits with eager longing for the revealing of the sons of God.'[4] That verse pairs well with another one from 2 Corinthians 4: 'For this light momentary affliction is preparing for us an eternal weight of glory beyond all comparison.'"[5]

"Does the Bible give any specifics about what heaven is like?" Suresh was curious about the differences between the Eastern view of nirvana and the Christian concept of heaven.

"It tells us some things." She turned a few pages. "This comes from the end of the Bible, in the book of Revelation, chapter 21."

> Then I saw a new heaven and a new earth, for the first heaven and the first earth had passed away, and the sea was no more. And I saw the holy city, new Jerusalem, coming down out of heaven from God, prepared as a bride adorned for her husband. And I heard a loud voice from the throne saying, "Behold, the dwelling place of God is with man. He will dwell with them, and they will be his people, and God himself will be with them as their God. He will wipe away every tear from their eyes, and death shall be no more, neither shall there be mourning, nor crying, nor pain anymore, for the former things have passed away." And he who was seated on the throne said, "Behold, I am making all things new." Also he said, "Write this down, for these words are trustworthy and true." And he said to me, "It is done! I am the Alpha and the Omega, the beginning and the end. To the thirsty I will give from the spring of the water of life without payment."[6]

---

3. Ps 23:4 (ESV).
4. Rom 8:18–19 (ESV).
5. 2 Cor 4:17 (ESV).
6. Rev 21:1–6 (ESV).

All three found themselves weeping at these words as they gazed at Angelo. Allison was crying as well, the tears running down her cheeks and splashing on her hand as it clenched Angelo's.

The words were devastatingly beautiful and heartbreaking at the same time.

Each friend spent a few moments privately with Angelo, saying their goodbyes, telling him how much they cared about him, thanking him for his friendship.

They thanked Allison and said their goodbyes. She promised to notify them of any changes in Angelo's condition.

They walked silently to the garage and went their separate ways.

* * *

Two days later, they received a remarkable text. In a message that nearly exceeded the maximum allowed characters, Allison excitedly recounted how Angelo suddenly began making marked improvement twenty-four hours prior. Within hours, his organs returned to full function, and his blood pressure stabilized. The doctors removed him from the sedative that was keeping him comfortable, and a few hours later, he woke up. They removed his breathing tube, and with a raspy voice, he asked for something to eat.

Angelo was expected to recover.

* * *

Suresh, Hannah, and Zach felt like the sun had broken through the clouds after weeks of overcast weather. Happiness returned to their daily routines, and they found themselves counting the days until they could see him again.

Exactly two months after they thought they had said their final goodbye to their friend, he walked through the door of Brews Brothers with a huge smile on his face. He was thin, but the color in his face was good. Allison held his arm, her face glowing, a beautiful ring sparkling on her left hand.

Angelo had a book in his hand. As he approached the table, he said in a strong, clear voice, "I have a great suggestion for our next book! Who's up for another reading group?"

THEORY

The narrative explored the role of worldview in one's understanding of death. The following discussion will unpack the various philosophical options for defining death, dealing with the fear of death, and the question of an afterlife.

Defining Death

A good way to begin any philosophical discussion is by defining our terms, so let's attempt to define what we mean by "death." This is one of those terms that everyone thinks they understand until you ask them to define it. Here are three possible definitions of death:

1. **Death is the end of your existence**. If mind-body physicalism is true, then there's no soul to survive the death of the body. Therefore, death is when the body stops functioning. For physicalists, death is the end of your story.
2. **Death is the departure of your soul from your body**. If mind-body dualism is true, then humans have an immaterial component that can survive the death of the body. On this view, death is the separation of the soul and the body. When the soul leaves the body, the body (usually) stops functioning, which is physical death, but the soul has the potential to live on.
3. **Death is the end of one of your many incarnations**. Eastern monistic religions like Hinduism and Buddhism hold that death is the cessation of one earthly life that will be followed by another earthly life. This is reincarnation. Reincarnation might sound like a good thing, but to Hindus and Buddhists, it signifies rebirth into another lifetime of suffering.

It's hard to find anything that all three views have in common. Cessation of bodily functions is a necessary component of the first view but not of the second, since the soul can conceivably leave the body without the body ceasing to function. The soul leaving the body is a necessary component of the second view, but adherents of the first view reject the existence of the soul. Reincarnation is a necessary component of the third view but not of the first or second. Finding a definition of death that works with all three types of worldviews is difficult.

Criteria for a Declaration of Death

If we can't pin down a general definition of death, perhaps we can at least figure out what conditions need to be fulfilled in order to know when death has occurred. Those who work in biomedical ethics discuss four possible criteria for determining whether someone has died.

1. **Departure of the soul:** One possible criterion is the departure of the soul from the body. This, of course, assumes dualism, which would be objectionable to physicalists. Even assuming dualism is true, there doesn't seem to be any empirical way to know whether the soul has departed. Therefore, this is not a practical criterion for determining when someone has died.
2. **Cardio-respiratory failure:** Another possibility is the cessation of heart and lung functioning. On this criterion, a person is dead if and only if she stops breathing and her heart stops beating. This is a traditional criterion of death. It used to be commonplace to check for breathing and a pulse, and if they weren't found, to declare the person dead. However, there are insurmountable problems with this view. First, a person's brain often continues to function after the heart and lungs cease functioning. Second, modern technology can prolong bodily life and brain function even when the heart and lungs are not functioning and have been removed from the body. When someone undergoes a heart and lung transplant, there is a period of time when neither the heart nor the lungs are working, but the patient is kept alive by receiving a continuous flow of oxygenated blood from a cardiopulmonary bypass machine. Therefore, cardiorespiratory failure is not a sure sign of death.
3. **Whole brain death:** A third possibility is irreversible cessation of all brain functions—"whole brain death." There are specific factors

that a physician uses to determine whether there is whole brain death.[7] This has become the standard criterion in the healthcare industry and is endorsed by many biomedical ethicists. It could be used to determine the death of a patient who is being kept alive by a ventilator or even a cardiopulmonary bypass machine. Nonetheless, there are some objections. One comes from physicalists who object that although the brain may not be functioning, if the body is still functioning, it seems wrong to say that the body is not alive. Since physicalists view the body as the person, it is consistent with physicalism to view general bodily function as an indication of life even if some specific part of the body (i.e., the brain) is not functioning. The other objection comes from dualists who wonder if the absence of brain function guarantees that the soul has departed. However, in defense of this view is the fact that if a person who is in a state of whole brain death is taken off the apparatus that is keeping him alive, he will lapse into cardiorespiratory death and in short order the entire body will die.

4. **Neocortical death:** The fourth possible criterion is irreversible cessation of functioning of the neocortex, the part of the brain that is most involved in higher brain functions like sensory perception, cognition, and communication. Some people argue that these higher functions are what differentiate a human from other animals and that they are the locus of personhood. Therefore, they reason, it is the loss of neocortical activity that indicates death. In 1986 the American Medical Association recommended that neocortical death be accepted as a criterion of death.[8] A concern with this is that although it seems likely that cessation of neocortical functioning is a **necessary condition** of death, it's not clear that

7. See Ajay Kumar Goila and Mridula Pawar, "The Diagnosis of Brain Death," *Indian Journal of Critical Care Medicine* 13, no. 1 (2009): 7–11, https://doi.org/10.4103/0972-5229.53108.
8. Mark L. Foreman and Lindsay C. Leonard, *Christianity and Modern Medicine: Foundations for Bioethics* (Kregel Academic, 2022), 158.

> it's a **sufficient condition**.[9] Since the body can go on living after the neocortex dies, physicalists have reason to suspect that there may be life even when the neocortex is dead. Dualists, on the other hand, object that a damaged neocortex does not guarantee that the soul has departed. Finally, there are problems with identifying personhood with any physical feature, as was discussed in chapter 21. For these reasons and others, neocortical death has not been widely accepted as a criterion of death.

You can see that settling on a criterion of death isn't easy. Nonetheless, medical professionals need a criterion, and whole brain death seems to easily beat out the other contenders. If this is an adequate criterion for death, that must be because it reflects the nature of death. So maybe we can use this to develop a definition of death. Perhaps we can define death thusly: "Death is the state wherein all brain functions have irreversibly ceased." While not requiring the death of the whole body, it does focus on physical death without any reference to an immaterial self, so this definition may be acceptable to physicalists. And while it makes no mention of the soul, it doesn't exclude the soul, either. It could be that when all mental functions cease, the soul leaves. On the other hand, it could be that the departure of the soul causes or contributes to the cessation of all mental functions. Either way, this definition is compatible with dualism. Dualists might want to make a modification, though: "Death is the state wherein the soul has departed from the body, which can be determined by the irreversible cessation of all brain functions."

The Fear of Death

Most people fear death, but that's not necessarily a bad thing. Fear of death serves several constructive purposes, like motivating us to take good care

---

9. A "sufficient condition" is something that, all by itself, is enough to cause a proposition to be true or show that a proposition is true. For example, ice on the road is usually a sufficient condition for the road to be slippery. A "necessary condition," on the other hand, is something that is absolutely required in order for a proposition to be true. For example, the temperature being freezing or below is generally a necessary condition for ice to form on the road. Something can be both a necessary and a sufficient condition, one or the other, or it can be neither.

of our personal health and to avoid foolishly risking our lives. But the fear of death can be quite burdensome, so people seek ways of coping with it. Some of these are more reasonable than others. Philosophical analysis can help us find our own ways of dealing with this fear. People fear death for a variety of different reasons.

1. **Fear of the process of dying:** One reason people fear death is that the process of dying could be unpleasant. Most people hope to die a peaceful, painless death, but many people die in painful ways. Concern about a premature, painful, or prolonged death is understandable.
2. **Fear of the unknown:** It's common to feel apprehensive when facing something you've never experienced before. Death is perhaps the most extreme example of this (if there's no reincarnation), and it will radically affect you. Hence, it's understandable that people feel intense apprehension about dying.
3. **Fear of unfulfilled responsibilities:** A significant type of fear of death for many people is the fear that their deaths will have a significant detrimental effect on their loved ones. This is why people spend hundreds, even thousands, of dollars each year on life insurance. Other people fear leaving their life's work incomplete, whether that be a work of art, a charitable cause, or anything else that someone is heavily invested in.
4. **Fear of annihilation:** In mind-body physicalism, the death of the body is the end of one's existence. Hence, death completely annihilates the person. Nothing survives. Your story ends.
5. **Fear of punishment:** Many theists believe that after people die, they are judged and then either rewarded or punished according to how obedient or disobedient to God they were.
6. **Fear of reincarnation:** Adherents to Eastern religions that teach reincarnation, like Hinduism, Buddhism, Jainism, and Sikhism, fear the possibility that their next life will be worse than the present one. You could even come back as some lower form of animal life rather than as a human.

Addressing the Fear of Death

Here are some ways that people have tried to deal with the fear of death.

1. **Social immortality:** Some people feel that when they die, they will live on through their children. What they mean by this varies; certainly their genes are passed on and so are some of their traditions and values. Some people seem to mean more than that, as if somehow some part of them is reincarnated in their children. They find this belief comforting. However, at best it only helps to deal with a few of the reasons why people fear death.

"I don't want to achieve immortality through my work: I want to achieve immortality through not dying." –Woody Allen

2. **Cultural immortality:** Some believe that when they die, they will live on through their creations, memorials, or contributions to society. Every painter wants one of their paintings to be admired like the Sistine Chapel, and every author wants to pen a bestseller so they will be remembered after they die. But at best, this only addresses the fear of being forgotten—and that only temporarily.
3. **Cosmic immortality:** Some say that long after you die and your body has returned to the dirt, when the sun goes supernova and the Earth is reduced to dust, your ashes will mingle with the dust of the universe and you will become one with everything. Some find this comforting, though others find it scary.
4. **Scientific immortality:** Some believe that science will eventually find a "cure" for death. The cells that make up our bodies are constantly dying and being replaced by new ones. It only takes about seven years for most of the cells in your body to be replaced. Hence, your body is never much older than seven years. Nonetheless, the body ages and will eventually die. However, some scientists believe that there is a DNA sequence that controls aging and that it may be possible to turn aging off. That would halt the aging process so you

will stay perpetually young.[10] But since aging isn't the only cause of death, you could still die from a disease, accident, violence, or something like that. Science may eventually find cures for every disease, too, but that still falls far short of guaranteed immortality.

5. **The natural process argument:** Some have argued that death is a natural part of life, and therefore, it should be accepted without fear. We don't fear the other stages of life—birth, infancy, adolescence, etc.—and we shouldn't fear death, either. But although this argument makes a good point, it doesn't address the reasons to fear death that were presented earlier.
6. **The necessity argument:** Some argue that death is necessary for us to appreciate life. This argument also makes a good point: If not for death, life might be taken for granted. However, it, too, fails to address the previously mentioned reasons to fear death.
7. **The agnostic argument:** Some argue that since we don't know what death is like, we shouldn't assume that it is unpleasant. Rather, we should adopt a wait-and-see attitude and neither fear it nor desire it. On the other hand, some argue that we have data about what death is like from religious sources and near-death experiences. Additionally, this argument doesn't address fear of the process of dying, of the unknown, and of unfulfilled responsibilities.
8. **Epicurus' argument:** Epicurus argued that death cannot harm you, because when you die, you no longer exist to be harmed. He was a metaphysical materialist, and therefore, regarding the mind-body problem, he was a physicalist who viewed the death of the body as the end of your existence. He believed that once you die, nothing can harm you since you no longer exist. This would be rejected by dualists, naturally. Even for physicalists it fails to address the fear of the process of dying and the fear of unfulfilled responsibilities.
9. **Life after death:** Perhaps the most widespread and persistent way that people have attempted to deal with the fear of death is the

---

10. This is discussed in Venki Ramakrishnan, *Why We Die: The New Science of Aging and the Quest for Immortality* (HarperCollins, 2024).

belief that death is not the end of a person's existence but instead a doorway to another life. Let's take a closer look at that strategy.

Life After Death

The belief that death is a doorway to a new life has comforted people for millennia. However, there are challenges. One is that many believe that the afterlife may be worse than the present life, rather than better. Of course, it's also possible that it will be as good as or better than the present life. Perhaps the most significant challenge is proving that the afterlife is real rather than wishful thinking. The following have been advanced as evidence for an afterlife:

1. **The argument from ultimate justice:** Kant argued that life experience shows that justice and injustice are real. However, life isn't fair: Good deeds go unrewarded and evil deeds go unpunished. Since justice isn't achieved in this life, there must be an afterlife in which it is.[11]
2. **Near-death experiences (NDEs):** Some who have experienced clinical death and been resuscitated have reported that their cognitive functions continued after death. They may feel a warm presence, see a bright light, or talk to a deceased loved one. Sometimes there are out-of-body experiences followed by recounted details of what transpired while they were dead. There is a considerable body of literature on this.[12] If any of these accounts is veridical, that would support the belief that consciousness sometimes continues after death.
3. **The resurrection of Jesus of Nazareth:** Perhaps the best docu-

---

11. Immanuel Kant, *Critique of Practical Reason*, trans. Mary Gregor (Cambridge University Press, 2015), ch. 1. See also Andree Hahmann, "Kant's Critical Argument(s) for Immortality Reassessed," *Kant Yearbook* 10, no. 1 (2018): 19–42, https://doi.org/10.1515/kantyb-2018-0002.
12. In a 2022 *Up First* program on NPR, Rachel Martin interviews someone who had an NDE and a psychiatrist who has studied NDEs for fifty years. This thought-provoking program can be listened to online: Rachel Martin, "Changed by a Near-Death Experience," *Up First*, July 17, 2022, https://www.npr.org/2022/07/15/1111686005/changed-by-a-near-death-experience.

mented case of life after death is that of Jesus, the founder of Christianity. Some scholars believe that the evidence for his resurrection is strong.[13] If Jesus rose from the dead, it proves that life after death is possible.

4. **Transcultural belief:** Belief in life after death appears throughout recorded history, among people groups around the world, regardless of religion and culture. This raises the question of "why?" A possible evolutionary answer is that belief in an afterlife has survival value: It enables us to survive in a hostile environment. However, that seems counterintuitive. Belief in an afterlife could instead cause us to struggle less ardently to survive since this life may be followed by a better one. An answer with a Marxist flavor is that belief in an afterlife helps us to bear the difficulties of this life, hoping that a better life awaits us. It's an "opiate of the masses," as Marx described religion. However, this is incompatible both with the theistic belief that the afterlife will involve judgment and even punishment for some people and with the Hindu and Buddhist belief that life after death is an evil to be (eventually) escaped. Another possible answer is that people all over the world believe in an afterlife because there really is one, and, one way or another, they have figured that out. They may have figured it out through revelation, through hearing about other people's near-death experiences, by reasoning about the benevolent nature of God, by thinking about the indissolubility of the soul (as did the ancient Greeks), or some other way. Regardless of how they arrived at this conclusion, if this is the best explanation of the widespread phenomenon of belief in the afterlife, then here we have an abductive argument in support of that belief.
5. **Pan-religious agreement**. Most religions include belief in an afterlife. If any of them is true, then belief in the afterlife is true. Logically, this argument is a categorical syllogism:

---

13. See, for example, Michael R. Licona, *The Resurrection of Jesus: A New Historiographical Approach* (IVP Academic, 2010).

a. The beliefs of religion X are true beliefs.
b. Belief in an afterlife is a belief of religion X.
c. Therefore, belief in an afterlife is a true belief.

This is a valid syllogism, and the minor premise (b) is true of most religions. The major premise (a) is controversial, and we don't have the space to try to answer this question even provisionally. However, if an individual is justified in believing that some religion is true, and if that religion teaches that there is an afterlife, then he is justified in believing in an afterlife.

Worldviews and Death

There is a reciprocal relationship between a person's worldview and the position that he or she takes on any major worldview issue. We should always want our beliefs to be in agreement with the best evidence. Both worldviews and positions on specific issues are clusters of beliefs supported by evidence, but both can serve as evidence, too. So the relationship between worldviews and major worldview-forming issues is a bit complicated.

"A man who has truly spent his life in philosophy is probably right to be of good cheer in the face of death and to be very hopeful that after death he will attain the greatest blessings yonder." —Socrates

Naturalism and belief in an afterlife don't fit well together. In part that's because naturalism implies mind-body physicalism, which rules out a spiritual afterlife. The same is generally true for pantheism: no spirit, so no afterlife. On the other hand, theism, deism, polytheism, and other dualistic worldviews are compatible with an afterlife, for they generally hold that humans have souls that can survive the death of the body.

Most people seem to look at death as something to be feared. That outlook has its benefits: We shouldn't be rushing to die. But each of the perspectives on death that we've studied has given us some reason for optimism as we face the end of life. With Epicurus, naturalists can view death as peaceful nonexistence. For theists, there's the hope of eternal life with God. In the Eastern religions, there's the hope of progressing toward escape from the cycle of rebirth. Since these views are mutually incompatible, they cannot all be true without violating the law of noncontradiction. Furthermore, the perspective on death found in each worldview also contains negatives. But the picture is not totally bleak.

The authors of this book are theists who believe in an afterlife. As Christians, we are convinced that we will face God and receive judgment in accordance with our relationship with Jesus Christ. Hebrews 2:14–15 suggests that one of Jesus' purposes was to deliver people from fear of death.[14] We have personally experienced that and wish it for our readers.

14. "Therefore, since the children share in flesh and blood, he likewise shared in their humanity, so that through death he could destroy the one who holds the power of death (that is, the devil), and set free those who were held in slavery all their lives by their fear of death" (Heb 2:14–15).

QUESTIONS TO PONDER

- What is death? How would you define death?
- Are you afraid of death? Why, or why not?
- Do you believe in life after death? Why or why not?
- Do you consider death a good thing, a bad thing, both, or neither?

TERMS TO KNOW

- death
- departure of the soul
- cardiorespiratory failure
- whole brain death
- neocortical death
- sufficient condition
- necessary condition
- social immortality
- cultural immortality
- cosmic immortality
- scientific immortality
- natural process argument
- necessity argument
- agnostic argument
- Epicurus' argument
- argument from ultimate justice
- NDEs
- resurrection of Jesus
- transcultural belief
- pan-religious agreement

FOR FURTHER READING

Jones, Clay. *Immortal: How the Fear of Death Drives Us and What We Can Do About It*. Harvest House, 2020. This is a Christian reflection on death, the fear of death, and attempts to address that fear.

Melkonian, Markar, ed. *The Philosophy of Death Reader: Cross-Cultural Readings on Immortality and the Afterlife*. Bloomsbury Academic, 2019. This is a good multi-cultural anthology.

Timmerman, Travis and Michael Cholbi, eds. *Exploring the Philosophy of Death and Dying: Classical and Contemporary Perspectives*. Routledge, 2021. This is a large and diverse anthology.

CONCLUSION

The authors of this book hope that, just as Zach, Hannah, Suresh, and Angelo progressed in their understanding of philosophical issues by studying together, you have progressed from studying with them. This book is purposefully written to help you grasp philosophical topics in conversation with various worldviews. It is useful to see the contrast between Eastern thought, naturalism, theism, and other worldviews. People with differing worldviews see philosophical issues quite differently. When we get together and talk about these differences, we gain perspectives we might not have been able to understand before. This can lead to more dialogue and harmony in society because the issues that divide people are often philosophical at their root.

Another perspective that we hope you have gained through this book is that philosophy and religion are not completely distinctive spheres. While they each have their own concerns, it is clear that most (perhaps all) religions and worldviews have metaphysical, epistemological, and ethical commitments that set them apart from each other. Dialogue with people outside your tradition will help you understand alternative ways of viewing reality. Therefore, we encourage you, dear reader, to consider joining a philosophy discussion group. While this may sound far-fetched, these groups bring people of disparate belief systems together for meaningful dialogue. They can be found in any city and many suburban and rural locations. One of the authors of this book (Mark) launched a weekly group to read Nietzsche; it has been meeting for more than three years. "Read Nietzsche with Me" brings together atheists, agnostics, Christians, Jews, and people of other worldviews for the goal of mutual understanding and increased comprehension of philosophical ideas. Friendships have blossomed even while differences are debated.

Philosophy ought to be a search for truth, a "love of wisdom," even if it contradicts our beliefs or choices. We should read philosophy with the expectation that our beliefs will be challenged, and some may even be discarded, though others may be confirmed. One of the most difficult exercises is to accept something as true even if we don't *want* it to be true. Humans tend to adjust our beliefs to fit our feelings instead of the other way around; our hearts often override our heads. But it is both rational and wise to search out and adopt the beliefs, and the worldview, that most consistently and coherently offers intellectually and emotionally satisfying answers to important philosophical questions. Each of the authors did that at different times in their lives. To us the Christian faith, centered in salvation by grace through the incarnation, death, and resurrection of Jesus Christ, best answers the questions raised by philosophy and the human condition.

What comes next? We encourage you to advance your knowledge of philosophy, and we have provided a bibliography of suggested readings in the following pages. We hope you will plunder the treasures of that list and grow in your love of wisdom.

You may have become attached to the characters in this book, as we have. Since they're fictional, you can picture their futures however you want to. We like to think of them this way:

Suresh rose to *chef de cuisine* at the swanky New York restaurant Décadence, where he won a Michelin star for his creative spin on momo, a dumpling commonly found in Tibet. Two years later he returned to Greenfield and settled down, opening an exclusive sixteen-seat restaurant two blocks from the courthouse called *Penseur*, which is French for "thinker." He told his three friends they can eat for free whenever they want.

Zach remained at Bradley Pharmaceuticals as the senior lab scientist. He turned down multiple offers for administrative positions at other companies so that he could stay in Greenfield. Five years later he received the prestigious Distinguished Scientist Award from the American Academy of Pharmaceutical Scientists for his formulation of a drug given to gunshot victims that identifies undetected blood loss by turning the patient's lips hot pink.

Hannah received a grant to study the long-term effects of trauma as part of a doctoral program in psychology at a nearby university. It required her to move out of Greenfield, but she visits as often as she can. She has been writing a book about their ordeal and has three publishers interested. She and Mack Ryan have been dating for the last six months.

Angelo got accepted into law school and began his studies, but recurring long-term effects of his wounds forced him to drop out. He married Allison and they have two children. He completed a paralegal degree and works a modified schedule to accommodate his health struggles. He eats lunch at *Penseur* every day, much to Suresh's chagrin.

BIBLIOGRAPHY

Alston, William P. *Epistemic Justification: Essays in the Theory of Knowledge*. Cornell University Press, 1989.

Arcadi, James M., ed. *T&T Clark Handbook of Analytic Theology*. T&T Clark, 2021.

Arp, Robert, Steven Barbone, and Michael Bruce. *Bad Arguments: 100 of the Most Important Fallacies in Western Philosophy*. Wiley-Blackwell, 2019.

Audi, Robert. *Epistemology: A Contemporary Introduction to the Theory of Knowledge*. 3rd ed. Routledge, 2011.

Baggett, David and Jerry Walls. *Good God: The Theistic Foundations of Morality*. Oxford University Press, 2011.

Becker, Lawrence C. and Charlotte B. Becker, eds. *Encyclopedia of Ethics*. 2nd ed. Routledge, 2003.

Benedict, Ruth. "Anthropology and the Abnormal." *The Journal of General Psychology* 10 (1934): 59–82.

Bernecker, Sven and Duncan Pritchard, eds. *The Routledge Companion to Epistemology*. Routledge, 2011.

Bluedorn, Nathaniel, Hans Bluedorn, Rob Corley, and Tim Hodge. *The Fallacy Detective: Thirty-Eight Lessons on How to Recognize Bad Reasoning*. 4th ed. Christian Logic, 2015.

Bourke, Vernon. *History of Ethics*. 2 vols. Axios Press, 2007

Bullivant, Stephen and Michael Ruse, eds. *The Oxford Handbook of Atheism*. Oxford University Press, 2013.

Campbell, Joseph K., Michael O'Rourke, and David Shier, eds. *Freedom and Determinism*. MIT Press, 2004.

Campbell, Ronnie P., Jr. *Worldviews and the Problem of Evil: A Comparative Approach*. Lexham Press, 2019.

Cowan, Steven B. and Stanley N. Gundry, eds. *Five Views on Apologetics*. Zondervan Academic, 2000.

DePoe, John M. and Tyler Dalton McNabb, eds. *Debating Christian Religious Epistemology: An Introduction to Five Views on the Knowledge of God*. Bloomsbury Academic, 2020.

Dew, James K., Jr. and Mark W. Foreman. *How Do We Know? An Introduction to Epistemology*. 2nd ed. Questions in Christian Philosophy. IVP Academic, 2020.

Dilman, Ilham. *Free Will: An Historical and Philosophical Introduction*. Routledge, 1999.

Feinberg, Joel, Jules Coleman, and Christopher Kutz, eds. *Philosophy of Law*. 9th ed. Cengage, 2013.

Feinberg, John S. and Paul D. Feinberg, *Ethics for a Brave New World*. 2nd ed. Crossway, 2010.

Feldman, Fred, Jens Johansson, and Ben Bradley. *The Oxford Handbook of Philosophy of Death*. Oxford, 2013.

Finnis, John. *Natural Law and Natural Rights*. 2nd ed. Oxford University Press, 2011.

Fuller, Michael, Dirk Evers, Anne Runehov, and Knut-Willy Sæther, eds. *Issues in Science and Theology: Are We Special? Human Uniqueness in Science and Theology*. Springer International, 2017.

Fuqua, Jonathan, John Greco, and Tyler McNabb, eds. *The Cambridge Handbook of Religious Epistemology*. Cambridge University Press, 2023.

Gallagher, Charles A., ed. *Rethinking the Color Line: Readings in Race and Ethnicity*. 7th ed. Sage, 2022.

Gallagher, Shaun, ed. *The Oxford Handbook of the Self*. Oxford University Press, 2011.

Goetz, Stewart and Charles Taliaferro. *A Brief History of the Soul*. Wiley-Blackwell, 2011.

Goldschmidt, Tyron. *The Puzzle of Existence: Why Is There Something Rather Than Nothing?* Routledge, 2013.

Gould, Paul M., ed. *Beyond the Control of God? Six Views on the Problem of God and Abstract Objects*. Bloomsbury Academic, 2016.

Groothuis, Douglas. *Christian Apologetics: A Comprehensive Case for Biblical Faith*. 2nd ed. IVP Academic, 2022.

Hasker, William. *Metaphysics: Constructing a Worldview*. Contours of Christian Philosophy. InterVarsity Press, 1983.

Hawkins, J. Russell and Phillip Luke Sinitiere, eds. *Christians and the Color Line: Race and Religion After Divided by Faith*. Oxford University Press, 2014.

Hayden, Patrick, ed. *Philosophy of Human Rights: Readings in Context*. Paragon House, 2001.

Hoekema, Anthony. *Created in God's Image*. Eerdmans, 1994.

Holland, Richard A., Jr. and Benjamin K. Forrest. *Good Arguments: Making Your Case in Writing and Public Speaking*. Baker Academic, 2017.

Holmes, Arthur F. *Ethics: Approaching Moral Decisions*. 2nd ed. InterVarsity Press, 2007.

Hurley, Patrick J. and Lori Watson. *A Concise Introduction to Logic*. 13th ed. Cengage Learning, 2017.

Ishay, Micheline R. *The History of Human Rights: From Ancient Times to the Globalization Era*. University of California Press, 2008.

Jones, Clay. *Immortal: How the Fear of Death Drives Us and What We Can Do About It*. Harvest House, 2020.

Jones, Michael S. *Moral Reasoning: An Intentional Approach to Distinguishing Right from Wrong*. Kendall Hunt, 2017.

Jones, Michael S., Mark J. Farnham, and David L. Saxon. *Talking About Ethics: A Conversational Approach to Moral Dilemmas*. Kregel Academic, 2021.

Kahane, Howard, Alan Hausman, and Frank Boardman. *Logic and Philosophy: A Modern Introduction*. 13th ed. Hackett, 2021.

Kenny, Anthony. *A New History of Western Philosophy*. Clarendon Press, 2010.

Kitcher, Patricia. *The Self: A History*. Oxford University Press, 2021.

Kramer, Matthew H. *In Defense of Legal Positivism: Law without Trimmings*. 1st ed. Oxford University Press, 1999.

Lebens, Samuel. *Philosophy of Religion: The Basics*. Routledge, 2023.

Lehrer, Keith, ed. *Freedom and Determinism*. Random House, 1966.

Liggins, David. *Abstract Objects*. Cambridge University Press, 2024.

Loose, Jonathan, Angus J. L. Menuge, and James Porter Moreland, eds. *The Blackwell Companion to Substance Dualism*. Wiley-Blackwell, 2018.

Mackie, J. L. *Ethics: Inventing Right and Wrong*. Penguin, 1990.

Martin, Michael and Ricki Monnier, eds. *The Impossibility of God*. Prometheus, 2003.

Martin, Michael and Ricki Monnier, eds. *The Improbability of God*. Prometheus, 2006.

McCall, Thomas H. *An Invitation to Analytic Christian Theology*. IVP Academic, 2015.

McGlothlin, James C. *The Logiphro Dilemma: An Examination of the Relationship Between God and Logic*. Pickwick Publications, 2017.

McGrath, Gavin and W. C. Campbell-Jack, eds. *New Dictionary of Christian Apologetics*. IVP Academic, 2006.

Melkonian, Markar, ed. *The Philosophy of Death Reader: Cross-Cultural Readings on Immortality and the Afterlife*. Bloomsbury Academic, 2019.

Miller, Ed L. and John Jensen. *Questions that Matter: An Invitation to Philosophy*. 6th ed. McGraw-Hill, 2008.

Moreland, J. P. and William Lane Craig. *Philosophical Foundations for a Christian Worldview*. 2nd ed. InterVarsity Press, 2017.

Morris, Tom. *Philosophy for Dummies*. 2nd ed. John Wiley & Sons, 2022.

Mumford, Stephen. *Metaphysics: A Very Short Introduction*. Oxford University Press, 2012.

Naugle, David K. *Worldview: The History of a Concept*. Eerdmans, 2002.

Noonan, Harold. *Personal Identity*. 3rd ed. Routledge, 2019.

Peterson, Michael, William Hasker, Bruce Reichenbach, and David Basinger. *Reason & Religious Belief: An Introduction to the Philosophy of Religion*. 5th ed. Oxford University Press, 2012.

Peterson, Michael, William Hasker, Bruce Reichenbach, and David Basinger, eds. *Philosophy of Religion: Selected Readings*. 5th ed. Oxford, 2014.

Plato. *Socratic Dialogues: Meno, Euthyphro, Apology, Crito, Phaedo*. Translated by Cathal Woods and Ryan Pack. Broadview Press, 2024.

Pojman, Louis P. and James Fieser. *Ethics: Discovering Right and Wrong*. Wadsworth, 2011.

Rosenthal, David M., ed. *Materialism and the Mind-Body Problem*. 2nd ed. Hackett, 2000.

Sartre, Jean-Paul. *Existentialism is a Humanism*. Translated by Carol Macomber. Yale University Press, 2007.

Seachris, Joshua W., ed. *Exploring the Meaning of Life: An Anthology and Guide*. Wiley-Blackwell, 2013.

Shapiro, Stewart, ed. *The Oxford Handbook of Philosophy of Mathematics and Logic*. Oxford University Press, 2007.

Sire, James. *Naming the Elephant: Worldview as a Concept*. 2nd ed. IVP Academic, 2015.

Sire, James. *The Universe Next Door*. 5th ed. IVP Academic, 2009.

Smart, Ninian. *Worldviews: Crosscultural Explorations of Human Beliefs*. 3rd ed. Prentice-Hall, 2000.

Sterba, James, ed. *Do We Have a Logical Argument from Evil?* MDPI, 2024.

Steup, Matthias, ed. *Knowledge, Truth, and Duty: Essays on Epistemic Justification, Responsibility, and Virtue*. Oxford University Press, 2001.

Sunshine, Glenn S. *Why You Think the Way You Do: The Story of Western Worldviews from Rome to Home*. Zondervan Academic, 2009.

Sweis, Khaldoun A. and Chad V. Meister, eds. *Christian Apologetics: An Anthology of Primary Sources*. Zondervan Academic, 2024.

Swinburne, Richard. *Epistemic Justification*. Clarendon Press, 2001.

Taliaferro, Charles and Chad Meister. *Contemporary Philosophical Theology*. Routledge, 2016.

Tattersall, Ian. *Becoming Human: Evolution and Human Uniqueness*. Harcourt, 1998.

Taylor, Paul C. *Race: A Philosophical Introduction*. 3rd ed. Polity Press, 2022.

Taylor, Paul C., Linda Martin Alcoff, and Luvell Anderson, eds. *The Routledge Companion to Philosophy of Race*. Routledge, 2018.

Timmerman, Travis and Michael Cholbi, eds. *Exploring the Philosophy of Death and Dying: Classical and Contemporary Perspectives*. Routledge, 2021.

Timpe, Kevin and Daniel Speak, eds. *Free Will and Theism: Connections, Contingencies, and Concerns*. Oxford University Press, 2016.

van Inwagen, Peter and William Lane Craig. *Do Numbers Exist? A Debate About Abstract Objects*. Routledge, 2024.

Van Til, Cornelius. *A Christian Theory of Knowledge*. 2nd ed. Edited by K. Scott Oliphint. Westminster Seminary Press, 2023.

Vanden Berg, Mary L. *Aquinas, Science, and Human Uniqueness: An Integrated Approach to the Question of What Makes Us Human*. Cascade, 2022.

Wacks, Raymond. *Philosophy of Law: A Very Short Introduction*. 2nd ed. Oxford: Oxford University Press, 2006.

Wilkens, Steve. *Beyond Bumper Sticker Ethics*. IVP Academic, 1995.

Wills, Christopher. *The Runaway Brain: The Evolution of Human Uniqueness*. Basic Books, 1993.

Withey, Michael. *Mastering Logical Fallacies: The Definitive Guide to Flawless Rhetoric and Bulletproof Logic*. Zephyros Press, 2016.

Zack, Naomi, ed. *The Oxford Handbook of Philosophy and Race*. Oxford University Press, 2019.

Zegarelli, Mark. *Logic for Dummies*. John Wiley & Sons, 2007.

FUN PHILOSOPHY BOOKS

Abbott, Edwin. *Flatland: A Romance of Many Dimensions*. NuVision Publications, 2008. This short, mind-expanding book questions our assumptions about the nature of reality.

Baggett, David, Gary Habermas, and Jerry Walls. *C.S. Lewis as Philosopher: Truth, Goodness, and Beauty*. IVP Academic, 2008. This investigates the philosophical insights of C. S. Lewis.

Baggini, Julian. *The Pig That Wants to Be Eaten: 100 Experiments for the Armchair Philosopher*. Plume, 2006. This is a collection of mind-expanding philosophical puzzles. See also Baggini's *The Duck that Won the Lottery* and *The Philosopher's Toolkit*.

Bowen, Jack. *The Dream Weaver: One Boy's Journey Through the Landscape of Reality*. Longman, 2008. This novel introduces many philosophical ideas.

Boyd, Gregory A. and Edward K. Boyd. *Letters from a Skeptic: A Son Wrestles with His Father's Doubts About Christianity*. David. C. Cook, 2008. This is a fun introduction to Christian apologetics.

Gaarder, Jostein. *Sophie's World: A Novel About the History of Philosophy*. Farrar, Straus and Giroux, 2007. This novel introduces philosophers and philosophical concepts.

Gavaler, Chris and Nathaniel Goldberg. *Superhero Thought Experiments: Comic Book Philosophy*. University of Iowa Press, 2019. This explores philosophical ideas through comic book thought experiments.

Grau, Christopher, ed. *Philosophers Explore The Matrix*. Oxford University Press, 2005. This anthology explores philosophical issues related to *The Matrix*.

Haden, Gary. *You Kant Make It Up! Strange Ideas from History's Great Philosophers*. OneWorld Publications, 2011. The title sums this book up well.

Hösle, Vittorio. *Dead Philosophers' Cafe: An Exchange of Letters for Children and Adults*. University of Notre Dame Press, 2005. This is an entertaining introduction to famous philosophers and their ideas.

Irwin, William and David Kyle Johnson. *Introducing Philosophy Through Pop Culture: From Socrates to South Park, Hume to House*. Wiley-Blackwell, 2010. This uses pop culture to illustrate philosophical ideas.

Irwin, William, ed. *The Matrix and Philosophy: Welcome to the Desert of the Real*. Open Court, 2002. This is another book that discusses the philosophy behind The Matrix series. See also William Irwin, ed. *More Matrix and Philosophy: Revolutions and Reloaded Decoded*. Open Court, 2002.

Jones, Michael S., Mark J. Farnham, and David L. Saxon. *Talking About Ethics: A Conversational Approach to Moral Dilemmas*. Kregel Academic, 2021. This is a dialogue-style exploration of ethics written by the authors of *Talking About Worldviews*.

Morris, Tom. *Philosophy for Dummies*. Wiley Publishing, 1999. This is an easy but good introductory text.

Osborne, Richard. *Philosophy for Beginners*. Writers and Readers Publishing, 1992. This is a comic-book style introduction to philosophy.

Potts, Michael. *Aerobics for the Mind: Practical Exercises in Philosophy That Anybody Can Do*. WordCrafts Press, 2014. This is an insightful collection of mental exercises.

Smullyan, Raymond. *Five Thousand B.C. and Other Philosophical Fantasies: Puzzles and Paradoxes, Riddles and Reasonings*. St. Martin's Press, 1983. This is a dialogue-style exploration of philosophy.

Waller, Bruce N. *Coffee and Philosophy: A Conversational Introduction to Philosophy with Readings*. Pearson Longman, 2006. This novel does a great job introducing philosophy.

Watts, Alan. *Essence of Alan Watts, Vol. 7: Philosophical Fantasies*. Celestial Arts Publishing, 1975. This is a short, easy, and interesting introduction to philosophy.

Williamson, Timothy. *Tetralogue: I'm Right, You're Wrong*. Oxford University Press, 2015. This fun, dialogue-style book focuses on epistemology.

The publishing house Open Court has a large series of books on popular culture and philosophy, including titles such as *Facebook and Philosophy*, *Martial Arts and Philosophy*, *Zombies, Vampires, and Philosophy*, *Star Wars and Philosophy*, and *Harry Potter and Philosophy*. See http://www.opencourtbooks.com/categories/pcp.htm for a list of titles.

Wiley Publishing's philosophy and popular culture series: https://www.wiley.com/en-us/Humanities/Introduction+to+Philosophy-c-PL0100?pq=%7Crelevance%7Csubject%3ACU02.

The University Press of Kentucky's philosophy of popular culture series: http://www.kentuckypress.com/live/list_series.php?seriescode=PPCS&skip=0&max=5.

There are many other books that make philosophy fun. Look up any of these titles on Amazon.com and other, similar titles will be suggested to you!

INDEX

Q

R

U

V

W